Controversial Issues in Corrections

Edited by

Charles B. Fields
Eastern Kentucky University

Series Editor

Steven A. Egger
University of Illinois at Springfield

ALLYN AND BACON
Boston • London • Toronto • Sydney • Tokyo • Singapore

Editor-in-Chief, Social Sciences: Karen Hanson
Series Editorial Assistant: Heather Ahlstrom
Marketing Manager: Brooke Stoner
Senior Editorial Production Administrator: Susan McIntyre
Editorial Production Service: Ruttle, Shaw & Wetherill, Inc.
Manufacturing Buyer: Megan Cochran
Cover Administrator: Jenny Hart
Electronic Composition: Omegatype Typography, Inc.

Copyright © 1999 by Allyn & Bacon
A Viacom Company
160 Gould Street
Needham Heights, MA 02494

Internet: www.abacon.com

Library of Congress Cataloging-in-Publication Data
Controversial issues in corrections / edited by Charles B. Fields.
    p. cm.
    Includes bibliographical references.
    ISBN 0-205-27491-9
    1. Corrections—United States.   I. Fields, Charles B.
HV9469.C666   1999
364.6—dc21   98-22622
                                      CIP

Printed in the United States of America
10 9 8 7 6 5 4 3 2 1   04 03 02 01 00 99 98

Contents

iii

II. Sentencing and Policy Debates

III. Legal and Constitutional Debates

Preface

Controversial Issues in Corrections is one of a series of books published by Allyn and Bacon on selected social themes. The unique debate format allows both sides of a controversial topic, such as corrections, to be examined by academic experts and professionals in the field, allowing the reader a comprehensive view of the issue and to become better informed about topics of concern. Additionally, each of the authors provides a brief rejoinder that specifically addresses the arguments espoused by his or her opponent. Anyone with an interest in prisons and the correctional process should find this book an invaluable resource, including those who desire to broaden their understanding of contemporary correctional issues, students and faculty in a number of social science disciplines, and practitioners in the field. It could be used as a text in an advanced correctional policy course or as a supplemental reader in an introductory corrections or related class.

Sixteen topics are addressed in this book. When Series Editor Steve Egger and I began to discuss possible topics to include, we were immediately overwhelmed by the complexity of the subject and sheer number of potential debates. As is readily apparent, a number of important correctional issues are not dealt with here. Although no single work could possibly encompass all of the significant ones, a conscious effort was made to include those that were indeed among the most "controversial." We avoided those general issues (e.g., death penalty, incarceration versus probation, prison overcrowding) that have been adequately dealt with in other venues and focused on more specific problems (with but a few exceptions).

The book is organized around three broad discussion areas. The first section, "The Rehabilitation/Punishment Debate," contains six debates regarding the evolving correctional philosophies and innovations in treatment and punishment. The seven issues dealt with in the second section, "Sentencing and Policy Debates," revolve around treatment of different correctional populations (e.g., elderly inmates, juvenile and female offenders, and white-collar criminals) and recent attempts to make the system more efficient. The final section, "Legal and Constitutional Debates," deals with three of the most controversial issues in corrections, issues that continue to polarize public opinion.

The contributing authors come from a variety of backgrounds, academic disciplines, and perspectives. I wanted to include contributions from established scholars as well as those a little less known. They were each solicited because of their expertise and interest in their respective topics, as well as their enthusiasm for debating their colleagues on issues that, with few exceptions, are most contentious. All were very interested in this project from the beginning and, in some instances, agreed to argue their issue from a position that did not always fit with their own philosophical or ideological perspective. Not always an easy thing to do!

There are quite a few individuals to thank for the publication of this book. First of all, I should thank the chapter authors for their thought-provoking essays and rejoinders. Steve Egger, *Controversial Issues in Criminal Justice* Series Editor and long-time friend and colleague, also deserves much of the credit for the completion of this book. When he first approached me about this project, I was most enthusiastic about the opportunity to compile a collection such as this, and his support has been invaluable. Karen Hanson, Editor-in-Chief at Allyn and Bacon, and her assistant, Heather Ahlstrom, deserve a special note of thanks; their patience and support (undeserved at times) is most appreciated. Jennifer Fielder, Greg Coomes, and Stephanie Sims provided a great deal of clerical assistance in the initial editing and preparation of the manuscript. Finally, to the late Richter Moore, teacher, mentor, colleague, and friend, I dedicate this book.

Is Recidivism
a Valid Measure
of Correctional Success?

Presenting the YES argument is Kevin I. Minor. He is Professor of Correctional Services at Eastern Kentucky University and has a Ph.D. in Sociology/Criminology from Western Michigan University. He is the co-editor, with D. L. Williamson and J. W. Fox, of *Law-Related Education and Juvenile Justice* (Charles C. Thomas, 1997) and, with M. K. Carlie, of *Prisons around the World: Studies in International Penology* (Wm. C. Brown Publishing, 1992).

Thom Gehring and Carolyn Eggleston argue NO. Dr. Gehring has worked in adult and juvenile institutions, as a teacher, counselor, college coordinator, statewide education administrator, consultant, and researcher. He chairs the San Bernardino County Juvenile Justice and Delinquency Prevention Commission. Dr. Eggleston has worked in correctional education since 1975 as a special educator, supervisor, principal, and teacher trainer. She coordinates the special education program at California State University, San Bernardino (CSUSB). Together, they direct the Center for the Study of Correctional Education at CSUSB.

YES

KEVIN I. MINOR

When we ask whether recidivism is a valid measure of correctional success, three subquestions are implied: (1) What is meant by correctional success? (2) Can recidivism be measured validly? and (3) Given that correctional success is defined and recidivism can be measured validly, should recidivism be used to measure success? This debate is organized around these questions.

Correctional Success

A discussion of correctional success presumes a utilitarian view of punishment. Success is a meaningless term without reference to goals (Maltz, 1984). Because overall success is nebulous and multifaceted, correctional officials and researchers must operationalize the concept into specific, measurable goals and objectives, treating these as proxies for overall success. Indeed, specification of goals and objectives is a standard recommendation of the program development and evaluation literature (e.g., Gottfredson, 1984; Petersilia, 1996). The success of a correctional intervention, then, can only be estimated according to how well its goals are accomplished. When a program is unaccompanied by measurable (i.e., researchable) goals, empirical evaluation of its success is impossible.

Goals and objectives reflect multiple considerations, such as legal mandates, the target group, and the theoretical assumptions underlying interventions. Furthermore, goals and objectives are influenced by an agency's bureaucratic dynamics. These dynamics operate within the parameters of (1) broader political and economic forces and (2) historically grounded, culturally particular conceptions of what punishment/corrections can and should accomplish. All these factors help pattern correctional goals and thus the definition of success.

As Garland (1990) observes, cultural mentalities and sensibilities shape correctional bureaucracies, and the philosophies and practices of these bureaucracies in return shape culture. Historically, cultural artifacts of the Enlightenment conjoined with the positivistic, progressivist orientation of the late 1800s and early 1900s to promote a utilitarian image of what was traditionally retributive punishment. The utilitarian product, represented as corrections and correctional practice, in turn reinforced cultural views of what punishment should accomplish. We came to expect lofty, concrete outcomes from punishment (e.g., deterrence and rehabilitation). The very term *corrections* carries with it a promise to deliver, to correct; broadly construed, "corrected" implies some measurable level of success.

Recidivism and Validity

As used in correctional outcome studies, recidivism is generally defined as returning to illegal behavior after, and sometimes during, correctional intervention (Maltz, 1984). Recidivism research has received much criticism (e.g., Maltz & McCleary, 1977; Petersilia, 1996). Criticism arises partly because recidivism is problematic to measure and partly because recidivism has sometimes been used to the exclusion of other, more appropriate measures. Also, recidivism findings have often frustrated cultural expectations and produced disheartening news for advocates of specific approaches. Yet these points apply to many social science variables (e.g., social class) and do not necessarily render it impossible to measure recidivism validly.

Cook and Campbell's (1979, p. 37) widely adopted definition of validity is "the best available approximation to the truth...of propositions...." These authors distinguish four types of validity. **Internal validity** is the confidence with which a relationship between variables can be deemed causal and is largely a matter of ruling out plausible competing causes of measured outcomes. Before cause becomes relevant, a relationship between variables must first be established; covariation is a necessary, but insufficient, condition for causal inference. As an offshoot of internal validity, **statistical conclusion validity** refers to the truth of conclusions about covariance. One may err by concluding that covariance exists when it does not (a type I error) or by failing to detect covariance when it is present (type II error). Factors that improve statistical conclusion validity include the use of larger sample sizes and reliable measures. **External validity** is the degree to which a study's findings are generalizable outside its context (e.g., to other persons, places, or times). External validity is affected strongly by the procedures used to draw a study's sample. The concern is whether these procedures yield a sample that is representative of the desired target of generalization. As an instance of external validity, **construct validity** refers to the fit between a theoretical concept and the way the concept is defined for research purposes. At issue is the extent to which concrete empirical operations capture abstract theoretical referents.

Although many things can be done to counter threats to these types of validity, there is no way to eliminate every threat in any study. Validity is never proven; the likelihood of invalidity is only lessened (Hagan, 1993). The best that can be done is to ascertain which threats remain operative despite efforts to preserve validity and examine the implications of operative threats for conclusions. Studies of correctional recidivism can achieve as much internal, statistical conclusion and external validity as studies of other dependent variables, given adherence to established methods and procedures. Any study that features experimental design or a viable alternative, a large enough sample and reliable measures, and representative probability sampling may yield respectable internal and statistical conclusion validity; except for problems with construct validity, the study may be externally valid.

Compared with other kinds of validity, there are fewer established ways for preserving construct validity. Because of the abstract and complex nature of many concepts (including recidivism), construct validation can be an arduous process. Central to achieving construct validity in correctional outcome research is an operationalization of variables that accurately reflects the intervention and its goals. It is also essential to state goals in a way that enables them to be assessed with the data that are (or will become) available and to understand what factors may impact the data. If practical considerations compromise the operationalization of variables in regard to goals, the impact of compromise on findings must be examined. For example, if a stated program goal is "to reduce criminal behavior" after intervention and only data on subsequent court convictions are available, findings must be qualified to reflect two facts: First, not all instances of criminal behavior result in conviction. Second, some convictions are false. In this situation, a more researchable goal would be "to reduce criminal convictions." Even then, however, one would need to bear in mind that the process leading to conviction entails much discretion.

Maltz (1984) contends that recidivism is not appropriate for measuring every goal of corrections. He sees it as being useful, but of secondary importance, for evaluating goals pertaining to rehabilitation and incapacitation; he assigns recidivism primary importance for assessing specific deterrence. Thus, the most basic determination is whether recidivism is germane to a given intervention's goals and objectives. If it is not, then attention must turn to whatever constructs are of concern (e.g., education, employment, substance abuse). If recidivism is of concern, the question is how to best operationalize it in view of goals and objectives. Recidivism findings vary depending on how the concept is operationalized (Griswold, 1978; Hoffman & Stone-Meierhoefer, 1980), and this is why operationalization needs to reflect what the program was designed to accomplish. It is also why goals must be specific and measurable.

Besides practical considerations, only program goals can direct such decisions as the source of recidivism data used (e.g., self-reports of re-offending, new arrests, new convictions, technical violations, reincarceration), follow-up period length, and the recidivism criteria. Greater confidence about construct validity can be attained by using multiple data sources and comparing across these for patterns, but the source(s) selected should represent what the program sought to accomplish. Likewise, the length of the follow-up period should reflect whether the intervention was meant to promote longer- or shorter-term behavioral change. The most common recidivism criterion is binomial—the proportion of persons who recidivate over a constant period (e.g., one year). However, different survival or hazard models are also available. These models conceive of recidivism as the time to the recidivating event, thereby relaxing the assumption that all recidivists are recidivating at the same rate over time (see Bloom, 1979; Maltz, 1984; Maltz & McCleary, 1977; Visher, Lattimore, & Linster, 1991). No single criterion is appropriate for every study. The choice depends on the purposes of both the intervention and the study (cf. Bloom, 1979). It is possible to achieve acceptable construct validity in recidivism research, given close operationalization of concepts around the program and its measurable goals, careful explication of methods, and proper qualification of findings. Recidivism findings must be interpreted against the total methodological context from which they emerge, and attempts to compare findings across studies should be mindful of this (Griswold, 1978; Hoffman & Stone-Meierhoefer, 1980). Notice, however, that these statements apply to social science research generally; they are not unique to recidivism studies. For instance, findings and interpretations thereof are always dependent on concept operationalization. If one concludes that it is impossible to measure recidivism validly, to approximate it within an acceptable margin of error, then one would probably have minimal confidence in the measurement of most social variables.

Recidivism and Correctional Success

We have seen that success must be defined in terms of measurable goals and objectives and that, although often difficult, recidivism can be measured validly. It follows that if recidivism is relevant to a program's goals, it ought to be included as an indicator of program success. One may suggest, as does Maltz (1984), that evidence of recidivism indicates failure instead of success: "A measure of success should be based on positive accomplishments, not on the absence of negative findings" (p. 23). However, Maltz realizes that a lack of (or low) recidivism can be taken as evidence of success; cessation of, or reduced offending is a positive accomplishment. Alternatively, if the main goal of a correctional program is tight surveillance of high-risk offenders who are expected to re-offend, then high recidivism might be interpreted as evidence of success (Petersilia, 1996). Success and failure are different sides of the same coin, and whether a given finding is interpreted as evidence of success or failure depends on program goals.

Assuming the extant utilitarian orientation of corrections, the issue becomes whether recidivism control should be a goal of intervention. The position taken here is that it should be unless there is a compelling rationale to the contrary. That is, if program goals do not incorporate recidivism, justification should be given for exclusion. People are sent to correctional facilities because they were found or pleaded guilty to criminal behavior. From a legal standpoint, no other behavior or condition (e.g., educational or vocational deficits, mental disorder, alcohol dependency) can constitute sufficient grounds for corrections. Therefore, when considering what corrections is trying to correct, one is hard-pressed not to include criminal behavior. Future crime (i.e., recidivism) is one basis for gauging the utility of placement. When we acknowledge the utilitarian focus of contemporary corrections, we accept recidivism as a criterion for utility, given that crime is the legally mandated rationale for corrections.

Even advocates of Kant's nonutilitarian position should attend to recidivism and other outcomes of correctional intervention. Punishment remains a purposive undertaking when exercised as a right or obligation. Initially, the purpose may amount to no more than meeting an obligation, but once exacted, the punishment response starts consequences in motion. An obligation to punish is accompanied by a parallel obligation to consider the various consequences of punishment. To do otherwise is to sidestep accountability. In short, we should be mindful of the consequences of correctional intervention, and recidivism should generally be a consequence to which we attend.

Crime after correctional intervention often means victimization. Victims and others who finance intervention are likely to construe recidivism as a lack of correctional success. Claims that recidivism control should not be a goal of corrections (and, by implication, that recidivism should not be a measure of correctional success) are regarded with suspicion, at best. As Duguid, Hawkey, and Pawson (1996) conclude, "it is obvious...that the pressure to demonstrate effectiveness in [correctional] programs is not going to go away and that despite protestations the bottom line is that effectiveness in the popular and political imagination means lowering the rate of recidivism." Thus, "there is...a strong 'political' case to be made for using recidivism as a measure of program effectiveness" (p. 83).

Using recidivism as a criterion for success has other benefits. Recidivism findings stimulate inquiries about the reasons for findings, and these inquiries often generate better questions about correctional intervention. Decades of recidivism research have helped direct us away from asking sweeping questions about whether, or what, intervention "works." We have moved toward asking process questions about why particular interventions work, or fail to work, to the degree they do. In more general terms, recidivism is a universal correctional concept of sorts; nothing seems to provoke discourse about the vast range of interrelated correctional issues as well as recidivism findings.

Recidivism research also tends to prompt action as the implications of findings are pondered, and this research can inform efforts to improve programs. Successful correctional programs are not just "out there" for the adopting, and seldom will an agency achieve such a program on the first try. Rather, these programs are the product of careful, ongoing development efforts guided by evaluation research findings. Too often in the past, recidivism findings have been construed as the "final grade" (pass or fail) for interventions. It is more constructive to see these findings as feedback that, when combined with other measures of process and outcome, can be used for purposes of gradual program refinement (Gottfredson, 1984; Minor, Wells, & Jordan, 1997). For instance, recidivism findings can assist in the proper matching of program components to offenders' risks and criminogenic needs (Gendreau, Cullen, & Bonta, 1996; Maltz & McCleary, 1977). Our ultimate and shared concern should be to eliminate or reform correctional practices that are either noneffective or counterproductive with respect to their goals and to build on promising approaches. Recidivism research is one indispensable tool for this endeavor. At the same time, we must guard against using findings from this research to justify premature abolition of programs that have not received a fair test because of faulty implementation or faulty evaluation research.

When a thorough assessment of a correctional program's success is desired, recidivism should seldom be the only outcome measure considered; sometimes it should not even be the primary measure. Programs can be designed to attain worthwhile goals (e.g., literacy, employment, improved family relations) without being meant to affect recidivism significantly, although goals such as these are often conceptualized as avenues to recidivism control. Under these circumstances, recidivism can be a useful correlate or secondary measure instead of a primary measure (Maltz, 1984). Similarly, any program that targets recidivism as a primary goal seeks to impact it through some process, such as employment. Under these conditions, recidivism can be the primary outcome variable, and the process can be assessed with secondary measures. Whether used in the primary or secondary sense (as directed by program goals), recidivism can be measured validly and should generally be included as an indicator of correctional success.

REFERENCES

Bloom, H. S. (1979). Evaluating human service and correctional programs by modeling the timing of recidivism. *Sociological Methods and Research, 8,* 179–208.

Cook, T. D., & Campbell, D. T. (1979). *Quasi-experimentation: Design and analysis issues for field settings.* Boston: Houghton Mifflin.

Duguid, S., Hawkey, C., & Pawson, R. (1996). Using recidivism to evaluate effectiveness in prison education programs. *Journal of Correctional Education, 47,* 74–85.

Garland, D. (1990). *Punishment and modern society: A study in social theory.* Chicago: University of Chicago Press.

Gendreau, P., Cullen, F. T., & Bonta, J. (1996). Intensive rehabilitation supervision: The next generation in community corrections? In T. Ellsworth (Ed.), *Contemporary community corrections* (pp. 252–265). Prospect Heights, IL: Waveland.

Gottfredson, G. D. (1984). A theory-ridden approach to program evaluation: A method for stimulating researcher-implementer collaboration. *American Psychologist, 39,* 1101–1112.

Griswold, D. B. (1978). A comparison of recidivism measures. *Journal of Criminal Justice, 6,* 247–252.

Hagan, F. E. (1993). *Research methods in criminal justice and criminology* (3rd ed.). Englewood Cliffs, NJ: Prentice-Hall.

Hoffman, P. B., & Stone-Meierhoefer, B. (1980). Reporting recidivism rates: The criterion and follow-up issues. *Journal of Criminal Justice, 8,* 53–60.

Maltz, M. D. (1984). *Recidivism.* Orlando, FL: Academic Press.

Maltz, M. D., & McCleary, R. (1977). The mathematics of behavioral change: Recidivism and construct validity. *Evaluation Quarterly, 1,* 421–438.

Minor, K. I., Wells, J. B., & Jordan, F. S. (1997). Considerations for evaluating law-related education programs. In D. L. Williamson, K. I. Minor, & J. W. Fox (Eds.), *Law-Related Education and Juvenile Justice* (pp. 55–76). Springfield, IL: Charles C. Thomas.

Petersilia, J. (1996). Measuring the performance of community corrections. In T. Ellsworth (Ed.), *Contemporary Community Corrections* (pp. 312–326). Prospect Heights, IL: Waveland.

Visher, C. A., Lattimore, P. A., & Linster, R. L. (1991). Predicting the recidivism of serious youthful offenders using survival models. *Criminology, 29,* 329–366.

Rejoinder to Dr. Minor
THOM GEHRING AND CAROLYN EGGLESTON

In his essay, Professor Minor maintains that it is possible and desirable to use recidivism data to measure correctional success. We agree. Our essay focuses on whether it is practical, and politically possible, in field-based situations.

Minor discusses the meaning of correctional success by addressing traditional retribution and utilitarian deterrence and rehabilitation. He suggests that the very term *corrections* implies an agenda. We agree. Next he introduces definitions of validity as they pertain to recidivism findings. Minor suggests that, when applied selectively and carefully, recidivism data can help measure whether corrections is successful in its agenda. We agree.

Our NO essay presents ways in which data are manipulated with bias to meet the needs of key decision makers who use recidivism research to misinform, rather than to inform the public. We apply Wilber's approach to arrive at four summary questions that we now paraphrase for convenience. First, we ask whether recidivism reduction is an appropriate personal goal. We answer NO, thus agreeing with Professor Minor's corrections success-agenda concept.

Then we ask, "Do the justice systems respond fairly, treating all people equally?" We answer NO. (Minor's discussion of the difference between criminal behavior and criminal conviction may imply agreement.) Next we ask, "Has recidivism research been adequately rigorous?" and answer NO. (Similarly, Minor recommends that the "source of recidivism data" should be clearly identified. He writes the data should be "self-reports of re-offending, new arrests, new convictions, technical violations, or reincarceration.") Last, we ask, "Have the data been used to improve correctional programs?" NO. (Professor Minor's statement that recidivism has too long been a "pass or fail" "final grade" for corrections seems to parallel this view.)

We summarize "…until these questions are adequately addressed, the public and its correctional systems are vulnerable to demagogues." Again, we focus on the gap between the way this research can be used and the way it has been used.

Gaps such as this are common in social science research, partly because of the relationship between internal and external validity. Internal validity asks, "Does the treated data measure what it is supposed to measure?" and external validity asks "Will the findings generalize to others not in the sample?" These questions are inversely related, the subject of perennial compromise. Laboratory conditions can be structured to minimize threats to internal validity, but field-based practitioners cannot replicate those conditions. There is an inherent trade-off between internal and external validity. Professor Minor emphasizes whether recidivism data can be applied honestly; we emphasize whether it has been applied honestly.

In short, Professor Minor appropriately addresses theoretical implications of recidivism as a valid measure of correctional success, and we address practical implications. The YES and NO essays on this issue are not mutually exclusive but mutually confirming. We respect Professor Minor's views and admire the wealth of knowledge he brings to the issue.

NO

THOM GEHRING AND CAROLYN EGGLESTON

This debate has four parts: (1) Some themes of the recidivism research, (2) problems with recidivism as a measure of correctional success, (3) an examination of those problems based on Wilber's (1997) comprehensive or integral model for posing meaningful research questions, and (4) implications. We propose that recidivism is complex and that decision makers are not able to use relevant findings effectively.

Some Themes of the Recidivism Research

Each audience of recidivism has its own interests. For example, correctional employees have an interest in accurate data about the degree to which their work is socially useful and how its effectiveness can be enhanced. Offenders have an interest in transforming their lives, if only to avoid future confinement. Decent political and social leaders seek to improve the quality of life in communities by reducing crime. Conversely, political opportunists or demagogues seek to further personal interests by misrepresenting recidivism data. At the broadest level of abstraction, the interests of correctional employees, offenders, and social leaders are convergent. The problem is that demagogues have contrary interests. Instead of helping develop safe communities, demagogues misuse data to support divergent claims. Unfortunately, public ideas about recidivism have been influenced most by the group with the most selfish interests.

Petersilia addressed these concerns thoroughly in the Recidivism entry in the *Encyclopedia of American Prisons:*

> Despite the recognized importance of recidivism for criminal justice policy and practice, it is difficult to measure because there is no uniformly accepted definition for the term.... What has resulted is a research literature

that contains vastly different conventions—different outcomes, different time
periods, and different methodologies. Thus recidivism data reported in one
study are seldom comparable to the data in another. (McShane & Williams,
1996, 382)

Petersilia established research parameters that could result in improved and potentially useful data. However, she also reported that no national research guidelines have been developed (p. 383).

Ross and Fabiano began their book *Time to Think* with these words: "There
is very little evidence that crime prevention programs prevent crime; that rehabilitation programs rehabilitate; that deterrence deters; that corrections corrects"
(1985, 1). They then proceeded to quote (p. 2) several researchers who reported
findings parallel to Martinson's in 1974 that "almost nothing works." The whole
point of Ross and Fabiano's very effective book is that subsequent research has
successfully identified attributes of programs proven to reduce criminality and
recidivism.

Further developments were impressive. In 1984, Thorpe reported that New
York State inmates who earned college degrees recidivated significantly less than the
overall statewide return rate (p. 86). In 1994, Ryan and Mauldin found "solid support" for the claim that education reduces recidivism. Duguid, Hawkey, and Pawson
(1996) argued that prison programs, and especially education, should be politically
responsive "to the calls for accountability." They implemented a recidivism-oriented
evaluation model that provides specific information for program improvement. Another program evaluation model was developed by Tracy and Steurer (1995).

These observations indicate that a repertoire of guidelines can be applied to
make recidivism a less problematic, valid measure of correctional success. However, those guidelines will not be implemented unless decision makers and researchers apply them. To date, therefore, the problems have been almost overwhelming.

In general, the problems relate to the questions raised by Petersilia about
research definition and design, and those raised by Ross and Fabiano (1985),
Duguid et al. (1996), and others, about how recidivism data might be applied usefully. Additionally, there is always the cultural problem about justice—fairness and
equality for all people under the law. The next section addresses these problems.

Problems with Recidivism as a Measure of Correctional Success

One problem is that no one knows what the term *recidivism* means. Jurisdictions
apply different definitions. One state defines recidivism as recommitment to a
correctional institution within five years after release. An adjacent state defines it
as recommitment within three years. Still another state defines recidivism as re-

arrest within five years. Offenders, however, sometimes reside in one state but are incarcerated in another or move to another state after release.

At Elmira Reformatory before the turn of the century, releasees who died were counted as successes, because they did not recidivate (Eggleston, 1989, p. 92). In most states, a person can have an extensive juvenile record and be incarcerated as a first-offender adult. We surveyed ten jurisdictions in one part of a state so a county could define recidivism consistent with it neighbors. There was no overlap in the definitions applied by the relevant eight counties and two statewide systems. As Petersilia implied, only the federal government can define recidivism for all jurisdictions in the United States (p. 383).

A second problem is the lack of a repository for recidivism data and no universally accepted methodology for treating it. Even if a definition were imposed by the federal government, it would be meaningless without accepted procedures for data collection and treatment. For example, one state had five simultaneous procedures for data collection by: (1) type of offense (felony/misdemeanor), (2) the state's geographical regions, (3) type of inmate (state inmate, jail inmate, state responsibility inmate in a jail facility), (4) level of institutional security, and (5) each institution. This allowed officials to respond to questions by various audiences according to whatever point they wanted to make. Legislators who wanted to cut institutional budgets unless recommitment was reduced were quoted recidivism levels of 12 percent to 32 percent. Law-and-order advocacy groups who wanted to expand the program budget were given recidivism levels of 57 percent to 92 percent. Each response was technically correct, based on a different methodology.

Third, these technical problems result in recidivism reports for disinformation, rather than for public information. Some states use so many methodologies that informed observers perceive an arbitrary treatment of the data to hide the ineffectiveness of the justice systems. It is a prolonged process to become sufficiently informed about the issue so one can ask relevant questions. In general, it is impossible to remain well informed, because methodologies are subject to change without notice.

Fourth, even if all these technical problems were solved, the meaning of recidivism data would still be elusive. Even if there were an accepted definition of recidivism—with a data repository, methodology, and full disclosure of procedures—we still would not know the meaning of recidivism in regard to correctional success. The relationship among crime, arrest, and incarceration is subject to so many diverse influences that it is often perceived as arbitrary or based on cultural inequalities.

Despite the expense of recidivism research, there are tendencies to focus exclusively on one part and overlook other parts. For example, few would disagree with the truth that people should be able to live decently or responsibly in a community without committing crimes. That is the unstated assumption of current recidivism research. But there are other obvious issues.

While media direct attention to inner city and minority crime, gender and age are the best predictors of incarceration, and incarceration is the best predictor of recidivism. Media mixes messages for political impact, instead of focusing on the facts.

Fifth, if problems of interpretation could be resolved, there would still be no adequate explanation of how recidivism measures correctional success. We do not know whether recidivism measures the effectiveness of industrial, religious, security, or education programs. It might measure the value of the institutional medical program or the spacing of the windows. Recidivism is a nonspecific measure most frequently used to assess the success of a specific institutional program; education. Therefore, we now focus on recidivism to measure education program success.

Recidivism is not applied to local school education, and it is inappropriately applied to institutional education. Local schoolchildren recidivate when they drop out and later enroll in a GED program, but we never hear the term *recidivism* used in this context. Similarly, we never hear the term used when bypass patients return to the hospital for a pacemaker or when faulty cars are recalled. It is unfair that recidivism is mostly associated in the public mind with the effectiveness of institutional education. The association itself reveals bias.

Lack of education is related to, but does not cause, crime. Recidivism data often are presented so the reader will assume that education causes reduced recidivism. However, that causal influence was never proved. When enrollment is voluntary, education is associated with the pursuit of a social lifestyle. Offenders who are interested in improving their lives self-select for school; the uninterested deselect themselves. When enrollment is mandatory, education is treated like any other institutional program; we cannot isolate the role of education as a contributor to reduced recidivism. Education helps people pursue social aspirations; it does not make people into good community members.

Several years ago a state found that one educational program reduced recidivism by approximately 50 percent, so they developed an extensive program delivery capability. Recently another state found that education did not reduce recidivism, so they sought to terminate the education program. How far will this go? Why not extend the same perspective to food or sanitation facilities in the institutions? In the absence of accepted standards for collecting and treating recidivism data, the "political spin" that is applied seems almost as important as the actual research findings.

Though not necessarily related to education, the perspective on boot camps is a good example of "political spin." Despite findings that boot camps do not necessarily reduce recidivism, many decision makers support them (Morris & Rothman, 1995; MacKenzie, in McShane and Williams, 1996). The public seems to have adopted a "don't confuse me with the facts" attitude. This is not how research is supposed to be used.

Sixth, recidivism is currently a dichotomous, unsophisticated, terminal measure, incapable of determining incremental progress toward postrelease success. We do not know whether inmate graduates of the tenth grade recidivate less than do high school equivalency graduates. We do not know whether those who learn public speaking recidivate less than those who learn arithmetic. Even when applied to education, recidivism data are nonspecific. Yet without answering incremental questions, our ability to use recidivism to enhance corrections program effectiveness is immature. Currently, it is used only to detract from the program.

Recidivism measures only *yes* or *no* and is incapable of identifying shades of improvement. Few would suggest that a murderer who recidivates as a forger has not made progress, or that an armed robber who moves on to a career of mail fraud has not taken steps to eliminate coercive violence from his behavior. Recidivism is insensitive to such progress. Therefore, even if all the problems of research and interpretation could be solved, recidivism still would not measure real-life reintegration.

The seventh problem outlines aspects of Sutton's report for the United Nations. His language is concise, relevant, and appropriate to this essay: "…prisons not only teach what the system intends, they also teach criminality and alienation from the social system…life chances can on balance be reduced by the total effect of imprisonment, rather than increased by the educational element of that experience…. There is the increased likelihood of being arrested again after one or more previous convictions" (Sutton, 1992, 55). These seven problems of recidivism should prompt caution about research methodology and the use of study findings.

An Examination of the Integral Studies Approach to Recidivism

Wilber (1997) developed a system to help researchers ask comprehensive and meaningful questions. He used four quadrants on a chart divided two ways: interior–exterior and individual–collective. These parameters are shown in Table 1.1, with problems from the previous section in four concise questions.

Implications

Recidivism is a flawed measure of correctional success. Public attention has focused on one part of the issue, neglecting other important parts. That part is that criminals should stop taking advantage of others—they should transform themselves, or be transformed—they should stop being criminals. This is of course true, but it is only one dimension of the recidivism issue. In the popular understanding, recidivism measures the lack of correctional success. Too many confined offenders have returned to communities without being sufficiently transformed.

TABLE 1.1   Four Relevant Questions about Recidivism

Interior (Individual)	Exterior (Individual)
The Interpretive, Subjective "I" Validity Claim: **Truthfulness**	The Empirical, Objective "IT" Validity Claim: **Truth**
Question: Should released individuals be able to live decent lives in the free community responsibility, without committing crimes?	**Question:** Can recidivism be researched rigorously (is the term adequately defined— are there accepted standards for data collection/treatment/reporting)?
Answer: Yes	**Answer:** No
Question: In general, do North American criminal justice systems treat all people equally and fairly, regardless of race, ethnicity, gender, or socioeconomic class?	**Question:** Have recidivism data been used to identify the adequacy or inadequacy of specific correctional programs to facilitate program improvement?
Answer: No	**Answer:** No

Interior (Collective)	Exterior (Collective)
The Cultural, Intersubjective "WE" Validity Claim: **Justice**	The Social, Interobjective "IT" Validity Claim: **Functional Fit**

At least three other relevant questions should also be asked: What does recidivism actually measure? Has it been usefully applied? Is it a fair standard in an unfair world? At the very least, Wilber's integral model suggests that the issue is more expansive and complex than people usually think. At most, it raises important questions about the appropriateness of public policy based on unjustified assumptions about recidivism. Until the "get tough on crime" sentiment evolves into a "get smart on crime" agenda, decision makers should be cautious about recidivism as a measure of correctional success. The reason is clear: until these questions are adequately addressed, the public and its correctional systems are vulnerable to demagogues.

Correctional workers should be careful if visitors to their institutions even mention the word *recidivism*. Program supporters frequently ask, "What are your goals? How can I help?" By contrast, program detractors ask, "What is your recidivism rate?"

Everyone agrees that "getting out and staying out" is an important aspiration of inmates and correctional programs. Nevertheless, there are demagogic–opportunist detractors. They do not shrink from interpreting recidivism data to exacerbate problems of cultural confusion, poor research designs, and resource inadequacy. Recidivism data can be used to destroy, as well as to support institutional programs. Therefore, correctional decision makers and interested citizens should proceed with extreme caution.

REFERENCES

Duguid, S., Hawkey, C., & Pawson, R. (1996, June). Using recidivism to evaluate effectiveness in prison education programs. *Journal of Correctional Education, 47* (2), 74–85.

Eggleston, C. R. (1989). *Zebulon Brockway and Elmira Reformatory: A study of correctional/special education.* Richmond, VA: Virginia Commonwealth University (unpublished Ph.D. dissertation).

Morris, N., & Rothman, D. J. (Eds.). (1995). *The Oxford history of the prison: The practice of punishment in Western society.* New York: Oxford University Press.

McShane, M. D., & Williams, F. P. (Eds.). (1996). *Encyclopedia of American prisons.* New York: Garland Publishing Company.

Ross, R., & Fabiano, E. (1985). *Time to think: A cognitive model of delinquency prevention and offender rehabilitation.* Johnson City, TN: Institute of Social Sciences and Arts.

Ryan, T. A., & Mauldin, B. J. (1994, April 14). *Correctional education and recidivism: An historical analysis.* Columbia, South Carolina (unpublished paper).

Sutton, P. (1992). *Basic education in prisons: Interim report.* Hamburg, Germany: UNESCO Institute for Education.

Thorpe, T. (1984, September). Follow-up study of offenders who earn college degrees while incarcerated in New York State. *Journal of Correctional Education, 35* (3), 86–88.

Tracy, A., & Steurer, S. J. (1995, December). Correctional education programming: The development of a model evaluation instrument. *Journal of Correctional Education, 46* (4), 156–166.

Wilber, K. (1997). *The eye of spirit: An integral vision for a world gone slightly mad.* Boston: Shambhala.

Rejoinder to Drs. Gehring and Eggleston   KEVIN I. MINOR

Drs. Gehring and Eggleston divide their argument into three sections. In the first section, Some Themes of the Recidivism Research, they state that some audiences of recidivism research misuse the information to further selfish agendas. The authors also note that there are established guidelines for measuring recidivism validly, but they express concern that these guidelines may not be applied. There is little to disagree with here, because neither of these points invalidates recidivism as a measure of correctional success. Both points illustrate why it is essential to be precise and explicit about the goals a given program is meant to achieve. The points also show why it is essential to take proactive steps to ensure that recidivism research is competently conducted and responsibly interpreted, with an eye toward limitations of the research. Selfishness, incompetence, irresponsibility, and other negative characteristics of select officials and researchers do not demonstrate the invalidity of recidivism.

In the second section, Drs. Gehring and Eggleston elaborate on various problems with recidivism as a measure of success in corrections. They speak first to the problem of definition, something that is less problematic when we see that recidivism can be meaningfully defined only in relation to a program's goals. Given that different correctional programs have different goals, multiple definitions of recidivism are warranted. In fact, almost all social science variables have multiple operationalizations; definition depends on context. Along the same line, it is good that no central repository exists for recidivism data and there is no single agreed-on method for assessing recidivism. Formulation of the latter seems inadvisable, given that no social science method is problem free. Where possible, researchers should employ multiple methods to study the same thing, hoping that this will help compensate for the problems inherent in any single method. I see no convincing argument that recidivism is impossible to measure validly within an explicit, acceptable margin of error.

The authors also express concern over which aspect of correctional success (e.g., education, religion, security) is being assessed by recidivism as a "nonspecific measure." My response is that the all too frequent practice of using recidivism as a general, overall measure should be abandoned. Instead, recidivism should be operationalized as precisely as possible around program goals that are themselves as specific as possible. Vagueness and ambiguity over goals and corresponding outcome measures invite widely varying interpretations and thereby make the misuse of research findings convenient for the demagogues whom Drs. Gehring and Eggleston rightly criticize. The aspect of success/nonsuccess being assessed by recidivism measurement can be determined only by careful delineation of correctional goals and implementation of solid experimental or quasi-experimental design tailored around those goals.

The authors also object to recidivism on grounds that it is "dichotomous" and "incapable of measuring incremental progress." But the validity of this objection is entirely contingent on the operationalization and measurement of recidivism. One can measure recidivism as a continuous rather than categorical variable (e.g., number of self-reported offenses or new official charges filed over a specified time frame). In this manner, it becomes possible to speak of degrees of success, as opposed to talking in simple yes or no terms. This end can be further served by assessing the type and timing of recidivistic behavior.

In the final section, Drs. Gehring and Eggleston conclude that recidivism represents a flawed indicator of correctional success, an assertion that I do not believe is supported by the arguments advanced. It is possible to measure recidivism validly, and without any rationale to the contrary. Recidivism should generally be included as a correctional program goal. As an alternative to the questions posed by the authors in this section, I would suggest asking: "What are the program's goals? Is recidivism germane to these goals? If not, why not? If so, how can it be measured in a way that is most meaningful to assessing the goals?" I agree with them that we must proceed with caution, but I think we should do so in a way that remains cognizant of recidivism as a major aspect of success.

Shaming: An Innovative and Successful Approach to Punishment?

Ruth-Ellen Grimes argues YES. She is a member of the Criminal Justice faculty at California State University, San Bernardino, and received her doctorate in 1993 from the University of Toronto. Her major areas of research include youth violence and delinquency, racial discrimination in justice processing, and media coverage of criminal and civil trials.

Katherine J. Bennett argues NO. She received a Ph.D. in criminal justice from Sam Houston State University in 1996 and is currently Associate Professor in Criminal Justice at Armstrong Atlantic State University in Savannah, Georgia. Her research interests include prison litigation, inmate rights, crime and popular culture, and reintegrative shaming theory.

YES

RUTH-ELLEN GRIMES

Although Braithwaite's 1989 seminal work on shaming, *Crime, Shame and Reintegration,* is the most frequently cited contemporary volume on the topic, his theory has been empirically tested by a myriad of criminologists, including Baumer (1997), Hagan and McCarthy (1997), Grasmick and Bursik (1990) and Grasmick, Bursik, and Arnekiev (1993). These research efforts have generated a broader understanding of the nature of crime and delinquency, recidivism, and overall social control.

In addition, social theorists such as Tittle (1995) have systematically critiqued Braithwaite's integrative shaming model and found the work complex, rich, and a "pattern-setting document" (as the late Donald Cressey observes on the book's jacket). Tittle's analysis of Braithwaite's contribution to theoretical interaction, in particular, points to the merits of tackling the problem of predatory deviance by linking anomie/opportunity, control, subcultural, learning, and labeling theories through a bridging or "shunting" process called shaming (Tittle, 1995, p. 112).

Reintegrative versus Disintegrative Shaming in Cultural Context

For Braithwaite, *shaming* refers to the expression of disapproval, and invocation of remorse, in a sequential process, contrary to Tittle's reading that "shaming and reintegration must occur simultaneously" (Tittle, 1995, p. 115), in which the individual is confronted by significant others (peers, family, neighbors, teachers) in an effort to moralize the offender and explain the evil of such offensive behavior (Braithwaite, 1989). Reintegrative shaming is characterized by community efforts to build moral conscience and strengthen social bonds. These efforts to reaccept the contrite offender back into the fold are paramount to successful reintegration.

Disintegrative shaming falls at the other end of the continuum, an end point at which the stigmatization has alienated the offender from the community, has failed to provide any avenue for reconciliation with the community, and ultimately degrades the outcast to the point where the delinquency becomes "Master Status" (in George Herbert Mead's categorization).

When shaming inculcates mutual respect, encourages social networking in interdependencies, and provides symbolic significance in the redemption of the individual, Braithwaite argues it is an extraordinarily powerful, efficient, and just form of social control. He qualifies the condition in which positive shaming contributes to lower crime rates as one of communitarianism, a literal community of concern.

Social Solidarity and Criminality in Malta and Japan

Given Braithwaite's criteria for a communitarian society, one grounded in social solidarity and marked by a high degree of integration and traditional modes of family and religious life, researchers have identified such societies and have analyzed the rates of crime, incarceration, recidivism, and compliance with law. Baumer (1997) explored these patterns in the Republic of Malta, a small Mediterranean island that "…fits nicely with Braithwaite's portrait of a communitarian society" (p. 604). He found that the social–structural conditions led to remarkably low levels of crime and incarceration. One might hypothesize that the strong social institutions of family and church (measures of integration), combined with a significant social welfare system, which produced such low rates of criminality and institutionalization, should also produce low rates of recidivism. However, these conditions did not yield similarly low levels of recidivism.

Baumer finds that Malta's recidivism rates actually mirrored those of nations characterized by heterogeneity and lower levels of integration. He grapples with the issue and speculates that Malta did not have the reintegrative resources to facilitate community intervention in terms of reintegrating offenders on release from prison. This void, Baumer posits, in addition to evidence that offenders meet with significant disapproval/stigmatization, thus supports Braithwaite's thesis (Baumer, 1997).

For Braithwaite, the key communitarian society underscoring reintegrative shaming is Japan. "When an individual is shamed in Japan, the shame is often borne by the collectivity to which the individual belongs as well—the family, the company, the school—particularly by the titular head of the collectivity" (Braithwaite, 1989, p. 63). The Japanese criminal justice system works in concert with family and school in providing alternatives to punishment. Reliance on self-guilt assignment and reintegrative shaming allows for repentance and reunification. Social control is diverted back to the environment of the significant others—the family, school and workplace (Braithwaite, 1989).

Cohen's (1990) comparison of the ecology of identities in the United States and Japan questions, "Why group pressure is so much stronger in Japan than in the United States, and how exactly does group pressure work to make the Japanese so well behaved?" (p. 113). Cohen argues that Japanese immersion in the collectivity may be contrasted to American individualism and that Japanese law derives largely from continental European models (which) are reluctant to recognize collectivities as criminal actors (p. 114). Consequently, the collectivity is treated more as an object of informal social control than of formal legal control.

The discussion is relevant as Braithwaite moves beyond individual deviance to corporate wrongdoing in his work, questioning why compliance to regulatory agencies and other law-making groups may be more effective if the collectivities share significant interaction with one another. Indeed, Cohen cites a *New York Times* article in which Japan is described as

> [a] country that regards corporations as surrogate families for their employees …(and where)…the idea of buying or selling a company is fraught with negative implications…(and further as stated by a Japanese CEO equivalent) "You don't have so many deals traditionally because to put a company up for sale generally means there has been some kind of failure…It is very shameful" (Cohen, 1990, p, 115 [footnote 4]).

Cohen identifies four mechanisms that affect the moral composition of an ecological field: (1) recruitment—bringing together those morally prepared for acting with one another; (2) socialization—educating those as to the right moral attitudes;

(3) allocation (mobility)—allowance for acquisition of relevant moral attitudes based on perceived need in different positions; and (4) extrusion or disposal—removal of troublesome people with the wrong moral attitudes (Cohen, 1990, p. 117).

These phases clearly parallel Braithwaite's reintegrative shaming scheme, especially because #4 allows for the ability of one to return to the fold; it is a non-definitive event likened to Braithwaite's finite open-ended duration of shaming terminated by forgiveness. Therefore, the Japanese society presents a high degree of cultural homogeneity and a low degree of criminality because of the view of punishment as shameful versus boastful.

The Australian and New Zealand Experience

Further support for Braithwaite's theory, in a macrocorporate context, is found in his own work with Makkai (1994) on reintegrative shaming and compliance with regulatory standards in their study of Australian nursing homes. They also discuss juvenile justice reform in the guise of "family group conferences," a national policy in New Zealand since 1989, which is a Maori-based reintegrative shaming model centuries old. In the New Zealand setting, and now through the Australian community accountability conferences, the adjudication of youth in court is replaced by conferences involving mostly interdependent family members, the victim, and supporters who care about the victim (1994; pp. 363, 379).

In New South Wales' community accountability conferences, "It is not the police convening the conferences who are relied on to do the reintegrative shaming; it is the family members, friends, and football coaches, selected for attendance precisely because of their special bonds of care for the offender" (Makkai & Braithwaite, 1994, p. 379). The authors posit that, in the youth conferences and regulatory exchanges, the emphasis on the problematic issue in lieu of the wrong-doer, in the context of community concern and acceptance, creates the macro-structural context necessary to reintegrative shaming (p. 380).

Aboriginal Justice

An aboriginal justice paradigm stands in stark contrast to an American justice paradigm. American processing is essentially vertical, but Aboriginal justice is holistic. Whereas American legal dialogue is both rehearsed and conducted in English, indigenous justice encourages conversant fluidity, employing native language. The United States system relies on statutory codification, the Indigenous on oral customary law. The American system is adversarial and argumentative in nature, and the indigenous system fosters trust, resolution, and healing (Melton, 1995).

The American system encourages separation of power, separation of church and state, and the indigenous system views law and justice as a way of life in a spiritual realm. The United States model offers a fragmented, isolated approach to the problem of offending, and the indigenous model encourages comprehensive problem solving. The American process is time oriented, whereas the indigenous process values patience. Use of stranger advocates in the United States is replaced by extended family members in indigenous culture. The U.S. system is focused on individual rights, and the indigenous system is focused on victim and community rights. High degrees of punitiveness are stressed in the American context; accountability and responsibility is stressed in the indigenous system. Sanctions in the United States system are state driven, seen as retributive to society; indigenous sanctions are customary, seen as necessary to restore interdependencies. And finally, the American system protects the rights of the accused, especially against self-incrimination; as opposed to the indigenous obligation to verbalize accountability (Melton, 1995).

Aboriginal justice looks for alternatives. In *Voyage of Rediscovery* (1990), Phil Lucas reenacts the case of Frank Brown, a Heiltsuk community gang leader found guilty of robbery and assault. Brown was banished for eight months to an isolated island. Brown epitomized the aboriginal youths on reserves and in urban centers throughout Canada who are caught in the conflict between their native system and the foreign sociolegal political system imposed on them. First Nations' communities have fought back against forced alienation from enshrined traditions and often intervene on behalf of their youth in Anglo-Canadian courts. Brown found, through traditional banishment, a respect for self, family, clan community, future generations, the land, and the Creator. Ten years after his banishment, Brown felt adequately resocialized to hold a *quxua,* the washing off ceremony, in which he dramatized his experience on the island and his reentry into the Bella Bella community.

The ceremonial rite of passage was performed by song and dance over four stages: (1) having the problem; (2) recognizing the problem; (3) confronting the problem; and (4) overcoming the problem, moving past it, reflecting back, and moving forward. This dramatization of the evil behavior allowed Brown to fully recognize his shaming by the elders and feel the support of the people who believed in his resocialization.

The aboriginal culture recognizes the difficulty young people have in moving from childhood through adolescence to adulthood. Relationships are fostered to ensure successful reentry and restoration of traditional means of conflict resolution. Braithwaite's criteria for successful reintegrative shaming are met, complete with the washing off ceremony, which literally cancels out the degradation of the previous disposal.

Streetwise Delinquency

Hagan and McCarthy, in *Mean Streets: Youth Crime and Homelessness* (1997), follow in Braithwaite's tradition of investigating macro and micro sociological forces that impact on youthful offending. They argue that street youth are subject to severe parental (extralegal) and legal sanctions over their life course, "and that these childhood experiences of parental abuse and violence, and the resulting shame spirals these produce, may be predisposing life experiences that interact with later criminal justice sanctions to intensify involvements in crime" (p. 185). Hagan and McCarthy develop an interactive model of criminal behavior that explores the consequences of legal and extralegal sanctioning. They test Braithwaite's notion that deviance calls out either positive reacceptance or negative stigmatization, and they "propose that predisposing family contexts of parental abuse and violence interact with police sanctions to amplify involvements in secondary forms of street crime" (p. 185). They find this effect strongest among youthful males, but interestingly, it is also apparent among female street youth.

Shame and Embarrassment

Grasmick and Bursik (1990) neatly delineate between shame, a self-imposed punishment resulting from an individual's ability to feel guilt and experience remorse, and embarrassment, a social punishment resulting in a loss of respect from significant others, a consequence of the individual's transgression of norms held sacred by that group. They "propose that both conscience (internalized norms) and attachments to significant others (broadly defined to include friends, family, etc.) function as potential sources of punishments which, like state imposed legal sanctions, vary in both their certainty and their severity" (1990, p. 839). They developed parallel measures of the perceived threats of shame, embarrassment, and legal sanctions for three offenses: tax evasion, petty theft, and drunk driving. They found that threats of shame and legal sanctions did deter the motivation to commit all three offenses.

Grasmick et al. (1993) revisited their hypothesis in relation to individuals' self-reported reduction in drunk driving, and found that the threat of shame was the primary reason cited for this decrease. Interestingly, this phenomenon occurred after moral crusading legislative attacks against drunk driving had been launched in the research venue. They found a parallel to their concept of the threat of shame and Braithwaite's consciences, which internally deter criminal behavior. They conclude: "Shame, a variable with a long and recently revitalized tradition in sociology, not only appeared in the analysis as a greater deterrent than the threat of legal sanctions, but also accounted for the reduction in drunk driving over an eight-year period" (p. 62).

Conclusion and Suggestion for Shaming's Applicability in the United States Context

The effects of positive shaming on reducing certain criminal behaviors has now been put forward in theoretical and empirical review. Although the strongest case for reintegrative shaming was seemingly made in reference to Japan, I note a telling remark in Braithwaite's volume: "In establishing the relationship between communitarianism and crime, we rely far too heavily on qualitative evidence from Japan..." (1989, p. 105).

In my opinion, this allows for a serious reassessment of shaming's previously held ability to work more or less exclusively in highly integrated societies. If we look to increased community activism in American inner cities, we find grass roots efforts to reinculcate pride in neighborhoods, a growing climate of reconciliation, and the increasingly visible development of a moral sense. Myriad programs call for accountability and responsibility. Organized community activists openly defy drug dealers and call for their shameful displacement.

I argue that the people who engage in this shaming should (1) care about the macro and micro outcomes and (2) care about the community, the individual victim, and the ultimate disposition of the offender—maintaining an option of return. Dysfunctional families remain a significant problem, but neighborhood churches and community organizations are more and more acting as supportive emotional units. The calls for fellowship and moral bonding should be heeded and supported by both the local residents and the dominant elites.

Gangs may be viewed not solely as negative entities, but, as Braithwaite states: "...sometimes these subcultures provide a social environment which is merely more tolerant of deviations from societal norms when opportunities arise to choose between gratification and compliance..." (p. 66). Systematic review of the dominant group's ability to alter the initial motivation to choose gratification should be examined. Economic opportunities that may change the subculture's motivation should not be ignored.

REFERENCES

Baumer, E. (1997). Levels and predictors of recidivism: The Malta experience. *Criminology, 31* (4), 601–628.

Braithwaite, J. (1989). *Crime, shame and reintegration.* New York: Cambridge University Press.

Cohen, A. (1990). Criminal actors: Natural persons and collectivities. In *New directions in the study of justice, law, and social control* (pp. 101–125). New York: Plenum Press.

Grasmick, H. G., Bursik, R. J., & Amekiev, B. J. (1993). Reduction in drunk driving as a response to increased threats of shame, embarrassment, and legal sanctions. *Criminology, 31* (1), 41–67.

Grasmick, H. G., & Bursik, R. J. (1990). Conscience, significant others, and rational choice: Extending the deterrence model. *Law and Society Review, 24* (3), 837–861.

Hagan, J., & McCarthy, B. (1997). *Mean streets: Youth crime and homelessness.* New York: Cambridge University Press.

Lucas, P. (1990). *Voyage of rediscovery*. (Review of the Canadian National Film Board's video program *Voyage of Rediscovery*). *First Nations: The Circle Unbroken*, 27–28.

Makkai, T., & Braithwaite, J. (1994). Reintegrative shaming and compliance with regulatory standards. *Criminology, 32* (3), 361–383.

Melton, A. P. (1995). Indigenous justice systems and tribal society. *Judicature, 79* (3), 126–133.

Tittle, C. R. (1995). *Control balance: Toward a general theory of deviance*. Boulder, CO: Westview Press.

Rejoinder to Professor Grimes KATHERINE J. BENNETT

Professor Grimes argues that shaming *is* an innovative and successful approach to punishment. Focusing on Braithwaite's (1989) reintegrative shaming theory, Professor Grimes defines the key concept of reintegrative shaming, contrasting that with disintegrative shaming or stigmatization. She discusses empirical support for reintegrative shaming theory and then contrasts the aboriginal justice system with the American justice system. Although her argument is concentrated in large part on communitarian and aboriginal societies, she concludes by calling for a reassessment of shaming's potential for American society and suggests that the needed communitarianism may be evident in community activism in inner cities, particularly in neighborhood churches.

Professor Grimes presents a cogent review of reintegrative shaming theory and makes a compelling argument for reintegrative shaming's potential as a successful approach to punishment. In fact, I agree that *reintegrative* shaming does have much to offer in the way of explaining desistance from crime and as a crime prevention strategy. Braithwaite's theory of reintegrative shaming has received much attention and acclaim. The theory is broad in scope, and Braithwaite strives hard to establish its testability. However, what I have argued is that reintegrative shaming is not what is currently being practiced in the United States. Moreover, we too often confuse shame with some other emotion, and extant tests of reintegrative shaming theory are characterized by unclear concepts.

Professor Grimes refers to Makkai's and Braithwaite (1994) ethnographic field study of "community accountability conferences" with juvenile offenders in Australia and New Zealand as one source of empirical support for reintegrative shaming. These conferences are not direct experiments or tests of reintegrative shaming theory, although Braithwaite sees them as characteristic of reintegrative shaming ceremonies. As Makkai and Braithwaite note, the origins of this reform movement are to be found in Maori culture.

Another source of empirical support cited by Professor Grimes is Makkai and Braithwaite's (1994) test of reintegrative shaming in the realm of compliance with governmental regulatory standards. The authors observed in this article that this test is a first attempt to measure the concept of reintegration. More troublesome in this study, however, was the measure for the key concept of interdependency. The researchers' measure for interdependency was simply whether directors of homes had met inspectors before the regulatory encounter.

Professor Grimes also relies on research by Grasmick, Bursik, and Arnekiev (1993), who note that shame "is being revived as a central concern in the social and behavioral sciences in general and in criminology" (p. 42). Their research falls short by failing to distinguish among shame, guilt, and embarrassment. For example, in testing shame and embarrassment as informal deterrents, they state that shame "is experienced most immediately as the pain of feeling guilt or remorse, and it can occur even if no one but the actor is aware of the transgression" (p. 43). These authors describe shame as "a self-imposed sanction" that "occurs when actors violate norms they have internalized," unlike embarrassment, which "is a socially imposed sanction that occurs when actors violate norms endorsed by others whose opinions the actors value and who become aware of the actors' transgressions" (pp. 43–44).

The authors asked a sample to respond to the statement: "Generally, in most situations I would feel guilty if I drove an automobile while under the influence of a moderate amount of alcohol." To measure perceived severity of shame, the authors "asked respondents to imagine that they did feel guilty or remorseful and to consider how big a problem such a feeling would cause for their lives." These researchers, then, are using the feeling of *guilt* to capture the feeling of shame. However, the authors offered two feelings (guilt and remorse) to capture just how strong that feeling of shame would be. Embarrassment was measured by asking respondents "if most of the people whose opinions they value would lose respect for them if they drove while under the influence" (p. 51). This measure fits the authors' definition of embarrassment, but it still is an indirect measure—others' loss of respect. The authors noted a positive correlation between shame and embarrassment and suggest that this correlation is in keeping with Braithwaite's contention that what we call shame results from repeated experiences of embarrassment (p. 56). Braithwaite also sees shame and guilt as interchangeable concepts. Such research reflects confusion about these emotions and fails as appropriate tests of reintegrative shaming theory.

Tests of reintegrative shaming theory have been lacking. In particular, operationalizing key concepts has been haphazard, resulting in weak, inadequate measures. Further critical support for reintegrative shaming must depend on convincing tests of the theory.

I agree strongly that reintegrative shaming theory intimates promise. I also agree with Professor Grimes that there should be a reassessment of reintegrative shaming's potential as a sanction in the United States. Reintegrative shaming theory is particularly applicable to the restorative justice paradigm. Reintegrative shaming theory is socially significant, and further studies are needed, especially in light of the aforementioned criticisms of some of the tests. Also, it is crucial that the public shaming trend in this country, an irrational, unthinking, mean-spirited response to crime, *not* be confused with reintegrative shaming theory.

REFERENCES

Braithwaite, J. (1989). *Crime, shame and reintegration.* New York: Cambridge University Press.

Grasmick, H. G., Bursik, R. J., & Arnekiev, B. J. (1993). Reduction in drunk driving as a response to increased threats of shame, embarrassment, and legal sanctions. *Criminology, 31* (1), 41–67.

Makkai, T., & Braithwaite, J. (1994). Reintegrative shaming and compliance with regulatory standards. *Criminology, 32* (3), 361–383.

NO

KATHERINE J. BENNETT

An Arkansas housewife convicted of shoplifting a 99-cent tube of lipstick was fined 250 dollars, placed on probation for 12 months, and sentenced to five hours of walking in front of the store from which she shoplifted, wearing a sign that read: "I Got Caught Shoplifting at Fred's" (Russell, 1997).

A 62-year-old Illinois farmer, as one condition of his probation for assaulting another farmer, had a sign posted at the end of his driveway: "Warning A Violent Felon Lives Here. Travel At Your Own Risk" (Hoffman, 1997).

By a judge's order, a woman was permitted to spit in her former husband's face as part of the ex-husband's sentence for harassing her (Kahan, 1996).

A New Hampshire legislator sponsored legislation permitting bare-bottom spankings of juvenile offenders ages twelve and older (Bass, 1996).

This is a list of a very few examples of the public shaming sanctions that either are being delivered by judges throughout the United States or are being proposed by legislators. Academicians have noted a growing trend in American criminal justice systems for these "public shaming" sanctions. Such sanctions range from stigmatizing publicity to literal stigmatization to self-debasement penalties to contrition ceremonies (requiring offenders to publicly apologize for their actions) (Kahan, 1996). The sanctions are described as "public shaming devices" to teach offenders responsibility for their actions (Bass, 1996). Shaming sentences have been promoted at judges' conferences and are being popularized as low-cost, innovative, effective deterrents (Russell, 1997). Serious attention is given to sanctioning flogging, the pillory, electric shock, and whipping machines (Wiedeman, 1996). But is such shaming really innovative and successful? This chapter argues that:

1. Public shaming is not innovative.
2. Public shaming is probably not successful.
3. Public shaming is not reintegrative shaming.
4. Public shaming is based on confusion about emotions and may be harmful in itself.
5. Public shaming may result in sentences that violate certain moral constraints on punishment.

Shaming Is Not an Innovative Approach to Punishment

That public shaming is not innovative can be seen by any cursory glance through introductory history or corrections texts. In seventeenth-century America, punishments were harsh, humiliating, and public. Flogging, including whippings with a cat-o'-nine tails, were popular and were practiced until the mid-1900s (Welch, 1996). Public whippings, in fact, were the most commonly used sentence for both felonies and misdemeanors (Walker, 1980). Corporal punishment has long been permitted in many schools, and more recently, the caning of Michael Fay in Singapore received significant American support.

Other public punishments in colonial America included branding on the hand, cheek, or forehead (*T* for thieves, *R* for repeat offenders, *B* for blasphemy, *SL* for seditious libel, and *D* for drunkards) (Welch, 1996). In 1718, a law in Pennsylvania required those receiving public support to wear a large blue or red letter *P* on their sleeve (Walker, 1980). Instead of physically branding women, female offenders also wore letters on their clothing, such as the scarlet letter *A* for *adulteress*. Gossipers were publicly humiliated by being forced to wear the brank, a birdcage-like device fastened to the offender's head (Welch, 1996, p. 61). Ducking stools were also commonly used and involved tying the offender to the chair or plank and submerging them briefly into water, as a reminder to "keep your mouth shut" (p. 61). Offenders were also placed in stocks and pillories in the center of town, where townspeople threw rotten vegetables, eggs, and stones at those on display. The pillory was last used in Delaware in 1905. Clearly, there is nothing new in the rediscovery of public shaming.

The primary purpose of such punishments was public humiliation. This may have seemed quite sensible when crime and sin were seen as one and the same and there was no attempt made to rehabilitate or reform the individual (Walker, 1980). However, by the eighteenth century, the Age of Enlightenment, such thinking underwent profound change; enlightenment philosophers saw the criminal justice system as "savage and irrational" and turned to thinking about crime prevention and reforming the system of punishment. By the late 1700s, public humiliation in America was no longer viewed as useful, even if it was occasionally practiced.

Public punishments were infrequently employed by the twentieth century; indeed, by the 1800s, these punishments were regarded as a harsh, undignified spectacle, and the community was no longer perceived as a "paragon of morality." Less than two hundred years later, we have returned to punishment as spectacle. Our return to public shaming penalties is credited as beginning in the 1980s, "with mortified Wall Street traders appearing on the nightly news in handcuffs" (Hoffman, 1997). But is public shaming successful?

Shaming Is Not a Successful Approach to Punishment

The Arkansas housewife mentioned at the beginning of this chapter was described as "clearly angry and embarrassed" on the day of her walk, refusing to talk to a reporter (Russell, 1997, p. 103). The Illinois farmer was depicted as unrepentant and challenged the imposition of the sign. The Illinois Supreme Court subsequently overturned his sentence. Other offenders have described their sentences as unfair and violative of their civil rights. Shaming penalties lack empirical research testing their effectiveness, but some indication of what we might expect may be provided by a recent University of Maryland study. This study found that short-term programs such as boot camps and drug education classes had little impact on crime prevention, in part because of these programs' failure to fundamentally change thinking or behavior or improve conditions in which offenders live (Butterfield, 1997). The same criticisms may be applied to public shaming, and for these reasons, shaming is likely to be ineffective.

Public shaming is not without censure from criminal justice practitioners, scholars, and the judiciary. A Florida public defender suggests that public shaming can have far-reaching detrimental effects on the offender's family, subjecting family members and especially children to ridicule and scorn. Jenni Gainsborough, public policy administrator for the ACLU's National Prison Project, sees public shaming as appealing to the "basest instincts" in people. Mitzi Vorachek, the director of community education at a center for battered women, notes that requiring batterers to publicly apologize is not a solution. She observes that "batterers apologize all the time. And they make all the excuses batterers always make" (Russell, 1997, pp. 103–104). Toni Massaro, law professor at the University of Arizona, describes shaming penalties as "whimsical, coarsely drafted," and without "restorative components" (Hoffman, 1997, p. All). Objections from the judiciary include the Tennessee State Supreme Court's ruling against a trial judge who had ordered a sign placed in an offender's yard announcing that the offender is a child molester. The state court referred to state law mandating the purpose of probation as giving offenders the "opportunity to rehabilitate themselves and to be restored to useful and productive citizenship" (Russell, 1997, pp. 105, 138; Hoffman, 1997). The sign in the offender's yard, according to the court, was punishment that went beyond the scope of rehabilitation.

The public shaming sanctions just discussed are the antithesis of alternative sanctions such as reintegrative shaming, family conferencing, and conflict resolution. The next section discusses these alternatives, their merits, and how public shaming differs.

Public Shaming Is Not Reintegrative Shaming

Popular public shaming sanctions are directly antithetical to Braithwaite's (1989) theory of reintegrative shaming, a theory that may be applied to the concept of restorative justice, family conferencing, and conflict resolution education. These practices are serious, in-depth approaches to preventing and reducing crime. Family conferencing focuses on the offender accepting responsibility and "owning the behavior" in a positive setting and in a forum constructively aimed at repairing the harm caused by the offender's actions. Conflict resolution education recognizes that delinquency and violence are symptoms of the inability to handle conflict and seeks to provide the juvenile with lasting decision-making skills. These approaches reflect the idea of restorative justice, not public shaming, which is "justice that humiliates," according to Gainsborough (Hoffman, 1997, All).

Family conferencing in the United States is based on the practice of Australian conferencing. These Australian conferences are depicted as reintegration ceremonies, typifying the tenets of reintegrative shaming theory (Braithwaite & Mugford, 1994). They note that in reintegration ceremonies, "the more serious the delinquency of the young offender, the more likely it is to come out that she has had to endure some rather terrible life circumstances" (p. 145). This information changes the picture of the offender to more than just a stereotype; witnesses see the offender as a "whole person" (p. 145). Furthermore, reintegrative shaming provides a central role for the victim and addresses the victim's own possible shame and fear (p. 155). Braithwaite and Mugford further describe reintegrative ceremonies as practices that give victims a meaningful voice and also reintegrate offenders back into the community, with the consequence of reducing recidivism (p. 139). It has been claimed that restorative justice, community service, mediation, and family conferencing are "justifiable reactions" to criminal behavior because they are integrative in themselves (Boutellier, 1996). Reintegrative societies, according to Braithwaite, are societies characterized by cohesiveness, interdependency, and strong family systems. Interdependency increases the effectiveness of reintegrative shaming practices.

How does contemporary public shaming in the United States compare with reintegrative shaming? Very unfavorably. Public shaming sentences are described as status degradation ceremonies (Kahan, 1996; see also Garfinkel, 1956). Public shaming in the United States has no reintegrative component and no constructive place for the victim. The effect on the offender is instead disintegrative or stigmatizing shaming. Stigmatization only serves to weaken interdependency. Other factors that weaken interdependency include unemployment, breakdown of the family, and cultural diversity (Braithwaite, 1989). Factors that weaken interdependency apply particularly to American society, and public shaming penalties do not strengthen social cohesion.

A recent content analysis of newspaper articles found more evidence of disintegrative stigmatization than reintegrative shaming (Bennett, Johnson, & Triplett, 1997). Articles about community responsibility were rare. Politicians and public alike are bent on promoting the moral accountability of offenders, as reflected in Von Hirsch's philosophy of just deserts. But such a philosophy ignores the "moral obligation of society to care for the people involved" (Boutellier, 1996). Public shaming ignores community responsibility and the role that a fragmented community may play in crime causation.

Gainsborough notes that "When dealing with people who are already alienated from the community, public shaming alienates them even more" (Russell, 1997, p. 103). Psychologists also agree that public shaming has little deterrent effect on those people who have never conformed to society's norms and that shaming can, in some cases, cause more harm. Shaming makes matters worse when the shaming elicits the emotion of shame, rather than guilt or embarrassment. The public shaming touted today appears to be based on confusion about the emotions of shame, guilt, and embarrassment. The following section discusses the differences among these three emotions and why understanding these differences is important for public shaming.

Public Shaming Reflects Confusion about Emotions

While acknowledging the inexact state of differentiating among shame, guilt, and embarrassment, numerous theorists in various disciplines do make distinctions among these three emotions (Tangney, Miller, Flicker, & Barlow, 1996). Susan Shott (1979) emphasizes that sociologists must study the role of these emotions, which she refers to as reflexive role-taking emotions, to fully understand social behavior and social control.

Shame and guilt are part of the class of "moral emotions"—those regulatory emotions that are believed to promote moral behavior and to restrain moral violations (Tangney, 1995). However, despite the similarity in their function, clear distinctions can be made between the two emotions. The predominant distinctions involve the levels of feeling, each emotion's focus, and the events that elicit the two emotions.

Researchers note that shame appears to be a more intense emotion than guilt in being related to feelings of weakness, helplessness, and a strong (negative) effect on self-esteem (Lewis, 1992). In shame, the focus is on the entire self and the feeling that "I am unworthy, incompetent, or bad" (Barrett, 1995; Tangney, 1995, p. 117). Michael Lewis connects eliciting events with focus, observing that if the focus is on one's behavior and an evaluation of the specific actions, then guilt is likely to be produced. If the focus is on the entire self, however, and an evaluation of the total self, then shame may be the emotion elicited (1992, pp. 71–76). The way that public shaming is employed in the United States encourages focus on the entire self and may be the sort of event that elicits shame. The problem is that shame is the more maladaptive emotion.

Shame motivates the individual to hide or sever relationships with others (Barrett, 1995; Lewis, 1992; Lindsay-Hartz, DeRivera, & Mascolo, 1995; Tangney, 1995; Tangney et al., 1996). Lewis emphasizes that theorists from Darwin forward have recognized the desire to hide as one of the principal components of shame (1992, p. 34). Theoretical and empirical evidence also suggest that shame motivates humiliation, depression, defensive anger, rage, and a tendency to blame others (Lewis, 1992; Lindsay-Hartz et al., 1995; Tangney, 1995). Extreme feelings such as rage are "out of control" and do not allow rational attention toward overcoming the obstacle or making reparation (Lewis, 1992). Likewise, when feeling shame, individuals are less likely to feel empathy for others and are focusing entirely on their negative sense of identity and the conviction that others view them negatively (Lindsay-Hartz, et al., 1995, p. 296). The state of shame may be so intense that any behavioral change is impossible.

Guilt, however, may be more likely to induce corrective action. Research consistently shows that guilt functions to motivate the individual to make amends and take reparative action (Barrett, 1995; Lewis, 1992; Lindsay-Hartz et al., 1995; Shott, 1979). Lewis states that "Reparation is a clear marker of regret or guilt. It is not a marker of shame" (1992, p. 181).

When feeling guilt, individuals often describe feelings of tension, remorse, and regret, along with an "other-oriented focus" (Tangney, 1995). Rather than blaming others, as when feeling shamed, "people in the midst of a guilt experience take responsibility for their actions" (1995, p. 135). Reparative action such as confessing and apologizing is often taken (p. 118). Theorists have thus characterized guilt as motivating more adaptive responses than shame and as being the developmentally more mature emotion. Guilt, unlike shame, serves important functions of strengthening and maintaining relationships rather than distancing oneself from others. Embarrassment, like guilt, also appears to be more adaptive than shame, allowing people to overcome minor social transgressions (Miller & Tangney, 1994, p. 275). Evidence also supports other theorists' assumptions that "embarrassment follows threats to one's self-presentation, and shame follows threats to one's self-concept" (p. 284).

As previously discussed, one of the feelings invoked by shame is rage. Michael Benson, in his research with white-collar offenders, suggests that rage and hostility may serve as defense mechanisms used to overcome the "paralysis of shame" (1990, p. 525). He further notes that disintegrative shaming employed by the American criminal justice system may cause offenders to feel a lack of repentance. Even Dan Kahan (1996), assistant professor of law at the University of Chicago and a strong supporter of public shaming, allows that such shaming can result in a "crippling" loss of self-esteem (p. 638). Lewis (1992) cogently notes that rage as a by-product of shame can result in violence against other people and against property. He believes that the amount of violent crime in this country committed by poor, black males may be attributable in part to how those individuals living in poverty and of minority status are continuously shamed—by the culture, school systems, the criminal justice system, and the white majority (p. 158). Lewis labels much minority and underclass crime as "shame dependent" (p. 153) and notes that reducing the shame is not accomplished through punishment and humiliation (pp. 161–162).

The earlier discussion of distinctions between shame and guilt emphasized the more reparative nature of guilt compared with shame, which may prompt inaction or feelings of rage. What needs to be recognized is that although guilt prompts reparation, it is the sense of shame, or the capacity to feel shame, that also may serve an important function, namely, that of deterring individuals from committing some transgression. While the emotion of shame may be less adaptive than the emotion of guilt, the capacity to feel shame is in itself a positive quality in terms of its deterrent effect. Once the transgression has been committed, however, it is guilt that makes us try to repair the damage.

Parents who use shaming as a socialization technique accompanied with forgiveness and a focus on ways to make reparation may induce feelings of guilt in a child. Shaming accompanied with disgust and contempt may induce shame. The emotion produced is vitally important: guilt prompts reparation; shame prompts inaction or an irrational feeling of rage. Reintegrative shaming ceremonies, family conferencing, and restorative justice are socialization techniques that employ the type of shaming that is likely to induce guilt. The public shaming currently employed is destructive and shame-provoking rather than guilt-provoking. Furthermore, shaming by itself, in absence of reintegration, is not associated with desistance from offending.

Another real concern about public shaming sanctions is that these sanctions may invite and provoke hostility from public citizens toward the offender, thus exacerbating the problem. Our history of vigilante justice supports this contention, as does the fact that citizens often amused themselves in colonial America by taunting and throwing objects at offenders in the stocks and pillories. A recent newspaper account tells of Georgia public schools using cardboard enclosures as behavior modification and placing a third-grader behind cardboard panels for punishment. Not surprisingly, classmates teased the child and referred to her as "cardboard girl" (Anderson, 1996). Although this may seem to be a fairly mild incident, it shows how stigmatizing this kind of punishment can be and how readily the label is applied to the total person, not just the "bad thing done." Again, the emotion of shame is likely to be the result of this kind of shaming.

Even proponents of public whippings acknowledge that such punishment is detrimental if it stigmatizes and does not reintegrate. Some proponents suggest allowing first offenders to wear hoods during their punishment and not publicizing their names (Wiedeman, 1996). But the public shaming practiced now makes no attempt at providing anonymity and, in fact, encourages public exposure.

Public Shaming May Result in Sentences That Violate Certain Moral Constraints on Punishment

Finally, we might consider whether the rediscovered public shaming is a revival of the passion for strict moralizing of bygone eras. If so, we must be careful not to lose widely shared values to this moralism. Hyman Gross (1979) has stated the problem clearly:

> …punishment must not be…inhumane as a transgression of those civilized standards that tell people how they ought to treat one another. Finally the procedures followed by a system of criminal justice must be designed to find and then to respect the truth about matters bearing on liability, while at the same time conforming to principles of fair play and respect for human dignity when confronting individuals with the awesome machinery of the state. And one may include among the many ironies of criminal justice that it is least likely to be morally sound when it is carried on most moralistically (p. 33).

Public shaming is that kind of shaming that is carried on "most moralistically," and it displays no respect for human dignity. For example, letting a former wife spit in her husband's face because he has harassed her (Kahan, 1996) is a destructive, undignified spectacle that signifies nothing more than sinking to that offender's level.

Conclusion

Let us be clear about what has been argued. Contemporary public shaming is not reintegrative shaming. Public shaming sentences focus entirely on the individual offender and ignore the underlying causes of the offending behavior. They are easy, quick, knee-jerk, emotional responses and border on the draconian. Such sentences do not fit Braithwaite's concept of reintegrative shaming, because the reintegration component is entirely absent. Moreover, studies have empirically supported the finding that what may deter persistence in criminal behavior is not shaming but reintegration. Furthermore, public shaming engenders the maladaptive emotion of shame rather than the adaptive emotion of guilt.

A society with politicians and a public bent on encouraging "public shaming devices" bodes poorly for decreasing crime. Intelligent, rational responses to deviant behavior are provided in other practices such as family conferencing and conflict resolution education. Unfortunately, judges and legislators enamored over public humiliation may not give these rational alternatives a chance. Society incurs a risk when any change in the mode of punishment is introduced. C. L. Ten (1987) has expressed clearly these risks:

> But we should seek, as best we can, to reduce crime without sacrificing fundamental moral values. Crimes and criminals are too various to be fitted into any simple explanation. But each perceived increase in crime is likely to be met with demands for more and more severe punishment. We often claim that such punishment merely gives offenders what they deserve, but we have no coherent theory of deserts which justifies the claim. We also claim that severe punishment will deter criminals more, but we are often wrong, and are prompted not by respect for the facts, but by dark and dangerous passions (pp. 163–4).

Public shaming in America is that type of punishment that appeals to our dark and dangerous passions." It is not morally sound and is putting us on an imprudent course we had abandoned during the Enlightenment Age of Europe. There are good reasons for not reviving this practice, and we would do well to reverse our direction.

REFERENCES

Anderson, V. (1996, July 19). Newton county sued over classroom incident. *The Atlanta Journal Constitution,* C4.

Barrett, K. C. (1995). A functionalist approach to shame and guilt. In J. P. Tangney, J. Price, and K. W. Fischer (Eds.), *Self conscious emotions: The psychology of shame, guilt, embarrassment, and pride* (pp. 25–63). New York: The Guilford Press.

Bass, P. M. (1996, August 8). Public shaming coming back, and it works. *Houston Chronicle,* Sec. Outlook, 1.

Bennett, K. J., Johnson, W. W., & Triplett, R. (1997). Reintegrative shaming in the media: A content analysis. In F. Y. Bailey and D. C. Hale (Eds.), *Popular culture, crime, and justice.* Belmont, CA: Wadsworth Publishing Co.

Benson, M. (1990). Emotions and adjudication: Status degradation among white-collar criminals. *Justice Quarterly, 7* (3), 515–528.

Boutellier, J. (1996). *Beyond the criminal justice paradox: Alternatives between law enforcement and social policy.* Paper presented at the Annual Meeting of the American Society of Criminology, November 1996, Chicago, Illinois.

Braithwaite, J. (1989) *Crime, shame, and reintegration.* New York: Cambridge University Press.

Braithwaite, J., & Mugford, S. (1994). Conditions of successful reintegration ceremonies: Dealing with juvenile offenders. *British Journal of Criminology, 34,* 139–171.

Butterfield, F. (1997, April 16). Most efforts to stop crime fall far short, study finds. *New York Times.*

Garfinkel, H. (1956). Conditions of successful status degradation ceremonies. *American Journal of Sociology, 61,* 420–424.

Gross, H. (1979). *A theory of criminal justice.* New York: Oxford University Press.

Hoffman, J. (1997, January 16). Crime and punishment: Shame gains popularity. *New York Times,* A1, All.

Kahan, D. M. (1996). What do alternative sanctions mean? *The University of Chicago Law Review, 63* (2), 591–653.

Lewis, M. (1992). *Shame: The exposed self.* New York: The Free Press.

Lindsay-Hartz, J., De Rivera, J., & Mascolo, M. F. (1995). Differentiating guilt and shame and their effects on motivation. In J. P. Tangney, J. Price, and K. W. Fischer (Eds.), *Self-conscious motions: The psychology of shame, guilt, embarrassment, and pride* (pp. 274–300). New York: The Guilford Press.

Miller, R. S., & Tangney, J. P. (1994). Differentiating embarrassment and shame. *Journal of Social and Clinical Psychology, 13* (3), 273–287.

Russell, J. (1997, August). Shame! Shame! Shame! *Good Housekeeping,* 102–105; 138.

Shott, S. (1979). Emotion and social life: A symbolic interactionist analysis. *American Journal of Sociology 84* (6), 1317–1334.

Tangney, J. P. (1995). Shame and guilt in interpersonal relationships. In J. P. Tangney, J. Price, & K. W. Fischer (Eds.), *Self-conscious emotions: The psychology of shame, guilt, embarrassment, and pride* (pp. 114–142). New York: The Guilford Press.

Tangney, J. P., Miller, R. S., Flicker, L., & Barlow, D. H. (1996). Are shame, guilt, and embarrassment distinct emotions? *Journal of Personality and Social Psychology, 70* (6), 1256–1269.

Ten, C. L. (1987). *Crime, guilt, and punishment: A philosophical introduction.* Oxford: Clarendon Press.

Walker, S. (1980). *Popular justice: A history of American criminal justice.* New York: Oxford University Press.

Welch, M. (1996). *Corrections: A critical approach.* New York: McGraw-Hill.
Wiedeman, W. (1996). Comment: Don't spare the rod: A proposed return to public, corporal punishment of convicts. *American Journal of Criminal Law, 23* (65), 651–673.

Rejoinder to Dr. Bennett Ruth-Ellen Grimes

There seems to be no good argument against shaming! When asked to respond in the affirmative to the question of whether shaming is an innovative and successful approach to punishment, I systematically selected theoretical and empirically based research endeavors that supported the best of the shaming literature. That ultimate and final ostracization is dysfunctional is old news; Braithwaite's rejuvenation of labeling theory in support of ultimate reclamation of the individual is innovative in the contemporary analyses I reviewed.

Both Bennett and I point to a number of shaming initiatives (family conferencing, conflict resolution education, etc,) that call for responsibility and accountability on the part of both the "deviant/criminal/delinquent" and those parties who may inculcate positive change. Where Bennett and I differ is in the interpretation of Braithwaite's model. I clearly argued the benefits of real communitarianism—a broader macro impact that goes beyond individual public shaming antics to include real efforts to seek underlying social/economic/political causes.

Shaming is by definition equated with humiliation. And public shaming is not always and directly antithetical to Braithwaite's theory of reintegrative shaming. Bennett's examples of "popular public shaming" are extremely parochial; her discussion is limited solely to the United States and is selectively limited to extreme examples of "sound bite" spectacles.

Pennsylvania's Judge Leon Harris, by his own definition "Crazy Judge Harris," uses public shaming effectively in his juvenile courtroom. In the 1994 *Victory Over Violence* television series, Judge Harris' courtroom sets the introductory stage for an evaluation of thirty-three treatment programs which have documented success in delivering positive change to communities across the United States. Judge Harris begins a session by challenging the veracity of the fifteen-year-old youth before him, telling the boy he did not start stealing with the current charge against him (theft of a speed bike). The judge pushes the youth to confess to stealing first a Milky Way candy bar at age eleven, then orders him to apologize to his mother.

But Judge Harris is not finished. He then addresses the mother, ordering her to present the absent father within five days. The youth is handcuffed and jailed awaiting the father's arrival in court, at which time the judge orders him to tell his son about "the birds 'n the bees" and "drugs 'n the grave," to call his son daily, to visit him on weekends, and to take him fishing. Although this may sound "hokey," with judicial follow-up and parental involvement, Judge Harris succeeds in using a public shaming forum that humiliates all of the responsible parties while reversing negative behavior patterns. Public shaming exercises do not have to be permanently stigmatizing; not all degradation ceremonies result in permanent disaffection from society.

I strongly disagree with Bennett's didactic conclusion that "*public shaming sentences focus entirely on the individual offender and ignore the underlying causes of the offending behavior…*such sentences do not fit Braithwaite's concept of reintegrative shaming, because the *reintegration component is entirely absent*" (emphasis added).

Rational public shaming exercises necessarily involve the element of humiliation. The ability of the offender to achieve positive change in his/her behavior, born of a desire to reverse previous behavior patterns, then is realized through community responsiveness—which necessarily involves the elements of community responsibility, accountability, and forgiveness.

Is Electronic Monitoring a Successful Community Supervision Method?

James F. Anderson argues YES. Currently Associate Professor of Police Studies at Eastern Kentucky University, he received his Ph.D. from Sam Houston State University in 1995. He has published in several venues, including *Journal of Criminal Justice, Journal of Crime and Justice,* and *Journal of Offender Rehabilitation.* His current research interests are in the areas of gangs, crime and public health, shock incarceration, and other alternatives to incarceration.

Terry Wells argues NO. Currently Assistant Professor of Criminal Justice at Georgia College and State University, he received an M.P.A. from Appalachian State University and a Ph.D. from Sam Houston State University in 1997. He has lectured in the areas of community corrections, correctional administration, and criminal justice systems. Current research interests include halfway houses and issues involving community corrections. Recent publications have addressed the use of intensive probation supervision and jail administration.

YES

JAMES F. ANDERSON

Faced with increasing crime rates and prison overcrowding, many state correctional systems are seeking alternatives to traditional incarceration. Scholars contend that no area of the justice system has been under greater stress than corrections. For instance, there are more than 1.6 million inmates confined in jails and prisons in the United States. Diversion from prison is appealing because the cost of incarcerating offenders has skyrocketed, causing a strain on many state correctional budgets. Eskridge (1996) estimates that states pay more that $25,000 yearly to confine an offender in prison. As a result, the criminal justice system spends more than $18.1 billion annually to house inmates in correctional facilities (Camp & Camp, 1994). Therefore, to reduce exuberant budgets and accommodate huge numbers of offenders entering the system, correctional agencies have begun exploring alternatives, such as regular probation, intensive probation supervision, boot camps, halfway houses, electronic monitoring (EM), and other community-based programs. These alternatives have become popular in recent years because of their economic potential as being cost-effective and commitment to punishing offenders for past criminal behavior.

Diversions are sought after to punish offenders and deter potential law violators. However, EM, more than many other intermediate sanctions, appears to be a viable alternative because it has the potential to reform criminals by punishing them while simultaneously allowing them to remain with their families. This twin effect could ultimately satisfy both conservatives and liberals because it punishes and provides therapy by preserving the family unit. Despite this, very little is known about electronic monitoring and the benefits that this intermediate sanction provides.

The purpose of this chapter is to argue the merits of electronic monitoring. As such, it is divided into four parts. The first part provides a working definition and rationales behind electronic monitoring, and the second addresses the cost-effectiveness of these programs. The third part discusses those offenders who are most suitable for such programs, and the fourth provides findings from studies that report the effectiveness of electronic monitoring programs. In the final analysis, the author contends that electronic monitoring is a vitally needed correctional practice.

Electronic Monitoring

Electronic monitoring, mostly used in conjunction with house arrest, is a sentence imposed by the court that legally requires offenders to remain confined in their homes. Clear and Cole (1994) argue that it can be used as either a sole sanction or in combination with other penalties imposed at any time during the criminal justice process. For example, electronic monitoring is sometimes mandated during pretrial investigations, after a short term in jail or prison, or as a condition of probation or parole. Correctional scholars contend that house arrest involves using electronic devices (usually anklets or wristlets) to monitor the offender's presence in a given environment, where the offender is required to remain until his or her sentence is completely served or to verify the offender's whereabouts. It is an appropriate punishment because it provides elements of retribution, incapacitation, and rehabilitation. EM devices discharge signals to track the movement of offenders, probationers, and parolees. Offenders are also monitored by random telephone calls. EM provides greater community control.

Before receiving an EM sentence, an offender must agree to special conditions that are vigorously enforced. These conditions include paying (1) restitution, (2) family support payments, (3) a supervisory fee ($50 per month), and (4) performing community services (Baird & Wagner, 1990). Furthermore, offenders are required to write a log of their daily activities and make it available to their community control officer on request. They must have at least twenty contact visits per month with their community control officer. Moreover, as an attempt to make early detection of possible probationary or parole violations and new criminality, control officers discuss the status of offenders with neighbors, spouses, friends, landlords, employers, and others to acquire a holistic determination of the offender's activities. Despite the rigidity of EM, special conditions permit offenders to leave their homes. Such conditions typically stipulate that offenders are free to attend work, school, seek medical attention in cases of emergency, and purchase household necessities (Rackmill, 1996).

Rationale for Electronic Monitoring

The rationales for these programs are fourfold. These include alleviating high correctional costs, allowing needed bed space for serious offenders, reducing the negative influences of traditional incarceration that undermine successful reintegration to society, and reducing recidivism. First, EM programs enjoy widespread popularity because of their potential to save states money. Clear and Cole (1994) argue that EM has experienced dramatic growth in Florida and other states. Moreover, the National Institute of Justice reports that in 1987, there were 826 offenders being monitored electronically; however, by 1989, the number had increased to 6500 (Renzema & Skelton, 1990). Lilly (1995) reports that between 50,000 and 70,000 people are monitored each day in the United States. Furthermore, Lilly argues that all states have had at least one program, and approximately 1800 federal offenders were monitored in 1993. Perhaps the biggest attraction to EM is its ability to reduce the high costs of traditional incarceration. The Edna McConnell Clark Foundation (1993) reports that states pay $8000 dollars each year to keep an offender under house arrest instead of paying $25,000 for traditional confinement and an additional $54,000 to build each cell. This figure does not include food and medical services that are provided by private companies under contract with prisons (Camp & Camp, 1994).

Second, with large numbers of offenders receiving an EM sentence, more bed space can be allocated to those offenders who commit serious offenses. However, those offenders who commit acts of violence or crimes against children should never qualify for such programs. Incarceration statistics indicate that a disproportionate number of offenders who engage in drug offenses and property crimes are given a sentence to traditional incarceration each day. Therefore, a tremendous amount of bed space could be appropriated for hardened offenders if first-time property and drug offenders are diverted to these programs.

Third, a traditional sentence to incarceration exposes offenders to experiences that negate any kind of rehabilitative potential that incarceration might provide. Sykes (1958) argues that while imprisoned, inmates endure the pains of imprisonment. These include deprivation of (1) liberty; (2) goods and services; (3) heterosexual relationships; (4) autonomy; and (5) security. He adds that imprisonment leads inmates to engage in behavior within prison that reduces their prospect for postrelease adjustment. If offenders are to become productive members of society after their incarceration, perhaps the experience of confinement does more harm than good. The benefit of EM is that the offender does not have to face reintegrating into society because he or she never leaves. The offender is allowed to serve the sentence at home. This affords the offender the opportunity to maintain his or her livelihood by retaining job and family ties. Therefore, it diverts the offender from the stigma attached to being labeled a criminal. Unfortunately, many offenders have a difficult time finding employment after release from prison. It is believed by many that this is what invariably pushes many parolees back into a life of crime; EM prevents the family from becoming dismantled. As a result, the family does not face financial hardship because offenders are allowed to keep their jobs. This practice could reduce the number of families that seek public assistance and welfare provisions.

Fourth, recidivism studies consistently report that most offenders released from jail and prison eventually return. This adds to already strained state correctional budgets because prisons serve as a "revolving door" to many offenders. The U.S. Department of Justice estimates that nearly 30 percent of releases are returned to prison for either committing additional crimes or violating a condition of parole (Bureau of Justice Statistics, 1994). Ex-offenders have consistently higher levels of recidivism than others. A sentence to EM could prove more beneficial than a traditional sanction.

Electronic Monitoring Is Cost-Effective

Though initially expensive, the price of EM can be offset by having offenders defray the costs of the entire monitoring process. This includes having monitoring telephones installed. In most programs, offenders pay for their own supervision. These fees vary depending on the state where one resides, but the maximum fee is typically $15 daily. Moreover, it proves cost-effective when offenders are able to keep their jobs, support their families, and pay their fines. For example, Quinn and Holman (1992) report that offenders sentenced to house arrest in Florida were able to pay in excess of $9 million in fees associated with home detention. Furthermore, they argue that in Maryland, seven dollars per day provides an offender with a staff, transportation, and equipment, whereas it costs forty-five dollars each day to house an inmate in the county jail. Maryland reported saving over $1 million in the first two years of this program.

Offenders Most Suitable for Electronic Monitoring and the Case for Inmates with "Special Needs"

Critics argue that EM is a form of "net widening" that places low-risk offenders in diversion programs who would have otherwise been sentenced to probation, but this is not necessarily true. For example, Baird and Wagner (1990) found in a comparison study of offenders on regular probation, in jail and prison, that offenders sentenced to the Florida Community Control Program were more serious than those placed on regular probation or in jail. However, they were less serious than offenders sentenced to long-term imprisonment. They reported that offenders in Florida who are typically selected for EM disproportionately committed drug, property, and personal offenses. Moreover, EM programs across the country report having "real" offenders in their programs.

Criminal justice experts, as well as citizens in the lay public, have recognized that the justice system has become punitive in its dissemination of punishments. For example, some of the justice system's arsenal include strict incarceration policies, such as mandatory sentencing and "three strikes and you're out" policies. Because these sentences are final and expensive, they add continued cost to already strained state correctional budgets by requiring that offenders spend their remaining days incarcerated. Although punitive and typically given to offenders who have committed serious offenses, these policies do not appear to have a deterrent effect, because the behaviors that warrant strict incarceration policies are continuously committed. We should reconsider imposing such expensive sentencing. Nonetheless, any offender who has received a strict incarceration sentence should not be considered for EM.

Perhaps offenders (in addition to personal, property, and drug offenders) who are more suitable for EM are those found within "special needs" inmate populations. Because they require constant medical attention and medication that is mandated of all correctional facilities by the Americans with Disabilities Act of 1990 and constitutional protections, special needs inmates are very expensive to confine. These inmates cost correctional facilities hundreds of millions of dollars each year. Some of these offenders are pregnant women, offenders who are terminally ill, geriatric convicts, paralyzed offenders, blind offenders, and those who are mentally retarded. Electronic monitoring programs would serve as an appropriate sentence for these offenders because they are no longer threatening to the general public or to their respective communities.

Releasing and placing these offenders under EM relinquishes the state of the burden of having to subsidize their existence by providing them food, clothing, shelter, medical treatment, medications, and security needs. Moreover, two of the most expensive "special needs" groups to keep confined are geriatrics and inmates with acquired immune deficiency syndrome (AIDS). These groups are the most expensive because geriatric inmates require constant medication and expensive surgery, and treating inmates with AIDS costs correctional facilities $50,000 yearly per inmate. This could present serious problems for correctional administrators, because it is estimated that there are nearly 80,000 inmates infected with the AIDS virus (Cauchon, 1995). These groups should be released; geriatric inmates have aged out of crime, yet they remain incarcerated because of strict sentencing guidelines. AIDS inmates are sometimes incapacitated because of complications with the disease, and they pose no threat to the general public by being placed under house arrest. Therefore, EM could save states millions by monitoring these offenders for the remainder of their prison sentence.

The Effectiveness of Electronic Monitoring

The effectiveness of EM is illustrated by evaluations of these programs in several states that have implemented such devices to monitor offenders. Three states that employ such devices are Mississippi, Louisiana, and Indiana. First, Gowen (1995) reports that in an evaluation in the Southern District of Mississippi, electronic monitoring programs achieved excellent results before and after at-risk offenders participated in this intermediate sanction. He argues that even when stringent entrance requirements were invoked, most of the high-risk offenders completed their terms. Many of these offenders were drug violators and others who are considered noncompliant offenders. Gowen's research shows that substance abusers and offenders who violated technical conditions of probation were suitable candidates for EM. Second, Gould and Archambeault (1995) argue that participants of Computer Assisted Monitoring of Offenders (CAMO), the experimental group, had lower rearrests or recidivism levels than those in the control group. Therefore, they contend that it may be concluded that CAMO is a more effective program for reducing recidivism than traditional probation.

Third, while examining the effects of Electronically Monitored Home Detention Program (EMHDP) in Lake County, Indiana, Roy (1995) reported significant findings from a recidivism study on juveniles. Because juveniles consistently recidivate more than older offenders, Roy's conclusions are compelling. He reports that 81 percent of the offenders in the program successfully completed their sentence. He argued that, of the program's targeted sample of 285 juveniles, 63 percent had been convicted of a felony. He found that younger offenders (ages 15–17) with a history of drug abuse and a vast number of priors were more likely to fail EMHDP. These three studies of EM are few, but they are representative of what has been reported by many other successful EM programs around the country.

Conclusion

Electronic monitoring programs serve a vital function to the criminal justice system as well as to offenders sentenced to these programs. These programs divert offenders from the stigma of long-term imprisonment, help alleviate the need to build more prisons, reduce expensive correctional costs, are cost-effective, and reduce recidivism. Furthermore, this sentence would be ideal for "special needs" inmates. Electronic monitoring offers the offender a second chance to be law-abiding by remaining in his or her community and retaining employment and family ties. This sentence also allows offenders to pay restitution, support their families, and perform community services.

REFERENCES

Baird, C., & Wagner, D. (1990). Measuring diversion: The Florida community control program. *Crime and Delinquency, 36* (1), 112–125.

Bureau of Justice Statistics. (1994). *Prisoners in the United States.* Washington, DC: Author.

Camp, C., & Camp, G. (1994). *The corrections yearbook 1994: Adult corrections.* South Salem, NY: Criminal Justice Institute.

Clear, T. R., & Cole, G. F. (1994). *American corrections.* Belmont, CA: Wadsworth Publishing Company.

Cauchon, D. (1995, March 31). AIDS in prison: Locked up and locked out. *USA Today,* 6A.

Eskridge, C. W. (1996). *Criminal justice: Concepts and issues.* Los Angeles, CA: Roxbury Publishing Company.

Gould, L. A., & Archambeault, W. G. (1995). Evaluation of a computer-assisted monitoring (CAMO) project: Some measurement issues. *American Journal of Criminal Justice, 19* (2), 255–273.

Gowen, D. (1995). Electronic monitoring in the southern district of Mississippi. *Federal Probation, 59* (1), 10–13.

Lilly, J. R. (1995). "Electronic monitoring in the U.S." In M. Tonry and K. Hamilton (Eds.), *Intermediate sanctions in overcrowded times.* Boston: Northeastern University Press.

Quinn, J., & Holman, J. (1992). The efficacy of electronically monitored home confinement as a case management device. *Journal of Contemporary Criminal Justice, 7,* 128–134.

Rackmill, S. J. (1996). An analysis of home confinement as a sanction. In C. W. Eskridge (Ed.), *Criminal justice: Concepts and issues.* Los Angeles, CA: Roxbury Publishing Company.

Renzema, M., & Skelton, D. T. (1990). *The use of electronic monitoring by criminal justice agencies, 1989. Grant Number OJP-89-M-309.* Washington, DC: National Institute of Justice.

Roy, S. (1995). Juvenile offenders in an electronic home detention program: A study on factors related to failure. *Journal of Offender Monitoring, 8* (2), 9–17.

Sykes, G. (1958). *The society of captives: A study of a maximum security prison.* Princeton, NJ: Princeton University Press.

The Edna McConnell Clark Foundation. (1993, April). *Americans behind bars.* New York: The Edna McConnell Clark Foundation.

Rejoinder to Dr. Anderson   Terry Wells

Dr. Anderson's argument for electronic monitoring as a successful community supervision method is based on the premise that these programs are capable of solving several important problems facing the criminal justice system. Citing four of these difficult problems, he suggests that each can be attacked through the increased use of EM programs. According to the author, EM can reduce the costs of the correctional system, provide needed bed space for more serious offenders, assist in reintegration, and provide lower recidivism rates than traditional programs. Serious questions concerning the ability of EM programs to accomplish these goals are briefly examined.

In suggesting that EM can help reduce the cost of the correctional system, Anderson points out that many of the states require that an offender pay for part of the monitoring program. This raises two concerns. First, does this discriminate against those who cannot afford to pay? Research addressing this issue is currently not available, and statements that suggest that no discrimination is present are merely speculative. Second, some programs subsidize offenders who cannot afford to pay the fee for EM. When this is the case, the question becomes: How are cost savings realized?

Dr. Anderson also points out that offender fees also can be used to offset staffing, transportation, and equipment costs. Are these costs associated with *new* staffing and equipment? If the answer to this question is yes, no real cost savings are realized because staffing, a major component in cost consideration, is not reduced. Offenders in EM programs may not be costing the existing correctional system more for staffing and equipment, but until there is a reduction in personnel in this area, the implementation of EM programs only appears to alleviate problems associated with cost by not adding to them. Perhaps the most important issue concerning costs deals with two additional goals that Dr. Anderson argues can be accomplished by EM programs: reducing recidivism and creating bed space for serious offenders.

A reduction in criminal behavior is a major purpose of the criminal justice system, and EM is suggested to be one, but not the only, means by which to achieve this goal. There is insufficient research to support the hypothesis that EM is more effective than other traditional methods of supervision in reducing criminal behavior. If an electronic component does not add significantly to the success of programs such as regular or intensive probation, how can expanding its use reduce costs over any option excluding incarceration?

Addressing the issue of overcrowding, Dr. Anderson suggests that EM programs can make bed space available for serious criminals. To accomplish this goal, it is suggested that, in addition to personal, property, and drug offenders, inmates with special needs be placed in EM programs. Additional benefits are to be derived from saving the correctional costs associated with the special requirements and medical needs of these inmates. Several reasons against such a proposal can be suggested.

First, to suggest that offenders with special needs are less of a threat to the public implies that the offender is incapable of engaging in criminal behavior. Medical condition does not necessarily inhibit criminal involvement and should not be a major consideration in sentencing decisions. Second, the argument that releasing inmates with special needs relieves the state of the burden created by these offenders is not necessarily correct. The burden may simply be shifted to other state agencies. Many of the services once provided through correctional institutions will still be performed, but through a different state agency. Third, filling the empty bed space with more serious offenders cannot achieve cost savings. Savings can only result if empty beds are decommissioned.

A final comment is warranted concerning Dr. Anderson's proposal that EM should be used because it avoids the difficulty of reintegration associated with incarceration. All traditional methods of supervision currently available in the community attempt to achieve this goal, but they go beyond simply monitoring the movements of an offender. Electronic monitoring does little in the way of assisting in finding employment or in reconnecting to the community. Electronic monitoring without providing treatment or services has no great advantage over current community supervision methods.

NO

Terry Wells

Along with a number of intermediate sanctions, EM has experienced tremendous growth over the last decade (Schmidt, 1991). Expanding prison populations and an increased concern for fiscal restraint have been major factors in the move toward EM, specifically, and community corrections in general (Baumer, Maxfield, & Mendelsohn, 1993). Research does not support an expansion of programs such as EM, and this chapter argues that such programs often fail to live up to the expectations offered by their sponsors. A determination of the success or failure of EM as a community supervision method is dependent on the goals that these programs seek to accomplish. Although these goals have changed since the initial development, research supporting the ability of EM to achieve anything other than limited success is currently not present.

The stated goals of earlier EM programs were to reduce the criminal activity of the offender (deterrence) and facilitate therapy in a more humane environment than in prison. Today these initial goals have been replaced or supplemented by ones that stress reducing the costs associated with overcrowded prisons while still protecting the public (Renzema, 1992).

The argument against the success of EM as a supervision technique is made by the following statements directed at the current use of such programs:

1. Electronic monitoring programs are not successful in achieving the goals of reducing overcrowded institutions and cost savings. Staffing may not decrease as a result of electronic monitoring, and offenders who are better suited for regular probation may be placed in programs to reduce the risk of failures. This increases the cost of programs and expands the social control mechanism of the state.

2. Electronic monitoring has not proved to be a deterrent over other types of supervision and in some cases, because of an increase in technical violations, the rate of recidivism increases. In addition, because electronic monitoring is primarily a surveillance technique through the use of devices such as the telephone and not by visual observation, it does not prevent the continuation of criminal activity. Offenders may continue to sell drugs or abuse spouses within their own residence.

3. The goal of rehabilitation is often lacking and, when present, is secondary to the goal of punishment in most electronic monitoring programs. If treatment components are included, cost savings are reduced.

4. Electronic monitoring is a punishment, but one that may extend to other members of society such as friends and relatives who reside with the offender.

5. Legal decisions upholding the constitutionality of electronic monitoring do not dilute arguments that EM may discriminate against those who are poor.

6. Electronic monitoring is not foolproof, and advances in technology do not guarantee success.

The real success of EM lies in the fact that it continues to increase in use even though it fails to meet many of its proposed goals. The reason for this phenomenon is that EM accomplishes many latent goals that are not explicitly stated as reasons for the creation of such programs. The argument is made that EM is no more successful than traditional methods of supervision in successfully accomplishing many of the goals offered for its continuation and expansion.

The earliest experiments in the technology required for EM began in Harvard in 1963, and small pilot projects were initiated in New Mexico and Florida in the early 1980s (Renzema, 1992). Only approximately 800 offenders participated in EM programs in 1987, and the number of participants is currently estimated to be between 40,000 and 70,000 (Lilly, 1992). Virtually all states have EM programs, many coupled with additional sanctions such as house detention and intensive supervised probation. Typical programs last between 30 and 180 days, with a mean duration of approximately seventy-nine days (Renzema, 1992). Drug testing is often a component of the programs, because many of the participants have alcohol and substance abuse problems.

There are two general types of EM systems in use. The first type, referred to as continuous signaling devices, transmit a signal from a transmitter worn by the offender. The second type, programmed contact devices, place computer-generated calls at random to the home of the offender. In addition to these two types, there are hybrid systems such as cellular devices that are used to track offenders.

Although EM has been proposed as a means by which to accomplish a multitude of goals, the current research does not firmly establish that it is more successful than other forms of community supervision.

The Goals of Electronic Monitoring

According to Palumbo, Clifford, and Snyder-Joy (1992), EM programs suffer from a difficulty experienced by other alternative sanctions. By "promising too much to too many," EM is set up for failure. According to its supporters, EM can save money, protect the public, deter offenders from future criminality, punish, and rehabilitate.

Cost-Effectiveness and Prison Overcrowding

A recent survey of EM programs (Renzema, 1992) reported that the primary program goal was to reduce overcrowding. The second most frequent response given as a reason for implementing EM was to save money. Electronic monitoring may not be capable of accomplishing these two goals, for a number of reasons. First, unless only offenders who are truly bound for prison or jail are sentenced to EM, the overall cost may increase rather than decrease. Recent research suggests that many programs include offenders who, without the program, would have been placed on regular probation and that probation officers and judges are reluctant to select truly prison-bound offenders (Mainprize, 1992).

Second, as Palumbo, Clifford, and Snyder-Joy (1992) point out, discussions of cost savings also must be concerned with other factors in addition to whether the target population is prison bound. If prison beds, which are empty because of EM programs, are filled and if facilities within a correctional system are not decommissioned, then no savings result. Additional threats to the cost benefits of alternatives such as EM, according to the authors, comes from offenders who are reincarcerated as a result of technical violations and from programs that fail to operate at full capacity, each of which impact on operating expenses.

A third reason why electronic monitoring may not reduce cost is that an insufficient number of offenders are being diverted into a program to affect staffing requirements. Fears that new technologies such as EM would replace people has not resulted, and in most cases staffing has been affected, but in the opposite direction (Schmidt, 1991). A recent survey regarding the level of staffing associated with the implementation of EM suggests that staff size generally increases, rather than decreases, as a result of adding these programs (Renzema & Skelton, 1990).

Protecting the Public and Deterrence

Claims that EM can provide an alternative to incarceration that protects the public also fail to be supported by the available research. Monitoring systems are merely capable of detecting the presence or absence of the offender and cannot prevent violations (Baumer, Maxfield, & Mendelsohn, 1993). Corbett and Marx (1991), in an overview of studies concerned with the ability of EM programs to reduce recidivism, find little evidence of success. One study reported that more than one-third of the participants had either a technical violation or an arrest after six months, and no difference was reported in the arrest rate for offenders on probation with EM and those on regular supervision. An additional study cited by Corbett and Marx found no differences between EM and that of human monitoring. An eighteen-month pilot program in Georgia concluded that EM did not improve the level of supervision over intensive probation supervision (Erwin, 1990).

Until monitoring programs are implemented with concerns for reducing staff, lowering recidivism rates, and the potential for net widening, it is difficult to conclude that they are more successful than traditional techniques of supervision. If programs such as regular probation produce similar results, the use of EM increases costs without producing additional benefits.

Punishment and Rehabilitation

An original goal behind the use of EM was to provide an environment conducive to treatment. Currently the goal of rehabilitation, if present, is given little attention. Treatment programs have been recognized as an important component that may assist in increasing the impact of a surveillance program (Baumer & Mendelsohn, 1992). Renzema (1992) argues that most programs fail to provide rewards, such as an extension of curfew, for positive behavior. Electronic monitoring programs that do not include a rehabilitative component have not proved successful in reducing recidivism. As long as programs emphasize control over offenders and fail to include the rehabilitative potential of treatment, EM will remain unsuccessful.

Although many programs provide little in the way of treatment, they do appear to contain elements of punishment. The difficulty with this is that the punishment may extend to family members of the offender. Baumer and Mendelsohn (1992) report that offenders find EM to be no more punitive than manual monitoring but that it is more demanding and stressful on the offender's family than regular supervision. Family members voiced concerns over the intrusiveness brought about by late-night calls and the inconvenience of family members having to take on the responsibilities and duties normally relegated to the offender.

Electronic monitoring does not accomplish many of the goals advanced by its supporters. Prison populations have not been abated by the introduction of EM. Arguments that EM programs are cost-effective fail to consider hidden cost such as the possibility of an increase in the number of individuals under this new form of social control and the expanding staff needed to operate the new technology. Electronic monitoring is no more successful than regular supervision in deterring offenders and in providing rehabilitative treatment. Electronic monitoring punishes but goes beyond manual supervision in its intrusiveness into the lives of family members of the offender.

Additional Arguments against the Success of Electronic Monitoring

Beyond the failure of EM to accomplish the goals stated for its implementation, additional issues require caution in assuming that new programs should be instituted. These issues must be addressed before EM programs expand.

Constitutional Issues

Most legal challenges to the constitutionality of EM have not been successful, but this does not mean that none will arise in the future (Baumer & Mendelsohn, 1992). Many states now require that offenders pay supervision fees to cover the cost of monitoring. This raises the possibility that many who cannot afford to pay supervision fees will be excluded from the program, with incarceration as the alternative (Mainprize, 1992).

Growth of the Private Sector and Ethical Issues

The use of offender fees to defray the cost of EM is also connected to the increased involvement of the private sector in operating programs. Lilly (1990; 1992) reports a dramatic rise in the number of private vendors entering the electronic monitoring business. Lilly notes that the cost of monitoring equipment has decreased at a time when supervision fees are on the rise. With an increased reliance on private vendors to carry out criminal justice programs, concern must be directed at the way in which programs compensate for those who cannot afford an alternative to incarceration. Lilly also observes that corruption between prison officials and the private sector, attributable to the vast amounts of money involved in operating a program, is a potential threat to the success of EM.

Target Populations

Conceived as an alternative to incarceration for low-risk offenders, EM programs are now targeting a broader range of participants. This transition is taking effect without sufficient evidence that EM is equally effective across offender populations. Renzema (1992) noted increases between 1987 and 1989 in violent offenders, drug offenders, and property offenders. The use of EM also increased for offenders under pretrial detention during the same period. In an examination of differences among target populations, Baumer, Maxfield, and Mendelsohn (1993) reported a lower rate of arrest and a higher rate of successful completion of the program for postconviction offenders than those on EM at the pretrial stage. This suggests that EM is not suitable for all offenders, and more research on differential outcomes is needed before programs are extended to include new populations.

Technological Issues

As Corbett and Marx (1991) suggest, there are serious flaws in thinking that new technology will resolve long-standing problems. The idea that EM will perform better than older and traditional methods of supervision is not supported by current research, and established programs may face the threat of abandonment if the fight for scarce resources becomes intense. In addition, there are technical problems associated with the use of EM equipment that make it difficult to suggest it as foolproof. Telephone lines may not operate effectively, offenders may circumvent the equipment, and, as anyone who has operated a personal computer can attest, malfunctions in both hardware and software are a common problem.

Latent Goals of Electronic Monitoring

It has been suggested that the reason alternatives to incarceration such as Intensive Probation Supervision (IPS) are supported and expand is because they accomplish unstated or latent goals (Tonry, 1990). These goals may be located at the political, professional, or institutional level. Electronic monitoring programs also may be driven by such latent goals.

Politically, EM can be sold as a tough punishment, keeping a constant watch on offenders. Professionally, EM adds esteem through technological expertise, which can be quantified by probation and parole officers. Institutionally, EM allows for organizations to argue that it is tough and safe. Similar to programs such as boot camps and intensive probation supervision, the success of EM and its expansion may be attributed more to its ability to accomplish latent, rather than stated, goals.

Conclusions

In the brief period since their inception, EM programs have experienced tremendous growth. This expansion is not warranted by the available research, and a realistic approach to what electronic programs can accomplish is needed. Many of the issues associated with electronic monitoring programs may be resolved through careful planning, training, and implementation, but this appears unlikely to take place. As the case with prior correctional reforms, rhetoric, rather than empirical evidence, supports their proliferation. The success of electronic monitoring cannot be found in the goals stated for its use.

In a time when an individual's daily movements can be tracked by use of automatic teller machines, visits to the shopping mall, and accessing the World Wide Web over a personal computer, rights to privacy may lessen in importance. The home, often a major part of monitoring, is one of the few areas limiting electronic access, and critics who dismiss the malevolent nature of programs such as EM ignore the potential of technology to expand the control of the state over a larger segment of the population and to intrude into the daily lives of citizens.

REFERENCES

Baumer, T. L., Maxfield, M., & Mendelsohn, R. (1993). A comparative analysis of three electronically monitored home detention programs. *Justice Quarterly, 10,* 121–141.

Baumer, T. L., & Mendelsohn, R. (1992). Electronically monitored home confinement: Does it work? In J. M. Byrne, A. J. Lurigio, and J. Petersillia (Eds.), *Smart sentencing: The emergence of intermediate sanctions.* Newbury Park, CA: Sage.

Corbett, R. P., & Marx G. (1991). No soul in the new machine: Technofallacies in the electronic monitoring movement. *Justice Quarterly, 8,* 399–414.

Erwin, B. S. (1990). Old and new tools for the modern probation officer. *Crime and Delinquency, 36,* 61–74.

Lilly, J. R. (1990). Tagging reviewed. *The Howard Journal, 29,* 229–245.

Lilly, J. R. (1992). Selling justice: Electronic monitoring and the security industry. *Justice Quarterly, 9,* 493–503.

Mainprize, S. (1992). Electronic monitoring in corrections: Assessing cost effectiveness and the potential for widening the net of social control. *Canadian Journal of Criminology, 34,* 161–180.

Palumbo, D. J., Clifford, M., & Snyder-Joy, Z. (1992). From net widening to intermediate sanctions: The transformation of alternative to incarceration from benevolence to malevolence. In J. M. Byrne, A. J. Lurigio, and J. Petersillia (Eds.), *Smart sentencing: The emergence of intermediate sanctions.* Newbury Park, CA: Sage.

Renzema, M. (1992). Home confinement programs: Development, implementation, and impact. In J. M. Byrne, A. J. Lurigio, and J. Petersillia (Eds.), *Smart sentencing: The emergence of intermediate sanctions.* Newbury Park, CA: Sage.

Renzema, M., & Skelton, D. (1990). Trends in the use of electronic monitoring, 1989. *Journal of Offender Monitoring, 3,* 14–19.

Schmidt, A. K. (1991). Electronic monitors—Realistically, what can be expected? *Federal Probation, 55,* 47–53.

Tonry, M. (1990). Stated and latent features of IPS. *Crime and Delinquency, 36,* 174–191.

Rejoinder to Dr. Wells James F. Anderson

Wells asserts that EM programs are ineffective primarily because:

1. They are used as a means to widen the "net" of social control.
2. They lack rehabilitative components.
3. They do not reduce overcrowding and high prison costs.
4. They discriminate against the economically challenged.

Electronic Monitoring Programs Are Used as a Means to Widen the "Net" of Social Control

Wells raises a classic criticism leveled against all intermediate sanction programs. He argues that EM is just another mechanism the government uses to impose unnecessary control over citizens. The reality is that it is not used by the state for unnecessary social control, but rather, to monitor criminals. Social control is not sinister and does not have to be used in the context of conflict between state officials and citizens. Society has the right to counteract any threat to its survival. Therefore, one method of ensuring its survival is to punish law violators. Offenders sentenced to EM have committed a crime. Their past behavior warrants punishment.

Were it not for EM it is possible that these offenders would be in an overcrowded prison. However, I concede that if offenders who are sentenced to EM would have ordinarily received probation for their law violations, then this sentence is inappropriate. Nonetheless, research indicates that offenses resulting in sentencing to these programs are just as serious as those that result in traditional imprisonment. This sentence is imposed because of strained correctional budgets, lack of bed space, and the seriousness of offenders' criminality.

Electronic Monitoring Lacks Rehabilitative Components

Wells confuses rehabilitation with "reward" incentives. Rehabilitation is an intrinsic component of EM. Allowing participants to retain family ties and employment serves to rehabilitate them because neither are compromised because of their crime and punishment. Unfortunately, after arrest, offenders lose their jobs and suffer while their families disintegrate, especially if they were the sole providers. Moreover, after release, the stigma of incarceration makes it difficult for them to find employment, not to mention rebuilding the family structure. This inevitably causes some families to become recipients of welfare provisions. The costs of public assistance programs for dependent families far exceed the cost of EM.

Wells suggests that participants should be given "reward" incentives such as extended curfews for complying with the conditions of EM. I believe that these programs should not "coddle" participants, but rather, allow them to serve their full sentence. After all, a crime was committed, and this sentence is already considered a reprieve. Therefore, allocating rewards to offenders who have committed a crime might send the wrong message. This could undermine the deterrence component of EM.

Electronic Monitoring Does Not Reduce Overcrowding and High Prison Costs

Because participants in EM are "real" offenders, the programs save states money as a sentencing option. Were it not for EM, states could conceivably have two options for managing an influx of offenders. First, states could build more prisons. Second, states could seek other intermediate sanctions. I cannot think of any program that is less expensive than EM. As mentioned initially, the cost of building prisons is exorbitant, and for states facing financial hardship, this might not be feasible. Wells cites a study in which most offenders in a new program failed because they committed either a technical violation or a new offense after the first six months. The reality is that one study is not reflective of all EM programs. Perhaps studies that fail to track the progress of participants over an extended period produce inclusive results. Scientific research demands conscious observations, not hasty conclusions. If we omit this principle, we may overlook and discontinue programs that may prove effective.

Electronic Monitoring Programs Discriminate against the Economically Challenged

Wells maintains that the constitutionality of EM could be challenged on the basis that it is given to economically advantaged offenders. This presupposes that the unemployed will be excluded from participation. If this is true, these programs should be challenged because they discriminate against the poor. However, some states purchase electronic devices for destitute offenders. This ensures that everyone who qualifies can participate. Research shows that EM participants represent all offenders; it is not reserved for the privileged nor does it exclude minority offenders.

Boot Camps for Youthful Offenders: Are They Effective?

Elizabeth L. Grossi, Ph.D., takes the YES position. She is Assistant Professor at the University of Louisville, Department of Justice Administration, where she teaches courses in criminological theory and corrections. She has published articles on correction officer stress, boot camps, and criminal justice education. She is currently conducting a qualitative study of the boot camp experiences of women offenders.

Jonathan R. Sorensen, Ph.D., argues NO. He is Associate Professor of Criminal Justice at the University of Texas, Pan American and received a doctorate in criminal justice from Sam Houston State University in 1990. His recent research has focused on boot camps, criminal justice programs, the death penalty, predictions of dangerousness, and prisoner violence. He is currently attempting to capture voices from victims of the drug war.

YES

ELIZABETH L. GROSSI

Juvenile justice reform has always been more rhetoric than anything else. Some think we are caught up in cycles. The pendulum swings from toughness to permissiveness, from rehabilitation to incapacitation, and back again. In reality, however, the cycles exist only in rhetoric.

—Jerome G. Miller, 1991

As our society continues to grapple with the problem of juvenile crime, several communities have implemented boot camp programs. These programs, designed to provide offenders with a brief taste of military regimentation and discipline coupled with educational, counseling, and aftercare services, were conceived with two basic goals in mind: reduce recidivism and lower incarceration costs. Like their adult counterparts, these programs typically target young, first-time, nonviolent offenders. Boot camps for juvenile offenders have emerged across the country, and many jurisdictions without these programs are planning to implement a boot camp model in the near future. As the use of juvenile boot camps grows more popular among politicians and their constituents and the net of the criminal justice systems seemingly expands toward the infinite, one must carefully examine the progress of current programs. Detailed study and evaluation of boot camps is necessary to avoid the pitfalls of early programs as well as develop more effective and efficient means of addressing the criminal behavior of today's youth.

Most boot camp programs consist of several components, including military drill and ceremony, physical exercise, individual or group counseling, substance abuse treatment, life skills, vocational and education services, and to a lesser extent, aftercare. The amount of emphasis and time given to each component as well as the program content varies across boot camps. For example, the California Youth Authority LEAD program includes several core components such as GED preparation and testing, community service projects, a twelve-step substance abuse program, and military drills designed to assist offenders in developing leadership, esteem, ability, and discipline (Bottcher & Isorena, 1996). In Florida, various boot camp models are employed to meet the needs of the unique offenders and the communities in which they operate (Cass & Kaltenecker, 1996). Each of the Office of Juvenile Justice and Delinquency Prevention (OJJDP) demonstration sites operate independently and, although each site did not fully implement all planned components, the camps did provide the core components of military drills, education, and counseling (Peters, 1996a, 1996b; Thomas and Peters, 1996).

Adult and juvenile boot camp program outcome evaluations clearly indicate that boot camp participants have similar, if not higher, rates of recidivism than those for offenders who do not participate in these programs (Burns & Vito, 1995; Mackenzie and Souryal, 1994; Peters, 1996a, 1996b; Thomas and Peters, 1996). Recent studies conducted by the OJJDP indicate that participation in boot camp programs does not significantly reduce recidivism. For example, Thomas and Peters (1996) report that Cleveland, Ohio boot camp participants had higher rates of reoffending (71.8 percent) than the rate for the nonparticipants (50 percent). Data from the Mobile, Alabama, boot camp program indicate that although youth in the experimental group had lower rates of recidivism than those in the control group (60 percent versus 56 percent), the difference may be considered marginal at best (Peters, 1996a). Similarly, the study of Denver, Colorado, boot camp youth conducted by Peters (1996b) found only a slight difference in recidivism rates from experimental (39 percent) and control groups (36 percent).

Thus, on the surface it appears that boot camp programs have a negligible impact on recidivism rates for juvenile offenders. However, using recidivism as the sole measure for evaluating the effectiveness of juvenile boot camps fails to capture the more intricate aspects of contemporary shock incarceration programs. Although full-scale formal evaluations of most juvenile boot camp programs are lacking, the available data indicate there are components that are, or have a strong potential to, positively affect juvenile offenders.

For example, in each of the demonstration sites funded by OJJDP, there were marked increases in the participants' literacy skills. On average, offenders increased their reading, math, language, and spelling skills by at least one grade level. Beyond improving the literacy skills, the educational component also served to prepare participants for reentry into mainstream schools. For those participants for whom the General Equivalency Diploma (GED) was more appropriate, the educational component served to prepare them for entry into a GED preparatory program on release (Thomas & Peters, 1996).

Another positive aspect of juvenile boot camp programs relates to the increased employability of participants on returning to the community. According to the results of the OJJDP demonstration project evaluations, a number of boot camp graduates secured either full- or part-time employment during the aftercare phase (Peters, 1996a, 1996b; Thomas & Peters, 1996).

Perhaps before discarding boot camp programs because they fail to demonstrate marked reductions in recidivism we should more closely examine existing individual program components and issues related to implementation and service delivery. In addition, boot camp programs would be well served to model their aftercare programs after successful community-based programs already in existence throughout the country. In short, before labeling juvenile boot camps as ineffective, one should explore implementation issues as well as expand the indicators of program success. This chapter addresses these issues and lends support for further refinement and expansion of viable juvenile boot camp programs.

Aftercare: The Missing Link

Contemporary research of adult and juvenile boot camp programs indicates that military training alone does not reduce recidivism. The essence of military training should be captured; however, it also must be complemented by programs that address the individual needs of offenders. Furthermore, the short duration of boot camps does not lend itself to meaningful, long-term change; therefore, a continuum of services for offenders should be established to bridge the gap between correctional settings and the community. Educational accomplishments, anger management strategies, substance abuse treatment, and the like are much easier to attain and sustain within a highly structured and controlled environment. However, the true measure of the utility of these programs occurs outside of the prison walls— when the offender returns to the community. It is at this point that the offender requires the most comprehensive and intensive services.

Aftercare for juvenile boot camp offenders is essential if long-term change is to be achieved. Virtually every evaluation of existing boot camp programs suggests that if long-term change is to be achieved, more emphasis should be placed on improving and fully implementing aftercare services (Bourque, Felker, Han, & White, 1995; Cowles & Castellano, 1995). Making the transition from the rigid and controlled environment of the boot camp to the city streets, even under the best conditions, poses a special challenge to offenders and can best be addressed by providing continuity of care from the prison to the community. The design of aftercare programs should occur during the early stages of planning the boot camp program and should be initialized for each offender during the intake process.

Several contemporary boot camp programs include an aftercare component; however, most aftercare services suffer from a number of deficiencies (Cowles & Castellano, 1995). First, aftercare services are rather generic and often fail to meet the needs of the specific offender. Most institutional programs provide rudimentary services to participants that may not prove effective once the offenders return to a less structured environment. Efforts should be made to build on the skills and knowledge acquired by participants during the residential phase and assist offenders in developing mechanisms to address recurring, as well as emerging, difficulties relating to their unique situation. Second, many programs release offenders from the boot camp to an aftercare program without the benefit of a transitional phase, which often results in fragmented and ineffective service delivery. A recent National Institute of Justice research report indicates that only two of ten juvenile boot camp programs, the Cuyahoga County Juvenile Boot Camp, Hudson, Ohio, and the Leon County Juvenile Boot Camp located in Florida, provide transitional services to boot camp graduates. Third, many programs fail to use existing community resources or to develop partnerships with community-based service providers. Preliminary evaluations of the three OJJDP demonstration sites indicate several problematic areas, including staff turnover and training, participant absenteeism, and balancing rehabilitation and supervision services. Finally, most programs make no attempt or are unsuccessful in their efforts to involve the family members of the offender in aftercare services (Peters, 1996a, 1996b; Thomas & Peters, 1996).

Partnerships among community members, universities, local government, and the private sector continue to evolve and perhaps hold the greatest potential for effective prevention and intervention of delinquency. In 1992, a collaborative venture involving local policing agents and mental health professionals was undertaken in New Haven, Connecticut. Hailed by OJJDP as the "national model for police–mental health partnership," the Child Development–Community Policing

(CD-CP) program seeks to establish practical strategies to counteract the damaging effects of exposure to violence in the community and prevent the intergenerational transmission of violence among youth. The success of this program has sparked OJJDP to sponsor replications in Buffalo, Charlotte, Nashville, and Portland (Marans & Berkman, 1997).

Another example of a highly successful community-based program can be found in Allegheny County, Pennsylvania. Faced with an alarming rise in juvenile crime and heightened fear of victimization, the Allegheny County community has established an antiviolence program that includes law enforcement, judicial, community, and private sector agencies. Many of the elements of the Pennsylvania program could be included in boot camp aftercare programs. For example, the antiviolence program provided opportunities for the development of leadership skills among at-risk youth. Boot camp graduates could benefit from continued involvement in leadership programs as a means of reinforcing the training received during the boot camp program. Of perhaps greater import, boot camp graduates could conduct the leadership training or serve as mentors to other at-risk youth. Other elements of the Allegheny County program merit consideration for inclusion in boot camp aftercare programs such as the family support centers, mentoring, and substance abuse initiatives (Hsia, 1997).

The inclusion of a mentoring program also would benefit boot camp graduates. Typically used with disenfranchised youth, mentoring programs such as OJJDP's Juvenile Mentoring Program (JUMP) provide individualized support to children by linking community resources and positive role models with at-risk youth. Juvenile Mentoring Programs in cities such as Cincinnati, New York, Los Angeles, and Denver have employed diverse and comprehensive strategies to address the needs of local youth, including frequent and consistent contact with adult volunteers, educational initiatives, cultural awareness and sensitivity activities, pregnancy prevention, participatory and spectator athletic opportunities, and a police mini-academy. Initial evaluations of the Big Brothers/Big Sisters mentoring program show that many youth improved their academic performance, social skills, peer relations, and school attendance while involved in the program. Furthermore, participating youth were less likely to employ violence as a means of resolving conflict and less likely to use drugs and alcohol (Grossman & Garry, 1997).

The Intensive Community-Based Aftercare Program (IAP) also may ease the transition from boot camp to the community. The IAP model consists of three primary components: prerelease planning and preparation, institutional and aftercare staff participation throughout the residential and aftercare program, and reintegrative activities of a sufficient duration (Altschuler & Armstrong, 1996). To some extent these components are present in existing boot camp aftercare programs; however, there is little to suggest that these measures have enjoyed full implementation. Clearly the IAP model, properly designed and implemented, has the potential to provide the much-needed transitional services to boot camp graduates.

Conclusion

Although long-term outcome evaluations of prison boot camp programs for youthful offenders have yet to be conducted, initial studies demonstrate the promise of these programs. The process and impact evaluations conducted to date indicate that reduction in recidivism for boot camp participants is not as significant as initially envisioned and that the use of boot camps does not always result in reducing the costs of incarcerating juvenile offenders. However, most of the evaluations make note of implementation problems that hindered the employment of the original program design. Furthermore, most evaluations suggest that the lack of sufficient aftercare planning and programming was all too prevalent and served to diminish the effectiveness of the program. Given the problematic issues relating to boot camp design and implementation, one may feel compelled to repeat the all too familiar cry of *NOTHING WORKS*. But on closer examination, one may find that certain components of boot camps have made a difference in the lives of youthful offenders. One may further surmise that if minor adjustment were made within these programs it is likely that a much different outcome may result.

Juvenile offenders must be given a solid foundation within the residential boot camp, highly structured transitional services, and long-term support in the form of community-based collaborative programs if the boot camps are to be an efficient and effective means of reducing confinement costs. It is far too early to abandon the boot camp model—instead, we should continue to evaluate existing programs and modify future ones. The causes of delinquency are far too complex to expect simplistic solutions. Boot camp programs must employ a dynamic, integrated, collaborative, and community-based approach to be an effective remedy.

REFERENCES

Altschuler, D. M., & Armstrong, T. L. (1996). Aftercare not afterthought: Testing the IAP model. *Juvenile Justice, 3,* 15–22.

Bottcher, J., & Isorena, T. (1996). First-year evaluation of the California Youth Authority boot camp. In D. L. MacKenzie & E. E. Hebert (Eds.), *Correctional boot camps: A tough intermediate sanction* (pp. 159–178). Washington, DC: National Institute of Justice.

Bourque, B. B., Felker, D. B., Han, M., & White, R. N. (1995). *An implementation evaluation of the first incarceration shock treatment program: A boot camp for youthful offenders in Kentucky: Final report.* Washington, DC: American Institute for Research.

Burns, J. & Vito, G. F. (1995). An impact analysis of the Alabama boot camp program. *Federal Probation, 59* (1), 63–67.

Cass, E. S., & Kaltenecker, N. (1996). The development and operation of juvenile boot camps in Florida. In D. L. MacKenzie & E. E. Hebert (Eds.), *Correctional boot camps: A tough intermediate sanction* (pp.179–190). Washington, DC: National Institute of Justice.

Cowles, E. L., & Castellano, T. C. (1995). *"Boot camp" drug treatment and aftercare intervention: An evaluation review.* Washington, DC: National Institute of Justice.

Grossman, J. B., & Garry, E. M. (1997). *Mentoring—A proven delinquency prevention approach.* Washington, DC: Office of Juvenile Justice and Delinquency Prevention.

Hsia, H. M. (1997). *Allegheny County, PA: Mobilizing to reduce juvenile crime.* Washington, DC: Office of Juvenile Justice and Delinquency Prevention.

Mackenzie, D. L., & Souryal, C. (1994). *Multisite evaluation of shock incarceration.* Washington, DC: U.S. Department of Justice.

Marans, S., & Berkman, M. (1997). *Child development–community policing: Partnerships in a climate of violence.* Washington, DC: U.S. Department of Justice.

Miller, J. G. (1991). *Last one over the wall: The Massachusetts experiment in closing reform schools.* Columbus, OH: Ohio State University Press.

Peters, M. (1996a). *Evaluation of the impact of boot camps for juvenile offenders: Mobile interim report,* NCJ 160926. Washington, DC: Office of Juvenile Justice and Delinquency.

Peters, M. (1996b). *Evaluation of the impact of boot camps for juvenile offenders: Denver interim report,* NCJ 160927. Washington, DC: Office of Juvenile Justice and Delinquency.

Thomas, D., & Peters, M. (1996). *Evaluation of the impact of boot camps for juvenile offenders: Cleveland Interim Report,* NCJ 160928. Washington, DC: Office of Juvenile Justice and Delinquency Prevention.

Rejoinder to Dr. Grossi

JONATHAN R. SORENSEN

Yes, I am one of the pessimists, or perhaps more appropriately, realists, referred to by Dr. Grossi in her essay in defense of boot camps. I am not "optimistic" that a draconian correctional punishment involving intensive physical and psychological control over the bodies and minds of young, relatively nonserious offenders will result in their normalization. Given the findings from current empirical studies and the lack of any persuasive logical rationale for continuing, correctional boot camps should be relegated to the status of a failed experiment, a footnote for distant penology texts.

As she notes, the two basic goals of correctional boot camps are to reduce recidivism and lower incarceration costs. Regarding the first goal, I concur with Dr. Grossi, who has obviously waded through the seemingly endless stream of empirical studies before stating that "Adult and juvenile boot camp program outcome evaluations clearly indicate that boot camp participants have similar, if not higher, rates of recidivism than those offenders who do not participate in these programs." Regarding the second goal of reducing cost, I also agree with her statement that "As the use of juvenile boot camps grows more popular among politicians and their constituents and the net of the criminal justice system seemingly expands toward the infinite, one must carefully examine the progress of current programs."

The comments taken from my adversary's text clearly show that boot camps have not been effective at achieving their stated goals. Why then would Dr. Grossi support the expansion of boot camps in the correctional treatment of young offenders? Her reasoning appears to rely on the assumption that positive aspects of boot camp programming such as improved literacy skills and increased employability would have a beneficial effect if proper aftercare programs were implemented. The author supports her position by discussing the results of many other types of successful community programs that could be used in conjunction with boot camp aftercare. This logic does not validate the need for boot camps, but instead suggests the need for emulating these successful components whenever community-based programs are implemented. These studies also suggest that if boot camps are to be successful, it will be for reasons other than the military-style training.

In Dr. Grossi's essay, we find no compelling reason to expand boot camp programming for youthful offenders. Indeed, implementing boot camp programs for youthful offenders should not be seen as a harmless experiment, but rather, as I outline in the next section, part of a symbolic, ideological-driven plan of human engineering with potentially devastating social consequences.

NO

JONATHAN R. SORENSEN

What was then being formed was a policy of coercions that act upon the body, a calculated manipulation of its elements, its gestures, its behaviour. The human body was entering a machinery of power that explores it, breaks it down and rearranges it. A 'political anatomy', which was also a 'mechanics of power', was being born; it defined how one may have a hold over others' bodies, not only so that they may do what one wishes, but so that they may operate as one wishes, with the techniques, the speed and efficiency that one determines. Thus discipline produces subjected and practised bodies, 'docile' bodies. Discipline increases the forces of the body (in economic terms of utility) and diminishes these same forces (in political terms of obedience).

(Foucault, 1979: 138)

While Foucault was interested in the rise of prisons and other disciplinary institutions as general instruments of social control nearly two centuries ago, correctional boot camps implemented recently in the United States emanate from the same historical forces. Just as penal detention in a panopticon was considered to be the disciplinary mechanism par excellence of the early nineteenth century, correctional boot camps appear to be the disciplinary mechanism par excellence of the late twentieth century. To understand why correctional boot camps fail, it is necessary to first examine the principles on which their regimen is based and the functions they are to intended to serve from an historical perspective.

Historical Antecedents

Bentham dreamed of an "inspection-house" in which strict partitioning and constant surveillance would render its inhabitants powerless to resist its normalizing influence. The principle controlling influence over the inhabitants was rooted in the architectural composition of the inspection house. In the panopticon, a circular building with individual cells situated around the periphery and an observation tower in the middle, the cells would have windows to the outside so that supervisors in the central tower could observe each charge in his cell, without themselves being seen. The constant visibility of the charge, whether a criminal, madman, school child, or worker, from the view of countless anonymous inspectors in the tower, assured a perfect exercise of power. Such an arrangement was to instill a constant vigilance in the inhabitants, who in the face of such seemingly omnipresent surveillance, would in essence become their own captors, significantly reducing the actual need for supervision. These austere and complete institutions were to provide a model for the functioning of the entire society while normalizing, correcting, and controlling potentially, or actually, recalcitrant citizens. With the diffusion of such disciplinary mechanisms throughout other social institutions, the general citizenry would be rendered obedient and productive. Since the configuration of the panopticon, disciplinary mechanisms have flourished.

Penitentiaries were introduced into the American cultural landscape as a respite from the perceived social disorganization of the young Republic. Designed in the monastic tradition wherein penitent offenders could reflect on their past misdeeds, penitentiaries were also to serve the function of restoring order to society, while disciplining errant citizens through its regimen of obedience, separation, and labor (Rothman, 1990). Soon after their introduction, however, penitentiaries degenerated into warehouses of human misery.

During the Reconstruction era, a new institution aimed at reforming young offenders with a program of educational and vocational training. The goal of these Reformatories was to transform errant young adults into disciplined and productive members of the industrial workforce (Brockway, 1910). The flame died out fairly quickly as these institutions failed to fulfill their intended goal of reformation through training.

The Progressive era of the early twentieth century ushered a new model into the field of corrections, typically referred to as the medical model. In the medical analogy, offenders would be free from the disease of criminality when healed of the illness that had caused them to commit their crimes. At the height of the medical model in the 1960s, correctional institutions across the United States focused on the task of rehabilitating offenders. In only slight deviation, the movement toward community-based corrections in the 1970s resulted from a belief that offenders could best be reintegrated into society if the ties that bound them were not entirely severed. However, with increasing crime rates, a series of evaluations finding correctional treatment ineffective, inequities in prison terms under indeterminate sentencing, and a general conservative shift in American public opinion, the medical model and its close relative came under attack.

A punitive backlash signaled a return to a custodial model of imprisonment, one in which warehousing inmates in a safe and efficient manner has become the predominant concern (DiIulio, 1987). The crime control model, now pervasive in the criminal justice system, led to more widespread use of imprisonment and lengthier prison sentences in an effort to deter, incapacitate, or simply punish offenders (Irwin & Austin, 1997). Ironically, extreme growth in the prison population led to an increased reliance on community-based alternatives to incarceration, not for the lofty purpose of reintegration, but rather as a pragmatic solution to the paradox of overcrowded prisons caused by an unrelenting public clamor for punitive sanctions. This paradox led to the creation and implementation of certain intermediate sanctions lying somewhere on the continuum between probation and prison (Morris & Tonry, 1990). For these sanctions not to be perceived by the general public as being "soft" on offenders, proposed alternative sanctions had to incorporate punitive characteristics, hence the development of intermediate sanctions such as electronic monitoring, shock incarceration, and boot camps.

As during previous eras, the development of recent correctional policies has been influenced by broader social changes. With the perceived failure of each wave of correctional reform, Americans seek out new disciplinary mechanisms to effectively normalize their deviant countrymen. Once again Americans are relying on specific correctional programs—boot camps—as panaceas. The specific features of the boot camp have been reconstituted from the disciplinary mechanisms of previous eras. The appeal of boot camps to the American public in general, and hence politicians in particular, lies in the extremity of its disciplinary regimen.

Failure of the Correctional Boot Camp Model to Induce Positive Behavioral Change

Correctional boot camps are typically designed for first-time youthful adult offenders. Emulating the atmosphere of the military boot camp, correctional boot camps purport to correct young offenders by inducing their conformity to a military style of discipline. Proponents tout the military model's ability to change attitudes in a prosocial direction, and also to habituate offenders to a conformist lifestyle through its regimen of daily physical exercise, hard labor, drill, and ceremony. Proponents suggest that, beyond serving a punitive function, boot camps are beneficial in reforming individuals and deterring them from further criminal acts.

The best means of gauging the specific deterrent and reformative effects of a sanction is by examining the attitudes and behaviors of program participants. Researchers have found that those leaving boot camps tend to have more prosocial attitudes and higher self-esteem on release, suggesting that the short-term objectives of the boot camp may have been met in some instances (Ethridge & Sorensen, 1997). However, the best indicator of any lasting effect is the behavior of former boot camp participants on their release back into the community. Overall, it appears that recidivism rates for those sentenced to correctional boot camps are similar to recidivism rates of control groups—those sentenced directly to probation, prison, or another alternative sanction (MacKenzie & Souryal, 1994). Boot camp programs that do result in lower rates of recidivism typically offer the most educational, vocational, and reintegrative programming, suggesting that the military style of discipline in these programs should not be credited for their success (Reid-MacNevin, 1997). Although military-style discipline makes the boot camp sanction retributive, it accomplishes little in terms of deterring or reforming program participants. Rather than using worn out military euphemisms, this evidence suggests that intermediate sanctions based on a reintegrative model of programming and training would be more effective at reforming criminal offenders (Welch, 1997).

Even though overall recidivism rates among boot camp participants are as high as among those receiving prison terms, the boot camp could possibly be deemed a success for accomplishing the same results in a shorter time for less money. While relatively short terms in boot camps appear to be less expensive than longer prison terms, potential cost savings have not been realized. One reason that savings are elusive is that a high number of program failures typically end up serving the remainder of their term in prison, as do boot camp graduates who recidivate in the community. Additionally, the only way in which any cost benefits can be realized is if the offender had truly been prison bound. Because boot camps are designed for young offenders with some hope of change, entrance criteria often restrict admission to first-time offenders who have committed nonviolent offenses. Along with the demand in many districts that these programs be fully utilized—operation at capacity often being the official measure of success—stringent entrance requirements increase the probability that participants were not diverted from prison. For offenders who would have previously received only a probated term, the boot camp becomes a form of probation enhancement. This widening or strengthening of the correctional net prevents promised savings from materializing.

Some may argue that the normalizing effects on those who successfully complete the program are more important than recidivism rates. If the dogmatic adherence to a rigid hierarchical power structure in the boot camp translates into the graduates' acceptance of the power differentials in unfair social arrangements and the occupational structures to which most of them will be subjected on release, the military regimen of the correctional boot camp may be deemed successful, in Foucault's terms, as a disciplinary mechanism. In another sense, successful acceptance of power differentials by graduates would be particularly devastating for those whom the graduate perceives as being of lesser status. In the military model, those of higher rank are to be obeyed, and those of lower rank are to be given orders. This is particularly problematic for females, given that all-male institutions foster the pervasive social view, especially among lower- and working-class males, of females as subordinates. In combination, authoritarian personality characteristics and sexist attitudes engendered by the military model in corrections will likely have a far-reaching, negative social impact—witness the recent charges of sexual discrimination, harassment, and assault in the military.

Nothing Succeeds Like Failure

According to Jeffrey Reiman (1995), the criminal justice system is succeeding, not in dispensation of justice, but in the ideological functions it serves. Boot camps, like most other current correctional practices, serve to promote certain ideas that benefit current social structural arrangements. First, boot camps do not significantly reduce recidivism; therefore, their failure assures a reoccurring stream of deviants who can be marginalized and sacrificed to sooth the collective conscience (Durkheim, 1964). Furthermore, boot camps squarely place the blame for criminal activity on the offenders. Pushing a routine of corrective discipline suggests that individual offenders have chosen to commit criminal acts because of a lack of self-control (Gottfredson & Hirschi, 1990). According to the logic of this theory, once the patterned discipline of the boot camp model is internalized, offenders will assert their self-control, thereby avoiding criminal activity. The proposed causal relationship between self-control and crime, and its solution, ignore the bulk of theory and research, which place the main determinants of juvenile delinquency and criminality within the economic and structural context.

Although individuals may exert free will in choosing life behaviors, this freedom of choice is bound by their cultural and structural milieu. Boot camp programming ignores the unforgiving social environment in which most of the recruits grew up, and will be returning to after their short stint in the program. They are not headed off to war, but returning to an environment in which legitimate opportunities for success are lacking, but in which illegitimate avenues often loom large. Real solutions that address the social structural causes of delinquency and criminality, such as training individuals for careers, providing legitimate opportunities, and eliminating discrimination, are ignored. Offering hope in place of a bleak future by providing a stake in conformity would be more effective than using a stick to promote conformity.

Boot camps for youthful offenders, just like correctional experiments of the past, have served as a means of managing a potentially volatile segment of the population, the underclass. Boot camps are politically manipulated symbols, especially effective at assuring the middle and upper classes that the status quo will be protected. Explaining lower-class criminality as a lack of self-control eliminates structural imperatives by placing blame directly on the individuals. The moral failure remains situated within the individual as opposed to society. Criminality unabated, the populace, led by ignorant or unscrupulous politicians, cries out for ever more punitive sanctions as the war against the underclass rages on.

REFERENCES

Brockway, Z. R. (1910). The American reformatory prison system. In C. Henderson (Ed.), *Prison reform: Correction and prevention*. Philadelphia, PA: Wm. F. Fell.

DiIulio, J. J. (1987). *Governing prisons: A comparative study of correctional management*. New York: Free Press.

Durkheim, E. (1964). *The division of labor in society*. New York: Free Press.

Ethridge, P. A., & Sorensen, J. R. (1997). An analysis of attitudinal change and community adjustment among probationers in a county boot camp. *Journal of Contemporary Criminal Justice, 13,* 139–154.

Foucault, M. (1979). *Discipline and punish: The birth of the prison*. New York: Vintage Books.

Gottfredson, M. R., & Hirschi, T. (1990). *A general theory of crime*. Stanford, CA: Stanford University Press.

Irwin, J. & Austin, J. (1997). *It's about time: America's imprisonment binge* (2nd ed.). Belmont, CA: Wadsworth.

MacKenzie, D. L., & Souryal, C. (1994). *Multisite evaluation of shock incarceration*. Washington, DC: National Institute of Justice.

Morris, N., & Tonry, M. (1990). *Between prison and probation: Intermediate punishments in a rational sentencing system*. New York: Oxford University Press.

Reid-MacNevin, S. A. (1997). Boot camps for young offenders: A politically acceptable punishment. *Journal of Contemporary Criminal Justice, 13,* 155–171.

Reiman, J. (1995). *The rich get richer and the poor get prison: Ideology, crime and criminal justice* (4th ed.). Boston, MA: Allyn & Bacon.

Rothman, D. J. (1990). *The discovery of the asylum: Social order and disorder in the new republic* (rev. ed.). Boston: Little, Brown.

Welch, M. (1997). A critical interpretation of correctional bootcamps as normalizing institutions: Discipline, punishment, and the military model. *Journal of Contemporary Criminal Justice, 13,* 184–205.

Rejoinder to Dr. Sorensen

ELIZABETH L. GROSSI

Dr. Sorensen's argument that boot camps are nothing more than another vehicle of the capitalists to criminalize and exploit the social dynamite of contemporary society is firmly embedded in the historical and theoretical literature. However, this position is myopic, lacks empirical support, and fails to provide for viable policy alternatives. Indeed, placing the primary, if not sole, responsibility for crime and delinquency on the existing social structure is to ignore the complex nature of human behavior. Furthermore, it is unrealistic to expect that major changes in the social structure alone will result in a significant reduction in crime. I do not contend that the existing social structure is without problems—it has and continues to be less than ideal; however, I do take issue with Dr. Sorensen's failure to adequately consider the individual factors that contribute to criminal behavior. The crime problem facing American society extends far beyond the socially constructed boundaries of race, class, age, and gender.

His position that boot camps do not address the social environment of the offender is inaccurate. Evaluations of existing programs clearly indicate the importance of aftercare services to offenders returning to their communities, and many programs have made significant strides in addressing the social and economic issues facing offenders. Furthermore, correctional administrators and policymakers have become increasingly aware that society's response to criminal behavior must be more comprehensive and are adopting a "continuum of care" philosophy, which is intended to further service the offender on release.

Dr. Sorensen suggests that boot camps are considered a "panacea." Clearly, a review of the extant literature indicates that programs such as boot camps were not designed to solve the crime problem. Instead, they are considered another available tool to address the unique needs of young offenders. Boot camp programs certainly will not work for everyone—but they can and do work for some offenders. Thus, we should continue to use boot camp programs. Furthermore, as I argued earlier, these programs must be comprehensively evaluated to identify existing imperfections and develop subsequent modifications to ensure that offenders are offered the most promising rehabilitative modalities.

Dr. Sorensen's argument that criminal behavior is a result of the "economic and structural context" of society, to some extent, parallels those he appears to despise—those who contend that criminal behavior results from impulsive actions of members from lower-class, single-parent families. Both positions fail to grasp the intricacies of human behavior and do not address the interactionist nature of criminal and delinquent behavior. Furthermore, far too many researchers have relied on quantitative methods that lack the ability to capture, or fully account for, the factors that contribute to deviance, delinquency, or criminality. Perhaps at this juncture the most appropriate course of action would be to refrain from making further ill-informed legislation and correctional policies and return to more ethnographic research—research that brings us closer to those who are most effective by our laws, policies, and programs. Of course, a moratorium on correctional "band-aids" is only necessary if we *really* want to understand and address the problems of crime and delinquency.

In sum, I am convinced that we need to continue to examine boot camp programs before summarily dismissing them as yet another failed experiment. Furthermore, I contend that future program evaluations require a more balanced blending of qualitative and quantitative research methods. Indeed, it is time to move beyond the rhetoric and earnestly pursue the answer to the proverbial question of "What works?"

Is It Still Practical to Incarcerate the Elderly Offender?

Irina R. Soderstrom argues YES. She is Assistant Professor in the Department of Correctional Services at Eastern Kentucky University and has a Ph.D. in Educational Psychology, Statistics and Measurement from Southern Illinois University (1997). Her current research includes methodological development in Logistic Regression, assessment of juvenile and adult boot camps, as well as scale validation in corrections.

W. Michael Wheeler presents the NO position. He received his doctorate from the University of North Carolina, Chapel Hill (1992) and is currently Associate Professor at Southwestern Oklahoma State University, Social Sciences Department, and Director of the Gerontology Program. He teaches courses in gerontology and geography. Dr. Wheeler has published several articles on aging prison populations and a book examining elderly and residential perception.

YES

Irina R. Soderstrom

Certainly, arguments can be made from all punishment rationale perspectives regarding the incarceration of some elderly offenders. Whether it be an argument of retribution, incapacitation, resocialization and reintegration into the community, or rehabilitation, there will be obvious cases in which incarceration of the elderly offender is the appropriate response to criminal activity. These same arguments apply to younger offenders and thus are not laid out in terms of their theoretical foundations.

In fact, rarely does the literature on elderly offenders discuss whether old convicts should be incarcerated. To the contrary, the primary debate seems to focus on whether special programming or treatment should exist for this small subgroup of the general inmate population (e.g., see Cavan, 1987; Durham, 1994; Goetting, 1983; Kratcoski & Pownall, 1989; McShane & Williams, 1990; Vega & Silverman, 1988; Walsh, 1992).

Because of the expense of providing special programming and treatment for any inmate subpopulation, it seems strange to single out the elderly subgroup for debate. It has never been, and never will be, practical, in an economic sense, to incarcerate the elderly. But then that same argument could be made for the practice of incarceration in general. Given current projected average cost-per-prison-bed construction costs as we move into the twenty-first century—$116,000 (maximum security), $88,000 (medium security), $49,000 (minimum security)—incarceration, for most types of offenders, does not seem to be economically practical. Thus, this debate focuses on the practicality of providing special programming and treatment for elderly inmates, given the fact that this "forgotten minority" (Goetting, 1983) will continue to grow because of sentencing guidelines that provide for mandatory and longer sentences, as well as the larger societal trend of human beings living longer than in the past.

Elderly Inmates Often Are Violent Offenders

Studies of elderly offenders (often defined as age fifty years or older) have tended to categorize older inmates in a number of different ways, including first time incarcerated versus multiply incarcerated (Teller & Howell, 1981); first time incarcerated during elderly years vs. first time incarcerated during younger years (but aged while serving long-term sentences) vs. multiply incarcerated (Vega & Silverman, 1988); and geriatric versus nongeriatric (Walsh, 1992). How this inmate subgroup is defined differentiates the criminal history profile associated with the older inmate.

Generally speaking, first-time incarcerated offenders tend to have current sentences resulting from crimes committed against others, often in a spontaneous fashion, and thus do not view themselves as criminals. Conversely, multiply incarcerated offenders typically are locked up for premeditated crimes and do in fact view themselves as criminals (Teller & Howell, 1981). In fact, Goetting (1983) discussed in her report on survey findings regarding the existence of special policies, programs, and facilities for elderly inmates in United States prisons, that available data does link elderly inmates, especially the first-time incarcerated, to crimes of violence. McShane and Williams (1990) studied an elderly inmate population that comprised 60 percent violent offenders. Even an article disputing this prevalence of violent criminal activity among elderly offenders reports a figure closer to 13 percent (Kratcoski & Pownall, 1989), which, albeit small, is still a percentage that indicates that a predominantly sympathetic image of the "old con" probably is not warranted.

Current statistics indicate that criminally charged senior citizens, fifty years and older, constituted 4.2 percent of all arrests in 1994. Furthermore, this age-group was responsible for 3.6 percent of all violent crime (defined as murder, nonnegligent manslaughter, forcible rape, robbery, and aggravated assault) arrests in 1994. Their total proportion of arrests for all eight index crimes computes to 3.2 percent (Bureau of Justice Statistics, 1995). Although these percentages are rather small, they do indicate that an identifiable amount of serious crime is being committed by senior citizens, and sometimes these crimes are of a violent nature. (Thus, the need to incarcerate some elderly offenders is arguable, given the seriousness of the criminal activity exhibited by at least a proportion of this older criminal subpopulation).

In fact, it has been predicted that by the year 2005, approximately 16 percent of the nation's inmate population will be a member of the fifty years or older age-group. It is no wonder that as this elderly subgroup continues to grow, correctional policies and administration practices will have to address the special needs inherent to elderly inmate status.

Right to Appropriate Medical Treatment Already Established

The U.S. Supreme Court affirmed the rights of inmates to have their medical needs met in *Estelle* v. *Gamble* (1976). In this case, the Court stated that "...deliberate indifference to the serious medical needs of prisoners constitutes the 'unnecessary and wanton infliction of pain' proscribed by the Eighth Amendment." Whether economically practical or not, it clearly has been established through case law that correctional systems must provide a vast array of health care services, including medical, dental, nutritional, acute, and long-term care (Kratcoski & Pownall, 1989, p. 32).

But these health care services will not come cheaply. As reported by Durham (1994), a 1990 study by Larry Sullivan found that physical and mental health costs for the elderly inmate increased from an average annual cost of $23,000 (for a nonelderly inmate) to $70,000. But given the costs to society and families of victims, especially in the cases involving violent crimes, it may be as practical to make these health care expenditures as opposed to some alternative reaction to older offenders' behaviors.

Specialized Programming and Treatment Already Exists for Elderly Inmates

According to available information, correctional systems increasingly appear to be responding appropriately (Kratcoski & Pownall, 1989) to the specialized needs of older offenders. The Federal Bureau of Prisons led the way in implementing geriatric care units for elderly inmates, particularly with its creation of a medical unit for male inmates (the Dallas Unit, previously called the Comprehensive Health Unit) located in Fort Worth, Texas. This specialized unit had 57.6 percent inmates in the 51 or older category according to 1986 figures. Additionally, as reported in Kratcoski and Pownall (1989), the U.S. Department of Justice provided the following list of criteria that characterized the ideal geriatric unit:

1. Special diets, nutrition monitoring
2. Special exercise needs for prevention of bone deterioration, etc.
3. Personal hygiene issues, i.e., problems of incontinence
4. Decline in sight, hearing and memory impairment
5. Slowing of physical and mental responses
6. Modified work and leisure programs
7. Monitoring for special problems, such as cardiovascular diseases, diabetics, digestive ailments
8. Modification of physical environment to facilitate walkers, wheelchairs, other physical aids
9. Ultimately, constant bed care and intensive medical supervision (p. 39).

Since the late 1970s, the Federal Bureau of Prisons has designated correctional goals to implement these ideal geriatric unit components. Typical programs in such a geriatric facility have included stress management, health wise, drug facts, and positive mental attitude (Kratcoski & Pownall, 1989). Thus, it seems that whether economically practical or not, the Federal prison system has accepted the inevitable need to provide extended and specialized services to the elderly inmate.

Only a Small Minority of Elderly Offenders Will Require Specialized Services

Current data suggest that only 10 percent of elderly offenders can be classified as geriatric and in need of these expensive specialized programs. The other 90 percent of elderly offenders will not exhibit geriatric complications until the very last stages of their incarceration (Walsh, 1992). Some expensive health services will be necessary for a small number of older offenders at any given correctional facility, but the required resources should not be that great, particularly when compared with the special health needs of other subgroups of inmates (e.g., inmates with AIDS or tuberculosis).

In fact, Kratcoski's and Pownall's (1989) review of Federal Bureau of Prison programming for elderly inmates indicated that most older inmates are encouraged to participate in most prison programming, including education, work, and exercise. They posit that even when an older inmate cannot participate in a sport such as basketball or football, they still can participate in other activities such as walking, light aerobic exercises, and a full range of more sedentary recreational activities.

Problems with Age-Segregated Facilities

There are a number of arguments against the use of age-segregated facilities, which would be the most costly of methods to handle elderly inmates. Because of the small number of geriatric inmates that would truly be in need of age-segregated conditions of confinement, the creation of geriatric courts and other types of age-segregation treatment in the criminal justice system would stereotype all elderly offenders as being feeble and incapable of withstanding regular incarceration conditions (Cavan, 1987).

Furthermore, considerable evidence suggests that older inmates actually provide a stabilizing effect on the general inmate population (e.g., Rubenstein, 1984; Wiltz, 1973). In fact, McCleery (1961) described the inmate hierarchy as being somewhat based on seniority, with "old cons" initiating daily prison life norms and occupying leadership roles. It appears the older inmates serve as unofficial sources of information necessary for successful prison adjustment by younger offenders who tend to be unfamiliar with or unprepared for the rigors of prison life. It has even been suggested that older inmates are respected by younger inmates for their accumulated wisdom regarding the workings of daily prison life, which allegedly allows them to manipulate the correctional system to their advantages (Wiltz, 1973). Additionally, Goetting (1983) describes a study by Wooden and Parker (1980), which found that older inmates were more stable in their jobs, tended to work in more substantial jobs, were more likely to have trades and skills as well as a positive attitude toward work, were more accustomed to maintaining standard work hours, were more mature in their approach to work, and generally were trusted more for roles of responsibility by prison staff than their younger counterparts. This superior inmate status, coupled with elderly inmates' economically advantaged position (many receive monthly Social Security income in addition to occupying the best-paying prison jobs), places them in a favorable position within the prison social structure (Goetting, 1983).

Contrary to the myth that older inmates are more vulnerable to victimization by younger inmates, studies have indicated that older inmates are less likely to be victimized than younger inmates. And even when older inmates cited incidences of violence, it typically was an incident involving the witnessing of a violent act, rather than actual participation in the act (Vega & Silverman, 1988).

Furthermore, Kratcoski and Pownall (1989) pointed out most federal elderly inmates had been previously incarcerated, so they certainly were not naive about prison life. The combined implication of these findings is that there does not appear to be justifiable cause to move toward a separate geriatric justice system nor the costly construction of age-segregated facilities.

Problems with Diversion Programs

Some authors have approached the problem of incarcerating the elderly from a least restrictive alternatives correctional philosophy (Cavan, 1987). These alternatives could include modified arrest procedures (e.g., citations to appear in court rather than usual arrest and booking procedures; pretrial release without bail unless offender is a clear threat to others), probation and suspended sentences (including supervision, counseling, and possibly a Big Brother/Big Sister type of program), diversion to residential treatment centers (particularly for alcohol detoxification) without formal charges, and diversion to community programs requiring community service work and counseling (Cavan, 1987).

The primary problem with attempting to divert elderly offenders from the correctional system pertains to the paucity of local agencies either willing or able to accommodate the special needs of geriatric offenders. In fact, Goetting (1983) discussed how many elderly inmates prefer not to be paroled because of problems on the "outside" such as unavailability of housing and work. Even agencies designed to facilitate community reintegration of ex-convicts are often unable or unwilling to take on the complex and diverse problems associated with the elderly inmate (particularly alcohol-, medical-, and financial-related problems).

Wiltz (1973) discussed how the prison environment even might serve as a more suitable place for the elderly inmate as opposed to the societal environment of his "free" counterpart. This discussion was premised on the fact that the prison system does not have compulsory retirement, and thus, elderly inmates do not feel "useless" as they often do in free society, where they often are forced to make the transition from an active work role to one of idleness.

Making Incarceration of the Elderly More Practical

A number of resolutions to the problem of the expense of incarcerating the elderly have been suggested. The following are just a sample: (1) the private sector should confer for suggestions as to containing spiraling medical costs; (2) cooperative efforts should be encouraged between state departments of health and medical universities to provide low-cost specialized geriatric and gerontological services for inmates and training for prison staff; (3) the use of cost-effective mobile units to accommodate the specialized needs of geriatric inmates should be pursued; (4) volunteerism should be encouraged of senior citizen groups, private organizations, and public organizations to implement low-cost educational and recreational programs (Walsh, 1992); (5) increasingly more medical and social services should be contracted from the private sector (as has been occurring at the federal level) as a cost-effective way of providing for special needs of elderly inmates (Kratcoski & Pownall, 1989); (6) increased use of split sentences, which would provide for a shorter incarceration followed by a period of probation; and (7) the establishment of work-fare type government-sponsored programs (such as Green Thumb in Richmond, Kentucky, for elderly nonoffenders), which put the elderly to work doing community and public service–type jobs (e.g., cleaning parks, stuffing government envelopes for large mailings).

In summary, it does not appear to be the case that the needs of elderly offenders will create such a burden on the correctional system that it will become impractical to incarcerate them. This is not to say that some of the specialized programming will not be costly—indeed, it will be. But rather than choosing a seemingly simple solution of diverting elderly offenders from prisons, it is more reasonable to look to plausible alternatives for funding the specialized programming and services that will be required by this steadily increasing subpopulation of inmates. In fact, it can be argued that correctional administrators have no choice in the matter. There is no getting around the fact that the percentage of elderly inmates is on the rise, and their rights to have their medical needs met have been affirmed by the U.S. Supreme Court. As Ann Goetting (1983) stated, "It is in the best interest of corrections administrations to accommodate the needs of their elderly residents, if not for humanitarian purposes, to avoid legitimate charges of civil rights violations."

References

Bureau of Justice Statistics. (1995). *Sourcebook of criminal justice statistics, 1994*. Washington, DC: Government Printing Office.

Cavan, R. S. (1987). Is special treatment needed for elderly offenders? *Criminal Justice Policy Review, 2* (3), 213–224.

Durham, A. M. III. (1994). *Crisis and reform: Current issues in American punishment*. Boston, MA: Little, Brown & Co.

Goetting, A. (1983). The elderly in prison: Issues and perspectives. *Journal of Research in Crime and Delinquency, 20,* 291–309.

Kratcoski, P. C., and Pownall, G. A. (1989). Federal Bureau of Prisons programming for older offenders. *Federal Probation, 53* (2), 28–35.

McCleery, R. H. (1961). The governmental process and informal social control. In D. Cressey (Ed.), *The prison: Studies in institutional organization and change*. New York, NY: Holt, Rinehart and Winston.

McShane, M. D., & Williams, F. P. III (1990). Old and ornery: The disciplinary experiences of elderly prisoners. *International Journal of Offender Therapy and Comparative Criminology, 34* (3), 197–212.

Rubenstein, D. (1984). The elderly in prison: A review of the literature. In E. S. Newman, D. J. Newman, and M. L. Gewirtz, (Eds.), *Elderly criminals*. Cambridge, MA: Oelgeschlager, Gunn and Hain.

Teller, F. E., & Howell, R. J. (1981). The older prisoner: Criminal and psychological characteristics. *Criminology, 18* (4), 549–555.

Vega, M., & Silverman, M. (1988). Stress and the elderly convict. *International Journal of Offender Therapy and Comparative Criminology, 32* (2), 153–162.

Walsh, C. E. (1992). Aging inmate offenders: Another perspective. In C. A. Hartjen and E. E. Rhine (Eds.), *Correctional theory and practice.* Chicago, IL: Nelson-Hall, Inc.

Wiltz, C. J. (1973). *The aged prisoner: A case study of age and aging in prison.* Kansas State University, unpublished M.A. thesis.

Wooden, W. S. & Parker, J. (1980). Age, adjustment and the treatment process of criminal behavior. Paper presented at the annual meeting of the National Gerontological Society, San Diego, California.

CASES

Estelle v. *Gamble,* 97 S. Ct. 285, 291 (1976).

Rejoinder to Dr. Soderstrom

W. MICHAEL WHEELER

After carefully reading Dr. Soderstrom's arguments that incarcerating the elderly offender is practical, clearly we agree on a number of important issues. First, there are always going to be a certain number of offenders regardless of age who need to be incarcerated. Second, the current number of elderly inmates is relatively small. Third, elderly inmates, just as any inmate, have basic needs that by law must be meet. Finally, the cost of providing for the basic needs of the elderly including housing, medical, and dietary needs, and the training of correction officials to handle elderly inmates, is more costly than for younger inmates, and that cost will continue to increase.

However, several issues are directly related to some of these commonly agreed on issues that need to be addressed. With respect to the statement that the current number of elderly inmates is relatively small, the key word is "current." It is true that the current percentage of elderly inmates is relatively small, but the overall number of elderly inmates is one of the fastest, if not the fastest growing segment of the U.S. inmate population. As states implement policies such as life-without-parole, correction officials must assume that most of these individuals will eventually become elderly inmates. The result is that the cost of aging and geriatric care in correctional institutions will increase dramatically. Several states with life-without-parole laws are already seeing as much as 10 percent or more of their inmate population with this type of sentence. Additionally, "Truth in Sentencing" laws will further contribute to the increasing numbers of elderly inmates. The increase in elderly offenders will directly have a negative impact on corrections' resources. It is just not practical from an economic or social point of view to keep many of these elderly inmates in prison for the duration of their natural lives.

Dr. Soderstrom and I agree that by law corrections officials have an obligation to meet the basic needs of inmates in general regardless of age. We tend to differ in the concept of "basic" versus "special" needs. Special means, if not implies, being unique or unusual. Just because the health care, medical, housing, dietary, exercise, and security needs of elderly inmates are different from those of the general prison population does not mean these needs are special. They are simply the basic needs this particular group of individuals require. Therefore, to not provide elderly inmates with these basic needs would be a violation of the law. The result is, if we demand that elderly inmates remain incarcerated, we must be willing to pay. From an economic standpoint, it just is not practical to require incarceration of many elderly inmates.

Furthermore, most elderly inmates are not violent and do not pose a criminal threat to society. Most elderly inmates are housed in minimum security facilities. Correction officials have known for years that most elderly inmates do not pose a serious threat. The greatest threat to society is more economic than anything. It would be less expensive to care for geriatric "ex-cons" outside of our correctional institutions simply because security and special training would not be required. Their needs are better and more cost-effectively met by existing facilities and resources external to correctional institutions. In addition, scarce corrections resources including money, facilities, and correction officials would be better spent on younger, more violent inmates.

It will not be practical, economically or socially, to keep all elderly inmates incarcerated. Strong consideration should be given to releasing elderly inmates, particularly those who no longer pose a criminal threat to society.

NO

W. Michael Wheeler

America's prison population is aging. National trends show a steady increase of approximately 6 percent annually for "older" or "elderly" inmates (Camp & Camp, 1991–93).[1] A number of factors contribute to this trend. First, corrections officials have been aware for some time that as the percentage of older persons in the general population increases, so does the number of older offenders. Given that the Baby Boomers, the birth cohort born between 1946 and 1964, are currently entering the age defined as elderly, it is safe to assume that a proportional increase in older offenders will result. Second, political and social pressure demanding legal sanctions such as truth in sentencing, minimum mandatory sentencing, three strikes and you're out, and life-without-parole result in longer incarceration for those convicted. These two trends alone virtually guarantee that increased numbers of older offenders will populate the criminal justice systems. The third trend, the inadequate funding and facilities of most, if not all systems, insures that these older offenders will be processed through conventional correctional methods and systems. Finally, with modern medical technologies and lifestyle changes, people, including offenders, are expected to live longer.

Given these trends in population and restrictive changes in our judicial system one must ask the following questions: Are we willing to pay for incarceration of elderly inmates? Can we afford incarceration of elderly inmates? Does it make sense in terms of cost and protection of society to incarcerate elderly offenders? What methods, alternative to incarceration, are most effective in dealing with elderly inmates?

Admittedly, some crimes committed by older offenders deserve and even require incarceration. However, nationally only about 6 percent of all prison inmates in 1993 were age fifty and older (Camp & Camp, 1991–93). Of those imprisoned, only a small percentage committed violent crimes. Incarceration of older inmates is in many cases a waste of limited resources, including money, facilities, and manpower. The result is that a relatively small number of older inmates is consuming a tremendously large proportion of prison monies. Therefore, I argue that incarceration of elderly offenders is not practical given that it is not cost-effective, and the use of limited resources would be better spent on younger, more violent offenders. Alternative methods of sentencing should be presented to our judicial system and applied where appropriate, particularly if the older inmate is not viewed as a threat to society.

Cost of Incarceration

"Basic" Needs and Programs

The courts have ruled that inmates have rights that are essentially dominated by the "basic" needs of all inmates. Adequate nutrition, medical care, and safety are a few of the rights determined by the courts to guarantee that basic needs are met. It is the responsibility of the correction officials to insure that these rights and "basic" needs are provided to the inmates.

State and federal governments and local institutions have also initiated programs for nonbasic needs that serve multiple functions. Educational and training opportunities are available in an attempt to provide inmates with work skills that should help reduce recidivism. Work programs in institutions translate into reduced sentences. Therapy and counseling programs are used to "rehabilitate" and again attempt to reduce recidivism. These are just a few of the programs provided by many institutions for incarcerated individuals.

The programs that meet the "basic" and "nonbasic" needs of older inmates are essentially the same as for younger inmates. However, there is a difference between what is required to meet the basic and nonbasic needs of younger versus older inmates. Following are examples of some discrepancies that exist between the inmate's needs that result in specialized programs. It is these specialized programs that will needlessly consume the limited corrections' and taxpayer's monies.

Health Care Needs

One of the most important, if not the most important, factors to consider with respect to incarceration of elderly offenders is the cost of health care. In a survey of the Department of Corrections in all fifty states, twenty-seven of the thirty-one institutions that responded identified medical needs and related factors as the most important or significant variable attributed to the cost of aging inmates (Wheeler, Connelly, & Wheeler, 1994). As people age, there is a definite shift in the number of incidences, the types of illnesses, and the effect that the illness has on the individual. With advancing age, the number of incidences of acute illnesses (temporary or relatively short in duration) decreases, and the number of chronic illnesses (long-term, permanent, possibly disabling or terminal) increases. It should be pointed out that even though the incidence of acute illnesses decreases with age, they tend to impact older individuals more than younger individuals, resulting in a greater risk of complications. For example, a cold is more likely to develop into pneumonia in an older individual. These complications translate into longer, more costly recovery periods (Atchley, 1994).

With respect to chronic illnesses, approximately 80 percent of all individuals age sixty-five and older have one or more chronic illnesses that require some form of long-term care. The older you become, the greater the likelihood of acquiring a chronic illness and the greater the cost of treating the ailment and meeting the basic needs of the individual. A recent article by Flynn (1992) suggests that the social, psychological, and physical health care needs of older offenders are greater than those of the elderly population in general. A review of ninety-three older inmates' medical records in the Limited Duty Unit at the Columbus Correctional Facility in Columbus, Ohio, contained the following list of age-related illnesses: twenty-one cases of essential hypertension; twenty-four cases of chronic heart disease; nineteen cases of degenerative arthritis; three cases of confirmed cancer; two cases of epilepsy; two cases of decubitus ulcers; one case of colostomy and ileostomy; two cases of unspecified tuberculosis; and eighteen cases of senility (Ham, 1980). According to Sullivan (1990), "…the elderly convict suffers from an average of three chronic illnesses, tripling the cost of his care from a yearly average of $23,000 to over $70,000" (1990). Furthermore, Flynn (1992) cites a 1989 U.S. Department of Justice finding on the future health care needs and costs in federal prisons. According to the study, older offenders will "…have many chronic health problems requiring specialized, continuous health care, including special diets, pharmacy services, physical therapy, skilled nursing care, and other supportive services" (p. 83). This is primarily the result of the offender's lifestyle.

Research suggests that possibly the healthiest older inmates will be those who have aged in prison because they had access to better medical care, diet, exercise, rest, and in general a better lifestyle than many individuals outside of correctional institutions (Panton, 1984). "Older prisoners are not exposed to heavy industry, hard labor, or heavy drinking" (p. 157). With the legal sanctions demanding longer incarcerations, these older inmates will reside in the correctional institutions even longer than those incarcerated later in life.

As inmates age and the number of chronic illnesses increases, so does an individual's chance of needing hospitalization and geriatric care. At the farthest end of the health care continuum, and possibly the costliest, are such health problems as strokes, Alzheimer's disease, and other forms of dementia that increase with age (Atchley, 1994). These illnesses require specially trained personnel and twenty-four-hour care, the type of care offered in nursing homes.

Finally, dietary concerns, particularly those related to older inmate's health, are an important program consideration (Alston, 1986; Flynn, 1992; Goetting, 1984). Diabetes, hypertension, and chronic heart conditions are only a few of the illnesses that require special dietary programs.

These are just a few of the health care–related costs that currently and will continue in the future to face correction officials and society if we demand incarceration of elderly offenders and do not allow for alternative methods of sentencing.

Housing Needs

As the age of older offenders increases, whether from aging within prison or entering prison at an older age, their physical, social, and health care needs change. Accordingly, modifications must be made with respect to the prison itself. Clearly, most prisons that exist today were not constructed or designed with the needs of older offenders in mind. "Prisons have historically been designed for young, healthy, dangerous, and violent offenders...Large, spartan, multi tiered cell blocks are ill suited for aging inmates who may be physically frail, mentally impaired, in need of canes, walkers, or wheelchairs" (Flynn, 1992, p. 86). Cold, damp buildings of concrete and steel can easily affect the health of older inmates.

Admittedly, the idea of barrier-free environments and prisons sounds like an oxymoron. In reality it is not. Maybe a more appropriate term would be "elderly-friendly" environments. Prisons, at great cost, are going to have to be designed or renovated to provide elderly-friendly environments that will meet the physical, psychological, and social needs of older offenders. Ramps for wheelchairs and doorways wide enough to allow access; grab bars near toilets; hand rails in hallways; beds fixed at a height suitable for the older offender; improved lighting, reduced distances between housing and cafeterias, canteens, places of work, recreational and medical facilities; and the separation of older offenders from younger offenders, as the situation warrants, are all examples of what will be needed to meet the basic housing needs of older inmates. Many older offenders will need wheelchair-accessible environments, canes, walkers, and personal assistance in movement, resulting in the need for barrier-free or elderly-friendly physical environments. Once again, already scarce resources will be consumed.

Safe Guarding the Older Offender

Housing older inmates with the general prison population can place them in an environment that jeopardizes their safety. Older offenders are outnumbered and more vulnerable to attack. They are viewed as prey by younger, more aggressive inmates. Golden found that older inmates often view their younger counterparts as being noisy, abusive, and harassing, and that older offenders are often the victims of robbery or assault (Newman, Newman, & Gewirtz, 1984, p. 146). "… [older inmates] are at the mercy of younger more aggressive, and difficult prisoners who tend to frighten, ridicule, or even harm them. The older prisoners become depressed, anxious…" (Panton, 1984, p. 157).

Providing housing that will meet the basic needs of older incarcerated inmates or simply providing for their safety is not cost-effective. Again, alternative methods to incarceration should be considered.

Training Staff

Currently, correction's staff are trained much as prisons have been designed, with young, violent offenders in mind. Older offenders present an entirely different population, with different needs that require special training. Morton (1993) recommends that the training of staff include the following objectives:

1. To enable participants to define older offenders and inmates with physical disabilities
2. To help participants understand the agency's mission, policies, and approved practices relevant to managing special needs of inmates
3. To sensitize participants to some of the physical and emotional difficulties encountered by older inmates and those with disabilities
4. To help staff identify problems encountered in working with these individuals and begin developing solutions specific to their institution. (p. 44)

Training should include knowledge and skills that are required to meet the needs of older offenders as well as an increased sensitivity to their needs and limitations, and the patience to deal with them. According to Welch (1987), "…staff members who work with elderly inmates will need specialized training in medical problems, in handling individual diets, and in simply being slower and more patient with their charges. Inmates can't stand up for head count anymore" (p. 8).

The bottom line is that it is not cost-effective to train future and retrain present prison staff to handle a relatively small percentage of incarcerated older offenders. There are less expensive and more effective ways of dealing with these problems.

Alternatives to Incarceration

The most common means of incarcerating older inmates is placing them in minimum security facilities. States that provide special housing programs for older inmates often concentrate them into one facility for two reasons: first, as a result of the relatively small number of older inmates and, second, as a cost-effective measure. Most facilities are minimum security, and, as long as they obey the rules, older inmates are often allowed more mobility (Alston, 1986; Flynn, 1992). In general, research has shown that administrators and officers view older inmates as being docile, obedient, respectful, and committing few rule violations (Alston, 1986). If older inmates are viewed as being minimal risk, and obviously they are, alternative forms of sentencing to incarceration should be considered. Because they are a low risk, many older offenders are good candidates for parole or probation. Research has shown that recidivism rates are lower for older offenders than for young offenders (Beck & Shipley, 1989).

In a study conducted by Goetting (1984), 52.72 percent of 248 inmates age fifty-five years and older, who were a subsample of 11,397, were incarcerated for their first offense. This included inmates who had committed their first offense before and after the age of fifty-five. Researchers have known for years that an inverse relationship exists between age and commitment of crime. Therefore, it is possible that even violent, young offenders, as they become older inmates, may no longer be a threat to society and should be considered for alternative methods of punishment.

Once again, consideration must be given to the most efficient use of limited resources in our corrections system. Alternative forms of sentencing that in many cases would be much more practical than incarceration of elderly offenders would include probation, parole, electronic monitoring, or house arrest. Judges, correction officials, and prison parole boards should be given the discretionary rights to apply alternative forms of punishment.

Summary and Conclusion

Obviously, for prison administrators, the costs of providing programs that will meet the "specialized" needs of elderly offenders are a major concern. For older inmates, often referred to as the "forgotten minority" (Aday, 1984, p. 305), meeting these specialized needs is essential not only with respect to the quality of their life but even for life itself. "If special privileges cannot be demanded on the basis of age alone, rights cannot be denied on that basis either" (Alston, 1986, p. 256). It is incumbent on administrators, legislators, and all who are concerned with the operations of correctional institutions to be creative and sensitive to meeting the needs of our aging prison population and the costs that they will incur. They must be allowed to identify those older inmates who are not a threat to society and use alternative methods to incarceration. Welch presents the following scenario: "Life-without-parole sentences raise the odd possibility of prisons becoming old-folks homes with geriatric inmates nodding away in their rocking chairs" (1987, p. 8).

The real threat of most older offenders to society is incarceration, particularly mandatory incarceration. A congressional conference committee recently "…approved the $32.4 billion crime bill, which will allocate millions for prison construction to states whose violent felons serve 85 percent of their sentences" (Plumberg, 1994, p. 16). How do we justify sentencing a seventy-five-year-old man to life-without-parole, whose only crime he has ever committed and will ever commit, is the mercy killing of his terminally ill wife, who is in excruciating pain and begs him to end her suffering?

The argument that it is not practical to incarcerate older offenders does not imply that they are not and should not be held accountable for their actions. It should first be determined whether they are a threat to society. If only 6 percent of the United States prison population in 1993 were age fifty and older, society needs to focus its limited resources on the 94 percent that is younger, violent, and clearly the greatest threat to society. Incarceration of elderly offenders simply because we have taken the human variable out of sentencing could be a greater crime than those crimes committed by older offenders.

NOTES

1. Because of the lack of a systematic approach of studying "older" offenders, and the great diversity that exists within the "older" offender populations, simply defining "older" or "elderly" inmates is quite difficult. For this discussion "older" or "elderly" inmates are identified as those aged 50 years and older, for the following reasons: A number of studies have used 50 as the chronological age for defining prevention of chronic illnesses (see, for example, Flynn, 1992; Morton, 1993). According to the Chief of Operations for the Health Service Division of the Federal Bureau of Prisons, "there is a 10-year differential between the overall health of…inmates and…the general population…[A] 50-year-old [inmate] will typically have the health problems of a 60-year-old person on the outside" (Durham, 1994, p. 92).

REFERENCES

Aday, R. H. (1984). Criminals. In *Handbook on the aged in the United States.* Westport, CT: Greenwood Press.

Alston, L. T. (1986). *Crime and older Americans.* Springfield, IL: Charles C. Thomas, Publisher.

Atchley, R. C. (1994). *Social forces and aging: An introduction to social geron-tology* (7th ed.). Belmont, CA: Wadsworth Publishing Company.

Beck, A. J., & Shipley, B. E. (1989). *Recidivism of prisoners released in 1983.* Washington, DC: Bureau of Justice Statistics.

Camp, G. M., & Camp, C. C. (1991–93). *The corrections yearbook.* South Salem, NY: Criminal Justice Institute.

Dunham, Alexis M. (1994) *Crisis and reform.* Boston: Litte, Brown & Co.

Flynn, E. E. (1992). The graying of America's prison population. *The Prison Journal, 72* (1&2), 77–98.

Goetting, A. (1984). Prison programs and facilities for elderly inmates. In E. S. Newman, D. J. Newman, & M. L. Gewirtz (Eds.), *Elderly criminals.* Cambridge, MA: Oelgeschlager, Gunn, & Hain.

Ham, J. N. (1980, July–August). Aged and infirm male prison inmates. *Aging,* 24–31.

Morton, J. B. (1993, February). In South Carolina: Training staff to work with elderly and disabled inmates. *Corrections Today, 42–47.*

Newman, E. S., Newman, D. J., & Gewirtz, M. L. (Eds.). (1984). *Elderly criminals.* Cambridge, MA: Oelgeschlager, Gunn & Hain, Publisher, Inc.

Panton, J. H. (1984, Winter). Personality characteristics of aged inmates within a state prison population. *Offender Rehabilitation 1,* 203–208.

Plumberg, D. (1994, July 30). Macy says new crime bill may worsen prison crowding. *Saturday Oklahoman & Times,* 16.

Sullivan, L. R. (1990). *The prison reform movement—Forlorn hope.* Boston, MA: Twayne Publishers.

Welch, R. (1987). Can this be life? The implications of life without parole. *Corrections Compendium, 11* (8), 1–8.

Wheeler, M., Connelly, M., & Wheeler, B. (1994). *The aging of the Oklahoma prison population: Problems and implications (Research Reference 94–194, AG131).* Oklahoma City: Oklahoma Department of Corrections.

Rejoinder to Dr. Wheeler
IRINA R. SODERSTROM

The primary problem with Professor Wheeler's argument that the elderly should not be incarcerated stems from the fact that he paints a sympathetic picture of the elderly offender. This can be most readily illustrated with the question he asks in his summary and conclusion section: "How do we justify sentencing a seventy-five-year-old man to life-without-parole, whose only crime he has ever committed and will ever commit, is the mercy killing of his terminally ill wife, who is in excruciating pain and begs him to end her suffering?" This heart-wrenching anecdote is hardly the norm when it comes to the particular reasons most elderly inmates end up in prison. Given the fact that older offenders (defined as fifty years and older) were responsible for 3.6 percent of all violent crime (defined as murder, nonnegligent manslaughter, forcible rape, robbery, and aggravated assault) in 1994, it is unlikely that mercy killing had very much to do with the prison sentences received by most older offenders. Certainly, Wheeler's need to use a sympathy ploy suggests the underlying weaknesses of his substantive arguments.

He does make four distinct arguments against the incarceration of the elderly, all of which relate to costs of incarceration. The common thesis of these four arguments is that incarceration of the elderly is a waste of limited prison resources because older inmates will consume a very large proportion of the total prison budget. I address each of these four cost-related arguments separately, but briefly.

The first argument was in relation to the cost of health care. Professor Wheeler discussed how 80 percent of offenders age sixty-five and older have one or more chronic illnesses, which leads to the tripling of yearly per prison bed costs. My response to this would be that there are many other types of special health circumstances that greatly increase the cost of caring for a variety of offenders. For instance, most prisons already provide for a number of special diets required by offenders, given various health problems (e.g., diabetes, hypertension). Furthermore, handicapped and chronically ill younger offenders necessitate considerable health care expenditures as well. Yet, we would not suggest that a violent, younger offender who was handicapped or chronically ill be allowed to go free, simply because it would be more cost-effective. Besides, as I already discussed in my initial argument, the right of all offenders to have their medical needs met has been established through case law.

In his second argument, he discusses the costs associated with making prisons more "elderly friendly." He provides a litany of expensive items such as ramps and wide doorways for wheelchairs, grab bars near toilets, hand rails in hallways, improved lighting, etc.... My thoughts on this are that we already have these types of facilities in place for handicapped and chronically ill younger offenders. It should be remembered that only a small proportion of elderly offenders would be placed in any particular prison (unless the prison is already set up to handle elderly and handicapped inmates and thus is the recipient of large proportions of these types of offenders), so it would not be that big of an expense to have a few prison cells equipped with the above-mentioned amenities in each institution.

Professor Wheeler's third argument focuses on the need to safeguard older offenders from victimization by younger offenders. But as I discussed in my initial argument, this perception of the elderly offender as being at the mercy of younger offenders has been determined to be a myth by several researchers. In fact, studies have suggested that the older offender presents a stabilizing factor in the prison subculture. Evidence has even suggested that younger offenders look up to older offenders and count on them as a source of information and guidance regarding adjustment to prison life.

The final argument against incarceration of the elderly concerns staff training. This argument seems to be the weakest of all given the fact that staff need to be trained in the handling of the special needs of all types of offenders. Many of these special needs will not be specific to elderly offenders, and thus will need to be learned for appropriate handling of handicapped and chronically ill younger offenders. Not to mention the fact that these skills will be required to manage offenders who will become geriatric in prison (there is no getting around the fact that there will always be a need to incarcerate some elderly persons).

In general, Professor Wheeler's argument against incarceration of the elderly is flawed because it paints a sympathetic and unrealistic picture of the typical older inmate. As I discussed in my initial argument, most older offenders will not be classified as geriatric until the very last stages of their incarceration. Thus, a more realistic picture of the elderly inmate is one of a repeat offender who has been incarcerated previously, who has been provided with better health care (and therefore is in better health condition) than many of his counterparts on the "outside," and who has learned to adjust to prison life as well as any inmate can. Given the various needs being met by our prisons for other special prison populations (e.g., handicapped and chronically ill), it seems inconsistent to argue that the elderly should be excused from their prison sentences just because it seems costly.

Should Incarceration of Pregnant Women Be Avoided?

Ken Ayers argues YES. He is Professor and Chair of Behavioral Science at Kentucky Wesleyan College and has presented and published a number of works on white collar crime, police behavior, and health care of pregnant inmates. Dr. Ayers received a Ph.D. from Sam Houston State University in 1984.

Laura J. Moriarty argues NO. She is Associate Professor of Criminal Justice at Virginia Commonwealth University. She received her Ph.D. in Criminal Justice from Sam Houston State University and has a Masters and Bachelors of Criminal Justice from Louisiana State University. Dr. Moriarty's research interests include victimology, fear of crime, and violent crime, and she is coauthor (with Robert Jerin) of a victimology textbook, *Victims of Crime* (Nelson-Hall, 1998).

YES

KEN AYERS

Women who are found guilty of committing crimes and who are pregnant should receive special treatment or consideration in sentencing. This special consideration for the pregnant inmate is due in part if inadequate medical facilities and health care exist in the institutions where the inmate will be housed. The issue of pregnancy does not necessarily need to be a major factor at sentencing, but it is a consideration that should be addressed. Whether a pregnant woman should be incarcerated encompasses several issues. Two major ones are addressed. The first focuses on pregnancy, specifically, the pregnant inmate and her coping with the condition of pregnancy and incarceration simultaneously. The woman and what is considered best for her and her needs during pregnancy is the primary concern. The second deals with the health of the woman and the fetus: specifically, the issue of health, medical, and prenatal care.

What do we know about pregnant inmates? First, research has established that women who are entangled in the criminal justice process tend to be young, single, uneducated, and incarcerated for drug–alcohol offenses, property offenses, and other nonviolent crimes (Snell, 1994). Second, these women, as a group, have a history of drug abuse, alcohol abuse, and prostitution, are impoverished, smoke, and do not have a habit of receiving the best medical or nutritional care (Ayers & Johnson, 1989). Women who are pregnant must deal with the stressors that accompany pregnancy. Women who are incarcerated must deal with the stressors of incarceration. Women who are pregnant and in prison have to deal with both. Finally, women who constitute the inmate population when they are pregnant are classic "high-risk pregnancies." Their lifestyle on the outside has created a situation that, without a change in their environment and lifestyle, could prove dangerous to them and their unborn child. Sometimes the inadequacies of the prison system are very dangerous, and incarceration needs to be balanced with the lifestyle of the inmate and what is best for the mother and the child.

Pregnancy

What is it about being pregnant and in prison that would require a sentencing alternative? Pregnancy is a very normal condition. It is not a sickness nor a disability. Pregnancy can be a developmental milestone in a women's life as well as a crisis. Pregnancy is a biological, psychological, sociological, and a transitional event. Erickson (1976) noted that all of the dimensions of pregnancy are interrelated, so when one aspect changes, it affects other dimensions. The physiological aspects of pregnancy influence the psychological and vice versa. Pregnancy is also a time in which inevitable inner conflict may occur, and the woman's response will either be adaptive or maladaptive. Adaptive responses would include attaining the maternal parenting role, and a maladaptive response may interfere with the development of the maternal–infant relationship. Research has shown that anxiety and conflict, stress, martial status, social support, employment, and self-esteem all can affect pregnancy.

Pregnant women with a combination of a high degree of crisis situations in life and low psychological assets will possibly have a greater potential for complications during pregnancy (Nuckolls, 1970). Also, the decrease in social support, life stresses, and emotional stress contribute to complications during pregnancy (Norbeck & Tilden, 1983). Prison can be a crisis situation for the pregnant inmate.

Pregnant Inmates

Women who are pregnant and in prison do not differ demographically from the general female prison population. They are young, single, and incarcerated for drug–alcohol offenses, property offenses, and other nonviolent crimes. The difference is found in the adjustment to incarceration, which may be harder for those who are pregnant.

Pregnancy and incarceration are crisis periods requiring major adjustment for the woman, and when a woman experiences both at the same time, there is potential for increased stress (Johnson, 1991). As previously noted, women constitute a minority of incarcerated adults, and the women who are pregnant and in prison are even a smaller minority. Approximately 6 percent of women in prison were pregnant at intake in 1991 (Snell, 1994). It is estimated that approximately 4000 women are pregnant when they enter prison. McHugh (1980) found that in twenty-six women correctional institutions, there were only 260 pregnant women during a one-year period. Ayers and Johnson (1989) found 1265 pregnant women were housed in thirty-eight correctional facilities in 1987.

Women in prison face a number of problems by virtue of being incarcerated. Prison life requires inmates to adapt to new situations. When the inmate is pregnant, adjusting to prison life may be more problematic, considering the issue of pregnancy requires additional coping by the woman. The woman who is pregnant and in prison has the same anxieties and doubts that all pregnant women encounter.

Were these inmates pregnant at the time of sentencing, or did they become pregnant after sentencing? Did they know they were pregnant? How did the Criminal Justice System find out about their pregnancy? Ayers and Johnson (1989) found that when prison health care administrators were asked how pregnancy was most often detected, 66 percent of the women's correctional institutions stated that self-reporting of pregnancy symptoms by the inmate was the most common method of detection. This information indicates that most women are possibly unaware of pregnancy at time of sentencing, or they became pregnant after sentencing and before prison, and some do become pregnant while incarcerated.

What happens when pregnancy is detected? Once pregnancy is diagnosed, inmates have several options available to them in most institutions. These options include (1) elective abortion; (2) delivery and placement of the infant with the inmate's family; (3) placement with the infant's father; (4) foster care; and (5) adoption (Ayers & Johnson, 1989).

Health and Medical Care

Health care and medical care are frequent concerns of women in prison. Health care may be defined as those activities that promote health and information provided to understand strategies to prevent illness. Medical care may be defined as those services provided that serve predominately to diagnose illness and disease and identify interventions. Often the services provided in prison fall into the medical services category, and there are few programs that focus on health promotion or health status improvement (Johnson, 1991).

Traditionally, health care within correctional institutions has been viewed as a privilege, not a right. Prison health care studies describe unsatisfactory health care delivery and health conditions within the prison system (Little, 1981). Few federal cases have delineated the medical rights for inmates but not health care rights. *Estelle* v. *Gamble* (1976) became the landmark case in outlining the states' responsibility in providing medical care to inmates. *Estelle,* however, does not specifically address the special medical or health care needs of incarcerated pregnant women. In fact, cases that identify the rights of pregnant inmates as being different from rights of other inmates are practically nonexistent. In a rare court ruling on the issue, a Federal District Court ruled that the state of Alabama had inadequate delivery conditions within the female prison (*Newman* v. *Alabama,* 1972). In *Morales* v. *Turman* (1974), it was ruled that the lack of prenatal care and postpartum counseling for pregnant girls may be creating conditions that violate the Eighth Amendment.

If we sentence convicted women to prison and these women are or become pregnant, are the health and medical services adequate enough to meet their needs? The answer appears to be that it depends in which state the women is incarcerated. McHugh (1980) cited glaring deficiencies in medical care of pregnant inmates. Holt (1980) inferred that the inmate usually does not receive a physical examination on admission to prison.

McHugh (1980) examined health care of pregnant inmates and concluded that services were less than adequate. Besides the lack of certain facilities, McHugh reported women had been forced to have abortions or had been denied them, and inmates are viewed as unfit mothers by staff. Holt (1980) stated that, although medical care may be available, it is, at times, withheld because of hostilities between staff and inmate.

Holt stressed that delivery facilities were not on site, and the inmates had to travel for delivery. Ayers and Johnson (1989) found all women institutions transferred inmates outside the institutions for delivery. Johnson (1991) noted "the maintenance of an on-site delivery facility is unrealistic and economically unsound, and travel to a distant facility for delivery is a common practice in the non-incarcerated population" (p. 12). It is not reasonable to expect prisons to provide the skilled and specialized care that a woman requires during pregnancy, labor, and delivery, and in the immediate postpartum period within the institution. These services require specialized equipment, trained personnel, and facilities that simply cannot be provided within the prison environment. Hospitals, in all parts of the country, are closing maternity units because of increasing costs of services as well as lack of qualified personnel.

Despite the assertions of inadequate medical care in women's institutions by McHugh (1980), Holt (1980) and Ayers and Johnson (1989) found that most prisons do meet the standards for prenatal care established by the American Academy of Pediatrics (AAP) and the American College of Obstetricians and Gynecologists (ACOG) (*Guidelines for Perinatal Care,* 1988). Although health care standards and accreditation processes for correctional institutions were established by the American Medical Association in 1973, health care practices within institutions vary from state to state. The implementation of health care services for prisoners has long been a concern of administrators. A major problem is lack of fundamental resources such as money, facilities, and personnel. This problem stems from the fact that state corrections departments must depend on state legislators for the resources needed to upgrade the quality of health care. It is this question: "How adequate are the medical and health care facilities within a state's prison system?" that should determine whether special considerations, if any, should be given to the pregnant inmate.

Another major problem in the delivery of health care to inmates has been the difference in the goals and objectives of health care personnel and corrections personnel. Novick (1987) emphasized that there is sure to be conflict in the mission and philosophy of the health care provider and the prison system in general. Corrections personnel tend to concentrate on control, containment, and isolation. In contrast, health care providers are concerned with the health needs and health promotion of the inmate (Mann, 1984). Health care for prisoners in the United States is influenced by two characteristics, according to Novick. He explained that health care in prisons is administered in a different environment separated from the traditional practice of medicine. He further stated that health care services in prison are more a product of the prison system than a product of the medical community (Novick, 1987).

There are some definite needs that are not being met. One area identified by McHugh and Holt that is still of concern is the nutritional status of the pregnant inmate. Nutritional state is known to be a very important factor in influencing the outcome of pregnancy. Many complications, including miscarriage, preeclampsia, intrauterine growth retardation, and others, are linked to inadequate diet. Nutritional counseling and diet changes would seem to be one intervention that would have great impact with minimal investment.

Prenatal Care

The inmate is in prison; she is pregnant; the Eighth Amendment mandates that medical care is a right; a medical care delivery system, with some flaws, is operational; and a health care system is present—now what? What about the pregnant inmate, the one who will have special needs? What do we do about her medical and health care needs? Make sure that she receives adequate prenatal care?

Prenatal care provides the best method of preventing birth defects, decreasing prematurity, and decreasing infant and maternal mortality and morbidity. This fact alone may have tremendous consequences when considering the financial impact of the cost of prenatal care and the long-term savings it may provide. Research into the prenatal care of pregnant inmates is all but nonexistent. Perhaps one of the reasons prenatal care of the inmate has received little attention by researchers is that it may be a fairly new need, encountered as the rate of incarcerated women increases and the age of the female prison population decreases. Mann (1984) stated that the number of incarcerated women in the younger age brackets on a national level has been increasing.

Prenatal care is especially important because most pregnant inmates will be classified as high-risk patients. A high-risk patient may be defined as one more likely to experience obstetrical, medical, or psychological complications of pregnancy and childbearing. The health status of inmates is often below that of the general population because of other sociological factors. The female inmate often has a history of drug addiction, prostitution, and poor nutrition and is a smoker. Any of these factors is enough to classify the inmate as a high-risk patient, and yet many inmates have each risk factor. The designation of "high risk" necessitates close follow-up and care during the pregnancy to, hopefully, prevent complications.

An infant born to a mother who has received inadequate care is twice as likely to require intensive care than an infant whose mother did receive adequate care (Nichols, 1988). The importance of the prenatal period in determining the outcome of the pregnancy and the long-term effect on the infant is well known. The reward for the system and the inmate of a healthy baby is not only a psychological one, but can also be viewed as a financial one—the fewer complications, the lower the health care cost to the State.

How adequate is the prenatal care within our correctional system? Again it depends on which prison system is offering the prenatal care. All women's institutions provide some type of prenatal care. The success of any program, however, is determined by its outcome. Pregnant inmates are considered high-risk pregnancies, and such pregnancies have a higher incidence of problems, such as lower than average birth weight and miscarriages, than normal pregnancies. Pregnant inmates have a miscarriage rate well below the usual rates reported in a nonincarcerated population (Ayers & Johnson, 1989). Knowing the prepregnancy history of inmates, one could conclude that inmates who are pregnant may have better outcomes to their pregnancy because they are incarcerated, but this could only be true if the prison provided adequate prenatal, medical, and health care.

Conclusion

A valid argument can be made that our society imprisons too many people; our prison bed space should be reserved for our "worst" criminals; repeat offenders should be incapacitated for long terms; women generally commit nonviolent crimes and, therefore, should not be incarcerated at the same rate as men; and we are attempting to build our way out of the prison population explosion, and a moratorium should be placed on prison construction. One could develop numerous arguments about what should be done to cope with our prison overpopulation problem. Avoiding the incarceration of a pregnant women because of inadequate facilities, prenatal care, medical care, and health care is one of them.

It has been established that some form of a medical and health care system is in place to deal with the pregnant inmate. These systems vary from state to state. Some are very comprehensive and some are not, and they include the entire pregnancy experience from diagnosis to delivery. Women who are in prison during their pregnancy have generally better health and medical care than those in the free world with similar high-risk factors, but the experience of being incarcerated and the effect that stress has on the pregnancy in general may outweigh any positive effects that incarceration could have. Not to incarcerate a woman or to show a woman special consideration because she is pregnant indicates an understanding about the nature of pregnancy and being pregnant in prison.

Women who deliver while in prison generally do not have the opportunity to fulfill the bonding experience. Bonding is very critical during the first few years of life. All too often the infant is removed from the mother before an emotional attachment can be made. Once again the conflict between correctional goals and health care goals occurs. From a security issue, the inmate needs to return to custody as soon as possible. From a health care issue, the mother should have time during the critical period after birth to experience motherhood. Generally the infant is not removed from the immediate family. Fathers, grandparents, or other relatives generally care for the infant. Of theses, grandparents are the most commonly used caregivers (Snell, 1994).

We should not make a sentencing decision on whether to incarcerate or not incarcerate based on the issues of pregnancy alone. Other, more relevant, factors should be considered in the decision-making process, such as the quality of care. During the sentencing process, every consideration needs to be given to ensure the intended outcome is best for the women, child, and society.

REFERENCES

Ayers, K., & Johnson, E. (1989, March). *Health care of pregnant inmates.* Paper presented at the annual meeting of the Academy of Criminal Justice Sciences, Washington, DC.

Erickson, M. T. (1976). The influence of health factors on psychological variables predicting complications of pregnancy, labor, and delivery. *Journal of Psychosomatic Research, 20,* 21–24.

Guidelines for perinatal care. (1988). Elk Grove Village, IL: American Academy of Pediatrics and American College of Obstetricians and Gynecologists.

Holt, K. (1980). Nine months to life: The law and the pregnant inmate. *Journal of Family Law, 20,* 523–543.

Johnson, E. G. (1991). *Pregnancy in prison.* Unpublished doctoral dissertation, University of Alabama at Birmingham.

Little, L. (1981). A change process for prison health nursing. *American Journal of Nursing, 81,* 739–742.

Mann, C. (1984). *Female crime and delinquency.* Birmingham, AL: The University of Alabama Press.

McHugh, G. (1980). Protection of the rights of pregnant women in prisons and detention facilities. *New England Journal of Prison Law, 6,* 31–63.

Nichols, P. (1988, April). *Obstetrical care in Kentucky.* Paper presented at the High Risk Pregnancy Workshop, Louisville, KY.

Norbeck, J. S., & Tilden, V. (1983). Life stress, social support, and emotional disequilibrium in complications of pregnancy: A prospective, multivariate study. *Journal of Health and Social Behavior, 24,* 30–46.

Novick, L. (1987). Commentary on health services in prisons. *Journal of Community Health, 12,* 1–3.

Nuckolls, K. (1970). *Psychosocial assets, life crisis, and the prognosis of pregnancy.* (University of North Carolina at Chapel Hill). University Microfilms No. 70-21, 219.

Snell, T. L. (1994). *Women in prison.* Washington, DC: Bureau of Justice Statistics.

CASES

Estelle v. *Gamble* 429 U.S. 97 (1976).

Morales v. *Turman* 383 F. Supp. 53 (1974).

Newman v. *Alabama* 349 F. Supp. 278 (1972).

Rejoinder to Dr. Ayers
LAURA J. MORIARTY

Dr. Ayers effectively argues to avoid incarceration of pregnant women based on two major positions. First, pregnancy is a high-risk situation for any woman, but those incarcerated will experience a decrease in social support while life and emotional stressors will increase, causing complications during pregnancy resulting in women finding it more difficult to adjust to incarceration. Second, health care and medical care, especially prenatal care, which are vital to the pregnancy, are often lacking in correctional facilities.

Although his arguments are persuasive and sound, I do not entirely agree with his viewpoints. I support his argument regarding pregnancy as a high-risk condition, making adjustment to prison more difficult than normal, but, as he points out, the medical and health care of inmates varies not only by institution but also from state to state. To assume that all facilities will be lacking in appropriate medical care, and as a result, pregnant women should not be incarcerated, is unreasonable.

As I point out in my NO argument, incarcerated women may have a positive pregnancy and childbirth as long as certain conditions are met. To reiterate, these conditions include participation in the decision-making process, detailed explanations about what is expected during pregnancy and childbirth, being responsive to the woman's pain, and keeping appointment waiting time to a minimum. These conditions are not inordinate, nor do they appear to disrupt daily prison routines, nor do they burden the institution with unreasonable demands. Consequently, it seems probable that such conditions will become more evident in the future.

As for Dr. Ayers' position that prenatal care is somewhat limited, I believe we should consider whether any prenatal care would be sought if the women were not incarcerated. As he points out, incarcerated females, as a group, are "young, single, uneducated, and impoverished, who smoke, and do not have a habit of receiving the best medical or nutritional care." These same females, on the outside, would not, by Dr. Ayers' own admission, pursue adequate health care. Perhaps services provided through the welfare system, including medical clinic visits, might be sought, but this assertion assumes (1) the woman knows she is pregnant, (2) the women knows about such medical treatment, and (3) the women will desire such care and continue to seek it.

I agree with him that we incarcerate too many individuals. However, as long as the dominant correctional philosophy is one of retribution, we will continue to incarcerate at alarming rates. What we need to do is prepare for the changing inmate population. With more women being incarcerated, we must plan for more pregnant women being incarcerated. This means standardizing the medical, health, and prenatal treatment provided not only throughout the states but also within each facility in the states. Good, consistent prenatal care can lessen the risks of pregnancy for both the mother and the child and would suggest that incarceration of pregnant females under these conditions is a viable sentencing option.

NO

Laura J. Moriarty

Pregnant women should be incarcerated if the facility has comprehensive maternity care for the inmates. This care must be properly planned and budgeted. The services provided should follow a "holistic, health-oriented model," and health care workers, with input from the inmate (patient), should develop the "obstetrical treatment plan" for the individual inmates (Hufft, Fawkes, & Lawson, 1993, p. 59). Moreover, if possible, a "multidisciplinary team comprised of a perinatal coordinator, nurse practitioner, physician, and nursing staff" should be used (Mills & Barrett, 1990, p. 55).

Hufft, Fawkes, and Lawson (1993, p. 58) list the conditions necessary for a female inmate to experience a positive pregnancy and childbirth. These conditions include allowing the inmate to participate in the decision-making process, providing detailed explanations to the inmate of what is expected during the pregnancy and child delivery, being responsive to the inmate's pain, and keeping appointment waiting time to a reasonable amount.

Furthermore, women who experience high-risk pregnancies can be incarcerated as long as the institution has effectively planned for such situations. Many institutions have designed contingency plans that allow inmates to be treated at a referral facility if the pregnancy is considered high-risk. One such example is the Federal Medical Center in Lexington, Kentucky; this facility is "uniquely capable of offering medical care for high-risk inmates. Lexington has an accredited hospital closely affiliated with the physicians and services of the University of Kentucky Medical Center. In addition, Lexington can house inmates of all security levels" (Hufft, Fawkes, & Lawson, 1993, p. 56).

According to Lillis (1994), who examined health care services in female institutions in the United States and Canada, forty-two systems provide obstetrical and gynecological care to female inmates. All those responding to the 1993 survey indicated that health care begins with an initial screening of the female inmates at intake. To a large extent, then, decisions to incarcerate pregnant women center on the medical services and provisions offered at the institution. With female incarceration rates steadily increasing, it is eminent that female institutions improve the medical care provided to inmates, especially those who are pregnant. When satisfactory conditions exist, incarcerating pregnant women is a viable sentencing option.

Proponents of incarcerating pregnant women also argue that the bonding process that usually takes place between the parent and the child does not have to suffer because of the incarceration of the mother. Two dominant arguments emerge: (1) the child needs to bond to someone not necessarily the mother; and (2) institutions have programs that initiate, sustain, and complete the bonding process between mothers and children. Each argument is discussed below.

Conventional wisdom tells us that a mother and child must form some sort of attachment to each other, if for no other reason than that the mother is usually the primary caregiver. The one who feeds, cleans, clothes, protects, shelters, and loves the child. As a society, we believe in this bond between a mother and child. We consider it sacred and seem to think that without such a bond, the child will suffer and perhaps not even survive. It is believed that incarceration of mothers negatively affects the mother–child relationship.

How important is the mother–child bond? Research indicates that it is the bonding process itself that is important. Not necessarily between the mother and child but between the child and a primary caregiver (Ainsworth, 1979). The quality of the substitute child care is the most important aspect of the bonding process. Consistent nurturing, stimulation, and individual attention to the young child are the cogent factors. Consider for a moment those children who are adopted at birth. They are not allowed to form a bond with their mothers, yet, for the most part, a bond does form between the adoptive mother (and father) and the child.

As early as the 1950s, researchers such as Margaret Mead (1954) maintained that the separation argument is offensive to even the mildest feminist. Citing Hilde Bruch (1952), Mead states that the mother–child bonding is a "new and subtle form of antifeminism in which men—under the guise of exalting the importance of maternity—are tying women more tightly to their children than has been thought necessary since the invention of bottle feeding and baby carriages" (Mead, 1954, p. 447). Mead found through her studies of different cultures that the most important aspect of child development is that the child is cared for by many warm and friendly people, not necessarily only the mother.

Focusing on the quality of care, it can be said that in some instances separation between the mother and child is positive. For instance, when a mother needs to sort out her own feelings and behavior regarding her children, separation gives her some time to think and reflect on the care provided (or not provided) to her children. Research conducted by Baunach highlighted the following positive effects of separation:

> For some mothers, an additional impact of the separation is to heighten their understanding of their own behavior and its effects on their children. Especially for mothers who had been involved in drugs or alcohol for prolonged periods, incarceration provided them with a chance to step back and take stock of the experiences their children have endured (Baunach, 1979, p. 121, as cited in Boudouris, 1996, p. 2).

Moreover, Rutter (1971), studying the short- and long-term effects of separation, "concluded that a child's separation from his family constitutes a potential cause for short term distress but separation is of little direct importance as a cause of long term disorder" (p. 255).

Furthermore, Richards (1992) contends that when assessing the effects of separation consideration should be given to how the child interprets the event, the quality and quantity of other relationships in the child's immediate circle, the impact the event may have on the material and social well being of the child, and other factors including the age, gender, and personality of the child. To conclude that a child will absolutely suffer from the separation caused by incarcerating mothers is illogical. To a great extent, it depends on the circumstances of the family dynamics (Ainsworth, 1979). For some children, separation is a valid and recommended alternative to the conditions at home.

Advocates of the mother–child bonding and limited separation perspective will be somewhat mollified when reading the next section. It provides a detailed listing of programs available in and out of prison specifically designed for incarcerated women to create and maintain the bond between mothers and their children.

Programs for Incarcerated Mothers

Most of the programs for incarcerated pregnant women focus on the philosophy that there is nothing more important than the mother–child bond. To encourage the development and sustainment of that bond, a range of programs exist both inside and outside the institution. According to research conducted by Boudouris (1996, p. 71), the types of programs available to incarcerated women can be grouped into seven headings: (1) prison nurseries, (2) overnight visits with children, (3) family visits/conjugal visits, (4) children's and day care centers, (5) parenting classes for inmates, (6) furloughs, and (7) community facilities for mothers and children.

Boudouris was involved in the most comprehensive and thorough examination of programs available to incarcerated mothers. In 1984, his research focused on day care centers and nurseries in prisons, and in 1996 he expanded it and examined 1174 state prisons, nine federal facilities, and three Canadian prisons to include "visitation policies and procedures, family units and conjugal visits, community facilities, supportive services for inmates with children and...penal colonies" (Boudouris, 1996, vi). His results are as follows:

Prison nurseries are currently operating in only one state, Nebraska, while Delaware has proposed such a program (pp. 71–81). Other states have tried prison nurseries or have had laws mandating such programs (Florida, Illinois, Kansas, Massachusetts, Pennsylvania, and Virginia), but none currently maintain such programs. One Canadian prison has a prison nursery (pp. 16, 81)

In England and Wales, as of 1990, three custodial institutions have facilities for inmate mothers and their children (National Association for the Care and Resettlement of Offenders, 1990). These three facilities can accommodate 39 mothers and their babies. The units are jointly staffed by nurses and prison officials.

Twenty-one of the fifty U.S states have at least one state institution that allows overnight visits with children, whereas two Canadian prisons allow overnight visits with children, and one grants extended visits but not overnight stays. Almost three-quarters (thirty-seven) of the states have at least one institution where family visits are allowed. Two Canadian prisons have family visits. Twenty states have children's and day care centers either currently operating or planned for the near future. None of the Canadian prisons have children's or day care centers. Forty-seven states have parenting classes for inmates or are currently planning such classes. This is by far the most frequently observed category of programs available in prison. All three Canadian prisons have parenting classes for the inmates (Boudouris, 1996, p. 81).

Clement (1993, p. 89) found in her survey of prison programs for incarcerated mothers that the parenting classes offered by the institutions differed significantly in terms of "length, depth [and] content" of the program. She also found that most classes were taught by volunteers. This means that for institutions to be successful at providing parenting classes, a core of dedicated, hard-working, professional volunteers is needed.

Twenty-seven of the states have some sort of furlough programs implemented. Furlough programs consist of (1) releasing mothers to spend time with their families, (2) emergency release, (3) work release, and (4) educational release. Different states have different types of furloughs. The most important are those that allow the mother to return to her home to rebuild her relationship with her family. Walker (1992) states that the British equivalent, "Home Leaves," have the purpose of linking the mother with her family. U.S. and Canadian furloughs in which the mothers are released to spend time with their families have the same goal. Twenty-seven states and all three Canadian prisons have furloughs (Boudouris, 1996, p. 81).

Seventeen of the states have community facilities for mothers and children. Community facilities are designed to handle female offenders in the community, when possible. Examples include work release centers, residential centers for low-risk female offenders, treatment programs for victims of physical and sexual assault, residential programs for pregnant women or those with young children, and programs that meet offenders' needs for drug treatment or other services (Kingi, 1993). None of the Canadian institutions have community facilities for mothers and their children.

Conclusions

Incarcerating pregnant women is a viable sentencing option as long as the facilities are medically equipped to handle such cases. Research indicates that comprehensive maternity care is available to inmates at certain facilities. The challenge is to incorporate such care to more correctional facilities.

Intuitively, it can be argued that there is nothing more important than the mother–child bonding (attachment) process. However, the empirical research conducted on incarcerated women and the bonding process is somewhat limited. Some have argued that separation from mothers may indeed be beneficial, especially when the mothers have personal issues to address such as drug addiction and poor parenting skills.

Prisons are developing programs to initiate, sustain, and maintain the bond between a mother and her child. Such programs can be grouped into the following categories: prison nurseries, overnight visits with children, family visits/conjugal visits, children's and day care centers, parenting classes for inmates, furloughs, and community facilities for mothers and children. The results of Boudouris' second study show a vast expansion of the programs available to incarcerated mothers. As long as individual states and institutions within the state continue to expand the programs available and make each program somewhat consistent in terms of length, depth and content, the incarceration of pregnant women should be less problematic than it has been in the past.

REFERENCES

Ainsworth, M. D. S. (1979). Infant-mother attachment. *American Psychologist, 34* (10), 932–937.

Baunach, P. J. (1979). *The separation of inmate-mothers from their children.* Unpublished manuscript (as cited in Boudouris, 1996).

Boudouris, J. (1996). *Parents in prison: Addressing the needs of families.* Lanham, MD: American Correctional Association.

Bruch, H. (1952). *Don't be afraid of your child.* New York: Farrar, Straus and Young.

Clement, M. H. (1993). Parenting in prison: A national survey of programs for incarcerated women. *Journal of Offender Rehabilitation, 19,* 89–100.

Hufft, A. G., Fawkes, L. S., & Lawson, W. T. (1993). Care of the pregnant offender. In *Female offenders: Meeting the needs of a neglected population* (pp. 54–59). Lantham, MD: American Correctional Association.

Kingi, V. (1993). Mothers in prison: The reality of their needs. *Criminal Justice Quarterly, 4,* 4–7.

Lillis, J. (1994). Program and services for female inmates. *Corrections Compendium, 19,* 6–13.

Mead, M. (1954). Some theoretical considerations on the problem of mother–child separation. *American Journal of Orthopsychiatry, 4,* 471–483.

Mills, W. R., & Barrett, H. (1990). Meeting the special challenge of providing health care to women inmates in the 1990s. *American Jails, 4,* 55–58.

National Association for the Care and Resettlement of Offenders (1990). *Mothers and babies in prison.* London: Author.

Richards, M. (1992). The separation of children and parents. In R. Shaw (Ed.), *Prisoners' children: What are the issues?* New York: Routledge.

Rutter, M. (1971). Parent–child separation: Psychological effects on children. *Journal of Child Psychology and Psychiatry, 12* (4), 233–260.

Walker, N. (1992). Introduction: Theory, practice, and an example. In R. Shaw (Ed.), *Prisoners' children: What are the issues?* New York: Routledge.

Rejoinder to Dr. Moriarty
KEN AYERS

The author, in taking the "no" position, makes assumptions that quality care is available and, because it is available, no special consideration in the incarceration decision should be given to women who are pregnant. Research does not support her position. The care she mandates is not available within our penal system. The case she attempts to make about quality of services are services that are needed by all pregnant women, not just inmates, and most women are not necessarily provided them. Simply, the idea that because an individual has access to medical care everything is all right is not accurate. To support her position, the author suggest that FCI Lexington is an example of a prison capable of providing quality care. FCI Lexington, however, does not provide on-site obstetric services for pregnant inmates. Instead, they contract out that service. It is not feasible to expect a prison hospital to provide all possible types of health and medical care to inmates when local and area hospitals can be contracted.

What about bonding? How important is it? It is true that the infant can bond with anyone. This is particularly true if the infant will not be returned to the birth parent. But in most cases the infant and mother will be united after her prison sentence is finished, and the mother will be the primary caregiver. How would the child respond to a mother that he or she never had the opportunity to bond with? How would the mother respond to the child? The process of bonding is a two-way street. We should not be so narrow in our analysis that we only focus on the infant. What about the birth mother? Is it beyond the realm of possibility that mothers in prison benefit from a bonding experience with their child? If we expect the inmate to function as a mother after incarceration, we must provide them the opportunity to develop a relationship with the infant.

Research has established that because a woman is in prison does not necessarily mean that she is a bad mother, and research has established the importance incarcerated women place on family. Attempting to make an assumption that bonding is only important to the "primary caregiver" supports the common view that prison mothers are bad mothers and do not have the right to be mothers to their children. If we, criminal justice professionals, are concerned about the future of the mother, then we should be very interested in this issue. Success after prison is enhanced by having strong family ties between the inmate and her family. Not to consider mother–infant bonding as important narrowly focuses the issue beyond reasonable conclusions.

Finally, the author discusses a number of programs that are available within our women's penal system. These programs are very effective in what they attempt to accomplish, but these programs are for women and their children. These programs were not designed to include infants. The needs of infants and their mothers are very different from the needs of older children and their mothers.

Overall, the author seems to miss the issue to be discussed: "should incarceration of pregnant inmates be avoided?" Instead she focuses on the medical needs of the inmates and not the psychological needs. Caring for pregnant inmates is no different from caring for any women who are pregnant. True, pregnant inmates have a higher proportion of high-risk pregnancies, but this still is not different from dealing with high-risk patients in the real world.

Has the Privatization Concept Been Successful?

Sam Torres says YES. He is Associate Professor of Criminal Justice at California State University, Long Beach, and has a Ph.D. in Criminal Justice from the Claremont Graduate School (1983). He began his career with the Orange County Probation Department in California and later was appointed a U.S. Probation Officer in Los Angeles, where he remained for 22 years. His primary areas of interest are corrections, theory, and drug abuse issues.

David Shichor argues NO. He is Professor of Criminal Justice at California State University, San Bernardino. He has published articles and book chapters dealing with corrections, juvenile delinquency, victimology, white-collar crime, and punishment policies. He is the author of *Punishment for Profit: Private Prisons/Public Concerns* (Sage, 1995), and he co-edited (with Dale K. Sechrest) *Three Strikes and You're Out: Vengeance as Public Policy* (Sage, 1996).

YES

SAM TORRES

Prison overcrowding continues to increase at record levels and at exorbitant cost to the taxpayer. Such high costs are diverting resources from other much-needed services such as education, health, and transportation. Many of these services, especially prevention and treatment, are the very ones needed to combat crime and delinquency in an aggressive proactive fashion. Privatization represents a viable solution to many of the problems confronting corrections. Privatization is not new to corrections. It has been an important component of community corrections for more than thirty years and has generally provided services, such as halfway house pre-release programs, in an efficient and cost-effective manner. Although privatization in community corrections has existed without much public fanfare, the entry of private companies into the operation and management of private jails and prisons has raised serious questions. However, there exists substantial evidence, that, at least in the operation of minimum security facilities, the private sector can generate annual savings of 20 percent for construction and 5 to 15 percent for operation. Private firms can open new facilities more quickly, encourage competition among contractors, and enhance accountability. Numerous other advantages are also noted in this chapter. Although critics raise a number of concerns, a cursory examination of correctional history in the United States shows a disturbing tradition of brutality, lack of accountability, rampant corruption, physical, sexual, and mental abuse, inhumane conditions, poor security, riots, substandard medical care, and poor fiscal management. We can do better.

Correctional institutions in the United State are confronting critical over-crowding problems. The number of prisoners has nearly doubled in the last ten years. In 1985, jails and prisons held an estimated 313 inmates per 100,000 residents. At midyear, 1996, this rate had increased to 615 inmates per 100,000 residents. More than 1.6 million men and women were incarcerated in our jails and prisons at the end of June, 1996. At midyear, 1996, there were 1,112,448 state and federal prisoners, and an additional 3.7 million offenders were also on probation and parole. Between July 1, 1995 and June 30, 1996, the total number of persons incarcerated grew by 4.4 percent: 4.3 percent for federal prisons, 5.6 percent for state prisons, and 2.3 percent for local jails (Bureau of Justice Statistics, 1996).

Privatization Is a Viable Solution

One promising solution to the costly problem of prison overcrowding is the transfer of correctional responsibility to the private sector. The vast amount of literature on privatization of corrections is evidence that this process is already under way and will continue to become an increasingly important force in American corrections. Although controversial, privatization in corrections is not new. The private sector and many nonprofit organizations, such as the Salvation Army, have been involved in community corrections for over three decades. The operation of halfway houses, which are often minimum security prerelease facilities, have largely been contracted out to the private sector, with generally favorable results. There are problems inherent in the operation of correctional facilities, be they private or public. However, there is no reason to believe that the problems of privately operated jails and prisons will be any greater than presented under government control. In fact, there is reason to believe that private prisons and jails can be operated more cheaply, safely, and more efficiently than government-run facilities. That government will monitor private correctional facilities at levels that it does not monitor itself is hardly in dispute. Nonetheless, it is in the privatization of jails and prisons that the debate intensifies.

Studies conducted by the National Institute of Corrections in the 1980s reveal that contracts with private industry are already common in most states. The interest in privatization displayed by major research funding organizations makes clear that there is an increasing national awareness of the potential advantages of private sector initiatives to cope with some of the problems associated with prison overcrowding (Durham, 1988).

The operation and management of small, specialized facilities has been touted as a possible role for the private sector in the nation's correctional system. By using small (500-man) facilities that offer prerelease programs, lawmakers are taking major steps toward preparing inmates to live outside prison walls (Folz & Scheb, 1989; Johnson & Ross, 1990). The question, therefore, should not be whether the government should or should not contract for correctional services. Private entrepreneurs have been involved in the correctional enterprise since the 1960s, and such involvement, by all measures, is expanding. The major advantages of privately operated prisons are that such prisons provide the same or better level of care as the government, but more cheaply and with greater flexibility (Clear & Cole, 1997). Thus, our efforts should be aimed at assuring that these private facilities are cost-effective and are operating at the standards established by the American Correctional Association (ACA).

The privatization enterprise has demonstrated an ability to operate community-based correctional facilities at a high standard and in a cost-effective manner. The expansion of privatization to jails and prisons is a great idea and deserves the opportunity to show that it can do at least as good a job as the government and at a lower cost. Certainly, a strong argument could be made that the private sector can hardly do worse. There are many reasons for concluding that privatization sounds like a great idea. A brief overview of the major justifications for privatization of jails and prisons is offered.

Cost-Effectiveness

The potential for cost savings drives much of the current argument in support of privatization. The biggest selling point of private companies has been that they have the ability to provide a total facility cheaper than the government can. Studies find savings of 20 percent for private construction and 5 to 15 percent for private enterprise (National Center for Policy Analysis, 1995). A study of the Hamilton County Tennessee Jail demonstrated savings of at least 8 percent. Hamilton County found that contracting out prison management generated annual savings of at least 4 to 8 percent, and more likely in the range of 5 to 15 percent, compared with the estimated cost of direct county management (Cripe, 1997).

The major reason that it is cheaper to privatize corrections is that approximately 85 percent of the costs of running a jail come from personnel expenditures. Private companies pay less and provide fewer benefits, particularly retirement. In addition, savings are obtained through centralized management and a significant reduction in governmental red tape (Cripe, 1997). Corrections Corporation of America (CCA) charges Harris County, Texas, and the Immigration and Naturalization Service only $35.25 per inmate per day to operate a 350-bed minimum security facility in Houston, Texas, a charge that includes recovery of the cost of building the facility. Operating costs for government-run prisons can be twice that amount even without taking construction and land costs into account (National Center for Policy Analysis, 1995). Most states generally have provisions that services be provided at a lower cost and the same quality as the state provides (Florida Correctional Privatization Commission, 1996).

In 1993, the Florida legislature created the Correctional Privatization Commission (CPC) for the express purpose of entering into contracts for the construction and operation of private correctional facilities. In its 1996 Annual Report, the CPC recommended that the construction and operation of new facilities should be privatized. The commission also recommended that a comparative evaluation system be established that could be conducted on an ongoing basis (Florida Correctional Privatization Commission, 1996). In Texas, the Sunset Advisory Commission concluded that private prisons were operating at 14 percent less than the state costs (Ethridge & Marquart, 1993).

These studies clearly demonstrate that privatization, with proper monitoring and evaluation, can result in considerable savings in taxpayer dollars. Requirements for the awarding of such contracts are conditional on providing the same or better quality of service as the state provides. There is no insurmountable legal obstacle to total privatization of prison operations. Unlike government agencies, private firms must know and account for all of their costs, including long-run costs. If they can do so and still operate for less than government, and all indications are that they can "then government should set punishments for felons and let the private sector supply prisons" (National Center for Policy Analysis, 1995).

Private Firms Can Open New Facilities More Quickly

Private companies can relieve the tremendous overcrowding by constructing jails and prisons much faster than can be accomplished by the government. The biggest selling point of private firms has been that not only can they build prisons much faster than the government, but that they can do it more cheaply. They have also claimed that they can build and get a facility open and running more quickly than the government can. This latter claim seems to be supported by experience, because private companies are not bound by governmental red tape that tends to slow down prison construction. The private sector has also shown that they can get the funding to build new institutions more quickly from private investors or from lenders, whereas the government moves much slower, getting appropriations from the legislature, or going through a bond-issuing process (Cripe, 1997).

Privatization Will Enhance Competition and Accountability

By enhancing competition, privatization encourages companies to minimize costs to obtain government contracts in the first place, and then to hold on to them. Government contracts are usually awarded for short periods of between one and three years. The short life of contracts creates an incentive to provide quality service so that those contracts are renewed. The need to show a profit is a powerful incentive to reduce waste and increase productivity (Logan & McGriff, 1989).

There will be greater accountability with the private management of prisons and jails because justice agencies have already demonstrated with community corrections contracting that there is intense scrutiny of contract compliance by private vendors. It has already been said than the government appears more willing to monitor and control a contractor that it is to monitor and control itself. Law enforcement and correctional agencies are also held accountable to the rule of law. There is no reason to believe that a private contractor will be held any less accountable to comply with existing due process requirements in their control and treatment of inmates. Contracting will also encourage accountability because private firms will want to perform well to have their contracts renewed.

It cannot be overemphasized that close, careful monitoring of all aspects of private performance is essential to good contract operation (Cripe, 1997). In Florida, the Correctional Privatization Commission (CPC) uses an on-site monitor at each of two private correctional institutions it contracts. The on-site monitors are employed by the CPC and submit monthly reports. In addition, CPC contracts with an independent annual monitoring for each of the facilities it contracts. The primary purpose of monitoring is to assure that the contractor is complying with the terms of the contract and is adhering to American Correctional Association (ACA) standards. Before renewing a contract, the Florida Department of Corrections is required to assure that substantial savings are being realized, comparisons to determine such savings shall include all components associated with inmate per diem, the auditor general is required to review the methodology used, and the quality of services must be evaluated to assure that they are, at least, equivalent to those offered by the Department of Corrections (Florida Correctional Privatization Commission, 1996). In Texas, private firms and the Texas Department of Corrections spent a great deal of time and money in reaching agreements on how to carry out the contracts properly. Ethridge and Marquart (1993) encourage policymakers contemplating prison privatization to study the current situation in Texas in an effort to avoid costly problems by failing to adequately monitor adherence to the contract requirement.

Public Response to Privatization

A major problem in overcoming barriers to privatization is the public's resistance to the operation of jails and prisons by private entrepreneurs (Funke et al, 1992; Logan, 1997). More recently, however, the public's willingness to support experimentation with privatization appears to be increasing (Cullen, 1986; Jengeleski, 1986). The public's responsiveness to privatization seems to be influenced by the private sector's strong drive for efficiency to maximize profits; there is a strong incentive to make private correctional facilities secure while also providing treatment programs and doing so in a more cost-effective manner as compared with government-run facilities (Cullen, 1986).

Conclusion

We learned long ago that there are no panaceas in the control and treatment of criminal offenders. Privatization of correctional institutions is no exception. However, unlike other correctional fads (intensive supervision, community service, electronic monitoring, and boot camps), privatization has been employed for over thirty years. It has been successfully used in the operation of halfway houses for prerelease prisoners and for detention facilities that hold immigration violators. Although it is not suggested that privatization enter the realm of maximum security prisons, at least not at this time, the literature seems to provide ample support for private operation of minimum security and perhaps even some medium security prisons.

One of the most significant features of imprisonment is that it is tremendously expensive. The cost of building a prison can be as high as $100,000 per cell, not including financing. Each personnel position is usually about twice the cost when considering medical and retirement benefits. The average cost of processing an offender is about $20,000 in direct costs and about $30,000 when factoring indirect costs. Therefore, prison crowding, combined with fiscal restraint, has produced profound concern about correctional expenditures (Clear & Cole, 1997). Privatization offers a viable solution to this problem.

Although private companies have been involved in corrections for three decades, their responsibility has generally been limited to involvement with community corrections facilities, such as halfway houses. However, we can say that the era of privatization in institutional corrections has now arrived. Since around 1980, twenty-five states have passed legislation authorizing private companies to contract for the operation of prisons. In 1980, there were no states that allowed the private sector to contract with the government to operate jails or prisons. Today, approximately 50 percent of the states have passed legislation allowing for the operation of prisons and jails by private companies. Furthermore, in the past decade there has been a substantial growth in the number of states recognizing the potential of privately run prisons (Pollock, 1997).

Critics of privatization raise questions of propriety, quality of services, flexibility, security, liability, accountability, and corruption. A cursory examination of correctional history in the United States through the present reveals a disturbing tradition of brutality, lack of accountability, rampant corruption, physical, sexual, and emotional abuse, inhumane conditions, poor security, riots, substandard medical care, and poor fiscal management. Surely, we can do better.

REFERENCES

Bureau of Justice Statistics. (1996). *Corrections statistics.* Washington, DC: Government Printing Office.

Clear, T. R., & Cole, G. F. (1997). *American corrections* (4th ed.). Belmont, CA: Wadsworth Publishing.

Cripe, C. A. (1997). *Legal aspects of correctional management.* Gaitherburg, MD: Aspen Publishers.

Cullen. F. T. (1986, June). The privatization of treatment: Prison reform in the 1980's. *Federal Probation, 65*–70.

Durham, A. M. (1988). Evaluating privatized correctional institutions: Obstacles to effective treatment. *Federal Probation, 50,* 8–16.

Ethridge, P. A., & Marquart, J. W. (1993). Private prisons in Texas: The new penology for profit. *Justice Quarterly, 10,* 29–43).

Florida Correctional Privatization Commission. (1996). *Annual report: An assessment of Florida's privatization of state prisons.* Tallahassee, FL: Author.

Folz, D. H., & Scheb, J. M. (1989). Prisons, profits, and politics: The Tennessee privatization experiment. *Judicature, 73,* 98–102.

Funke, G. S., Miller, N. & Greiser, R. (1992). The future of correctional industries. *Prison Journal, 42,* 37–51.

Jengeleski, J. L. (1986). Corrections: A move to privatization. In B. I. Wolford and P. Lawrence (Eds.), *Issues in correctional training and casework.* College Park, MD: American Correctional Association (ACA).

Johnson, B. R., & Ross, P. P. (1990). The privatization of correctional management: A review. *Journal of Criminal Justice, 18,* 351–358.

Logan, C. H. (1997). Well kept: Comparing the quality of confinement in private and public prisons. In J. W. Marquart & J. R. Sorensen (Eds.), *Correctional context: Contemporary and classical readings.* Los Angeles, CA: Roxbury Publishing.

Logan, C. H., & McGriff, B. W. (1989). *Comparing costs of public and private prisons: A case study.* Washington, DC: National Institute of Justice.
National Center for Policy Analysis. (1995). *Bringing down costs through privatization.* Dallas, TX: Author.
Pollock, J. M. (1997). *Prisons: Today and tomorrow.* Gaithersburg, MD: Aspen Publishers.

Rejoinder to Dr. Torres

DAVID SHICHOR

The major argument for the privatization of prisons is economic as was emphasized by Dr. Torres. The major claim is that private companies can finance, build, and operate prisons cheaper than government agencies can. Financing by securing loans in private market usually involves the circumvention of the voters because the loan payments can be buried in the operating budget of the government agency; thus there is no voting on issuing bonds for the building of correctional facilities. Also, loans received on the open market usually are more expensive than the interests paid on bonds. It is true that private companies can build faster and cheaper; however, they often get tax breaks from local governments, which are not calculated into cost of the building, but they are a loss in revenues for the authorities.

There are conflicting reports regarding the operating costs of private prisons. Most reports confirm that the cost per capita in private prisons is cheaper than in government run prisons. As Dr. Torres correctly pointed out, most of the savings are materialized because of lower labor cost, but there are also other related factors, such as less training expenses, attempts to change staffing formulas, and using more mechanical security devices. Regarding changes in the staffing, in some cases private companies back out from the contract, like Wackenhut did in the Monroe County Jail in Florida in 1991, because the staffing was determined by the state standards and the company was not able to alter it. Problems related to training were recently revealed in the Brazoria County Jail in Texas, where correctional officers in the privately operated facility were kicking, beating, and dragging inmates by their hair. Problems such as this have, besides quality of service, economic consequences as well.

The maintenance of specified services by government authorities, which may be needed in emergencies, is costly, but usually is not included in the cost analysis. Government authorities have to maintain services that can effectively intervene if there are problems of fire, natural disasters, or prison riots. These services remain the government responsibility, and they are a government expense.

Effective monitoring by government agencies, which is claimed to enhance accountability, may be too expensive and may reduce considerably the savings suggested by privatization. Besides the extra cost involved with monitoring, there is also the problem of potential co-optation of government monitors by the private contractors. Promises of future employment, hiring of family members of monitors, and even bribery may seriously impede monitoring. The effectiveness of monitoring is also dependent on the availability of suitable replacement for a company if it has to be replaced because of poor performance, violation of the contract, abuse of inmates, or for any other reason. It is possible that another company is not available, or if one is lined up, it is only ready to take over for an increased price.

Finally, the continued lobbying for more and longer sentences of incarceration that private companies are involved in over the long run will increase the share of corrections in the general budget. The industry's efforts to expand and to get more business is clearly seen in the organization of the Annual Privatizing Correctional Facilities Conference for correctional companies, brokerage firms, investment banks, insurance companies, mutual funds, and state correctional administrators. The advertisement for the 1997 Conference included statements such as: "Prisons have created more than $1 billion a year industry for privatization initiative" and "In the past 2 years alone, capacity in private adult correctional facilities has doubled! Additional facilities must be constructed to accommodate the growing number of incarcerated persons. We have to achieve efficiencies in the design, construction, financing, and operation of these facilities. Privatization is the key." It is more than feasible that the private prison industry will make every effort to make sure that more offenders will be incarcerated for longer periods and that attempts to find alternative methods to deal with offenders will be reduced to the minimum.

Punishment is a government function, and it should stay in government hands. It does not mean that the government should not do a better job; on the contrary, it means that all efforts should be focused on the improvement of government services and not on creating a new industry that will impinge on the ability of the government to formulate correctional policies.

NO

DAVID SHICHOR

For several decades during the twentieth century, rehabilitation was the leading principle of American corrections. However, since the early 1970s there has been a growing disillusionment with and criticism of the idea of rehabilitation. This was the result of the general perception that rehabilitation policies did not reduce crime and were not very successful at changing offenders' behavior. The conservative turn of the sociopolitical climate in the 1970s prompted the introduction of social control policies based on the principle of incapacitation, which in its modern version means the locking up of offenders for a period during which they are not able to harm society. The change in punishment policies coupled with the public's demand for law and order and the declaration of "war on drugs" resulted in an unprecedented increase in imprisonment during the 1980s and early 1990s. The large-scale increase in the number of prisoners, which Irwin and Austin (1994) refer to as "America's imprisonment binge," has resulted in major prison overcrowding in spite of efforts to build more facilities and enlarge existing institutions. There was also a steep increase in correctional expenditures, which outpaced even the growth of prison population. For example, between 1980 and 1992, the number of prisoners in state and federal institutions showed 168 percent growth, but in the same period correctional cost increased by 306 percent. To confront this situation, there was an urgent need to search for new measures that would ease the pressure on the correctional system.

One of the possibilities in this regard that received a great deal of consideration was the privatization of prisons. Since the 1970s, many state departments of corrections had contracts with private corporations to supply medical, educational, vocational, culinary, and various other services that traditionally were the domain of government agencies. During the 1980s, private for-profit corporations started to operate entire prisons. This development was supported by the American tradition of distrust and negative view of "big government" and a strong belief in the efficiency and resourcefulness of the private sector. Also, the precedents from the early history of American prisons in the nineteenth century, when many of them were run by private entrepreneurs (see Shichor, 1995), helped to make the idea of privatization acceptable.

The operation of entire prisons by private companies raises several important issues. Some are theoretical; others are practical.

Theoretical and Legal Issues

Punishment is a legally imposed deprivation or suffering. It "must be for an offense against legal rules," and "it must be imposed and administered by an authority constituted by a legal system against which the offense committed" (Hart, 1968, pp. 4–5). Accordingly, punishment is inherently a governmental function. Supporters of privatization accept this premise, but they try to make a distinction between the sentence meted out by the courts that determines the nature and the extent of the punishment, and the actual administration of punishment, which, according to their claim, can be delegated to the private sector (Logan, 1990). They maintain that the punishment remains under the authority of the government, whose major task is to supervise its administration by the private contractor. This delegation of government authority to private entities was found to be constitutional by the courts.

Formally, the private company that operates the prison only administers the punishment and should not have any influence over it; however, informally, it does have an impact on it, through the setting and enforcing of everyday institutional rules. Although disciplinary hearings of inmates who violate rules are usually conducted by government agents who monitor the facility, the disciplinary write-ups are made by the private companies' employees who are in charge of enforcing the rules. The disciplinary procedure may influence the conditions of confinement and also the length of it by having an influence on the amount of "good time" that inmates can earn. Similarly, reports of institutional adjustment and behavior prepared by the staff may have an impact on parole decisions. Thus, the employees of a private prison corporation do have "quasi-judiciary" position determining certain aspects of punishment. Critics also point out that because private companies have a strong financial interest in keeping their facilities full at all times, they might use disciplinary reports to maintain the level of their population if there is a decline in the incarceration rates. Although at present this situation is only hypothetical, this possibility should be kept in mind. There is a vested interest of private correctional corporations in constantly growing incarceration rates, and this fact should be taken into consideration when the various issues of correctional privatization are analyzed.

As mentioned, on constitutional grounds, the state, without abdicating its penal authority, may delegate power to private companies to administer punishment. However, the opposition holds that on legitimate and moral grounds "the authority to govern those behind bars, to deprive citizens of their liberty, to coerce (and even kill) them, must remain in the hands of government" (DiIulio, 1990, p. 173). It is also pointed out that the symbols surrounding punishment, such as the uniforms of police and correctional officers and robes of the judge, are expressions of the inherently public nature of punishment. Although supporters of privatization dismiss this argument and claim that the substance of punishment is more important than the symbolism of uniform, symbolic meanings of punishment may influence not only prisons, but may have an impact on society as a whole. Garland (1991) observes in this regard that punishment "relics on meanings and representations that construe its own actions and weave them into belief systems, sensibilities, and cultural narratives of the social actors and audiences involved" (pp. 192–193).

In spite of the fact that the government can delegate its power to private companies to operate prisons, legally it remains responsible for what is happening in the facilities. This means that although government agencies do not have full control over the everyday operations, they do carry the ultimate liability. In prisons, where sometimes physical force has to be used to control violent inmates and in extreme situations even "deadly force" may be applied, this issue is an important one. This legal liability, in light of the large number of the civil rights suits filed by the inmates a last the correctional system, may create serious problems for the government authorities and underscores the importance of the contracts between the government and the private companies and its monitoring. They serve as a safeguard against potential legal and financial claims against the state.

Issues of Contract and Monitoring

A clear and detailed contract is a key element in the contracting out of prison oper-ation. The contract has to be flexible enough that it can be terminated if a legitimate reason arises. Every contract has to make sure that the company carries enough in-surance to cover civil liabilities. However, currently when civil judgments often reach seven figures, being able to afford a policy that could cover all possible dam-ages may be very hard, and some companies may balk at doing so. As noted, the ul-timate liability remains with the government, who has the "big pocket."

Effective monitoring of prisons, whether they are public or private, is impor-tant. Prisons are not visible institutions, and the public hardly knows what is going on behind the prison walls every day. In fact, most people really do not care much what happens within a facility that houses inmates who are generally considered to be not worthy of any consideration or concern, and who are politically powerless to command any major attention to the conditions of their confinement. Public interest focuses on prisons only in extreme situations, such as in escapes of violent offend-ers or when riots occur. There is a need to ensure that private contractors follow operational guidelines set by government agencies, not only because of the legal re-sponsibility of these agencies, but also because in a democratic society convicts have to be treated decently in accordance with the law.

Rigorous monitoring of private prisons is costly, because government agents have to be on the premises on a permanent basis. Private companies may have an interest in coopting monitors, usually not by direct bribes, but by promises of fu-ture employment after their retirement. Another factor that may impede effective monitoring is that the files of correctional companies are private, and they may refuse to open them for scrutiny.

Another concern of critics is the likely entrenchment of private corporations in the operation of prisons. To exercise effective monitoring, it is essential that government agencies have a backup capability in case of a major or consistent vi-olation of a contract. These agencies have to be in a position that they can step in and take over the operation in a short notice, because finding another private com-pany that is able to replace the previous one may take some time. If the govern-ment does not have this option available, its ability to enforce the contract is compromised. However, if government has to maintain a backup contingent for emergency situations, it may defeat the economic purpose of privatization.

Another potential problem relates to the division of authority between the management of the private prison and the government officials in charge of mon-itoring. "Unless care is taken to define the respective roles of public and private managers, two organizations are responsible, but neither may be clearly account-able" (Mullen, Chabotar, & Carrow, 1985, p. 75). Matthews' (1989) view con-cerning the effectiveness of monitoring is worth considering, he states: "To a large extent, the effectiveness of the monitors...will depend upon the levels of sanctions that they can ultimately utilize and the degree of critical autonomy they can maintain from the organization being monitored" (p. 4).

Economic Issues

The major argument for prison privatization is economic. Private corporations claim that they can operate prisons at a lower cost than government agencies do without lowering the quality of service. They suggest doing so by using private sector management techniques, more practical staff deployment, allowing the downsizing of personnel because they are not bound by civil service regulations and union contracts, and by more flexible procurement practices. Furthermore, they claim that they can also finance and build confinement facilities faster and cheaper than government agencies can. This analysis focuses on the operational aspect of privatization, because that is the most controversial issue; thus, the questions concerning financing and the construction of facilities will not be dealt with currently.

So far, there is no firm consensus whether privatized prisons save money for the government, and if they are, how much is the saving? Some reports and estimates indicate that private prisons cost less than government-operated prisons; others do not find any significant differences in cost (see, for example, U.S. GAO, 1996). Several reports find the cost comparison inconclusive. For example, in 1995 the Correctional Facilities Task Force dealing with this issue in Delaware in its recommendation against privatization stated that the state probably would not realize any savings from the privatization of prison operations; the only possible area of savings would be in the construction of facilities by private companies.

In general, the calculation of correctional costs is a complicated task. Cost estimates of government-operated prisons are usually underestimated, because the institutions often receive services from other government agencies that are not included in the prison budget. For example, the state education department may run academic or vocational programs in prisons, and government hospitals may care for sick prisoners. Usually, there are hidden costs accruing to the government in the operation of private prisons as well. These may include monitoring expenses, legal work involved in preparation of the contracts, legal expenses involved in settling contract disputes (Shichor & Sechrest, 1995), other costs that may accrue in unusual circumstances, such as in the case of bankruptcy of the private company, unexpected breaking off of contracts, and by tax benefits granted to private corporations and to their investors (Borna, 1986). In addition, a certain proportion of the maintenance of public services used for emergency situations, such as riots, fires, and natural disasters, can be considered as government costs.

Concerning labor cost, privatization advocates claim that private companies can manage prisons at a lesser cost than the government does by "side-stepping of government bureaucracy in building and operating of prisons, better staff motivation, the utilization of modern management techniques, and increased flexibility in the hiring and firing of employees" (Borna, 1986, p. 328).

Corrections is a labor-intensive industry. Between 60 and 80 percent of the operational cost is labor related. Thus, to make prisons profitable, private corporations have to cut their labor cost considerably. They do so by paying lower salaries, providing fewer fringe benefits, limiting promotions, reducing staff, and requiring less training. Supporters claim that labor cost savings are achieved mainly through flexible staffing, the use of more electronic surveillance devices, and by substituting fringe benefits with profit-sharing arrangements. Critics, however, maintain that these practices may result in reduced safety in institutions and in less security for surrounding communities. Many suggests that correctional staff in private facilities will be "ill trained, undereducated, poorly paid, and unprofessional" (DiIulio, 1991, p. 184). Others point to a high staff turnover rate, which may affect the quality of services.

Privatization supporters point to the managerial differences between the private and public sectors that impact prison costs: "Profit-and-loss incentives differ fundamentally from budget-driven bureaucratic incentives. Entrepreneurs are competitively motivated to provide maximum satisfaction at minimum cost. In contrast, bureaucrats are rewarded not so much for efficiency, but in direct proportion to the size and total budget of their agencies" (Logan, 1990, p. 84). Thus, public administrators do not have incentives to save cost; in fact, they may gain status by increasing their budget and their expenses. Similarly, as noted earlier, private companies are more flexible in their procurement practices by not being bound in long-term contracts to suppliers, by not having to go through bureaucratic channels to make purchasing decisions, and by shopping around and using their centralized buying power nationwide.

Political Issues

Privatization in general is related to the classical–liberal ideal of the "minimal state." This view contends that the state has usurped too much power; therefore there is a need to scale down state intervention in many aspects of social life. This concept, among others, questions the principle of centralized state monopoly over crime control. The minimal state concept claims that all rights are basically individual and the state does not have any legitimate authority by itself, but only rights transferred to it by individual citizens. This philosophical approach is ingrained in the Anglo-American sociopolitical tradition and tends itself to the promotion of private involvement in many governmental functions that in other societies are the sole domain of governments. This orientation is inherently related the ideals of laissez-faire and free market economics, which are the cornerstones of the capitalist system. According to these ideals, everyone can pursue his or her private interest that will serve the common good. Following this way of thinking, the involvement of private companies in the operation of correctional facilities may not only be acceptable, but it even can be beneficial.

Private correctional companies are in the "prison business" to make money. The most important ones, Corrections Corporation of America and Wackenhut Correction Corporation, for example, are traded in the stock market. Obviously, to be profitable, they have an interest in keeping their facilities full, as much as possible, and to expand the legislation and implementation of incapacitation-oriented punishment policies. In the pursuance of their interest, they will use the same political venues as other major corporations use in a capitalist society. They already have lobbyists in Washington and in several major state capitols, and they will continue to channel campaign contributions to political parties and to individual candidates to get support for maintaining incapacitation-oriented punishment policies. At a time when budgets for social services are seriously curtailed, when thousands are losing welfare benefits, the expansion of prisons supported by the private prison lobby may conflict with the general societal interest.

Private prison management companies are a part of the correctional subgovernment. Traditionally this includes legislators, various interest groups, and corrections officials. Although previously these subgovernments were by and large operating on a consensual basis through the state legislatures, the addition of private for profit corrections companies may introduce conflict into the correctional decision-making process by their pursuance of direct material gains from the adopted policies (Stolz, 1997).

Conclusion

Private management of prisons raises theoretical and pragmatic questions on ethical, economic, legal, and operational grounds. Schiflett and Zey (1990) in their organizational analysis make a comparison between private product-producing organizations and public service organizations. Private product-producing organizations receive their revenues from business activities; therefore, their customers have a strong control over them because they can shop around and take their business wherever they find better deals or services. Thus, these organizations have to be accountable to them. Public service organizations receive their finances from government agencies; their actual clients in general, and prison inmates in particular, are not able to shop around for better services. Therefore, these organizations are less accountable to their clients, in fact, the clients are greatly dependent on the public service provider mainly because they are poor, politically powerless, and low-status people. Public service organizations, because of their source of financing, are more dependent on their social environment than are private product-producing organizations and, therefore, they are more open to public scrutiny because their records are public.

The entrance of private for-profit organizations into the "prison business" introduces an extra factor to this area of public concern, the factor of profit seeking, which, besides the ethical issues related to the concept of "punishment for profit," raises a host of other concerns that make the already complex issue of punishment even more complicated, troublesome, and controversial.

References

Borna, S. (1986). Free enterprise goes to prison. *British Journal of Criminology, 26,* 321–334.

DiIulio, J. J., Jr. (1990). The duty to govern: A critical perspective on the private management of prisons and jails. In D. C. McDonald (Ed.), *Private prisons and the public interest.* New Brunswick, NJ: Rutgers University Press.

DiIulio, J. J., Jr. (1991). *No escape.* New York: Basic Books.

Garland, D. (1991). Punishment and culture: The symbolic dimensions of criminal justice. In A. Sarat and S. S. Sibley (Eds.), *Studies in law, politics, and society, 11.* Greenwich, CT: JAI Press.

Hart, H. L. (1968). *Punishment and responsibility.* Oxford: Clarendon.

Irwin, J., & Austin, J. (1994). *It's about time: America's imprisonment binge.* Belmont, CA: Wadsworth.

Logan, C. H. (1990). *Private prisons: Cons and pros.* New York: Oxford University Press.

Matthews, R. (1989). Privatization in perspective. In R. Matthews (Ed.), *Privatizing criminal justice.* London: Sage.

Mullen, J., Chabotar, K., & Carrow, D. M. (1985). *The privatization of corrections.* Washington, DC: National Institute of Justice.

Schiflett, K. L., & Zey, M. (1990). Comparison of characteristics of private product producing organizations and public service organizations. *Sociological Quarterly, 31,* 569–583.

Shichor, D. (1995). *Punishment for profit: Private prisons/public concerns.* Thousand Oaks, CA: Sage.

Shichor, D., & Sechrest, D. K. (1995). Quick fixes in corrections: Reconsidering private and public for profit facilities. *The Prison Journal, 75,* 457–478.

Stolz, B. A. (1997). Privatizing corrections: Changing the corrections policy-making sub-government. *The Prison Journal, 77,* 92–111.

United States General Accounting Office. (1996). *Private and public prisons: Studies comparing operational costs and/or quality of service.* Washington, DC: GAO.

Rejoinder to Professor Shichor SAM TORRES

In presenting his view on the privatization of corrections, David Shichor asserts that "private management of prisons raises theoretical and pragmatic questions on ethical, economic, legal, and operational grounds." The last sentence of his essay concludes, in part, that privatization introduces an extra factor of "profit seeking, which, besides the ethical issues related to the concept of 'punishment for profit,' raises a host of other concerns that make the already complex issue of punishment even more complicated, troublesome, and controversial."

Shichor and I could not be more in agreement. The privatization of prisons does indeed raise theoretical and pragmatic questions on all of the above issues. However, I believe that advocates of private corrections have addressed each of these concerns adequately and concluded that on each issue privatization performs at least as well as government-run prisons, if not better. In addressing punishment as inherently a government function, he responds on this critical legal issue by properly pointing out that "this delegation of government authority to private entities was found to be constitutional by the courts."

I also agree with Professor Shichor that "punishment for profit" raises a host of other concerns that make a complex issue more complicated, troublesome, and controversial. The punishment of law violators has always been complicated, troublesome, and controversial. Some argue for a treatment approach, and most argue for a punishment model, and others argue for both punishment and treatment. A majority of citizens support the death penalty, yet some are vehemently opposed to it. Recently, there is growing support for shaming of offenders; however, there are those who say this punishment will diminish their ability to be reintegrated into society. Today, many politicians are supporting the removal of weights in prison, the use of chain gangs, passage of "three strikes laws," sex offender notification laws, elimination of parole, mandatory minimums, elimination of conjugal visits, and even corporal punishment. For each one of these controversial issues, there is a vocal segment of society that strongly oppose these approaches. I could go on and on ad infinitum but, I believe, the point is clear. That is, correctional strategies *are* inherently complicated, troublesome, and controversial.

I found Shichor's essay to be a lukewarm NO. Rather than finding substantial opposition to my YES position, I found considerable support. Although he does eloquently present the "troublesome" issues related to privatization, he does not appear to openly reject the concept. Instead, he pointedly presents specific issues that, if addressed, would enhance the implementation of privatization, and in this regard, we are in full agreement. The areas of disagreement have already been addressed in my YES arguments. Professor Shichor does present several criticisms of privatization, but most of these seem to apply equally to the government operation of corrections.

For example, he reports that staff in private prisons will be "ill-trained, undereducated, poorly paid, and unprofessional," and staff turnover will be great. However, one need only pick up any text on corrections or penology to discover that persons employed in our government-run prisons tend to be poorly trained, undereducated, poorly paid, and unprofessional, and the turnover rate is high. In addition, research on corrections cite low morale and an antagonism between administration and line staff.

Shichor is also concerned with the potential lobbying activities of private corrections. He states, "they already have lobbyist(s) in Washington and in several major state capitols, and they will continue to channel campaign contributions to political parties and to individual candidates to get support for maintaining incapacitation-oriented punishment policies." In California, Professor Shichor's home state, the California Correctional Officer's Association (CCOA) has one of the strongest and most influential lobbies in the state. As any strong lobby, the CCOA acts in the best interest of its members by channeling campaign contributions to political parties and to individual candidates to get support for legislation that supports maintaining incapacitation oriented punishment policies. At $55,000 a year (without overtime), correctional officers in California are among the highest paid in the nation. Since the early 1980s, California has been involved in the largest prison-building program in the United States. In California, we now spend more for corrections than we do for higher education.

Perhaps the strongest argument made by Shichor and those who oppose privatization is that the state's authority to punish should not be delegated and, in this regard, I also share concern about this most fundamental of governmental functions. However, this argument is simply inadequate as a rationale for not *experimenting* with privately run minimum and medium security prisons. As I said previously, "a cursory examination of correctional history in the United States through the present reveals a disturbing tradition of brutality, lack of accountability, rampant corruption, physical, sexual, and emotional abuse, inhumane conditions, poor security, riots, substandard medical care, and poor fiscal management." The cost of running government prisons is exorbitant. In seems to me that privatization has no place to go but up. If the experiment fails, we can always revert back to a fully operated government system.

"Three Strikes and You're Out" Legislation: A Cheap and Effective Crime Control Initiative?

Robert A. Jerin argues YES. He is currently Chair of the Law and Justice Department at Endicott College and has a Ph.D. from Sam Houston State University (1987). A former juvenile detention officer for the State of Connecticut, Dr. Jerin has also taught at North Georgia College, Salem State College, and Appalachian State University. He is presently involved in research on restorative justice and crime prevention and has just published (with Laura Moriarty) *Victims of Crime* (Nelson-Hall).

Dale K. Sechrest argues NO. He is Professor of Criminal Justice at California State University, San Bernardino. He earned his D.Crim. in 1974 from the University of California at Berkeley. From 1975 to 1984, Dr. Sechrest developed national standards for corrections and procedures for their application in an accreditation program for the American Correctional Association. He is co-editor (with David Shichor) of *Three Strikes and You're Out: Vengeance as Public Policy* (Sage, 1996).

YES

ROBERT A. JERIN

'Three Strikes' is a model of strict and evenhanded justice. It demands accountability, reflects common sense, presents a clear and certain penalty, and uncompromisingly invests in public safety.

—Dan Lungren, Attorney General of California (1996)

On October 1, 1993, twelve-year-old Polly Klaas was last seen alive. Over the previous twenty years Richard Allen Davis was allowed to plea bargain, receive probation, early release, good time, and parole for an assortment of crimes including robberies, burglaries, sexual assaults, kidnaping, and assaults with deadly weapons (Bidinotto, 1996). Had "three strikes" been in place, Polly Klaas would be alive today, and many other crime victims would not have had to suffer at the hands of Richard Allen Davis. An unknown number of victims, survivors, and their families would have been safe from this man's sadistic violence.

The terrifying rampage of Leslie Allen Williams finally came to an end in 1992, when he was caught and confessed to four murders and eleven rapes. This serial murderer and rapist had been in and out of the criminal justice system for over twenty years. He had been paroled four separate times before he went on his killing rampage (Bidinotto, 1996). He had been allowed to serve less than half his sentences, violate his paroles without punishment, plea bargain serious offenses down to minor ones, and continue to walk free in society killing and raping innocent victims because the justice system would not keep him incarcerated.

In November 1993, the federal three-strikes law was first approved in the Senate. The first person convicted under this statue, Tommy Farmer, had a twenty-five-year criminal career that included assaults with dangerous weapons, aggravated batteries, robberies, and murders (Butterfield, 1995). By using the federal statute, Tommy Farmer was sent to prison for life instead of walking free in a few years, preventing him from continuing to terrorize and kill innocent citizens.

After thirty years of increasing crime rates and violence, society has demanded that something be done with habitual offenders. Beginning in 1993 in Washington State, legislatures across the United States and the federal government have responded with statutes that provide for a life sentence for persons convicted of three felonies, some without the possibility of parole. Most of the new laws require courts to impose mandatory sentences for habitual offenders, with very few retaining some judicial discretion (Edwards, 1995). For a summary of the various types of legislation that are considered to be three strikes' statutes, see, for example, Turner, Sundt, Applegate, and Cullen (1995).

Is Three Strikes Cost-Effective?

What are the costs associated with "three-strikes," and what does it mean to effectively control crime? In the previously discussed cases, failure to imprison these criminals cost people their lives, innocent citizens suffered emotional and physical trauma, and society was subjected to additional criminal acts that should not have occurred. Although it is estimated to cost upwards of $700,000 to imprison a person over their lifetime (Butterfield, 1995), the costs associated with failing to imprison someone who later kills, rapes, robs, or assaults an innocent citizen are astronomical. What was the cost to society to lose Polly Klaas and others as productive members of the community? What were the costs incurred by the country for the physical and emotional harm inflicted by the murder of Polly and others who are victimized by habitual offenders? What are the costs of the investigations into the additional crimes these offenders commit? What are the costs associated with bringing the offenders to trial again and again, and how much is it costing to incarcerate and sentence them for their additional crimes? All of these factors must be taken into account when examining the question: "Is three strikes cost-effective?"

It has been estimated that the cost to imprison someone for one year is approximately $30,000. If these habitual offenders go on to kill someone, as happened in the cases of Richard Allen Davis and Leslie Allen Williams, and are then faced with the death penalty, the costs go even higher. In Florida, it costs taxpayers six times as much to execute someone (over $3 million dollars) than to keep them in prison for life (Spangenberg & Walsh, 1989).

Although the costs associated with putting habitual offenders in prison for life are easily measured, the costs associated with the additional victimization of innocent citizens are largely ignored. The intangible costs associated with victimization such as lost quality of life, pain, suffering, and fear must be counted when assessing a cost-benefit analysis of life imprisonment versus additional victimizations. It has been shown that when the intangible costs associated with victimization are counted in a cost–benefit analysis, the use of more prison time actually is less expensive.

In 1996, the National Institute of Justice (NIJ) examined the question of what does crime cost (Miller, Cohen, & Wiersema, 1996). In this comprehensive evaluation of all of the costs associated with criminal victimization, NIJ estimated that the total cost to victims in the United States for crimes against individuals and households amounted to $450 billion annually. Even this staggering sum does not include two of the largest costs associated with crime: "the cost of operating the criminal justice system and the cost of actions taken to reduce the risk of becoming a crime victim; costs incurred directly by or on behalf of the crime victim" (pp. 16–17) are part of their calculations.

Additional cost savings occur from the general reduction of crime that occurs when high-rate offenders are locked away. As has been seen in California, where three-strikes legislation has resulted in more than 15,000 prosecutions, the crime rates have plunged since the enactment of the new law. It is estimated that the citizens of California saved an estimated $4 billion in additional costs to the potential victims and the State in just one year of crime reduction (Lungren, 1996). Although not all the reduction can be attributed to the new legislation, it is hard to believe it is just a coincidence.

Is Three Strikes Effective in Controlling Crime?

The deterrent effect of three strikes legislation is a source of heated debate. The concepts of deterrence focus on two separate, but intertwined notions, specific deterrence and general deterrence. Specific deterrence proposes that a sentence has the effect of preventing the individual on whom it is imposed from committing any future criminal acts. General deterrence proposes that a sentence, once known to the general population, will be an example to others so that they will not commit any future crime.

There is no doubt that if a person is locked up for life they are unable to commit any additional crimes against innocent citizens. The ability of high-rate offenders to re-offend has been taken away from them with the use of three-strikes sentences. Parole boards can no longer set free the habitual violent offender to rape and murder innocent victims. No longer will violent offenders serve only a small portion of their sentences. The likelihood of a three-timer returning to crime once they are released has been estimated to be greater than 75 percent (LaCourse, 1994), and these are only estimates based on known crimes.

The impact on other offenders who have been convicted of two previous violent felonies is harder to measure, but through various research, anecdotal information, and common sense, certain conclusions can be put forth. In interviews with offenders who were released after having been convicted of two prior violent felonies, the potential impact of facing a life sentence has altered some futures (Thomas, 1995). Offenders have started to take the criminal justice system seriously once they know that the system itself cannot be manipulated any further.

Another example of the deterrent effect of three strikes can be seen in the migratory patterns of felons on parole in California. Paroled felons flowed into California at a greater rate than those who left the state before the passage of three strikes legislation. Since the passage of the three strikes legislation, parolees have been leaving California in greater numbers than those entering (Lungren, 1996). All this is occurring at a time when the population is increasing, and the economy in California is getting better.

According to the Rand Corporation, the State of California could reduce serious adult felonies by up to one-third with their implementation of the three strikes sanction. Of these, one-third of the crimes reduced would be violent offenses (Greenwood et al., 1994). Even this percentage is significant when we examine the harm to innocent victims that is being eliminated. There has been no other crime control program that has produced the across-the-board reduction in crime that has been achieved since the introduction of the three strikes legislation.

In California, there have been reductions in crime of historical proportions. These decreases have occurred in all categories of crime throughout the state. Since the introduction of the three strikes legislation, California has experienced:

- The largest one-year drop in state history in the rate and number of crimes
- The largest two-year decline in the number of crimes
- the first two-year drop in all major categories of crime (homicide, rape, robbery, aggravated assault, burglary, and motor vehicle theft)

- The largest drop in the number of violent crimes
- The largest one-year drop in the rate and number of property crimes
- The largest one-year drop in the number of burglaries

(Lungren, 1996, p. 1)

And the crime rates keep dropping in California and across the country since the introduction of three strikes legislation. Although economic and other social reasons may be playing a part in this historical drop in crime, it would be negligent to suggest that three strikes has no part in this reduction.

Conclusion

Three strikes legislation is an emotional, controversial issue. The public by a wide majority supports mandatory sentences for convicted three-time felons, and legislatures have responded. The debate as to whether three strikes laws are cheap and effective crime control initiatives will depend on all of the factors considered. Is it cheap? No, but neither is allowing criminal acts to continue. The costs to innocent victims of crime and to society are only now being quantified, and they far outstrip the costs of imprisoning habitual offenders for life. Billions of dollars in losses are incurred each year by innocent men, women, and children of all races because of the failure of the criminal justice system to control habitual offenders.

The amount of crime citizens have to fear and are affected by is finally being reduced, and the three strikes legislation is particularly responsible. Offenders and would-be third-time felons are now on notice that the public will not tolerate their criminal activities any more. Society has decided to get serious with the individuals who have been given multiple chances to change, but have decided that the criminal way of life is the easier alternative. The need to provide a criminal justice system that responds to the wishes of the law-abiding community is just becoming a reality.

REFERENCES

Bidinotto, R. J. (1996). *Freed to kill: How America's "revolving door" system of justice fails to protect the innocent.* Washington, DC: Safe Streets Coalition.

Butterfield, F. (1995, September 11). First federal 3-strikes conviction ends a criminal's 25-year career. *The New York Times,* B11.

Edwards, M. (1995). Mandatory sentencing. *CQ Researcher, 5* (20), 465–483.

Greenwood, P., C. P. Rydell, A. F. Abrahamse, J. P. Caulkins, J. R. Chiesa, K. E. Model & S. P. Klein. (1994). *California's new three strikes law: Benefits, costs and alternatives.* Santa Monica, CA: Rand Corporation.

LaCourse, D. (1994). Commentary. *Journal of Interpersonal Violence, 9* (3), 420–426.

Lungren, D. (1996). Three cheers for 3 strikes. *Policy Review, 80,* 34.

Miller, T. R., Cohen, M. A., & Wiersema, B. (1996). *Victim costs and consequences: A new look.* Washington, DC: National Institute of Justice.

Spangenberg, R. L., Walsh, B. (1989). Capital punishment or life imprisonment? Some cost considerations. *Loyola of Los Angeles Law Review, 23,* 45–58.

Thomas, J. (1995). Scared straight: Interview with a second striker. *Youth Outlook,* 2–3.

Turner, M. G., Sundt, J. L., Applegate, B. K., & Cullen, F. T. (1995). 'Three strikes and you're out' legislation: A national assessment. *Federal Probation, 59* (3), 16–35.

Rejoinder to Dr. Jerin
DALE K. SECHREST

No one doubts the importance of locking up serious criminal offenders. As I noted in my statement, laws designed to deter serious, habitual offenders have been in existence for many years in most states. Curiously, the thirty years of "increasing crime rates and violence" cited have been decreasing for several years, probably more for demographic reasons than because of the three strikes laws or any sentencing innovations. Violent crime, according to the *Uniform Crime Reports,* had gone up 41 percent from 1982 to 1991, whereas *National Crime Victimization Survey* data showed a rather constant level and slight decline in violent crimes against households during the same period. The murder rate has dropped 23 percent since 1993, although this is usually attributed to an increase in the chances of being arrested, convicted, and sentenced to prison. In California, crime began dropping two years before the three strikes law was passed (1994) and continues to decline. The evidence for the specific crime reduction effects of three strikes laws is mixed based on comparisons of states with and without such laws.

No one doubts the importance of bringing criminals to justice, especially serious offenders. It has long been the case that 70 percent of stranger-to-stranger rapists do time in prison or jail, and violent offenders have usually done about half their sentences. In fact, three strikes laws have simply become another tool in the arsenal of prosecutors to see that these individuals are taken off the streets, which has always been their job. Most offenders who get sentenced for a second or third strike deserve it, just as they have in the past. But at what cost? Special prosecutorial units have been set up across the country to manage three strikes cases. In San Diego County, California, the "three strikes prosecution team" is made up of eight deputy district attorneys, two investigators, two investigative specialists, and a "priors" clerk. Nine public defenders work with three courts and their associated judges and staff. Considerable time is taken to determine the following: the seriousness of the current offense, whether the priors are remote in time, whether the defendant has no recent criminal history, whether the defendant has never been to prison, whether the underlying facts of the strike priors do not reflect the criminal behavior normally associated with such charges, whether the current offense is a petty theft involving food for consumption, and whether the defendant has no history of violence or history of weapons possession or mental illness.

With all of these activities, which increase costs of prosecution, fewer than one-fourth of second-strikers in California were admitted to prison for a violent or serious offense. The most common offenses are possession of a controlled substance, petty theft with a prior theft, and second-degree burglary. Slightly more than half of third-strikers were admitted to prison for a violent or serious offense, the most common being robbery and first-degree burglary, which are considered violent offenses. Laws that target specific offenses, such as use of a handgun in a robbery, may be far more effective as a deterrent.

The law has simply become another tool for prosecutors to screen offenders into the prison system. In California, prosecutors cannot plea bargain, but they can strike prior strikes. Rather than use the law as it is written, prosecutors are "justifying" its use in most cases to improve system efficiency. Also, many of these offenders are older and may be nearing the end of their criminal careers at this stage. Is this cost-effective? Many of them will devolve into very expensive geriatric cases in our prison systems. Is this the most effective deterrent to future crimes? It is generally acknowledged that the baby "boomerang" of the next decade will lead to increases in violent juvenile crime; yet three strikes laws are not designed to manage this potential problem.

Finally, as one ponders potential dollar savings from the three strikes laws, the human element must be considered. There is evidence that these laws target disadvantaged and minority groups. They also allow society to comfortably abrogate its responsibility for crime prevention and the duty to assist offenders who can benefit from programs. It is doubtful that the law provides justice in instances in which a third strike is not a serious felony, such as forgery or petty theft with a prior. It is a more effective use of time and resources to get less serious cases out of prison and reserve scarce, expensive prison space for truly violent offenders, such as armed robbers, child molesters, and rapists.

NO

DALE K. SECHREST

The rationale for three strikes laws is defective. Social policy based on mandatory sentencing laws are detrimental to society, offenders, and to the criminal justice system. These laws have negative social, moral, and practical implications for society. They portend many long-term detrimental effects on society and the operation of the criminal justice system, especially in the allocation of fiscal resources to the crime problem, which is a social problem. The American Society of Criminology has developed a policy statement on the subject (Adler, 1995) that will be summarized along with other legal and scholarly sources (see Shichor & Sechrest, 1996).

Before the "strikes" term became popular, these laws were referred to as "habitual offender laws," and several states had them. Estimates are that thirty-four states have habitual offender laws requiring enhanced prison terms for repeat felony offenders (DiMascio & Mauer, 1995, p. 19), and twenty-four have three strikes laws. The federal government has a "truth in sentencing" law requiring violent offenders to serve at least 85 percent of their sentences. Generally, these laws require long sentences for second offenders and 25 years-to-life sentences for offenders involved in a third felony, sometimes regardless of its seriousness. However, they are rarely used and appear to have had little effect on crime rates.

The mandatory minimum laws became quite popular in the 1990s, especially in California, where 17,000 offenders have been sentenced under the three strikes law since March 1994. Most sentences are for second strikes, which call for a doubling of the original sentence and reductions in "good time" credits that will ensure that inmates serve 80 percent of their sentences. Alternatives, such as probation, are eliminated for second-time violent felons—they will go to prison. The argument is that such laws will control persistent, serious, and violent offenders and in doing so reduce crime (see Shichor & Sechrest, 1996).

Why are such laws necessary? Shiraldi, Sussman, and Hylan (1994) note the paradox of stable crime rates in California since 1977 and a media-driven public fear of crime that led to the law, which is seen as "governance by hyperbole." Feeley and Kamin (1996, p. 135) take the broader view, placing the law in the context of similar laws that constitute "moral panics or symbolic crusades with only marginal instrumental value in terms of improving the effectiveness and efficiency of crime control." Basing the management of criminal offenders on periodic adventures into publicity-inspired retribution seems a flawed method of managing the crime problem.

Legal Issues

Three strikes laws can constitute cruel and unusual punishment. Or can it? The U.S. Supreme Court has provided little good guidance on whether three strikes laws constitute cruel and unusual punishment. The major concern is proportionality. Is the sentence consistent with the harm caused by the crime? For example, in *Harmelin* v. *Michigan* (1991), the Court reversed itself on the issue of when proportionality review can be applied and returned to the principles espoused in *Rummel* v. *Estelle* (1973), which essentially upheld three strikes laws as long as parole was available. It now appears that states must develop their own interpretations of these laws.

Crime Reduction

These types of laws have not reduced crime. In California, the crime rate had been declining for two years before the passage of the law (since 1992), in keeping with national trends (Mauer, 1996). A national study reported that between 1994 and 1995, "both violent and overall crime rates dropped more in the thirty-seven states without three strikes laws than in the thirteen that had such laws" (Associated Press, 1997), including California.

It is suggested that the demographic shift resulting in fewer 15 to 25-year-olds is the reason for reduced crime rates, not the three strikes laws. We may soon know the answer to this question as the crime-prone age-group is increasing, up an estimated 29 percent by 2004 (Ostrom, 1997). Based on the increases in violent juvenile crime that began in 1988, this trend already appears to be in place. Snyder, Sickmund, and Poe-Yamagata et al. (1996, 14) report that 19 percent of the person entering the justice system in 1994 for a violent crime were younger than age 18, which is below the mid-1970's 23 percent but above 1988's 15 percent. In California, the juvenile population between the ages of ten and seventeen will increase over 30 percent by 2004 (Trask II, 1996).

Cost and Benefits

The RAND assessment of California's three strikes legislation points to its potential for reducing serious and violent crime, but at an estimated cost of about $5.5 billion over the next twenty-five years, or about $300 per taxpayer (Greenwood, Model, Rydell, & Chiesa, 1996). Most of the funds would be used to construct and operate new prisons. If all the projected prisons were built, costs would almost consume the budget for higher education in California. Smith (1997) summarized Washington State's twelve years of experience with the "fixed sentence" by citing several costly problems, to include more requests for jury trials, crowded jails, overloaded prosecutors and public defenders, civil case delays, prison expansion to rates higher than the entire country, the greatest increase in corrections costs in the nation, and no decrease in reported crimes or arrests. Delaware reports similar results. O'Connell (1995) provides some reasons why mandatory sentences have not acted as a deterrent to crime in Delaware, citing the economic benefits of drug sales as the key force causing offenders to risk long prison terms.

A second long-term effect on costs will be the unprecedented growth of the elderly population in prisons, which will contribute to higher costs because of their health needs (expected to be double or triple that of inmates from the general population). In fact, Californians have rejected new prison construction initiatives or any new funding for the law. Pressure has mounted to put these scarce dollars into improving schools and developing prevention programs for juveniles, which one would think might be the better approach to controlling crime and prison construction.

Other impacts on states and specific areas of the criminal justice system will be felt, some of which are unintended consequences. For example, some law enforcement personnel report that potential three strikers have nothing to lose and may be more dangerous. Evidence from a state-sponsored study of eighteen California jails shows increased violence rates in local jails since the passage of the law. Assaults by inmates against jail staff have risen 26.7 percent, from 333 to 427 during the first nine months of the three strikes law (McConnell, 1995).

Questions of Justice

Justice suffers from three strikes laws. Short-term effects of this legislation include a clogged court system, causing rising court costs and intolerable delays in civil cases; early release of sentenced felons to make room for three-strikes detainees; and increased discretionary power for prosecutors. Judges in some jurisdictions have been reassigned from civil to criminal dockets. In Los Angeles, there is evidence that after three years civil trials are returning, largely because of the implementation of a trial delay reduction plan. The plan protects defendants' rights and has helped reduce jail crowding (Harris, 1997).

Contrary to the expectation that prison populations would rise markedly, jail crowding is up as offenders seek trials in anticipation of long sentences. Estimates for California are that the number of trials will double. However, estimates are that one-third of all people now booked for less serious crimes in California are released early because of lack of jail space (Ostrom, 1997). Are these unintended consequences desirable?

The law casts too wide a net. Individuals who have committed offenses not considered serious, such as the U.S. Supreme Court cases cited above, will be imprisoned longer than necessary to achieve the result of less criminal activity. Several of these cases are documented by Shiraldi et al. (1994). In California, the third strike need only be a felony, and not one on the serious or violent list that defines the two earlier strikes. Also, three strikes offenders are older and are the poorest targets for longer sentences. Younger offenders who are just beginning their criminal careers would be better prospects from the standpoint of reduced crime and greater public safety.

The most important issues surrounding the implementation of mandatory minimum laws is the types of offenders involved. The law is not targeting serious offenders. California has incarcerated 75 percent of its cases under the law for nonviolent third offenses (e.g., property, drugs).

The law targets minorities disproportionately. Mauer (1994) found that African American men were overrepresented in charging for three strikes cases in Los Angeles; although they constitute 20 percent of the felony population, they make up 43.6 percent of those charged under the three strikes law. State prison figures (California Department of Corrections, 1996) found the following for offenders sentenced under the law: 43.9 percent African American, 27.1 percent Hispanic, 25.3 percent white (see also Moffitt, 1996).

Conclusion

Fixed sentencing is bad social policy. The federal determinate sentencing policy is seen as a failure. Taking discretion away from judges is counterproductive, as seen in California Supreme Court decisions that return some discretion to judges. As the editorial in the *L.A. Times* stated after the *San Diego* v. *Romero* (1996) decision, "the California Supreme Court Thursday unanimously called a halt to the unfairness and massive chaos that the 'three strikes and you're out' law has wrought since it took effect three years ago" (p. B8). In the case, the judge had dismissed two prior felony convictions for burglary and attempted burglary when sentencing Romero for cocaine possession for six years. In a later case (*People* v. *Alvarez,* 1997), judges were allowed the discretion to determine whether a "wobbler" was to be considered either a misdemeanor or a felony.

Clearly, some offenders require incarceration. Scarce prison space should be reserved for the sexual assaulter, the child molester, and the murderer. There is evidence that serious habitual offenders can be controlled by three strikes laws. However, for most offenders, judges should be allowed to judge, as they have in the past, to consider the facts and circumstances of individual cases and the use of appropriate sentencing alternatives. As Feeley and Kamin (1996) suggest, and history supports, the criminal justice system will adjust to the new circumstances. In California, practitioners have already begun to adjust to new circumstances as defined by the courts.

Fixed sentencing takes attention away from crime prevention and early intervention, especially for youths and first offenders. It is not only a "quick" fix; it is an easy fix. Incarceration has never been and never will be a solution to the types of social and individual problems that yield crime. As stated by the American Society of Criminology (Adler, 1995), categorical sentencing schemes, such as three strikes, are contrary to existing knowledge regarding the relationships between age, future crime, and recidivism, which declines with age.

Prevention is the more desirable strategy. The cost-effectiveness of early intervention with individuals moving toward a life of crime is addressed in a RAND report (Greenwood et al., 1996). Interventions do cost money but are cost-effective. Based on this report, Moffitt (1996) concludes that the "war" on crime is not only cruel but fiscally insane. As concluded by Shichor and Sechrest (1996), the ultimate tests for the effectiveness of any of these measures will be substantial and continuing declines in crime rates and increased levels of public safety. If not, then three strikes will be "another costly and failed attempt to deal with a major symptom of severe social ills without trying to address in serious and fundamental ways the underlying problems that are plaguing American society" (p. 276). It appears that California legislators who face staggering prison costs are beginning to get this message.

REFERENCES

A return of judgment to the judging process. (1996, June 21). *Los Angeles Times,* p. B8.

Adler, F. (1995, November/December). Critical criminal justice issues: Task force reports from the American Society of Criminology to Attorney General Janet Reno. *Criminologist, 20* (6): 3–16.

Associated Press. (1997, March 7). Study says '3-strikes' laws made no difference in crime levels. *San Bernardino Sun,* p. A5.

California Department of Corrections. (1996). *California prisoners and parolees, 1995.* Sacramento, CA: Author.

DiMascio, W. M., & Mauer, M. (1995). *Seeking justice: Crime and punishment in America.* New York: Edna McConnell Clark Foundation.

Feeley, M. M., & Kamin, S. (1996). The effect of "Three strikes and you're out" on the courts: Looking back to see the future. In D. Shichor & D. K. Sechrest (Eds.), *Three strikes and you're out: Vengeance as public policy.* Thousand Oaks, CA: Sage Publications.

Greenwood, P. W., Model, K. E., Rydell, C. P., & Chiesa, J. (1996). *Diverting children from a life of crime: Measuring costs and benefits.* Santa Monica, CA: RAND Corporation.

Harris, M. D. (1997, April 15). After strikes deluge, civil trials return. *Los Angeles Daily Journal,* p. 1.

Mauer, M. (1994, October). *Racial disparities in the charging of Los Angeles County's third 'strike' cases.* San Francisco, CA: Center on Juvenile and Criminal Justice.

Mauer, M. (1996). Three strikes policy is just a quick-fix solution. *Corrections Today, 58,* 23.

McConnell, T. (1995, February). *Three strikes jail population report.* Sacramento, CA: State Sheriffs' Association Detention and Corrections Committee and Board of Corrections.

Moffitt, B. (1996, July 12). Testimony before the United States Commission on Civil Rights, for the National Association of Criminal Defense Lawyers.

O'Connell, J. P. Jr. (1995, Winter). Throwing away the key (and state money). *Spectrum,* 28–31.

Ostrom, M. A. (1997, March 9). "3 strikes" prison influx a no-show. *Sacramento Bee,* Forum 3.

Shichor, D., & Sechrest, D. K., (Eds). (1996). *Three strikes and you're out: Vengeance as public policy.* Thousand Oaks, CA: Sage Publications.

Shiraldi, V., Sussman, P. Y., & Hylan, L. (1994). Three strikes: The unintended victims. San Francisco, CA: Center on Juvenile and Criminal Justice.

Smith, A. L. (1997, Spring). Fixed sentencing a failed policy. *ACRIM Newsletter.*

Snyder, H. N., Sickmund, M., & Poe-Yamagata, E. (1996). *Juvenile offenders and victims: 1996 update on violence (statistics summary).* Washington, DC: National Center for Juvenile Justice, Office of Juvenile Justice and Delinquency Prevention.

Trask, G. II. (1996). *California task force to review juvenile crime and the juvenile justice system response.* Sacramento, CA: Author.

Cases

Davis v. *Davis,* 601 F.2d 153 (4th Cir. 1979) (en banc).

Harmelin v. *Michigan,* 501 U.S. 957 (1991).

People v. *Alvarez,* 60 Cal. Rptr. 2d 93 (1997).

San Diego Co. v. *Romero,* S. Ct. S045097 (June 20, 1996).

Rummel v. *Estelle,* 568 F.2d 1193 (5th Cir. 1978).

Solem v. *Helm,* 463 U.S. 277 (1983).

Rejoinder to Dr. Sechrest ROBERT A. JERIN

Dale Sechrest states that the rationale for three strikes laws is defective and is detrimental to society, offenders, and to the criminal justice system. To validate this belief, he uses almost exclusively questionable data and examples from California, ignoring the valuable information found in the other twenty-three states that enacted new laws using the "three strikes" label. According to the National Institute of Justice, the vast majority of California "strikes" inmates have been sentenced under the two-strikes provision and for nonviolent crimes. When three-strikes was proposed and implemented throughout the country, it was intended to attack the violent, habitual offender, and it has succeeded.

Crime rates continue to plummet as states and the federal government take a hard line against habitual, violent offenders. Tougher new sentencing policies, such as three-strikes, better law enforcement, a growing economy, and crime prevention programs have reduced violent crime throughout this country to thirty-year lows. While the short-term benefits multiply, tougher sentencing policies such as three-strikes are establishing a foundation for long-term rewards.

Three-strikes laws are not cruel and unusual punishments against violent habitual offenders; however, the failure to remove these criminals from society is a cruel punishment inflicted on the innocent crime victims they will create. Justice does not suffer from three strikes laws; it flourishes. The elimination of potential victims of violence is one of the most important results of the three-strikes legislation. The protection of society from someone who has continually proved to have violated their social contract with the rest of community is the foundation of our laws and the cornerstone of our justice system. Professor Sechrest even laments that the number of trials may double: I ask, is this not a better opportunity for true justice than plea bargaining and back room deals?

Another area of concern expressed by the NO side is the impact on the prison systems. The most recent research from the National Institute of Justice, which examines all states that have enacted three-strikes legislation, finds that "early evidence shows that with the exception of California, most of the laws will have minimal impact on those States' prison systems because they were drafted to apply to only the most violent offenders. Only broadly defined two-strikes provisions like California's have the potential to drastically alter existing sentencing practices." Even Sechrest acknowledges the RAND assessment of California's three strikes legislation, which finds potential for reducing serious and violent crime. Little impact on the system, reduction in crime—these are the types of legislation the criminal justice system has been wanting for decades.

Since the enactment of three strikes, crime, especially violent crime, is going way down, and prisons and the criminal justice system are only minimally impacted. There are many less victims of violence, so the costs to the potential individuals and society are being reduced by an increase in the quality of life they have to look forward to. We know, as even Sechrest reports, that the evidence shows that serious habitual offenders can be controlled by three strikes, and with the addition of prevention programs, many less crime victims will have to suffer the injuries associated with criminal violence.

Can We Continue to Lock Up the Nonviolent Drug Offender?

Stanley W. Hodge argues YES. Recently returning to private practice, he served as Judge of the Superior Court of California beginning in 1990. Mr. Hodge has been active in the field of criminal law throughout his professional career and, in addition to his judgeship, has served as both a prosecutor and defense counsel. He has a Master of Arts in Political Science from the Ohio State University and a J.D. from the University of Southern California. He has been Adjunct Instructor in the Department of Criminal Justice at California State University, San Bernardino, and has provided numerous continuing education courses for attorneys.

Victor E. Kappeler argues NO. He is Professor of Police Studies and Director of Criminal Justice Programs in the College of Law Enforcement at Eastern Kentucky University of Richmond, KY. Dr. Kappeler is the editor of *Justice Quarterly* and has published several journal articles. He is the co-author of several books; two of the most recent titles on the topic debated here include *The Mythology of Crime and Criminal Justice* (1996) and *Constructing Crime: Perspective on Making News and Social Problems* (1998), both with Waveland Press.

YES

STANLEY W. HODGE

In this chapter, I argue that the answer to the question is a definite YES. The reasons for incarcerating these offenders are the traditional reasons for imprisoning any criminal. First, imprisonment will have a deterrent effect on those contemplating future drug involvement. Second, the state is affirming a moral proposition about illicit drugs by imposing custody time for these offenders. Those involved in drug trafficking must be given lengthy sentences as retribution for their crimes and to segregate them from the rest of society. Even drug abusers guilty of simple possession or use must be given some custodial time for these same reasons and to prevent them from committing other crimes. Lastly, varying amounts of incarceration are useful tools for attempting to rehabilitate drug abusers.

By the term "nonviolent drug offender," I mean any defendant who has not been arrested for an assaultive crime in his current prosecution. His offense can range from manufacturing or selling large quantities of drugs to simple possession. Finally, I do not contend that incarceration should be meted out to serve the paternalistic purpose of "saving them from themselves." These offenders must be given various terms of imprisonment because of the harm they do to *other* people.

The question of what to do about drug offenders is a problem confronting decision makers daily. The issue of who to incarcerate assumes a great deal of importance because custodial resources are limited. The issue is complicated by the fact that there are so many different drugs being consumed, each with its own pharmacological and behavioral consequences. Also, the degree and type of involvement of the individual violator varies greatly. Because these variables directly affect the propriety of incarcerating an individual, it is important to begin the discussion by setting forth the author's assumptions about incarceration in general.

One's position with regard to the incarceration of nonviolent drug offenders depends to a great degree on how the drug problem is perceived. The situation in the 1990s can only be described as a crisis. The dimensions of the drug situation are staggering. The Office of National Drug Control Policy estimates that in 1990 drug consumers in the United States spent $41 billion for illegal drugs (Bureau of Justice Statistics, 1992). A 1991 study found that 29 percent of high school seniors had used illicit drugs within the past year and that 12.6 million people had used them within the past month (National Institute on Drug Abuse, 1991).

The latest drug to gain widespread use is methamphetamine. The western states are currently experiencing of influx of "meth." A National Institute of Justice study found that 37.1 percent of arrestees in San Diego, California, tested positive for methamphetamine. In Phoenix, Arizona, 21.9 percent tested positive, and in Portland, Oregon, 18.7 percent (Fecht & Kyle, 1996). Methamphetamine's effects are similar to cocaine, but it is cheaper.

Large numbers of people spending a great deal of money on illegal drugs is only relevant to the criminal justice system if the usage results in harm to others. If all of these people are only hurting themselves, perhaps the state should approach drug use as a public health problem. The reality of the situation is, however, that drug manufacturers, dealers, and users do harm others. Their activity directly harms others in the form of other crimes being committed against persons and property. Additionally, children are neglected and abandoned in large numbers because of their parents' involvement with drugs.

Drugs and Crime

The relationship between drugs and crime has been the focus of many studies over the years. The evidence of the positive relationship between illicit drugs and crime is most persuasive. The 1995 Drug Use Forecasting Program (DUF) of the National Institute of Justice surveyed over 20,000 adult male arrestees at twenty-three sites in metropolitan areas in the United States and more than 8000 female arrestees at twenty-one of the sites. The study found that 31 percent of both male and female arrestees were under the influence of drugs or alcohol at the time of their alleged offense. Furthermore, 40 percent of men and 48 percent of women arrestees tested positive for cocaine (National Institute of Justice, 1996).

Earlier studies by the Drug Use Forecasting Program produced even more startling results. The 1990 DUF Program found that 60 percent or more of the males arrested for the property crimes of burglary, larceny, vehicle theft, and robbery were found to be positive for drug use, as were 50 percent of the females arrested for the same offenses (Bureau of Justice Statistics, 1992).

The sheer number of crimes committed by narcotics addicts indicates the strength of the drugs–crime relationship. A study of crime by heroin addicts in Miami, Florida (Inciardi, 1986), tallied the crimes of these addicts by "crime days." A "crime day" is defined as any day in which an addict committed a crime. The results were impressive. The mean number of "crime days" per addict per year from 1973 to 1978 were 255, 244, 259, 257, and 336, respectively. We can only conclude that most addicts commit a crime on most days! It was also learned that fewer than 1 percent of all offenses reported by addicts resulted in arrest and that narcotics abusers engaged in criminal activity for an average of two years before their first arrest. Finally, the number of "crime days" were drastically reduced during periods when the abusers were not actively addicted, dropping from 255 to 65 (Bureau of Justice Statistics, 1992).

Drug Use and Violence

We treat violent crimes more seriously than crimes against property. Inflicting pain and suffering or even death on others are obviously more deserving of punishment than a property crime. But what about the "nonviolent" drug offender? Should we assume that drug usage is a precursor to violence and take preemptive steps to punish him? The answer lies in the fact that there is a significant connection between violence and the use of the currently most popular drugs. The 1990 DUF found that 48 percent of men and 50 percent of women who committed an assault tested positive for drugs (Bureau of Justice Statistics, 1992). Furthermore, the relationship between amphetamine abuse and violence is quite clear. Observers of the caseload in any western court can attest to the violence caused by the paranoid thinking induced by amphetamine use. Over and above such anecdotal evidence are the results of scholarly research in this area. Researchers have confirmed the connection. One study (Ellinwood, 1971) found that amphetamine use led directly to the commission of the homicides studied. The reason: paranoid thought patterns and delusions induced by methamphetamine use. A subsequent study has confirmed that delusional paranoia and social isolation due to amphetamine use led to homicides (Asnis and Smith, 1978). Moreover, the use of amphetamines has been found to have produced a culture of violence among users (Smith, 1972).

The connection between drugs and crime and drugs and violence has been noted by the United States Supreme Court. In *Harmelin* v. *Michigan* (1991), the Court upheld a mandatory life without possibility of parole sentence for possession of 1.5 pounds of cocaine against a challenge that the severity of the term violated the Eighth Amendment proscription of cruel and unusual punishment. In his concurring opinion, Justice Kennedy wrote:

> Studies bear out these possibilities and demonstrate a direct nexus between illegal drugs and crimes of violence (See, generally id., at 16–48). To mention but a few examples, 57 percent of a national sample of males arrested in 1989 for homicide tested positive for illegal drugs (National Institute of Justice, 1989 Drug Use Forecasting Annual Report 9 [June, 1990]). The comparable statistics for assault, robbery and weapons arrests were 55, 73 and 63 percent, respectively. Ibid. In Detroit, Michigan, in 1988, 68 percent of a sample of male arrestees and 81 percent of a sample of female arrestees tested positive for illegal drugs (National Institute of Justice, 1988 Drug Use Forecasting Annual Report 4 [March, 1990]). Fifty-one percent of males and seventy-one percent of females tested positive for cocaine (id., at 7). And last year an estimated 60 percent of the homicides in Detroit were drug related, primarily cocaine related (U.S. Department of Health and Human Services, *Epidemiologic Trends in Drug Abuse 107* [December, 1990]).

Drug Use and the Children of the Users

In 1992, an estimated 221,000 American women who delivered live babies had used illicit drugs while they were pregnant. These women victimized their children even before birth. The phenomenon of "crack babies" suffering through withdrawal is well known. But other drugs also harm babies. Expectant mothers who use amphetamines cause a delay in fetal growth, low birth weight, and premature birth. More than half of the babies exposed to amphetamine in utero exhibited abnormal visual reflexes a year after birth (Dixon, 1989). Babies born to mothers who used PCP during pregnancy have gone through withdrawal and suffered birth defects (Golden, Kuhnert, & Sokol, 1984).

Children who have escaped from fetal drug abuse also suffer because of their parents' use. The disintegration of crack cocaine smokers' psychosocial functioning is predictable. The compulsion to smoke crack becomes more important than maintaining employment. It comes as no surprise to anyone that drug usage is harmful to the user—and to the user's family. Daily in courts around this country judges appoint relatives and friends of drug abusers to act as guardians of the users' children. Typically, the children have been dropped off by their parents to be cared for by others. Guardianships are then necessary so that the children can be cared for and protected while their parents are "on drugs." Worse, if no one is available to volunteer to provide care for these children, they are declared dependent children of the state and maintained at public expense. The extent of this phenomenon is demonstrated by the fact that a large number of women cocaine abusers do not adequately care for their children.

Incarceration of Nonviolent Drug Offenders

At the top of the drug trafficking pyramid sits the "big time" drug manufacturer and dealer. These are people who deal in quantities ranging from pounds to hundreds of pounds of illegal drugs. They do not engage in the trade to support their own habit, but to make money. And they make huge amounts of money. The answer to our question is easy regarding these nonviolent drug offenders—when apprehended and convicted they should be sentenced to *lengthy* prison terms. Severe sentences in these cases serve the purpose of general deterrence by providing an example to those who may be tempted to enter the drug trade. The sentence also punctuates the moral statement that wrecking untold numbers of lives is deplorable and calls for the severest of punishments. The retributive function of sentencing is also served. The general public can see that the scales of justice are somewhat balanced by an onerous prison sentence.

State legislatures have created gradations of punishment in recognition of the fact that traffickers in more substantial amounts of illicit drugs deserve more severe punishment. In California, for example, the punishment for cocaine trafficking increases as the amount involved increases. Imprisonment starts at a four-year maximum and is increased until twenty-five years are added for dealing in 80 kilograms or more (*California Health and Safety Code, § 11370.4*, 1992). Michigan has provided for a mandatory life sentence for possession of 1.5 pounds or more of cocaine.

Defendants punished under these statutes deserve every day that they get. They have earned them. All the suffering by drug users and their victims begins with these people. Retribution is in order. Also, these sentences are required if a deterrent effect is to be achieved. A moral message is also delivered: no one can create the level of human suffering caused by the illegal drug trade without paying dearly.

Like all commodities, drugs have to be transported to market. Typically the large manufacturer or distributer will hire someone (a mule) to transport the drug.

These "mules" are essential to the drug trade and when caught must be sentenced to a prison term. The reasons are essentially the same as for the "big time" people for whom he works. The example of his sentence serves to deter others. The moral point is again made. Even though others may take his place, for the terms of imprisonment *this* mule will be out of business. Importantly, this defendant deserves the retribution visited on him because of his participation in the misery trade.

The next step down the drug trafficking structure is the user–dealer. This offender is likely to have a drug habit of his own and sells small amounts to help support his own habit. The type of sentence that should be given in these cases depends largely on the personal circumstances of the defendant. No one wants to impose a prison sentence on these defendants until efforts at rehabilitation have been made. If he or she has no criminal record, it is likely that probation will be granted. In the event that probation is granted, incarceration will be limited to some moderate amount of time in a local jail as a condition of probation. This sentence serves a general deterrent function. More important in these cases is the effect of jail time on the individual, that is, the specific deterrent effect. The probationary term should be imposed to dissuade the defendant from reentering the trade on release. Also, in the case of the probationary, sentence, the custodial experience, along with other terms of probation, serves to aid in the rehabilitation of the offender. It is important to let the probationer know that there is a serious downside to reoffending.

If a prison sentence becomes necessary for this offender, it need not be as long as those of the more substantial traffickers discussed above. Nevertheless, rehabilitative efforts having failed, a prison sentence must be imposed for retributive and general deterrence purposes. Here too, this defendant will be out of circulation for a time. He or she will not be dealing drugs or stealing while locked up.

The nonselling drug abuser is at the bottom of the drug trafficking pyramid. He or she is the ultimate consumer of the product. Assuming that no diversionary program is available, this person is entirely likely to be granted probation. Imposition of some custodial time is essential for this defendant. The goal of a probationary sentence is to rehabilitate the offender. The substances currently in vogue are *extremely* addictive. The brain yearns for the euphoria that drug consumption brings. If this offender is to be dissuaded from further use, we must impose sufficient discomfort initially to prevent relapse. Otherwise, all the other efforts to rehabilitate will be futile. Here, too, jail time simply must be imposed.

Conclusion

The United States is experiencing a drug crisis. Trafficking in, and the use of, illegal drugs produce crime and violence. The children of users are the immediate victims of parent's drug use. The criminal justice system cannot ignore the fact that innocent people are being victimized. Incarcerating nonviolent drug offenders affirms society's moral disapproval of drug involvement and its correlative criminal behavior. Incarceration also serves the purposes of retribution, segregation, deterrence, and rehabilitation.

We can, and indeed, we must continue to incarcerate the nonviolent drug offender.

References

Asnis, S., & Smith, R. (1978). Amphetamine abuse and violence. *Journal of Psychedelic Drugs, 10,* 317–377.

Bureau of Justice Statistics. (1992). *Drugs, crime and the justice system.* Washington, DC: United States Department of Justice.

Dixon, S. (1989). Effects of transplacental exposure to cocaine and methamphetamine on the neonate. *Western Journal of Medicine, 150* (4), 436–442.

Ellinwood, E. (1971). Assault and homicide associated with amphetamine abuse. *American Journal of Psychiatry, 127,* 90–95.

Fecht, T. E., & Kyle, G. M. (1996). *Methamphetamine use among adult arrestees: Findings from the drug use forecasting (DUF) program.* Washington, DC: National Institute of Justice.

Golden, N., Kuhnert, B., & Sokol, R. J. (1984). Phencyclidine use during pregnancy. *American Journal of Obstetrics and Gynecology, 148* (3), 254–259.

Inciardi, J. A. (1986). *The war on drugs: Heroin, cocaine and public policy.* Palo Alto, CA: Mayfield.

National Institute of Justice. (1996, June). *1995 drug use forecasting.* Washington, DC: Author.

National Institute on Drug Abuse. (1991). *National household survey on drug abuse: Population estimates.* Washington, DC: Author.

State of California. (1992). *California Health and Safety Code, Section 11370.4.*

Smith, R. (1972). Speed and violence: Compulsive methamphetamine abuse and criminality in the Haight-Ashbury. In C. Zarfonetis (Ed.), *Proceedings of the International Conference.* Philadelphia: Lee & Febiger.

Cases

Harmelin v. *Michigan.* (1991) 501 U.S. 957.

Rejoinder to Mr. Hodge
Victor E. Kappeler

Mr. Hodge raises several issues in taking the position that we continue incarcerating nonviolent drug offenders. There seem to be three general themes running through his position. He argues that incarceration serves several basic functions and should be used because the use of controlled substances have harmful effects on users and innocent others and because there is a causal link between drug use and crime. These assertions are less than convincing, and volumes of research and literature have addressed these assertions in detail. I will briefly touch on the rationalizations for punishment as they concern drug users.

Four of the rationalizations Mr. Hodge uses for punishing nonviolent drug offenders have been subjected to scientific scrutiny for decades. The assertion that incarceration serves a deterrent function, either general or specific, is unimpressive. One need only look at the research on the death penalty to find that punishment, even in this extreme form, has no general deterrent effect on crime. Some research even suggests that the use of the death penalty results in higher rates of violence. It is therefore an inappropriate inference to argue that incarceration, a lesser form of punishment, has a general deterrent effect on lesser crimes such as drug use. If this were the case, we would incarcerate ourselves right out of the so-called drug crisis. The specific effect of deterrence is even more suspect when one considers that drug offenders have very high recidivism rates. Drug offenders are among those people incarcerated that are most likely to repeat their crimes once they leave the correctional setting. These observations lead to some logical inferences about rehabilitation. If prisons and jails rehabilitate and deter drug offenders, then we would expect to find low rates of recidivism among these offenders.

This is simply not the case. Compounding the inadequacy of the argument is the observation that few scholars familiar with the research on correctional rehabilitation would even attempt to argue that prisons attempt rehabilitation. Scholars and researchers alike are quite clear on this topic. Today, the American correctional system warehouses, but does not rehabilitate, offenders. This practice of warehousing is referred to by Mr. Hodge as *segregation,* but researchers more often use the term *incapacitation.* Proponents of incapacitation argue that incarceration should be used to protect society from criminality. There are many complex problems associated with this argument (including how to predict who will be dangerous in the future), but two simple observations undermine the credibility of this rationalization for punishment. First, about 97 percent of the people incarcerated in our correctional system will one day be released from prison, and most will continue their criminality. Second, just because people are incarcerated does not mean they stop engaging in crime. One of the most frequent crimes in prison is drug use, not to mention victimization of inmates and correctional officers. Existing research quickly dispatches these basic radicalizations for punishment.

These remarks leave us with the final two radicalizations for punishment—moral education and retribution. In a novel undertaking, Mr. Hedge argues that, "When a crime is committed the values society holds most dear have been compromised." By punishing offenders he continues "...courts are reaffirming the importance of society's moral judgments." His own observations on drug use undermine this argument. If we are experiencing what he calls a "drug crisis," and millions of Americans are consuming drugs, then whose values are we affirming? Society is composed of all its members, including the millions of drug users who cross all social and demographic characteristics. Further weakening the argument are pragmatic considerations.

Prisons do not educate, save for the values and techniques conducive to further criminality. Even if the moral education argument could be made, it is quite an expensive proposition. The cost of incarceration is not much lower than the cost of an ivy league education. Might there be better places for moral education and reaffirming moral judgment than the courthouse or the big house? These observations leave us with retribution as the sole rationalization for punishing nonviolent drug offenders. One can hardly use research to refute the moral assertion that we should abandon logic and allow those who have the power to punish inflict harm for harms sake alone. The radicalizations and arguments used to support the retribution position, however, rest on two myths that make the idea of retribution socially acceptable: *drugs cause extreme social harm* and *drugs cause violent crime.* Let me be clear about the these two assertions. The best available research indicates that drugs *do not* cause the level of personal and vicarious harm necessary to rationalize incarceration, and drugs *do not* cause violent crime. To continue to incarcerate nonviolent drug offenders seems, at best, misguided.

NO

Victor E. Kappeler

The question "Can we continue to incarcerate nonviolent drug offenders?" is enmeshed with a number of assumptions about the desirability, utility, and forms of punishment a civilized society should employ in an attempt to gain control over undesirable behavior. Before one can begin to answer the question, it is necessary to come to terms with the assumptions and meanings embedded within the question. Because of the highly politicized nature of the drug war and the labels ascribed to people associated with this problem, the characterization of someone as a drug user is to assign them a master status that carries with it a multitude of constructed images and meanings.

When the term *drug offender* is invoked, we automatically conjure up images of those who abuse controlled substances rather than those who abuse legal substances. In like fashion, the mind also calls up very selective images of highly stylized media depictions. More often than not, the image we see when we think of the "drug offender" is the IV drug abuser shaking in a corner or perhaps the cocaine addict scrambling behind a toilet to retrieve a dropped vial. We seldom think of the Supreme Court nominee, banker, lawyer, or college professor who smokes marijuana or uses powder cocaine at a party well beyond the reach of law enforcement. Images such as the former carry with them a variety of presuppositions about the people who use drugs, their motivations and behaviors, and the threat they present to society. The individuality of drug use is lost in the political, media, and policy constructions of the "drug offender."

One serious problem in the policy debate of whether to continue to incarcerate nonviolent drug offenders is the failure to demonstrate the question into its various parts. In the construction of social problems, the labeling of similar but conceptually distinctive behaviors into an aggregate allows for distortion and stereotyping, which allows for the emergence of social problems and often formal legal responses (Kappeler, Blumberg, & Potter, 1996). We must be careful to demonstrate the meaning of terms and phrases that have become household words aggregated into what is commonly referred to as "the drug problem."

The drug problem is composed of numerous behaviors by a variety of actors as well as a number of policy descriptors that have become associated with the policy debate. There are, for example, distinctions between the host of actors involved in the drug problem; two obvious distinctions are between drug users and drug traffickers, recreational users and addicts.

Likewise, there is a need to delineate the language that encircles the complex relationships between drugs, crime, and other social issues. Drug use, alone, does not cause the hysteria necessary to invoke a criminal justice response. In the social construction of problems, it is seldom sufficient to rely on a single well-defined behavior to invoke a formal and often violent social response. To motivate a formal response, such as incarceration, the behavior under consideration must be extended to other social issues and become defined as threat to a significant segment of the population (Kappeler, Blumberg, & Potter, 1996). This requires that the construction of the drug problem be linked to other social issues that are more likely to impact a large audience. This is the case with drug use and the debate surrounding the relationship between drugs and other social issues. In the drug debate, drug use has been rhetorically linked to worker's productivity, workplace violence, high school dropout rates, violent and property crime, violence against women, and just about any other contemporary social concern. This, of course, is done with very little empirical evidence, and even existing evidence often fails to make clear definitional distinctions.

There are differences between, for example, drug users and drug offenders, drug-related crime and drug-induced crime, as well as a clear distinction between the types of drug users and the variety of behaviors that make up crime. The term *drug-related,* a popular policy term, is a poor descriptor and is misleading in that it makes no distinction between crimes caused by the psychotropic experience of using some drugs and crimes caused by the prohibition of drug use itself. In this distinction, we often focus on the drug-crazed killer or in similar simplicity the "turf wars" associated with drug trafficking. Yet, we often fail to consider crime related to drug policy. The violent acts of law enforcement officers who are waging war on drugs, the extortion, bribery, and corruption of public officials generated by illegality and sale of poisonous drugs because of a lack of regulation are all forms of criminality related to drug policy. Seldom are long terms of incarceration the justice system's response to drug policy crimes.

Our simple construction of the drug user also fails to acknowledge that many crimes committed by drug users have nothing to do with drug use. Most research on drug users and crime finds that drug users are no more criminal than ourselves or were engaged in criminality long before the onset of drug use (Beirne & Messerschmidt, 1991; Goode, 1984). It is interesting that researchers have had to focus on heroin users in an attempt to advance the drug–crime connection rather than studying marijuana users. For that matter, about 97 percent of Americans, including both drug and non–drug users, have engaged in behaviors for which an incarceration could have been the consequence had it been detected (Bohm, 1986).

In our construction of the drug user, we also have a tendency to focus exclusively on illegal drugs and their harm. The debate on the harmfulness of drug use to the individual drug user, however, is beyond the scope of the essay save to say that there is considerable evidence that the real harm associated with the use of controlled substances pales in comparison to the harm caused by abusing legal drugs. Alcohol and tobacco cause approximately 400,000 deaths per year, whereas all illegal drugs combined only cause about 3,500 deaths a year (Nadelmann, 1989; Kappeler et al., 1996). This makes the harm from abuse of legal drugs well over one hundred times greater than the harm from controlled substances.

The simple distinction between violent and nonviolent drug users further clouds the debate on appropriate social response to the issue. For example, many nonviolent drug users engage in criminal activity, and many violent drug users are not engaged in the forms of property crime sometimes associated with nonviolent drug use. These distinctions have become blurred and intentionally aggregated to constitute the drug problem and forge its relationship to the "crime problem." Public policy has flowed from these and other socially constructed conceptions of drug users.

To adequately answer the incarceration question, one must be mindful of these distinctions and their effects on our constructions of the harmful aspects of drug use and the effects they have on drug control policies themselves. Constructions of this nature sanitize the effects of using the criminal justice system as a response to this social issue.

Now, if we are considering the incarceration of people who are nonviolent recreational illegal drug users, those who come to the attention of the criminal justice system, we can begin to answer the question of whether a formal criminal justice response to their behavior is warranted or should continue. It is necessary, however, to first consider just what we have been doing and what we are advocating to continue.

Making and Responding to Drug Offenders

A simple fact of the drug debate is that our drug policies make drug offenders in highly selective fashion. About 22.6 million people use controlled substances every year, and about 77 million people have used illegal drugs over the course of their life time (SAMHSA, 1993). These, of course, are conservative figures, because the desirability of reporting oneself as a drug user has certainly diminished over the last two decades. Illegal drug use crosses all ages, races, and ethnic boundaries. Yet, the drug war has been blatantly racist. About half of all arrests for drug offenses are African Americans (Walker, 1994), although African Americans make up only 14 percent of all drug users and National Institute on Drug Abuse data show the prevalence of drug use is almost identical among whites and African Americans (Walker, 1994). In fact, Randolph Stone states: "All reports indicate that the percentage of illegal drug use is the same among racial groups. But the drug problem among blacks and Hispanics is dealt with in the criminal justice system. Among whites, it's dealt with largely as a health problem" (Marx, 1995, p. 2).

Consider cocaine: crack is predominately found in the inner city, powder cocaine in middle- and upper-class suburbs. Three of five powder offenders are white; nine of ten crack offenders are African American or Hispanic (Editorial, 1995). As Nkechi Taifa of the ACLU states, the law "punishes poor people and people of color more heavily" (Smolowe, 1995, p. 45). The U.S. Sentencing Commission affirmed the uneven treatment: 88.3 percent of federal crack distribution convictions were for black defendants; only 27.4 percent of cocaine convictions. The average crack prison sentences are three to eight times longer than powder cocaine sentences. The Commission stated, "Issues of fairness or just punishment result when relatively low-level crack retailers receive higher sentences than the wholesale-level cocaine dealer from whom the crack seller originally purchased the powder to make the crack" (Smolowe, 1995, p. 45). The disparity in sentencing resulted from the drug panic of 1986, when crack sales spread rapidly through urban areas. Janet Reno opposed changes in the guidelines: "I strongly oppose measures that fail to reflect the harsh and terrible impact of crack on communities across America" (Smolowe, 1995, p. 45). Perhaps, the Attorney General should look at the harsh and terrible impact of currently mandated sentencing.

In 1982, prisoners serving time for drug convictions were about 22 percent of the federal inmate population. Today, because of mandatory sentences, that percentage has increased to well over 61 percent. One-third of federal prisoners are nonviolent, low-level offenders with no criminal record. Drug inmates typically serve longer federal sentences than those convicted of sex offenses or manslaughter.

The American experience at the state level is not much better. In two decades, the total number of inmates held in prison and jail facilities has quadrupled.

In the last decade, the number of incarcerated drug offenders rose 510 percent. In 1990, when the number of individuals incarcerated in U.S. jails and prison facilities reached 1.1 million, the cost of incarcerating these individuals was approximately $20.3 billion. In the last decade, the percentage of drug offenders incarcerated in state prisons rose from 7 percent of the prison population to over 22.5 percent.

These increases in the American prison population need to be understood in the context of the overall prison population and crime. In 1992, for example, new court commitments for drug offenses were about 102,000; this is an increase from about 8,900 in just 12 years. During this time, the number of people incarcerated for drug offenses was almost as large as the number incarcerated for property offenses and far greater than that of violent and disorder offenses. Over thirty percent of new court commitments in 1992 were drug offenders, up from 6.8 percent just 12 years before. Overall, the increase in the incarceration rate of drug offenders accounted for about 46 percent of the total growth in new court commitments since 1980. Our current imprisonment binge is squarely on the backs of drug offenders, and if these trends continue, the United States will have built more prisons in the last twenty years of the century than it had the previous 200 years.

The Consequences of Incarceration

Incarceration in our society has always been and remains a harsh and painful experience. Make no mistake, incarceration is violence rationalized by the philosophies of punishment. In recent decades, the experience has become even more unpleasant. Nonetheless, legislators and the public continue to seek ways to further increase the level of discomfort under the rhetoric of penal harm. Whether this entails reinstating "chain-gangs" or placing drug offenders in boot camps, the motivation is similar: incarceration is punishment. Most correctional authorities and inmates have long understood: doing time in America's prisons is not now and never has been easy. Each year, about $22 billion dollars is spent operating the nation's prisons. When drug offenders are incarcerated, we are paying about $18,000 a year to hold each one of them, and we are inflicting violence on them.

Drug use is a social problem that is constructed in such a manner to make the criminal justice system seem a viable solution. The simple matter is that the formal punishment does not always fit the crime, deterrence is not a rational basis for the incarceration of drug users. Perhaps most importantly, the people who use drugs and are swept into the correctional system are not all equally reprehensible drug users. Some are innocent, some are old and harmless, some are unfortunate, and some are, in fact, incorrigible. Anyone who has ever driven after drinking more than the legal limit, shoplifted, or taken something of value from work could all find themselves in our correctional system. Rather than ignoring (or denying) possible similarities between "us" and "them" by segregating the offenders in prisons and increasing their distance from us, perhaps we should take another look at what we want the correctional system to accomplish. The more we understand the behavior that offends and attempt to look at the offender rather than resorting to predetermined stereotypes, the better the chances of reaching rational alternatives to prisons that offer no programs, no opportunities, and no hope.

REFERENCES

Beirne, P., & Messerschmidt, J. (1991). *Criminology.* New York: Harcourt Brace Jovanovich.

Bohm, R. (1986). Crime, criminals, and crime control policy myths. *Justice Quarterly, 3* (2), 193–214.

Editorial. (1995, March 30). The elusive logic of drug sentences. *Chicago Tribune,* Sec. 1, 20.

Goode, E. (1984). *Drugs in American society.* New York: Alfred A. Knopf.

Kappeler, V. E., Blumberg, M., & Potter, G. W. (1996). *The mythology of crime and criminal justice* (2nd ed.). Prospect Heights, IL: Waveland.

Marx, G. (1995, April 27). Swift Justice. *Chicago Tribune,* Sec. 5, pp. 1–2.

Nadelmann, E. (1989, September). Drug prohibition in the United States: Costs, consequences and alternatives. *Science, 245,* pp. 939–947.

SAMHSA. (1993). *National household survey on drug abuse.* Washington, DC: Department of Health & Human Services.

Smolowe, J. (1995, June 19). One drug, two sentences. *Time,* p. 45.

Walker, S. (1994). *Sense and nonsense about crime and drugs* (2nd ed.). Belmont, CA: Wadsworth.

Rejoinder to Dr. Kappeler

STANLEY W. HODGE

Dr. Kappeler, while not specifically addressing the points made in my initial essay, has raised several objections to antidrug efforts. I will address a few of his arguments. He does not successfully challenge the position that incarceration should continue to be used with regard to nonviolent drug offenders.

He objects that antidrug efforts are premised on misconceptions about who drug users are. Drug users are doctors, business people, lawyers, cops, truck drivers, and housewives. They are also young people—some starting as young as grammar school. Virtually anyone is eligible to be destroyed by illegal drugs. The impetus to use incarceration as a tool in the antidrug effort does not come from hysteria about figures from the fringes of society lurking in the shadows. It does not stem from any artificial "construction" of the problem. The response with punitive sanctions is just that, a response. Public officials have been presented with a problem of enormous proportions. Recall that the use of many of those drugs leads to depression, paranoia, and hallucinations. Violence results. Additional crime of all kinds results. The human carnage caused by drug trafficking and use has produced the response that includes incarceration, not any mistaken "construction" of the drug problem.

He also asserts that, regarding drug offenders, "punishment does not always fit the crime" and that not all users punished are "equally reprehensible drug users." Merely to state these propositions demonstrates their truth. They are truisms. As I made clear in my opening piece, not all drug offenders should be treated alike. Their ages, records, and degree of involvement differ. As I pointed out earlier, the severity of the response should also differ. An eighteen-year-old first offender caught with a small amount of cocaine should not be treated similarly to the sophisticated dealer transporting kilos of cocaine. Moreover, they are not in fact treated alike. The legal system employs probation, counseling, and some incarceration with the former and incarceration with the latter. We have the tools available to us to make the punishment fit the crime according to how "reprehensible" the particular offender is. It is up to prosecutors, probation officers, judges, and defense lawyers to make sure it is done right!

The charge that efforts to combat illegal drugs are "racist" must be taken seriously. Are minority groups being singled out by the government for disparate treatment? No. The United States Sentencing Commission recently released data regarding the ethnic background of drug trafficking defendants. The results are enlightening. Indeed, 88.3 percent of traffickers dealing in crack cocaine are black. Only 2.9 percent of such defendants are white and 4.6 percent Hispanic. Conversely, 84.2 percent of defendants trafficking in methamphetamine were white and only 1.5 percent black. Interestingly, 48.8 percent of heroin traffickers were Hispanic and 48.2 percent of marijuana traffickers were white. The implications of these data are clear: different illegal drugs are currently popular among different ethnic groups. Also, the abuse of some drugs is regional in nature. Methamphetamine use is predominately a problem in the western states.

The proportion of any ethnic group prosecuted for a particular drug offense is not the result of racism. It is the product of use in that particular community. It would be unconscionable to abandon any community to the drug traffickers. Those inflicting drug-related suffering on blacks, Hispanics, or whites must be opposed.

The judicial system is intolerant of criminal defendants being treated in a disparate fashion on the basis of race. In fact, if a defendant can show that he or she has been prosecuted for an offense while others have not been prosecuted because of his or her race, his case must be dismissed. To make a colorable claim of discriminatory prosecution, a defendant must show that similarly situated individuals of a different race were not prosecuted. Anyone alleging that enforcement of drug laws is "racist" is obliged to present evidence that race is the criterion used to treat defendants in a disparate fashion. That demonstration has not been made.

The problems created by the trafficking and use of illegal drugs call for an energetic response. Incarceration is a tool that must be a part of that response.

Is Incarceration an Appropriate Sanction for the Nonviolent White-Collar Offender?

Arguing YES is Gilbert Geis. He is Professor Emeritus, Department of Criminology, Law and Society, University of California, Irvine. A past-president of the American Society of Criminology and recipient of its Edwin H. Sutherland award for research, he has also received research awards from the Association of Certified Fraud Examiners, the Western Society of Criminology, the American Justice Institute, and the National Organization for Victim Assistance. Dr. Geis has edited three editions of *White Collar Crime* (the third with Robert Meier & Larry Salinger) and (with Ezra Stotland) a collection of original articles on the subject.

Michael B. Blankenship argues NO. He is Associate Professor and Chair of the Department of Criminal Justice and Criminology at East Tennessee State University. He has previously published an edited volume entitled *Understanding Corporate Criminality* (Garland, 1993) and a coauthored article on media coverage of violent white-collar crime (*Crime & Delinquency,* 1995). His current research focuses on juror comprehension of sentencing instructions in capital cases.

YES

GILBERT GEIS

Let's first convert the general issue into illustrative specifics. Consider these cases:

> Robert Vesco acquired control of a Swiss-based complex of mutual funds known as Investors Overseas Services. He siphoned off $224 million from the company and placed the money in banks that he controlled in Luxem-

bourg and the Bahamas. When the SEC began to investigate him, Vesco filled an attache case with $200,000 in $100 bills and covertly donated the money to President Nixon's reelection campaign. Later, Vesco fled the country, making investments in places such as Costa Rica to buy his way out of extradition to the United States (Dorman, 1975).

Ivan Boesky, a leading Wall Street arbitrage deal-maker, often traded on the basis of illegally acquired insider information. Boesky made huge profits on tips from Dennis Levine, a highly placed merger and acquisitions specialist with the Wall Street firm of Drexel Burnham Lambert. In one deal, Levine told Boesky of the prospective takeover of Houston Natural Gas. The day before the takeover, Boesky purchased 301,800 shares of Houston. He sold the shares two weeks later at a $4.1 million profit. Boesky was sentenced to three years in prison and fined $100 million. The relatively light sentence was a payback to Boesky for having told federal authorities about the involvement of others in insider trading deals (Stevens, 1987).

Jim Bakker, an evangelist, used his television program to solicit donations, allegedly to support missionaries and other church-related causes. But much of the money sent to him went for the huge salaries that Bakker and his wife paid themselves (about $2.5 million a year), for fancy cars, several mansions, a houseboat, and luxurious trips. Television viewers were persuaded to donate millions with the assurance that the money would entitle them to annual stays at Heritage USA, a Christian resort and amusement park under construction in South Carolina. Tens of thousands more partnerships were sold in Heritage USA than could possibly be accommodated by the facilities. Bakker was convicted on twenty-four fraud and conspiracy charges, sentenced to forty-five years in prison (later reduced significantly), and given a $500,00 fine (Friedrichs, 1996).

Lest these seem overly high-profile examples, let's add to the roster two of the thousands of more routine white-collar crimes:

Milton Zitin of Bala-Cynwid, Pennsylvania, was convicted of mislabeling hundreds of hams that were injected with water beyond the limit permitted by law. For fifteen years, he sold his product nationally to delicatessens, which used it for lunch meat. Zitin was sentenced to six months in prison, a leniency granted because he cooperated with the prosecutor. He also was ordered to pay $1.5 million in fines.

A New Jersey dermatologist pled guilty to a twenty-count indictment for Medicaid fraud. He was ordered to repay the state $60,000 in addition to a $30,500 fine. The judge sentenced the doctor to twenty years in prison but suspended the term in favor of two days per week free service at a hospital.

The state Medical Licensing Board took a firmer stand, revoking the doctor's license. The Board maintained that his behavior shook the confidence of the public in the Medicaid system and created "a gap between this individual's conduct and that which the public has a right to expect from a physician" (Jesilow, Pontell, & Geis, 1993, p. 129).

I carry no brief in favor of prisons, but if we are going to imprison street offenders, such as burglars and auto thieves, it seems to me that we clearly ought to treat upper-echelon criminals, such as those portrayed in the earlier paragraphs, in the same manner. Are white-collar criminals to be exempted from the fate accorded less powerful persons because they dress and talk better and otherwise play a respectable role in the community? Clearly, they exact a much greater financial toll on the community than the more traditional kinds of criminals.

Why Should White-Collar Offenders Be Privileged?

As it is, well-heeled white-collar offenders are notably difficult to catch at their dirty work. They avoid being implicated in illegal acts by tactics that create a paper trail that is very difficult to follow to their desk. Underlings in the corporation commit the crimes; those in control shelter themselves against traceable evidence. And, as Kenneth Mann (1985) has thoroughly documented, high-powered defense attorneys (who invariably presume, almost invariably correctly, that their clients are guilty) are marvelously successful in derailing prosecutions before any information about their clients becomes public.

Obviously, well-off suburban white-collar crooks would not escape prison if they committed the kinds of nonviolent crimes that lead to a penitentiary term for working-class folk. But their social and economic position affords them the opportunity to engage in more elegant types of deceit. Who would not prefer to embezzle from a bank rather than to come in off the street and hold up the tellers with a machine gun? For one thing, the street offender will usually be easily identifiable and will face the considerable risk of being shot. Embezzlement is so much more genteel. Should the fact that the lower-class offenders are not in a position to engage in such things as antitrust violations and savings and loan depredations lead to their imprisonment and provide immunity from incarceration for those who have so much more and are able to steal so much more adroitly?

Justice and Equity

The basic issue is justice and equity. Is it fair that a person who steals a television set should do prison time while a person who bilks the government out of millions walks away with a fine or a community service sentence? There is enough injustice already in our country, where important aspects of existence are mediated by money: the least we can do is to try to minimize such inequity. The rich get better medical care, superior educations, and overwhelmingly live much more satisfying lives. And things are getting better for them as they use what they have—the power—to get more. Twenty years ago, for instance, corporate CEOs earned on the average forty times more than the median salary of their employees; today that figure has soared to 200 times. Similarly, of the several thousand persons earning more than a million dollars annually, some 20 percent of them have figured out how to pay no income tax whatsoever. At the very least, the wealthy white-collar person ought to be inhibited from using illegal means to gain further advantages over those less well situated by the prospect of being placed in prison if he or she does so.

Second, white-collar criminals probably are more threatening to the integrity of the society than run-of-the-mill traditional kinds of offenders. A street crime can serve to unite "good" citizens in condemning the offenders and what they have done and can serve to reinforce allegiance to conformity among the law-abiding. A white-collar offense tends to shred the fabric of social life. If those who have so much defy the law to get more, faith in the integrity of the social system is undermined.

It was for this reason that Jonathan Swift located a sensible custom in a land visited by Gulliver:

> The Lilliputians look upon fraud as a greater crime than theft, and therefore seldom fail to punish it with death, for they allege that care and vigilance, with a very common understanding, may preserve a man's goods from theft, but honesty has no defense against superior cunning (Swift, 1735/1785: pt. 1, ch. 6).

Third, there is the matter of *noblesse oblige*. Those who are fortunate enough to have more than others should have a correspondingly greater responsibility to live a law-abiding life. It is one thing for a ghetto minority youngster without wheels to steal an automobile; quite another for a physician with a fleet of elegant sports car and a $420,000 annual income to violate the medical insurance statutes to get enough money to upgrade his speedboat model. The society has a perfect right to demand more of its favored citizens and, not getting it, to at least see that those favored citizens suffer some significant consequences.

Specific and General Deterrence

The issue of specific and general deterrence is the fourth major consideration that dictates imprisoning white-collar offenders who commit financial offenses. People in high places are much more sensitive to the loss of prestige associated with being a guest of the government in a state or federal prison. Therefore, to the extent that they perceive that they are likely to be treated in this manner (as evidenced by the fact that others like them are so treated) they are more likely than street offenders to arrange their behavior in accord with the requirements of the criminal law.

Take the example of Oliver North. North tried to talk his way out of charges that he had illegally sold arms to Iran and earmarked the profits for the insurgents in Nicaragua. He granted, with some pride, that he had assumed that he would be the "fall guy," taking the "hit" for the operation if it unraveled. His explanation for why he had changed his mind and now was determined to tell his side of the story is instructive:

> I never in my wildest dreams or nightmares envisioned that we would end up with criminal charges," North told a Congressional investigating committee. "It was beyond my wildest comprehension." When North learned that his dutiful silence and his shredding of crucial evidence to protect his superiors might result in criminal charges, "my mind set changed considerably" (*Taking Sides*, 1987, pp. 207; 337).

Note also the remarks of a high officer of the Westinghouse corporation who had engaged in a blatant antitrust conspiracy, meeting with competitors to arrange prices on submitted bids for multi-million dollar contracts. This was the dialogue between the onetime executive and the U.S. Senate committee attorney questioning him:

> COMMITTEE ATTORNEY: Did you know that these meetings with competitors were illegal?
>
> WITNESS: Illegal? Yes, but not criminal. I didn't find that out until I read the indictment.... I assumed that criminal action meant damaging someone, and we did not do that.... I thought we were more or less working on a survival basis in order to make enough to keep our plant and employees (Conklin, 1977).

In addition, as John Braithwaite and I (1982) have pointed out, prison often is a training school that inculcates and sharpens the illegal talents of street offenders. But the skills of crooked accountants and other white-collar violators will become increasingly out of date as they languish behind bars.

Consequences of Imprisonment

Prison is much more likely to have a worthwhile effect on those who are unused to it than those who tend to be more adaptable to conditions of incarceration. Consider the extraordinary case of Charles W. Colson, a onetime special assistant to President Nixon. Colson was described by Herbert Klein, Nixon's intimate friend, as "one of the meanest people I ever knew." Caught up in the Watergate scandal, Colson negotiated a guilty plea to one count of obstruction of justice. He received a one-to-three-year prison sentence and was fined $5,000.

During his time as an inmate, Colson formed the Prison Fellowship, which sought to change the lives of convicts. He was so successful that two decades after his release he was awarded the Templeton Prize for Progress in Religion, an honor that carried a stipend of more than $1 million. "I see how God has used my life," Colson said when he got the award. "Sometimes the greatest adversities turn out to be the greatest blessings" (Colson, 1979). Similar blessings, hopefully with equally positive outcomes, ought to be imposed on all deserving white-collar offenders.

Note too that among the most impressive sources of information that we acquire on the deplorable state of our prisons are the writings of the articulate elite offenders who are compelled to serve time in them. In the past year, for instance, two books have offered highly critical portraits of what goes on in America's penal institutions. Sol Wachtler, a former chief judge of the New York State Court of Appeals, was sentenced to federal prison for attempting to extort money from a woman who had jilted him. On release, Wachtler told of his experiences and warned the public that "if the prisoner is made to feel like garbage when he is prison he will for certain not like garbage when he is released" (Wachtler, 1997, p. 114). He argued that sentences were too long, the mandatory sentencing guidelines a disaster, that offenders were being warehoused without hope of treatment, and that drug penalties were draconian.

A Massachusetts state senator from 1972 to 1975, Joseph Timilty spent four months in the Schuylkill Federal Prison after being convicted of a real estate scam. In the epilogue of the book about Timilty's prison experiences, he and his co-author note that Timilty "learned that the prison system is corrupt, ineffectual and largely meaningless.... He learned that the system cries out for complicated, painful reform measures" (Timility & Thomas, 1997, p. 247).

If enough important people are realistically afraid that they might spend some time behind bars, they could lead a long-overdue campaign to see that prison conditions are upgraded. In addition, once inside, if there are enough of them, they might help to change for the better the horrendous conditions that mark so many penal facilities. Note that when they did a brief stint in a county jail, the General Electric executives were credited by its warden with upgrading the record-keeping system beyond his fondest hopes (Geis, 1967).

Imagine what Richard Nixon would have accomplished if he had been given the extended stay inside a federal prison that he so well deserved.

REFERENCES

Braithwaite, J., & Geis, G. (1982). On theory and action for corporate crime control. *Crime and Delinquency, 28,* 292–314.

Colson, C. W. (1979). *Life sentence.* Minneapolis: World Wide.

Conklin, J. E. (1977). *"Illegal but not criminal": Business crime in America*. Englewood Cliffs, NJ: Prentice-Hall.

Dorman, M. (1975). *Vesco: The infernal money-making machine*. New York: Berkeley Books.

Friedrichs, D. O. (1996). *Trusted criminals: White collar crime in contemporary society*. Belmont, CA: Wadsworth.

Geis, G. (1967). The heavy electrical equipment antitrust cases of 1961. In M. Clinard & R. Quinney (Eds.), *Criminal behavior systems: A typology* (pp. 139–151). New York: Holt, Rinehart & Winston.

Jesilow, P., Pontell, H. N., & Geis, G. (1993). *Prescription for profit: How doctors defraud Medicaid*. Berkeley: University of California Press.

Mann, K. (1985). *Defending white-collar crime: A portrait of attorneys at work*. New Haven: Yale University Press.

Stevens, M. (1987). *The insiders: The truth behind the scandal rocking Wall Street*. London: Harrap.

Swift, J. (1735/1787). *The adventures of Captain Gulliver: In a voyage to the islands of Lilliput and Brobdingnag*. London: P. Osborne & T. Griffin.

Taking Sides. (1987). New York: Pocket Books.

Timilty, J. & Thomas, J. (1997). *Prison journal: An irreverent look at life on the inside*. Boston: Northeastern University Press.

Wachtler, S. (1997). *After the madness: A judge's own prison memoir*. New York: Random House.

Rejoinder to Dr. Geis
MICHAEL B. BLANKENSHIP

Professor Geis captures perfectly the major similarity between our positions when he writes that "The basic issue is justice and equality." Hopefully, only a few sad cases with twisted morals would agree that a defendant's financial and social standing should dictate whether incarceration is an appropriate sanction. He chooses, however, to "balance the books" in a rather curious manner—instead of reforming our attitudes toward criminals and concomitant penal policies, he recommends that we should incarcerate nonviolent white-collar offenders with greater frequency to increase sentencing parity between conventional and white-collar criminals.

The same sort of argument is heard from proponents of capital punishment who are confronted with evidence of racial, gender, and class disparity in meting out death sentences. Assuming that these extralegal differences exist (and the current crop of pseudo-conservatives rarely admit to such despite the empirical evidence to the contrary), the way to address any imbalance between the number of people of color who are sentenced to death or are executed is to make sure that a similar number of whites receive a similar fate. Because only one woman has been executed since 1977, while more than 400 men have been killed by the states, the obvious solution is to kill more women!

Obviously, this response falls far short of addressing why the racial and gender imbalances exist in the first place, nor does it ameliorate the injustice of allowing extralegal factors to influence sentencing outcomes. The same reasoning can be applied to the sentencing disparities that exist between conventional and white-collar criminals. Just because we overuse incarceration as a response to conventional criminality, we should not compound the problem by attempting to increase the number of white-collar criminals who fall into the clutches of an already overburdened system.

And this last point brings us to another pressing problem. The cost of incarcerating prisoners continues to skyrocket. We are hard pressed to provide housing and other basic staples at constitutionally and morally acceptable levels to those already incarcerated. Can we continue the current imprisonment binge while including a larger proportion of nonviolent white-collar offenders? If we are to continue this policy direction, we must either impose a substantial tax (or other revenue-generating mechanism) increase or continue to raid the funding of other government functions such as education and health and welfare.

However, fiscal constraints should not temper our concern over justice and equality. I share Professor Geis' concern over the inequity of our current sentencing policies. Where we seem to differ is in how we would address the problem. I would recommend that the entire issue of sentencing disparity be addressed systematically instead of piecemeal. If we are not willing to rationally sanction all offenders and then operate prisons that approach the comfort afforded animals ensconced in our zoos, then we must consider moral and constitutional alternatives to incarceration. But then perhaps he is being pragmatic in that he recognizes that the chance of implementing a rational sentencing policy bereft of racial, gender, and class considerations is practically nil. I enter a guilty plea to the charge of utopian thinking!

As I have attempted to show, we can achieve an adequate degree of retribution without adding to our already overburdened prison systems. The real problem facing criminologists will be convincing policymakers, the public, and the media that we need to balance the need for justice with the desire for a well-ordered society. Hopefully, debates such as those contained in this volume will facilitate an informed dialogue on this issue.

NO

Michael B. Blankenship

During a visit to a new federal correctional facility in Millington, Tennessee, I witnessed a rather nostalgic sight. Outside, on his knees doing some landscaping, was a *former* member of the Memphis City Council. I emphasize the phrase *former* because this individual was serving time after his conviction for some nefarious activities, including bribery associated with his official duties. The sight before me warmed the cockles of my heart—a white-collar criminal doing menial labor!

This new federal correctional facility was located at the U.S. Naval base in Millington. Part of the attraction in locating this correctional facility (it was not a prison if walls make a prison, because this facility lacked outer walls) on the naval base was that it supplied an inexpensive source of manual labor for the base. From raking sand traps on the golf course to unstopping plugged up toilets, approximately 150 nonviolent white-collar offenders were available to perform maintenance needed on the base.

Having grown up in the rural South, I was accustomed to seeing inmates working beyond prison confines. I even had some distant relatives who had served time on the chain-gang for some minor offenses! During my days as a graduate student in Huntsville, Texas, it was not uncommon to see dozens of unsupervised inmates performing a myriad of tasks in various parts of the city. However, this visit to the new correctional facility added a new dimension to my experiences with inmates. Seeing a former member of the Memphis elite digging in the dirt exemplified the current sentiment about punishing the upper class. Whether this attitude is based on a sense of social justice or resentment of status, it is somehow politically correct to demand the proverbial pound of flesh from the upper class (see, for example, Tom Wolfe's *Bonfire of the Vanities* for insights into this phenomenon).

Despite the nostalgic rhetoric of the times, that is the "let's get tough like we used to be" dogma espoused by the current crop of politicos, and the concomitant policies that result in institutions such as the one in Millington, is all we gain from punishing nonviolent white-collar criminals a sense of egalitarianism in our penal policies? Even this objective may be ethereal given that the available research suggests that punishment is typically reserved for less powerful organizational and occupational offenders (Clinard & Yeager, 1980; Goff, 1993; Sutherland, 1983; Wright, Cullen & Blankenship, 1995). In short, seeing a few white-collar criminals being forced to perform menial labor may satisfy a superficial sense of retribution. Is there more to this punishment issue than meets the eye?

Should we not consider the other punishment rationales, such as deterrence and rehabilitation? Does incarcerating nonviolent white-collar criminals facilitate achievement of these goals? Equally important, can these goals be achieved through other, less expensive, means? In the following sections, I examine briefly why incarceration may not be the best penal practice for dealing with nonviolent white-collar offenders.

Punishment Rationales

Most introductory criminal justice texts provide a brief overview of the rationales of punishment. With some small variations, these texts focus on retribution, deterrence, incapacitation, and rehabilitation as the main grounds for punishing offenders. We may, in effect, punish wrongdoers because they deserve to be punished (retribution) or in hopes of preventing future episodes of law breaking (incapacitation, deterrence, and rehabilitation). In most textbook treatments of this subject, each rationale is presented as if it is independent from the others. In reality, each rationale is pursued simultaneously; however, the emphasis each rationale receives varies across periods. For example, during the 1950s, rehabilitation was in vogue; today, retribution appears to be the philosophy driving penal policies. We must also bear in mind that policies that facilitate a specific rationale may work with one class of offender and not another, and that sometimes the rationales compete and conflict with each other. For example, retributive crime control policies may be counterproductive to efforts at rehabilitation.

In the sections that follow, each punishment rationale is examined in terms of what we know about its efficacy as a response to nonviolent white-collar crime. This analysis is premised on the proposition that we can achieve the justifications of punishment without resorting to incarceration.

Retribution

Retaliation is probably the oldest rationale for redressing a grievance, either real or perceived (Allen & Simonsen, 1998). Retaliation can take several forms that range from payment of money or goods to vendettas. The problem inherent in this rationale is knowing when one has satisfied the desire for revenge while avoiding retaliation from the original offender or his or her family and friends. Individuals who support retaliation for wrongdoing often cite the passage from *Leviticus* of an "eye for an eye" as a divine imprimatur. However, doing so is taking this biblical passage out of context.

We might think of retribution as a curb on retaliation. For example, the passage from *Leviticus* refers to punishing transgressors in proportion to the harm they inflicted on their victim. In essence, if a person is assaulted and losses vision in one eye, it is inappropriate to inflict punishment beyond the victim's loss, say, by taking the offender's vision in both eyes. Thus, retribution is premised on "compensating" the victim for his or her loss while reinforcing social values by condemning unacceptable behavior.

The problem facing retributivists lies in making determinations as to the amount and type of punishment proportionate to the harm inflicted. The issue of ordinality (parity among crimes and rank according to severity) and cardinality (magnitude of punishment) are problematic in determining criminal sanctions, and even more so for white-collar offenses (Schlegel, 1990).

The problem lies, in part, with determining the amount of harm white-collar offenders inflict on their victims. Unlike victimization by conventional criminals, victims of white-collar crimes may never realize their victimization or may become aware of their plight only with the passage of time. Further complicating matters is making a determination of who to punish. We must remember that the phrase "white-collar criminal" encompasses a tremendous array of occupational and organizational offenders. In short, the problem for retributivists is determining what categories of white-collar crimes are deserving of differing degrees of punishment, including incarceration, when compared with both conventional criminality and other white-collar criminality.

Deterrence

Unlike retribution, which is premised on an ideology of punishment for the sake of punishment, the three remaining punishment rationales are utilitarian in nature. That is, each of the remaining rationales holds the promise of some "greater good" resulting from the punishment, such as a reduction in future offending. The issue of deterrence occupies a dominant research problem among criminologists. We are concerned with two facets of deterrence in this essay. The first facet deals with the traditional definition of deterrence and its efficacy in reducing/preventing future white-collar crimes. The second aspect is directly related to the thesis of this essay: assuming that white-collar criminals can be deterred, can alternatives to incarceration produce deterrence similar to any generated by incarceration?

Depending on which text we refer to, we find that deterrence is generally divided into two broad categories. The first category is typically referred to as general deterrence, which means that by punishing some offender, other would-be offenders consider the consequences before committing an offense. The second category of deterrence, frequently termed specific deterrence, is distinguished from general deterrence by focusing on punishing an individual to dissuade that individual from committing future criminal acts.

Thus, deterrence can be classified as a learning theory. Potential offenders either learn about the certainty, swiftness, and severity of punishment through the process of penalizing other offenders (general deterrence) or by having been sanctioned previously themselves (specific deterrence) and decide whether to engage in future offending. Braithwaite and Geis (1982) opine that white-collar offenders should be more susceptible to deterrence because they have a potentially greater stake in conformity, and their criminal behavior is typically not embedded in their lifestyle. White-collar offenders also may be more easily deterred than conventional criminals given that rational decision making is frequently a part of their occupation and their offending.

Yet the evidence does not support these conclusions. Although a great deal more research is needed, Friedrichs (1996) concludes that is difficult, if not impossible, to demonstrate that the threat of punishment deters white-collar criminals. In fact, several studies have suggested that informal sanctions, such as negative publicity, may produce a greater deterrent effect than formal criminal sanctions (Elis & Simpson, 1995; Makkai & Braithwaite, 1994).

Friedrichs (1996) also notes that the pervasiveness of white-collar crime continues unabated. He argues that any deterrent effect may be negated by the perception that the probability of discovery and punishment of the crime is highly remote. In their seminal study of the impact of publicity on corporate offenders, Fisse and Braithwaite (1983) reasoned that the process of the ensuing investigation was itself a significant deterrent. Thus, much of the research has failed to detect a deterrent effect from formal criminal sanctions. We can then conclude, at least for the moment, that not only are white-collar criminals somewhat resistant to threats of formal sanctions, but that incarceration is likely to be an ineffective deterrent. Given the lack of evidence supporting deterrence, can we afford to incarcerate nonviolent white-collar criminals when other alternatives are available? We turn to this issue in the next section.

Incapacitation

Incapacitation is typically defined as imprisoning offenders to prevent them from committing crimes, at least during their period of incarceration. However, this rationale only works if we discount the crimes that offenders commit against other inmates and custody employees.

The latest incarceration data indicate that the prison population has reached about 1.2 million adults and is increasing with each passing year. The question is simple: can we afford to consume valuable prison space by incarcerating nonviolent offenders? Given the current attitude toward taxation, it is likely that public budgeting will continue to be a zero-sum process. That is, if one area, such as prisons, receives an increase in public funding, then some other area loses money. This process is well documented in a report by the RAND Corporation regarding the impact of "three strikes" legislation on prison budgets. Future of funding of colleges and universities in California is in serious jeopardy as money shifts from their budget to fund prisons. The consequences of this shift is that students will have to bear an increasing amount of the total cost of tuition in the future.

We are also faced with the problem of deciding who is worthy of incarceration. For example, how do we go about incarcerating a corporation? As one writer points out, corporations "have no soul to damn, no body to kick." Aside from dealing with this fictional entity, how should we determine responsibility for illegal acts? Take, for example, the case of defective products, such as in the pharmaceutical industry. Do we hold the chemists responsible for developing a drug that kills patients? What about the board of directors and the chief executive officer? Do stockholders incur any liability? Because of the definition of white-collar criminal, we have a difficult time in fixing blame and imposing a sanction on any group or individual.

Because of these problems, we must ask whether there are there other means of incapacitating nonviolent white-collar criminals without resorting to incarceration. Unlike many conventional criminals, white-collar criminals can be incapacitated without physical restraints. By definition, many white-collar criminals commit their crimes during the course of their occupation; therefore, they can be denied future access to opportunities to commit crimes by prohibiting them from further participation in their occupation. For example, a stock broker who steals from his or her clients (stock churning) can be barred from future activity as a stock broker. A physician who defrauds Medicaid or who performs unnecessary surgeries can lose his or her license to practice medicine. In short, white-collar criminals can be incapacitated by denying them the employment opportunities that facilitate their illegal acts.

Rehabilitation

The concept of rehabilitation has undergone dramatic change over time. The hallmark of early American prisons (the so-called Pennsylvania system) was punishment (isolation from the outside environment) to allow the offender to seek penitence. This early form of rehabilitation (changing an offender into a law-abiding citizen by imposing a prison sentence) eventually gave way as treatment programs were introduced based on the notion of the Medical Model of corrections.

The problem for white-collar criminals is that modern-day rehabilitative ideals are not designed with them as participants. Therapy to help inmates manage their anger, drug and alcohol counseling, job training, and educational programs that allow inmates to earn a GED or a college degree are not appropriate for most white-collar offenders (Friedrichs, 1996). The conditions that these and other similar programs are designed to ameliorate are typically not associated with white-collar offending.

However, the original intent of bringing about change through the imposition of punishment is fitting for white-collar offenders. However, this version of rehabilitation can be accomplished without resorting to incarceration. I want to emphasize that we need a better understanding of the punishment dialectic for white-collar criminals, but the evidence suggests that we can effect change among this group of offenders more effectively and at less cost by avoiding incarceration.

Alternatives to Incarceration

Because incarceration is both an expensive and a limited commodity, we must seek punishment alternatives that produce similar results at less cost and that are less destructive than incarceration. In addition to the conventional punishments that can be imposed on nonviolent white-collar offenders, a broad array of innovative and effective sanctions are available.

For example, as has been pointed out in previous sections, white-collar offenders who commit their crimes for economic gain can be precluded from future opportunities by disbarment or occupational disqualification (Friedrichs, 1996). Negative publicity also holds great potential as a specific deterrent to future illegal acts. And of course monetary fines, restitution, and community service provide opportunities for white-collar offenders to compensate their victims, the community, and the criminal justice system.

Perhaps the most innovative alternative to incarceration is self-regulation. A leading proponent of this concept is John Braithwaite (1982; 1990), who argues that government does not have sufficient resources to monitor all categories of business activities. Given this limitation, businesses would have the opportunity to influence regulatory rules and guidelines and then would be charged with compliance. Deviation from accepted standards and procedures would result in criminal prosecution. Businesses then would have a vested interest in compliance because they helped develop the standards and would ostensibly seek to avoid a criminal prosecution. This alternative would be problematic with smaller businesses, but it does offer the potential to address some of the most harmful nonviolent white-collar activity by focusing on larger businesses and corporations.

Conclusion

We must not repeat the same mistakes made in dealing with conventional criminality when deciding how to respond to nonviolent white-collar crime. Just as we need to reserve prison space for the most dangerous street criminals, we need to do the same for violent white-collar criminals. There are viable alternatives to incarcerating nonviolent white-collar criminals that produce the same, or better, outcomes as incarceration yet cost less and preserve prison space for serious offenders. As has been shown, some of the alternatives, such as informal sanctions, may be more effective in preventing future illegal acts than conventional punishments such as incarceration.

I believe that I have shown that the only justifiable rationale for incarcerating nonviolent white-collar criminals is retribution. However, we must not be seduced by the rhetoric of the times and the concomitant appearances of getting tough on criminals. I was taken in by the "Potemkin village" located in Millington. We must consider the practicality of incarceration and prioritize according to seriousness those we would send to prison or jail. The "bottom line" is that incarcerating nonviolent white-collar criminals should be the last option taken by the criminal justice system instead of the first.

REFERENCES

Allen, H. E., & Simonsen, C. E. (1998). *Corrections in America: An introduction* (8th ed.). Upper Saddle River, NJ: Prentice-Hall.

Braithwaite, J. (1982). Enforced self-regulation: A new strategy for corporate crime control. *Michigan Law Review, 80,* 1466–1507.

Braithwaite, J. (1990). Convergences in models of regulatory strategy. *Current Issues in Criminal Justice, 2,* 59–66.

Braithwaite, J., & Geis, G. (1982). On theory and action for corporate crime control. *Crime & Delinquency, 28,* 292–314.

Clinard, M. B., & Yeager, P. C. (1980). *Corporate crime*. New York: Free Press.

Elis, L. A., & Simpson, S. S. (1995). Informal sanction threats and corporate crime: Additive versus multiplicative models. *Journal of Research in Crime and Delinquency, 32*, 399–424.

Fisse, B., & Braithwaite, J. (1983). *The impact of publicity on corporate offenders*. Albany: State University of New York Press.

Friedrichs, D. O. (1996). *Trusted criminals: White-collar crime in contemporary society*. Belmont, CA: Wadsworth.

Goff, C. (1993). Sanctioning corporate criminals. In M. B. Blankenship (Ed.), *Understanding corporate criminality* (pp. 239–262). New York: Garland.

Makkai, T., & Braithwaite, J. (1994). The dialectics of corporate deterrence. *Journal of Research in Crime and Delinquency, 31*, 347–373.

Schlegel, K. (1990). *Just deserts for corporate criminals*. Boston: Northeastern University.

Sutherland, E. H. (1983). *White collar crime: The uncut version*. New Haven: Yale University Press.

Wright, J. P., Cullen, F. T., & Blankenship, M. B. (1995). The social construction of corporate violence: Media coverage of the Imperial Food Products Fire. *Crime and Delinquency, 41*, 20–36.

Rejoinder to Dr. Blankenship
GILBERT GEIS

If we put someone in prison, we ought to do so to accomplish something worthwhile. This seems to me to be an important matter whether the person is a nonviolent white-collar criminal or a so-called street offender. Professor Blankenship admirably outlines and examines some of the traditional aims of incarceration, matters such as retribution, incapacitation, rehabilitation, and deterrence of the person or of others who might be inclined to do what the imprisoned offender did. He concludes that evidence supports the view that putting nonviolent white-collar criminals in prison is not likely to accomplish anything worthwhile. Therefore, alternative and more benign methods of dealing with them ought to be sought.

There is an attractive core of common sense in the Blankenship position, and he sets it out convincingly, but I believe his thesis involves a bit of polemical sleight-of-hand. For one thing, of course, he assumes that the only reasonable aims of the administration of criminal justice and imprisonment are the four that he considers. For another thing, he fails to extend his reasoning to all kinds of violent and nonviolent crime and to consider the implications of such an extension. Imprisoning many murderers, for instance, serves none of the purposes that Professor Blankenship notes: If he were guilty, would it have done any good to put O. J. Simpson in prison? Simpson, presuming he did so once, is extraordinarily unlikely to kill again, and therefore represents no further threat to society. Nor are others likely to cut the throat of their former wives because Simpson did not do prison time. Therefore, using the punishment rationale paradigm, we ought not send most murderers, much less street offenders, to prison.

Perhaps so. The two of us might agree on this. Where we differ significantly is in our answer to the question he raises almost as rhetorical aside: "[I]s all we gain from punishing nonviolent white-collar criminals a sense of egalitarianism in our penal policies?" I would submit that the answer to this question should be a rousing "yes," and that such a gain, the quest for equal penal consequences flowing from equivalent behavior, should be basic in any society that seeks fairness, decency, and justice. I could not endorse a public policy that would have a nonviolent white-collar criminal spared time in prison while his blue collar, or no collar, equivalent (in regard to the harm done) is tucked away in a penitentiary cell.

Therefore, until sensible leniency is exercised for all offenders I cannot believe that it ought to be accorded to nonviolent white-collar criminals. They already have benefitted greatly by having more than their fair share of the goodies that our society so unequally distributes. Is their privileged position also to allow them to escape the kinds of consequences that befall others who commit offenses that are not notably different, except in the names attached to them, than theirs? There is an adage that should permeate the practice of criminal justice and the infliction of punishment: Not only must justice be done, but people must believe that it has been done. Equal treatment for equivalent behavior is a fundamental principle of justice. And it seems to me to provide a notably sound basis for rejecting Professor Blankenship's position and for feeding even greater numbers of white-collar offenders into the nation's prisons!

Should Violent Juvenile Offenders Be Routinely Tried as Adults?

Arguing YES is Eric Fritsch. He is Assistant Professor in the Department of Criminal Justice at the University of North Texas and teaches courses in juvenile justice, criminal justice policy, law enforcement, criminological theory, and criminal procedure. He has published in the areas of juvenile justice policy, including waiver to adult court, and his recent articles have appeared in *Crime & Delinquency, Law & Policy, American Journal of Criminal Law,* and *Juvenile and Family Court Journal.*

Taking the NO position is Clifford Dorne. Currently Associate Professor of Criminal Justice at Saginaw Valley State University, his teaching areas include juvenile justice, corrections, criminology, and restorative justice. He received a Ph.D. from the School of Criminal Justice, State University of New York at Albany, and has taught at Texas A&M International University, Laredo, and Indiana University at South Bend. Dr. Dorne is the author of *Child Maltreatment: A Primer in History, Public Policy and Research, 2nd Edition* (forthcoming from Harrow and Heston).

YES

ERIC FRITSCH

Over the past decade, there has been a significant increase in juvenile arrests for violent crime. From 1986 to 1995, arrests of juveniles for murder increased 90 percent, robbery increased 63 percent, aggravated assault increased 78 percent, and forcible rape decreased 4 percent (Snyder, 1997). Furthermore, there does not appear to be an end in sight. According to Snyder and Sickmund (1995), juvenile arrests for violent crime will double by the year 2010 if trends continue as they have during the past decade. These grim statistics have led juvenile justice officials, politicians, and citizens to question what can be done with violent juvenile offenders. In this chapter, it is argued that violent juvenile offenders should be routinely tried in adult court. Two reasons are provided and discussed as to why this is an appropriate option of what to do with violent juvenile offenders, including:

1. Violent juvenile offenders should be punished for their actions and incarcerated for long periods. Empirical studies provide support that violent juvenile offenders who have been waived to adult court receive longer sentences than are available in juvenile court; and

2. Juvenile justice systems were never designed to appropriately deal with violent juvenile offenders. However, juvenile justice systems are becoming more and more punitive in many states in response to violent juvenile offenders and turning away from their rehabilitative function despite the fact that violent juvenile offenders are few in number.

Violent Juvenile Offenders Deserve Long Terms of Incarceration

Violent juvenile offenders deserve punishment for their actions and should be incarcerated for long periods. Although waiver to adult court serves numerous purposes, the primary reason juveniles are waived to adult court is to impose longer terms of incarceration than are available in the juvenile justice system (Feld, 1989). The juvenile justice system is generally unable to impose long sentences of incarceration on juvenile offenders because the jurisdictional age limit of most juvenile correction agencies ends at twenty-one years of age. This means that these agencies must release individuals in their custody before their twenty-first birthday. Therefore, if a sixteen-year-old juvenile is accused of murder and the jurisdictional age limit of the juvenile corrections agency in the state is twenty-one, the maximum term of confinement in a juvenile institution would be five years. For many, this is not a long enough sentence for a juvenile offender convicted of murder. The adult system does not have a maximum jurisdictional age limit, and is thus seen as a better avenue to impose long terms of incarceration and punishment on violent juvenile offenders.

But just because the adult system is capable of imposing long terms of incarceration on juvenile offenders who have been waived to adult court, including sentences of twenty-five years, fifty years, life imprisonment, and even death, do juveniles waived to adult court for violent offenses receive longer sentences than are available in juvenile court? Some studies have found that juveniles waived to adult court do in fact receive shorter sentences than are available in juvenile court. However, there is a relationship between offense committed and sentence length. It is reasonable to assume that property offenders who are waived to adult court may receive shorter sentences of incarceration in comparison with violent offenders waived to adult court. Many of the studies that have concluded that waiver to adult court does not lead to longer sentences than are available in juvenile court only used aggregate data on sentences and did not break down sentences by offense. Therefore, one is unable to determine the sentences received by waived offenders convicted of murder, rape, robbery, and aggravated assault. This chapter is not concerned with sentences imposed on property offenders waived to adult court but violent offenders exclusively.

Therefore, it is important to understand how violent offenders waived to adult court generally fare. In a recent comprehensive literature review, Howell (1996) wanted to determine the extent to which waiver to adult court protects the public by incarcerating waived offenders. He concluded that "virtually every study has found that serious and violent juvenile offenders receive longer sentences in criminal court than in juvenile court, and serve longer prison terms" (p. 49). For example, Rudman, Hartstone, Fagan, and Moore (1986) compared violent juveniles waived to adult court from 1981 to 1984 in Boston, Newark, and Phoenix with violent juveniles retained in juvenile court after a waiver hearing. They found that 90 percent of the violent juveniles convicted in adult court were incarcerated. On average, violent juveniles waived to adult court received sentences that were five times longer than those who were retained in juvenile court. In Boston, violent juveniles waived to adult court received an average sentence of more than nineteen years, whereas violent juveniles retained in juvenile court received an average sentence of less than two years.

Although empirical studies show that violent juvenile offenders waived to adult court regularly receive lengthy sentences, the possibility exists that some violent offenders waived to adult court are treated leniently and given minimal terms of confinement, even probation. Even if the adult court does not impose long terms of incarceration on every violent juvenile offender waived to adult court, it does not mean that waiver to adult court was unnecessary or failed for those offenders who did not receive substantial sentences. The adult court does not substantially punish all violent adult offenders either. In 1994, only 62 percent of adult offenders convicted in adult court of a violent offense received a prison sentence, including 95 percent of those convicted of murder, 71 percent of those convicted of rape, 77 percent of those convicted of robbery, and 48 percent of those convicted of aggravated assault (Langan & Brown, 1997).

Furthermore, waiver to adult court of violent juvenile offenders allows the adult court to begin to accumulate an adult criminal record on juveniles as they continue their criminal activity as young adults. Violent crime peaks at age 18, but some violent adult offenders do not receive long terms of incarceration until their middle to late twenties, which is at or near the end of their criminal career. Boland (1995) argues that this lag in punishment occurs because prior criminal record is one of the most important factors in predicting the severity of sanction imposed on an offender. She argues that when violent offenders are at their peak, age eighteen, they are sometimes treated as first-time offenders by the adult court because of the confidentiality of juvenile court records. Therefore, the adult court is treating a chronic violent offender as a first-time offender despite several prior arrests and adjudications in juvenile court, even though the offender is at the peak of their criminal career. By waiving violent juvenile offenders to adult court, the accumulation of an adult criminal record is expedited, thus increasing the probability that the offender will be incarcerated during the peak of their criminal career rather than near the end.

Juvenile Justice Systems Are Becoming Punitive in Response to Violent Offenders

Juvenile justice systems were never designed to appropriately deal with violent juvenile offenders. However, juvenile justice systems are becoming more and more punitive in many states in response to violent juvenile offenders and turning away from their rehabilitative function despite the fact that violent juvenile offenders are few in number. Violent juvenile offenders have driven many state legislatures to enact laws to better deal with these offenders. These changes have generally involved two strategies. First, many state legislatures have expanded waiver provisions by either expanding the offenses eligible for waiver, lowering the age eligibility for waiver, or enacting automatic waiver provisions in an attempt to better manage violent juvenile offenders (Fritsch & Hemmens, 1995). Second, some state legislatures have completely revamped their juvenile justice systems by changing their orientation from rehabilitation to punishment in an attempt to deal with violent juvenile offenders. It will be argued that the former option is more appropriate, thus allowing violent juvenile offenders to be routinely waived to adult court.

States such as Florida have recently expanded their waiver statutes to deal with chronic and violent juvenile offenders. In 1994, the Florida Legislature expanded Florida's waiver law in three ways. First, a presumptive judicial waiver provision was added that mandates juveniles be waived to adult court if the juvenile has three prior adjudications for felonies and one involved violence or use or possession of a firearm, unless the court states reasons why the waiver should not take place. Second, a mandatory prosecutorial waiver provision was enacted mandating that the prosecutor file any case in adult court involving a juvenile who has three prior felony adjudications and has served three prior residential commitments. Third, prosecutorial waiver provisions were lowered from sixteen years of age to fourteen for several violent offenses (Lanza-Kaduce, Bishop, Frazier, &

Winner, 1996). These modifications were targeted at chronic and violent juvenile offenders and are expected to significantly increase the use of waiver to adult court in Florida. In fact, Lanza-Kaduce et al. (1996) estimated that an additional 14,500 juveniles would have been waived to adult court in Florida if the legislative changes made in 1994 were in effect in 1993. It is argued that the expansion of waiver and routinely waiving violent juvenile offenders to adult court as is the case in Florida is a better policy option than completely modifying the juvenile justice system to be able to appropriately manage violent juvenile offenders.

Some states, such as Texas, have undertaken a comprehensive revision of their entire juvenile justice system by changing its orientation from rehabilitation to punishment in an attempt to deal with violent juvenile offenders. When the concept of a separate juvenile justice system was developed, it was not designed to handle violent juvenile offenders. Therefore, significant changes had to occur if the juvenile justice system was going to appropriately deal with violent offenders. In 1995, the Texas Legislature enacted *House Bill 327* into law, which made over one hundred changes to the juvenile justice code in Texas. Although all the revisions are too numerous to discuss in this chapter, some of the most pertinent were the erosion of confidentiality provisions through the expansion of the ability to fingerprint and photograph juvenile offenders, the authorization to establish a statewide depository for juvenile records, and granting the public open access to juvenile court hearings as well as the expansion of the determinate sentence law.

Before the passage of *House Bill 327,* the determinate sentence law allowed a juvenile to receive up to a forty-year sentence if convicted of one of six specified offenses: capital murder, attempted capital murder, murder, aggravated sexual assault, aggravated kidnaping, or deadly assault on a law enforcement officer, corrections officer, court participant, or probation personnel. These juveniles were processed in juvenile court, not waived to adult court, and were sentenced to a Texas Youth Commission (TYC) institution until eighteen years of age. After a release hearing at eighteen years of age, the juvenile could be transferred to prison for the remainder of the sentence. *House Bill 327* expanded the determinate sentence law by making it applicable to twenty-one offenses. The expansion of the determinate sentence law was deemed necessary because it was argued that the determinate sentence law had not kept pace with the expansion of violent crimes such as drive-by shootings, aggravated robberies, and aggravated assaults being committed by juvenile offenders in recent years (Joint Interim Committee on the Family Code, 1994). In fact, most of the changes made by the passage of *House Bill 327* were made in response to violent juvenile offenders. Now the juvenile justice system in Texas does not resemble a traditional juvenile justice system that focuses on rehabilitation but an adult system that focuses on punishment and holding offenders accountable for their actions.

As stated previously, I believe the best policy option in response to violent juvenile offenders is to routinely waive them to adult court. I do not think the best policy option is to change the juvenile justice system to a punitive system to increase its ability to deal with violent offenders. For one thing, violent juvenile offenders are few in number, and to change an entire system in response to a few offenders does not appear to be a wise decision. In 1995, only 5.4 percent of all juvenile arrests were for a violent index crime (Snyder, 1997). The remaining 94.6 percent of the offenses were for such offenses as index property crimes, vandalism, liquor law violations, disorderly conduct, drug violations, curfew, and running away. In addition, Snyder and Sickmund (1995) found that only 41 percent of the juveniles referred to juvenile court return to juvenile court after their first referral. Therefore, 59 percent are never referred again.

As Gardner (1995) notes, "most delinquency is a symptom of adolescence that is generally outgrown and thus demands no lengthy attention in the name of social protection" (p. 109). These offenders do not need to be placed in a juvenile justice system that is punitive in orientation. Handling violent juvenile offenders in juvenile court hinders the system's ability to maintain its rehabilitative focus. If a juvenile offender cannot be handled in a juvenile justice system based on rehabilitation, then they need to be sent to a system that can deal with them, namely, the adult system. Now the State of Texas has a juvenile justice system that can adequately deal with violent juvenile offenders but does not have a system to effectively deal with less serious offenders. States are changing their juvenile justice systems to deal with a small number of offenders when they should maintain a more traditional juvenile justice system and the sanctity of it and waive to adult court those offenders that the juvenile justice system cannot deal with, especially, violent offenders. Most offenders are still status, minor, and first-time offenders, and now they will be in a system designed to deal with violent and chronic offenders. Do we want a juvenile justice system designed to deal with the 5 percent of juvenile offenders who are violent or the 95 percent who are not? I argue the latter, and the primary way to insure this happening is to routinely waive violent juvenile offenders to adult court.

Conclusion

Violent juvenile offenders need to be punished for their actions, and the adult court is in the best position to accomplish this objective. Research has shown that violent juvenile offenders waived to adult court receive significantly longer sentences in adult court than they could have received in juvenile court. In addition, the juvenile justice system was never designed to appropriately handle violent juvenile offenders, and attempts to make the main focus of the juvenile justice system punishment interferes with the system's ability to maintain a benevolent and rehabilitative orientation. For the following reasons, violent juvenile offenders should be routinely waived to adult court.

REFERENCES

Boland, B. (1995). Fighting crime: The problem of adolescents. In M. L. Forst (Ed.), *The new juvenile justice* (pp. 193–199). Chicago, IL: Nelson-Hall.

Feld, B. C. (1989). Bad law makes hard cases: Reflections on teen-aged axe-murderers, judicial activism, and legislative default. *Law and Inequality: A Journal of Theory and Practice, 8,* 1–101.

Fritsch, E. J., & Hemmens, C. (1995). Juvenile waiver in the United States 1979–1995: A comparison and analysis of state waiver statutes. *Juvenile and Family Court Journal, 46,* 17–35.

Gardner, M. R. (1995). Punitive juvenile justice: Some observations on a recent trend. In M. L. Forst (Ed.), *The new juvenile justice* (pp. 103–114). Chicago, IL: Nelson-Hall.

Howell, J. C. (1996). Juvenile transfers to the criminal justice system: State of the art. *Law & Policy, 18,* 17–60.

Joint Interim Committee on the Family Code. (1994). *A comprehensive review of the Texas family code.* Austin, TX: Texas Legislative Council.

Langan, P. A., & Brown, J. M. (1997). *Felony sentences in state courts, 1994.* Washington, DC: U.S. Department of Justice.

Lanza-Kaduce, L., Bishop, D. M., Frazier, C. E., & Winner, L. (1996). Changes in juvenile waiver and transfer provisions: Projecting the impact in Florida. *Law & Policy, 18,* 137–150.

Rudman, C., Hartstone, E., Fagan, J., & Moore, M. (1986). Violent youth in adult court: Process and punishment. *Crime & Delinquency, 32,* 75–96.

Snyder, H. N. (1997). *Juvenile arrests, 1995.* Washington, DC: U.S. Department of Justice.

Snyder, H. N., & Sickmund, M. (1995). *Juvenile offenders and victims: A national report.* Washington, DC: U.S. Department of Justice.

Rejoinder to Dr. Fritsch   CLIFFORD DORNE

Dr. Fritsch's essay contains two theses. The first involves the observation that "juvenile offenders who have been waived to adult court receive longer sentences than are available in juvenile court." I do not quibble with this point, and it does seem to be supported by the data. However, his statement does not squarely address the issue of whether violent juveniles should be routinely transferred to adult criminal courts. In fact, the statement leads us far astray. He should have focused on the issues of routinized statutory transfer and on which violent juvenile offenders should be transferred. Of course, there are exceptions to his observation that "sentences are longer for juveniles in the adult system when compared with the juvenile system" and he does concede this point (e.g., probation instead of prison).

Concerning Dr. Fritsch's second thesis, how does his observation that "juvenile justice systems have generally become more punitive" buttress the argument favoring routine legislative transfer? This does not make sense! I strongly suggest that his observation constitutes a good reason not to implement routine, across-the-board transfers because juvenile justice may already be harsh enough or at least moving in this conservative direction.

Granted, his statement that "violent juveniles deserve punishment for their actions and should be incarcerated for long periods of time" may be true. I must point out, however, that he is making a sweeping generalization that falls to consider the fact that some (or perhaps many) violent juveniles may not be living a criminal lifestyle or engaging in violence on an ongoing basis. Not all juveniles who commit acts officially constituting "violent crimes" are worthy of adult system processing. What about schoolyard fights? What about a youngster who hits another person in a fit of rage as an isolated act? Should all such juveniles be sent to adult prison, where they will probably learn toughness and physical prowess as a way of life? Justice in these instances must be individualized pursuant to *Kent* transfer hearings!

Murder cases are also mentioned by Dr. Fritsch. Admittedly, cases in which the facts meet statutory criteria for first- or second-degree murder should be handled by the adult system, and these cases can be transferred via *Kent* transfer hearings. But should cases of manslaughter be *routinely* transferred in advance by statute? I think not. Some cases should be transferred, and others should not.

Dr. Fritsch argues that the criminal records accumulated by transferred juveniles is socially constructive. I disagree. I can only concur with him in cases in which a juvenile has been through a *Kent* transfer hearing. He seems to ignore the fact that our society is not too forgiving when it comes to criminal records. I am currently engaged in a detailed study of the pardon process, and this point seems to resound in the data. Personal stigma, social exclusion, and restrictions from various types of lawful employment should not be taken lightly. If a juvenile is accused of a violent crime and is wrongfully transferred, the results for him or her in terms of stigma could be horrendous. Most importantly, many juvenile courts are opening their records to police agencies and to criminal courts so that such information can be used in later investigations and criminal sentencing processes.

A cogent argument is simply not made for routine, across-the-board legislative transfer. Indeed, he even goes so far as to explain that Texas's juvenile justice system can adequately deal with violent offenders by focusing on punishment and accountability! Then why would he want to transfer these juvenile offenders to an already overcrowded and expensive adult prison system *en masse*? Perhaps his position is predicated on the fact that Texas now has a "blended sentencing system" in which a juvenile could be sentenced in juvenile court to training school and then sent automatically to adult prison after age eighteen to complete a lengthy sentence. The blended system has advantages in that children are not placed directly into an adult facility, but it detracts from the qualities of individual justice offered by *Kent* transfer hearings. I would urge that juvenile court transfer hearings be required before any blended sentence is meted out.

I submit that we continue working to improve both the rehabilitative and punitive aspects of the juvenile justice system and retain *Kent* transfer hearings to deal with the violent 5 percent (figure offered by Dr. Fritsch) in the adult prison system. The policy of routine legislative transfers is not the way to go.

NO

CLIFFORD DORNE

Should juveniles accused of violent crimes be routinely transferred to the criminal justice system to be adjudicated and punished as adults? In this section, I shall contend that "transfer" should be retained as a policy but should not be implemented on a routine basis.

There are actually three methods by which juveniles may be processed in the adult criminal justice system, which, in effect, constitutes a transfer from (or waiver of) the less punitive, civil law–based juvenile justice system.

Judicial Transfer

An adversarial transfer hearing may be held in juvenile court that affords the juvenile court judge ultimate discretion to determine whether the accused juvenile is amenable to treatment in the juvenile correctional system or is better suited to criminal adjudication where he or she may be subjected to much harsher penalties. Generally, a probable cause standard of proof is used to evaluate evidence, which, of course, is a very low level of validation when compared with standards applied in civil and criminal adjudications such as clear and convincing evidence and proof beyond a reasonable doubt. The probable cause standard emphasizes the preliminary or preadjudicatory nature of the transfer hearing and, in some cases, serves to expedite the juvenile court judge's decision-making capacity. This approach individualizes justice, provides some due process to the defense to attempt to resist the transfer within an adversarial setting (including some cross-examination), and permits the juvenile court judge to consider all relevant aspects of the case. Such considerations should include the safety of the community and concerns of the victim or the victim's family. Often these issues must be balanced with the "best interest of the juvenile defendant" and his or her amenability to treatment in juvenile corrections.

Prosecutorial Transfer

Also termed "concurrent jurisdiction," the prosecutor is given transfer discretion by statute to determine whether to charge a juvenile in civil juvenile court or in adult criminal court. Such cases do not necessarily have to involve violent crimes, but they usually must involve a charge that is considered serious. Prosecutors have traditionally enjoyed an enormous amount of charging discretion and, in some jurisdictions, procedural statutes simply extend this tradition to juvenile transfer cases. Although this approach has the ability to individualize justice and adequately consider the juvenile's life situation and community safety issues, it does not involve an adversary process in which the defense can present evidence to an impartial judge that may mitigate against transfer.

Legislative Transfer

The third method most closely adheres to the concept of "routine transfer." That is, the legislature designates in *advance* the crimes that are serious enough to warrant the automatic transfer of juveniles over a certain age to the adult system. It is this method of transfer that most closely adheres to the current "get tough on crime" political movement. Under such laws, the accused juvenile never actually enters the juvenile justice system but instead is immediately processed into the criminal justice system. There is a recent trend in various states that already have these laws on the books to get increasingly tougher. They can do this by expanding the types of crimes that would prompt an automatic transfer or by lowering the age at which accused juveniles may be transferred. Some states have also added prior felony juvenile records as a criterion for automatic transfer. Forty-one states have made such statutory expansions since 1978 (Coordinating Council on Juvenile Justice and Delinquency Prevention, 1996, 22).

Currently, there is much variation from state to state with respect to transfer mechanisms. One-third of the states have adopted a singular model, and the remainder have enacted combinations of two or three of the models. New York seems to be the only state that has legislative transfer as its sole transfer mechanism, and at least twenty states use legislative transfer along with one or two of the other models. About sixteen states solely use judicial transfer pursuant to the Kent decision (CCJJDP, 1996, p. 23). Some states that have the legislative transfer model have also promulgated clauses that permit a "reverse transfer" so that a juvenile who has been sent directly into the criminal justice system may be subsequently transferred to the juvenile justice system under certain circumstances (CCJJDP, 1996, p. 22). If a state adopts the rigid model of legislative transfer, then these reverse transfer clauses should certainly be appended to the statute.

Legislative transfer is the most automatic procedure that in effect circumvents juvenile court decision making. Thus, it bypasses judicial analysis of important information about a particular case that should impact the transfer question.

The Juvenile Justice Mission and the Spirit of *Kent* v. *United States*

The fairest and most utilitarian transfer policy is the judicial model urged by the U.S. Supreme Court in the case of *Kent* v. *U.S.* (1966). This approach places the transfer decision squarely in the juvenile court, and it is in this environment where a juvenile defendant's overall background, family setting, and behavioral patterns can best be analyzed and debated.

Kent v. *U.S.* represented the beginning of the so-called "constitutionalist era" for juvenile courts as the U.S. Supreme Court called into question the benevolent (*parens patriae*) doctrine of these courts. While respecting the principle of the doctrine in a general sense, the Court questioned the juvenile court's actual implementation of informal procedures aimed at disposing of cases in the "best interest of the child." Before *Kent,* juveniles were not entitled to due process protections and were not getting the rehabilitative services that were promised as a justification for the lax, informal court procedures. This was expressed by Justice Fortas's famous observation that juveniles were receiving the "worst of both worlds" in the pre-*Kent* juvenile court.

The *Kent* case did involve facts that can be characterized as heinous: burglary and rape. The juvenile court in its original conception in 1899 (often called the "socialized juvenile court"), however, was mainly invented to deal with status offenses and nonserious delinquency cases. This unique court was designed to take a holistic view of the juvenile and to individualize or tailor case dispositions to his or her needs. This feature has been retained in modern juvenile courts despite the due process reforms imposed by the U.S. Supreme Court, mainly in the area of delinquency adjudications (see, for example, *In Re Gault,* 1967 and *In Re Winship,* 1970). But modern juvenile justice retains some important benevolent procedures that exist outside of the adjudication process, which are aimed at rehabilitation, such as case intake tribunals presided over by probation staff, pretrial diversion programs, deinstitutionalization of status offenders, and probation and aftercare (both of which can impose supervision on the entire family, unlike criminal justice probation and parole officers). Again, it was mainly in the areas of transfers and adjudications where the Court imposed some due process reforms.

The *Kent* case provides general procedures recognizing the profound seriousness of the transfer decision. In the Appendix to the case, criteria for transfer were set forth and may be paraphrased as follows: the seriousness of the offense, danger of the offender to the community, whether the offense was committed in an aggressive and premeditated manner, whether the offense was against property or person, extent of injury to victim, the prosecutive merit of the complaint/charge (evidence), the age of the juvenile defendant's crime partners, the sophistication and maturity of the juvenile, home environment, pattern of living, emotional attitude, prior crime record, and likelihood of rehabilitation in juvenile corrections.

A decade after the *Kent* decision, the Task Force on Juvenile Justice and Delinquency Prevention (1977, p. 103) recommended that transfer be considered if the juvenile defendant is sixteen years old or older at the time of the alleged commission of the crime, the crime is aggravated or heinous in nature, the crime is part of pattern of repeated delinquent acts, the juvenile is not amenable to treatment in juvenile corrections, and that such determinations are made pursuant to a

Kent due process transfer hearing. Clearly, both the U.S. Supreme Court and this Task Force were proclaiming that the transfer of a juvenile to the adult criminal justice system involves a *substantial constitutional liberty interest* and thus logically necessitates a court hearing in a due process adversarial format.

The Political Context of the "Get Tough" Movement and Juvenile Transfers

Although there have been problems throughout this century with the civil law juvenile justice system (e.g., rather mixed results on the deliverance of rehabilitative services), a large-scale or national implementation of routine/legislative transfer procedure has the potential to sound the death knell for the entire juvenile justice system. I am convinced that this would be a serious mistake, because juvenile justice has the potential to do more constructive work with troubled families when compared with its more punitive criminal justice system counterpart. Juvenile justice should be preserved because a total merger with criminal justice may result in a return to the nineteenth century practice of indiscriminately incarcerating children with adults. This merger would also result in a large-scale abandonment of public and private services to troubled children and their families. Such philanthropic abandonments have not been unknown to twentieth-century U.S. public policy. The massive deinstitutionalization of the mentally ill that resulted in hordes of untreated, homeless former psychiatric patients roaming city streets serves as a poignant reminder (Isaac & Armat, 1992).

I am not, however, contending that juvenile transfers to criminal justice be abolished. Clearly, there are cases in which a juvenile offender is simply too dangerous to be processed in the more benevolent and lenient juvenile justice system. I submit, nonetheless, that these heinous cases are not as common as many would tend to think—relative to cases of nonviolent juvenile crime and status offenses. Indeed, Wolfgang, Figlio, and Sellin's (1972) classic cohort study illustrated that a small proportion of juvenile offenders were committing a large percentage of the crimes (the much celebrated "chronic 6 percent"). Currently, research indicates that anywhere from 6 to 8 percent of all juvenile offenders account for a disproportionate amount of serious offenses (CCJJDP, 1996, p. 20).

Kent transfer hearings have the ability to both protect society and deliver the relatively small proportion of very dangerous juveniles into the adult prison system, where they may serve very long sentences in maximum security settings for purposes of retribution, incapacitation, and deterrence.

Of course, very little political veneration may be achieved by advocating the *Kent* Judicial Transfer model. Ostensibly, Judicial Transfer does not sound like a very tough policy, but it does highlight the complexity of youthful criminal behavior. Moreover, these transfer hearings do not have uniform outcomes because there are procedural variations across jurisdictions and juvenile court judges are vested with substantial discretion. Sweeping generalizations about dangers to the community are difficult to make from the vantage point of *Kent* transfer hearings. Clearly, gun-toting, crack-dealing youth gangs are more of a danger in some jurisdictions than others. Some juveniles involved in serious crime will mature out their street crime activities, and others will not. Policy proposals that do not lend themselves to certitudes are not easily sold to the public by elected officials. "Get tough" rhetoric, however, has the ability to galvanize a frightened public. Such shrill political exclamations may at times defy logic and often do not attend to specific problems of implementation. Political exhortations to routinize and expedite the juvenile transfer process must be understood in the context of a general "get tough on crime" trend that has prevailed for the past fifteen years or so. "Get tough" policies rarely have had any major problems in moving from bills to statutes in the legislative process. This movement, however, has been fraught with problems at the implementation level.

The Routinization of Legislative Juvenile Transfers as a Component of the "Get Tough Ideology"

It is difficult to historically pinpoint the actual genesis of the most recent "get tough on crime" political movement. Some may point to Richard Nixon's law-and-order presidential campaign, and others may cite the controversial findings of Robert Martinson and colleagues in the mid-1970s. Their research ostensibly indicated that most juvenile and adult correctional rehabilitation programs have no appreciable affect on recidivism (Martinson, 1974). Still others may plausibly point to Ronald Reagan's presidential victory in 1980. As of the early 1980s, there is little doubt that a wave of political conservatism suffused criminal justice public policy, and this in turn permeated juvenile justice. Whether a frightened electorate initially prompted law makers to move toward the political right in criminal justice policy, or whether some (or many) elected law makers inflamed existing public fears by exaggerating the threat of violent crime, is not the main issue here. Rather, the more relevant questions have to do with implementation and considerations of unintended consequences.

Some noteworthy manifestations of this "get tough" ideology include: three-strikes legislation, truth in sentencing laws, mandatory minimum sentencing, guideline/just deserts sentencing, abolition or reduction of parole releases, massive prison construction, a hastening of the appeals and *habeas corpus* processes in death penalty cases, the "war on drugs," and a limited abrogation of the Fourth Amendment (e.g., "good faith doctrine" in search and seizures). Legislative transfers, along with calls to continually toughen them, are part of this movement.

These policies have resulted in a sharp increase in the U.S. prison population; from 319,598 to 1,112,448 by mid-year 1996 (Bureau of Justice Statistics

[BJS], 1997, p. 1). The rate of prison incarceration is 615 inmates per 100,000 or 1 in every 163 U.S. residents serving prison time (BJS, 1997, p. 2). Irwin and Austin (1997) refer to this as "the imprisonment binge." They point out that annual spending on corrections has increased from $9.1 billion in 1982 to $32 billion in 1992 (1997, p. 14). Prisons have become the fastest-growing item in many state budgets and, according to a report issued by the National Association of State Budget Officers, have even detracted from higher education spending in some states (American Council on Education, 1994, p. 4).

Poverty-stricken citizens, the unskilled, the uneducated, and minorities have disproportionately borne the brunt of the imprisonment binge. With respect to race, at mid-year 1996, 58.4 percent of the prison population was nonwhite. Many have charged that this is the result of racial bias in criminal justice (Miller, 1996; Irwin & Austin, 1997) and, if there is some veracity to this claim, there is little reason to believe that a routinization of juvenile transfers would improve the situation. Making juvenile transfers to the adult system more routine and automatic would only serve to exacerbate the "imprisonment binge." This may, in turn, force departments of corrections to expand existing facilities or build new ones to accommodate such juveniles at a very high cost to taxpayers. Moreover, many states are now struggling with serious inmate overcrowding problems while under federal court supervision. Indeed, some states have been forced to pass laws for emergency inmate releases from prison to alleviate overcrowding problems and to comply with federal court consent decrees.

A significant increase in juvenile inmates incarcerated in adult prison systems also presents special challenges in areas of inmate classification, inmate gang activity (e.g., the aggressive recruiting of juvenile inmates into adult prison gangs), and inmate safety. A large influx of juvenile inmates would create many internal security problems as prison administrations struggle to protect juvenile inmates from the stronger and more numerous adult inmates. The now familiar tragedies that are characteristic of prison life, such as inmate-on-inmate extortion, rape, and forced homosexual prostitution, would only escalate. In addition, from a criminological perspective, both differential association and labeling may well operate to make transferred juveniles worse and less able to avoid recidivism on release. Such admonitions have long existed in criminology: that promiscuous and prolonged intermixing with hardened adult long-term inmates would most likely result in the inculcation of criminal values and extremely negative self-conceptions in juveniles. Most of these juvenile prison inmates will eventually be released and, if not infirm or elderly, may constitute substantial threats to the community.

These problems have not been lost on some criminal court judges who are faced with the task of sentencing transferred juveniles. For example, one New York City judge recently told *Newsweek* that he works to individualize justice for juveniles who have been transferred to his adult criminal court as much as possible. He believes that many of these juveniles are salvageable and sends about 60 percent of them back onto the street on five-year probation terms that include counseling. This same judge, however, has meted out life prison terms to juvenile murderers. He relies on *Kent*-like criteria, such as prior record, severity of the crime, and reports from probation officers, much like juvenile court judges after they receive input from both prosecution and defense during the transfer hearings. It should be noted that New York has legislative transfer as its sole method of moving juveniles to the adult system. This article was published on the heels of a bill pending in Congress that was sponsored by Representative Mike Mcullum (R–FL) offering $1.5 billion for the states if they toughen and routinize their transfer laws (Reibstein, 1997, p. 70). This bill has been criticized by child welfare advocates as an attack on children. As Olsson (1996, pp. 49–50) notes, there is a scarcity of research indicating that transferring juvenile offenders lowers recidivism rates. Research has not shown that community safety is enhanced by the routinization of transfers. There also are few systematic data that show what actually happens to such juveniles when they are sent to adult prisons.

To say the least, much caution should be exercised before passing any federal legislation that encourages more states to move in the legislative transfer direction; more research is imperative.

Getting Tougher in the Juvenile Justice System without the Routinization of Transfers

The "get tough" political movement has, to a large extent, filtered down to the civil juvenile justice system. This has occurred without altering the basic *parens patriae* foundation on which this system is predicated. Such reforms include juvenile curfew laws, "zero tolerance" for school violence (using arrests instead of intraschool disciplinary proceedings), holding parents liable for the delinquency of their children, and permitting juvenile court judges to engage in preventive detention before adjudication pursuant to *Schall* v. *Martin* (1984). Arguably, these policies have made the juvenile justice system somewhat tougher and better able to deal with juveniles who commit isolated crimes of violence (not occurring in the context of an ongoing criminal lifestyle), such as assaults on other juveniles with whom they associate in the neighborhood or at school. More to the point, these reforms have made the system more flexible and better able to deal with a wider variety of juvenile problems.

Such conservative reforms in juvenile justice are also congruous with the U.S. Supreme Court's decision of *McKeiver* v. *Pennsylvania* (1971). In this case, the Court had the opportunity to provide juvenile defendants with a Sixth Amendment right to jury trial in juvenile court adjudications. The Court declined to do so on the grounds that this would signal the end of the *parens patriae*–based juvenile justice system. The majority believed that, although juvenile justice has experienced some disappointments, the system still holds promise to help children in trouble. The relative procedural informality was viewed by the Court as an advantage with respect to dispositional flexibility and creativity in juvenile cases. It was concluded that state legislators can pass laws permitting juries in juvenile delinquency trials, but the U.S. Supreme Court was not going to carry due process reform to the point of eradicating the rather unique juvenile justice system altogether.

Most importantly, juvenile courts using the Judicial Transfer Model have clearly gotten tougher in the transfer decision process. There has been a large increase in the number of cases transferred to the adult system by juvenile court judges. Between 1989 and 1993, the number of cases involving crimes-against-persons processed by juvenile courts increased by 58 percent, whereas there was a 115 percent increase in judicial transfers of these cases. The Office of Juvenile Justice and Delinquency Prevention (1996, p. 28) lists "an increase in the willingness of juvenile courts to transfer eligible cases" as a major reason for this trend. Juvenile courts certainly have the ability to "get tough," but this should not be applied by routine a priori legislative mandate across the board for juveniles.

Maintaining judicial transfer as the primary model would reaffirm the spirit of *McKeiver* and do much to preserve the socially desirable attributes of the juvenile justice system to the general benefit of troubled children and their families. These characteristics include procedural flexibility, individualized justice, and hope for rehabilitation; at least more hope than a long prison sentence would offer in the adult criminal justice system. Moreover, juvenile courts can address the problems of an entire family much better than a criminal court. Juvenile justice is also in a better position to engage in restorative justice, such as alternative dispute resolution/mediation, than the more punitive adult criminal justice system. None of these assertions detract from the fact that, under the judicial transfer model that I strongly endorse, dangerous juveniles can be selectively placed into the adult system to serve lengthy prison sentences or even be placed on death row if the criminal court jury sends them there. Routinizing transfer on a grand scale to the point of abrogating the juvenile justice system's capacity to consider each juvenile's case is not the way to go. Judicial transfer, although not neatly fitting into the politically expedient "get tough" paradigm, should be retained as it individualizes justice while it maintains the option of transfer to the adult criminal justice system.

REFERENCES

American Council on Education. (1994). *Higher education and national affairs, vol. 43* (p. 18). Washington, DC: Author.

Bureau of Justice Statistics. (1997). *Prison and jail inmates at mid-year, 1996* (NCJ 162843). Washington, DC: Office of Justice Programs, U.S. Department of Justice.

Coordinating Council on Juvenile Justice and Delinquency Prevention. (1996). *Combating violence and delinquency: The national juvenile justice action plan (Report)*. Washington, DC: Office of Justice Programs, U.S. Department of Justice.

Irwin, J., & Austin, J. (1997). *It's about time: America's imprisonment binge* (2nd ed.). Belmont, CA: Wadsworth.

Isaac, R. J., & Armat, V. C. (1992). *Madness in the streets: How psychiatry and the law abandoned the mentally ill*. New York, NY: Free Press.

Martinson, R. (1974, Spring). What works?: Questions and answers about prison reform. *The public interest*, pp. 22–54.

Miller, J. (1996). *Search and destroy: African-American males in the criminal justice system*. New York, NY: Press Syndicate of the University of Cambridge.

Olsson, K. S. (1996). The juvenile justice dilemma. *Corrections Today, 58* (1), 48–51.

Reibstein, L. (1997, May 26). Kids in the dock. *Newsweek*, pp. 70–72.

Task Force on Juvenile Justice and Delinquency Prevention of the National Advisory Committee (1977). *Juvenile justice and delinquency prevention*. Washington, DC: U.S. Government Printing Office.

Wolfgang, M. E., Figlio, R. M., & Sellin, T. (1972). *Delinquency in a birth cohort*. Chicago, IL: University of Chicago Press.

CASES

In Re Gault, 387 U.S.1 (1967).
Kent v. *United States*, 383 U.S. 541 (1966).
McKeiver v. *Pennsylvania*, 403 U.S. 528 (1971).
Schall v. *Martin*, 467 U.S. 253 (1984).
In Re Winship, 397 U.S. 358 (1970).

Rejoinder to Dr. Dorne Eric Fritsch

Professor Dorne contends that waiver to adult court should continue to be used in the juvenile justice system but should not be used on a routine basis. After reviewing the three types of transfer to adult court, he argues that legislative transfer will be implemented routinely, and the other two will not. He challenges the use of legislative transfer and calls for the use of judicial transfer because of its ability to be individualized and its due process provisions. Although there are several challenges I can offer to the arguments presented here, I will limit my rejoinder to just a few comments.

He argues that legislative transfer will be implemented on a routine basis but juvenile and prosecutorial waiver will not. I strongly argue that the other two mechanisms of transfer to adult court can be used just as routinely as legislative transfer. For example, I discussed in my response to the question that an additional 14,500 juveniles would have been waived to adult court in Florida in 1993 if the legislative changes made in 1994 were in effect. Waiving over 14,500 juveniles to adult court in a single year certainly makes this practice routine. The legislative changes in Florida primarily centered around expanding prosecutorial transfer provisions by lowering the age from sixteen to fourteen years for several violent offenses.

Furthermore, the routinization of judicial transfer is not precluded by the fact that juveniles have the due process right to a transfer hearing. Professor Dorne makes the assumption that the due process provisions provided in judicial transfer will prevent the procedure from being used on a routine basis. I would argue that it is ill-advised to make such an assumption. For example, felons have the due process protection of receiving a grand jury hearing and indictment. Just because they have this right does not mean that indicting felons is not a routine practice. The use of grand juries is frequently criticized because they are merely a "rubber stamp" for the prosecutor's wishes. Other examples also exist within the criminal justice process, but the point is that providing a juvenile with a right to a transfer hearing will not prevent the routinization of transfer to adult court.

I believe this debate centered more around the issue of whether violent juveniles should be routinely waived to adult court regardless of the mechanism employed (i.e., judicial, prosecutorial, or legislative transfer), rather than the problems with legislative transfer and the benefits of judicial transfer. But because Professor Dorne drew this distinction, I believe it is important to briefly mention a few of the potential benefits of legislative transfer. In fact, I would argue that legislative transfer is a more appropriate mechanism than judicial transfer for transferring violent juvenile offenders to adult court, because it is designed to be nondiscretionary and will lead to greater consistency in processing violent juvenile offenders. Because legislative transfer is designed to be nondiscretionary, it can assist in diminishing bias in the juvenile justice process, including racial bias. Professor Dorne states that the routinization of waiver will not improve racial bias in the juvenile justice system but legislative transfer will if it is truly nondiscretionary. In addition, legislative transfer will also lead to greater consistency in processing violent juvenile offenders by decreasing the influence of discretion and justice by geography. Wide variation in judicial outcomes can occur because juvenile judges possess substantial discretion, and procedural practices vary between jurisdictions. Some jurisdictions frequently waive juvenile murderers and rapists to adult court, whereas other jurisdictions do so rarely. Therefore, legislative transfer can lead to consistency in judicial outcomes and can insure that violent juvenile offenders will receive appropriate punishment. Professor Dorne himself admits that judicial transfer hearings will not lead to uniform outcomes.

In conclusion, I challenge his claim that the routine transfer of violent juveniles will "sound the death knell" for the juvenile justice system. I will not belabor the points I made in my initial response to the question posed, but I strongly believe that the routine transfer of violent juvenile offenders to adult court is what will save the juvenile justice system, not lead to its destruction.

Should Female Correctional Officers Be Used in Male Institutions?

Richard Tewksbury argues YES. Tewksbury is Associate Professor of Justice Administration at the University of Louisville. His research focuses on correctional programming, gender identity, and sexual and gender deviance. Dr. Tewksbury is the author of *Introduction to Corrections* (Glencoe, 1997) and serves as editor of the *American Journal of Criminal Justice*. In addition, he has worked for the Ohio Department of Rehabilitation and Corrections and serves as a consultant for a number of corrections, public health, and social service agencies.

Mary (Hageman) Clement argues NO. She is Associate Professor of Criminal Justice at Virginia Commonwealth University and received a Ph.D. in Sociology from Washington State University in 1977. In 1990, she completed a dual degree in social work and law. Dr. Clement has published several textbooks on community-based corrections, police, community relations, and juvenile justice.

YES

RICHARD TEWKSBURY

Isn't it time to stop talking about gender differences?

—Lucie McClung, Correctional Service of Canada

The question of whether female correctional officers should be employed in institutions housing male inmates is a question that is asked only when the questioner relies on stereotypes and outdated assumptions about the nature and operations of correctional institutions. This is a question with such a clearly established answer that to even ask is to reveal one's lack of familiarity with correctional practices, legal rulings, and understandings about the gendered nature of social interactions.

However, this is a question that is still asked, despite the advances in equal employment opportunities and women's demonstration of ability and value in men's correctional institutions. In response, this discussion highlights the reasons why the answer is so clear. The use of female correctional officers in male correctional institutions is today a well-established, "normal" aspect of correctional administration. Since their first emergence in men's prisons in the 1970s, women correctional officers have fairly rapidly come to have a significant presence in most American prisons. The Federal Bureau of Prisons led the way, integrating female correctional officers in all but the few maximum security penitentiaries by 1975 (Feinman, 1986). In fact, by 1981, all but four states (Alaska, Pennsylvania, Texas, and Utah) employed women as correctional officers in mens' institutions (Morton, 1981). In 1995, 18 percent of correctional officers in adult correctional institutions are women (Camp & Camp, 1995, pp. 70–71). Female correctional officers are very similar to male correctional officers in almost all respects. In fact, one leading researcher on women in correctional work has concluded that the available research shows that "sex has little influence in the work-related attitudes, evaluations and performance of officers" (Zupan, 1992, p. 334).

In response to the question guiding this discussion, Perry Johnson (1992), then President of the American Correctional Association, identified two primary reasons for employing female correctional officers: need and fairness. I would add a third, dual-faceted, category of rationale for this practice: it only makes sense, and there are no valid reasons not to do so.

The remainder of this discussion highlights the reasons why it only makes sense to use female correctional officers in male institutions. The focus is on two areas of complementary rationales: (1) the positive contributions female correctional officers bring to male institutions and (2) the legal justification and support for such practices.

The Positive Contributions of Female Correctional Officers in Male Institutions

Female correctional officers bring patterns of interaction and interpersonal skills to the institution that are products of their feminine socialization. For some observers, this may be seen as a significant handicap, because stereotypical thinking would hold that this means women are "softer" on inmates, are less able to effectively respond to attacks or affronts, and are unable to exert effective means of control on males' behavior. However, research clearly shows that such assumptions are unfounded and simply wrong.

Female correctional officers are not, contrary to popular opinion, disadvantaged by an inability to physically respond in ways similar to their male counterparts, when such responses are necessary. Although female officers are consistently reported (by themselves and their male colleagues) to be less likely to resort to physical means to control inmates (Cadwaladr, 1993), this does not suggest that female correctional officers are unable or unwilling to do so. However, perhaps the first and most loudly voiced concern among male correctional officers regarding the inclusion of females on an institution's security staff is that men do not have confidence in a female colleague's ability to back them up in a crisis situation (Cadwaladr, 1993). Clearly, some female correctional officers may not be able to effectively control a violent male inmate using physical means; however, there are just as clearly a large number of male correctional officers who also cannot single-handedly physically control some violent male inmates. Contrary to popular belief, female correctional officers do not "back down" from physical confrontations with inmates, avoiding altercations or physical control of inmates when necessary.

Female correctional officers commonly bring to their jobs alternatives to male correctional officers' typical responses of physically controlling inmates. Female correctional officers have been repeatedly shown to react in a calmer and consequently more effective manner to volatile inmates (Cadwaladr, 1993; Kauffman, 1988). More specifically, female correctional officers rely more heavily on verbal skills to engage inmates in discussions and to "talk through" problems and issues that might otherwise trigger violent outbursts. The reasoning for this difference may come from two sources: first, women's differing socialization experiences, and second, such behavior may be (at least in part) the result of female correctional officers' higher level of education (Zimmer, 1986).

The differing styles of interacting with inmates and how female correctional officers generally respond to aggressive inmates is one of the major reasons why female correctional officers are less often victimized by male inmates than are male correctional officers (Cadwaladr, 1993; Kauffman, 1988). Male correctional officers are violently attacked by inmates as much as 3.6 times more often than are female correctional officers (Rowan, 1996). Furthermore, in contrast to the fears and predictions of some male correctional officers, the inclusion of women on an institution's security staff has no relationship to assaults on male correctional officers (Shawver & Dickover, 1986).

Overall, female correctional officers' adjustments to the stresses of correctional work are very similar to that of male correctional officers. Although some researchers have concluded that female correctional officers experience higher levels of work stress than male correctional officers (Cullen, Link, Wolfe, & Frank, 1985; Zupan, 1986), a large portion of this stress is related to interactions with colleagues, not inmates. Management of stress and perceptions of organizational commitment and how the job impacts one's personal life show few differences across sexes (Fry & Glaser, 1987) Consequently, the levels of job satisfaction male and female correctional officers experience are essentially the same (Cullen et al., 1985). This is important, because job satisfaction and how one copes with stress are well known to be related to job longevity and turnover. Based on the similarities of experiences, it can be expected that female and male correctional officers will have similar rates of turnover and length of service.

This is not to say that female correctional officers are "better" than male correctional officers. Nor is this a suggestion that male and female correctional officers experience their jobs significantly differently. Rather, this suggests that, just as in society in general, male and female correctional officers effectively complement one another's style and presence. Stated differently, having male and female correctional officers working side-by-side in correctional institutions creates a social environment that is, in at least some respects, similar to free society. The benefits of creating such an environment are clear: because the vast majority of inmates will someday return to society, it is desirable (if not imperative) to "correct" inmates in an environment that is at least roughly analogous to the society to which they will one day return.

Legal Issues

The legal status of female correctional officers in men's prisons has been well summarized by one scholar who points out that "case law dealing with female officers supervising male inmates generally supports women working almost all posts and performing nearly all tasks in an institution" (Collins, 1996, p. 301). Simply stated, women have the legal right to work in correctional institutions (both male and female), and although there may be some specific instances or situations in which administrators are discouraged from using female staff, there are very few legal restrictions on women's opportunities. This, however, has not always been the case. As recently as 1977, the U.S. Supreme Court ruled that under some circumstances women could and should be prohibited from holding correctional jobs in which they would have contact with male inmates (*Dothard* v. *Rawlinson,* 1977). This landmark case was largely based on the justices' unsupported belief that women's presence in an Alabama maximum security prison for men would be a threat to internal security and order. However, as has been discussed, this is a faulty belief. Whereas some feared that the *Dothard* case would establish a powerful precedent in correctional employment, in fact no other states have successfully relied on this case to restrict women's correctional employment opportunities (Zupan, 1992).

Legal challenges to the presence of female staff in male institutions have most commonly focused on issues involved in searches of inmates and female staff observing males using toilets or showers, or dressing. These legal challenges have generally not been fruitful for inmates. The generalized findings are that while there certainly are some restrictions placed on what female correctional officers can legally do, "what would otherwise be a reasonable search is not necessarily rendered unreasonable by virtue of the fact that the search was conducted by a person of the opposite sex, or in the presence of such a person" (Mushlin, 1993, p. 393; also see *Fillmore* v. *Eichkorn,* 1995; *Johnson* v. *Phelan,* 1995; and *Hayes* v. *Marriot,* 1995). In short, although the courts have imposed some restrictions allowing male inmates to maintain some degree of modesty and dignity, if correctional officials can show a need for female correctional officers to search or observe a male inmate partially or fully unclothed, then such actions are permissible.

The federal courts have declared that the legal determinations regarding complaints by male inmates about female officers working in all-male institutions need to be decided on the basis of inmates' privacy rights being balanced against the equal employment rights of correctional staff (*Avery* v. *Perrin,* 1979; *Riddick* v. *Sutton,* 1992), as well as the security needs of institutions.

One of the most common areas in which male inmates point to problems with female correctional officers is in the area of body searches. Female correctional officers conducting pat-down searches of male inmates or female correctional officers being present when male inmates are strip searched have been declared to not be violations of inmates' privacy rights, so long as female officers are not regularly performing or observing such actions (*Klein* v. *Pyle,* 1991; *Canedy* v. *Boardman,* 1994; *Michenfelder* v. *Sumner,* 1988).

Additionally, not only direct searches of inmates' persons, but female correctional officers' simple observation of male inmates in states of undress has raised legal issues. On this point, as with all other legal issues concerning cross-gender observation and contact in prison, the courts have been consistent and strong in their rulings. The assignment of female correctional officers to work stations where they may (or at times, must) observe male inmates dressing, undressing, showering, or using the toilet has been deemed as a minimal invasion of privacy and outweighed by the security needs of an institution (*Grummett* v. *Rushen,* 1985; *Jones* v. *Harrison,* 1994; *Michenfelder* v. *Sumner,* 1988; *Riddick* v. *Sutton,* 1992; *Timm* v. *Gunter,* 1991). Recently, the federal courts have further specified the conditions under which female staff can have opportunities to view male inmates, proclaiming that inmates' privacy rights are not violated if female officers regularly view male inmates only from the waist up, and if female correctional officers have "regular, predictable hours for patrolling" (*Strickler* v. *Waters,* 1993).

Similar issues, with similar judicial rulings, have been raised by female inmates concerning the employment of male correctional officers in women's prisons. Here too, as with cases involving females in male institutions, cases are determined based on issues of equal employment opportunities, definitions of privacy (and the right to privacy), and institutional security needs. One interesting case (*Jordan* v. *Gardner,* 1993) arising from a complaint by female inmates concerning pat down searches conducted by male staff concluded that to restrict such activities to only female staff would "create labor problems…conflict with the collective bargaining agreement...less effectively control the movement of contraband, and...could create security problems" (Mushlin, 1993, p. 96).

What is seen very clearly is that the courts have established a clear pattern in ruling that cross-gender supervision is a logical, nonproblematic, and fully acceptable practice in correctional work. Although some minimal restrictions have been placed on the tasks female correctional officers can and should perform in men's prisons, these restrictions are slight and designed to provide male inmates with a minimal degree of privacy rights. Prisons are environments in which privacy is assumed to be forfeited, as this is one of the long recognized "pains of imprisonment" (Sykes, 1958). Protecting an inmate's privacy rights, therefore, is not so much of a guarantee of his rights as it is the granting of a privilege.

Conclusion

In very clear and simple terms, employing correctional officers of different genders than inmates is a situation that clearly appears to be here to stay, as it should be. The reasons for having female correctional officers in male correctional institutions are clearly established, in both the social science literature and in case law. A job as a correctional officer is an employment opportunity, nothing more and nothing less. Although the job may present some fairly unique requirements and demands on those filling the post, these are not so specialized that there is a need to restrict more than one-half of the population from access to these jobs.

Based on this discussion, the question of "should female correctional officers be used in male institutions?" has a definitive answer: YES. There are a multitude of reasons for having women correctional officers in male correctional institutions, and there are no relevant legal, social, or scientific reasons not to have female correctional officers working in correctional institutions for men.

REFERENCES

Cadwaladr, M. I. (1993). *Breaking into jail: Women working in a men's jail.* Unpublished M.A. thesis, Department of Sociology and Anthropology, The University of British Columbia.

Camp, C. G., & Camp, G. M. (1995). *The corrections yearbook, 1995: Adult corrections.* South Salem, NY: Criminal Justice Institute.

Collins, W. (1996). Employee legal issues: Equal employment opportunities. In M. McShane and F. Williams III (Eds.), *Encyclopedia of American Prisons.* New York: Garland Publishing.

Cullen, F. T., Link, B. G., Wolfe, N. T., & Frank, J. (1985). Sex and occupational socialization among prison guards: A longitudinal study. *Criminal Justice and Behavior, 9,* 159–176.

Feinman, C. (1986). *Women in the criminal justice system* (2nd ed.). New York: Praeger Publishers.

Fry, L. J., & Glaser, D. (1987). Gender differences in work adjustment of prison employees. *Journal of Offender Counseling, Services and Rehabilitation, 12,* 39–52.

Johnson, P. M. (1992). Why employ women? *Corrections Today, 54* (6), 162–166.

Kauffman, K. (1988). *Prison officers and their world.* Cambridge, MA: Harvard University Press.

McClung, L. (1992). Gender balance. *Forum on corrections research, 4* (I). (Available at http://www.csc-scc.gc.ca/crd/forum/e04/e04lk.htm).

Morton, J. B. (1981). Women in correctional employment: Where are they now and where are they headed? In B. H. Olsson (Ed.), *Women in corrections.* College Park, MD: American Correctional Association.

Mushlin, M. (1993). *Rights of prisoners* (2nd ed.). Colorado Springs: Shepard's/McGraw-Hill.

Rowan, J. R. (1996). Who is safer in male maximum security prisons? *Corrections Today, 58* (2), 186–189.

Shawver, L., & Dickover, R. (1986). Research perspectives: Exploding a myth. *Corrections Today, 47* (6), 30–34.

Sykes, G. (1958). *The society of captives.* Princeton, NJ: Princeton University Press.

Zimmer, L. E. (1986). *Women guarding men.* Chicago: The University of Chicago Press.

Zupan, L. L. (1986). Gender-related differences in correctional officers' perceptions and attitudes. *Journal of Criminal Justice, 14,* 349–361.

Zupan, L. L. (1992). The progress of women correctional officers in all-male prisons. In I. Moyer (Ed.), *The changing roles of women in the criminal justice system* (2nd ed.). Prospect Heights, IL: Waveland Press.

CASES

Avery v. *Perrin,* 473 F Supp 90 (DNH 1979).

Canedy v. *Boardman,* 16 F3d 183 (7th Cir 1994), *revg* 801 F Supp 254 (WD Wis. 1992).

Dothard v. *Rawlinson,* 43 3 U.S. 3 21 (1977).

Fillmore v. *Eichkorn,* 891 F Supp 1482 (D Kan 1995).

Grummett v. *Rushen,* 779 F2d 491 (9th Cir 1985).

Hayes v. *Marriot,* 70 F3 d 1 144 (10th Cir 1995).

Johnson v. *Phelan,* 69 F3d 144 (7th Cir 1995).

Jones v. *Harrison,* 864 F Supp 166 (D Kan 1994).

Jordan v. *Gardner,* 953 F2d 11 37 (9th Cir 1992), *vacated & remanded,* 986 F2d 1521 (9th Cir 1993).

Klein v. *Pyle,* 767 F Supp 215 (D Colo 1991).

Michenfelder v. *Sumner,* 860 F2d 328 (9th Cir 1988).

Riddick v. *Sutton,* 794 F Supp 169 (EDNC 1992).

Strickler v. *Waters,* 989 F2d 1375 (4th Cir), *cert denied,* 114 S Ct 393 (1993).
Timm v. *Gunter,* 917 F2d 1093 (8th Cir 1990), *cert denied,* 111 S Ct 2807 (1991).

Rejoinder to Dr. Tewksbury Mary H. Clement

When in law school, we were taught to argue the law if the law was on our side. If not, then argue the facts. In anticipation of your excellent review of the literature and the law, I conceded that the law was on your side of permitting women to legally work in an all-male facility in the very beginning of my debate. Perhaps this argument is not so much a yes-or-no formatted answer but more in line with: "when should you (my sister, my daughter, my female student) take a job in an all-male correctional institution (prison)?" Thus, I will continue to argue the reality of the situation—the facts.

Richard, did you notice that we both agree that women correctional officers experience higher levels of work stress and that a large portion of this stress is related to interactions with colleagues, not inmates? I do not disagree that female correctional officers in male institutions make positive contributions. I only question the cost to her—emotionally, physically, and mentally. Whereas I would agree that men and women working side-by-side as in normal society sounds "nice," the reality is that men and women are not working as co-equals. The same hidden, subtle discrimination that plagues our society is also represented in the microcosm of the prison. If one's coworkers have been trained in the military they make good "guards" but they are lacking in effective experiences with working with women.

The literature you cited for job satisfaction comes mainly from 1984 to 1986. It is based on prison populations then—not now. Today, the statewide overcrowding, the abolishment of parole, and "three-strikes-you're-out" sentencing has made work for all correctional officers much more stressful. In addition, prison structures are being misused. For example, in Virginia, we have five or six new facilities that were developed as minimum security facilities in Maryland. However, in Virginia, we have doubled-bunked the dorms so that now there are one hundred inmates per side, not fifty. These inmates are not classified as minimum security risk; they are murderers and rapists. But, the design permits more inmates at a lesser cost to the state. However, the only officer in the control booth that was designed to be elevated has his or her view obstructed by the double bunks for each side of the control booth. Unintentional blind spots make all officers vulnerable to assaults. Women, however, have a different vulnerability; that is why victorious armies rape the conquered women.

Several decades ago, when I began teaching in this field, I came out of graduate school thinking that juvenile correctional facilities should be coed. Later, when I learned about developmental stages, I realized the error in my thinking. Well, the same kind of "let's-make-things-equal" has now been applied to male correctional facilities, and I question the real intent. I recognize that inmates do not have privacy rights, but they should. Legal cases have supported minimal invasion of privacy of male inmates because security needs of the institution outweigh those rights. Yet, when I do a role reversal, it is not there. For example, in an all-female correctional setting, men are present as guards but mostly female correctional officers do the acts considered invasion of privacy. Male police officers do not do strip searches on women, so why should the institution's failure to hire enough officers change the balance of the equation? Thus, I wonder. Could it be that this is another way to continue the pains of imprisonment by emasculating the male at the expense of the female officer? Could it be that by showing her off when she's the warden's favorite toy, a more subtle form of torture is being used?

I recognize the fact that research of the 1980s and law cases support your argument. However, I visit prisons in my area, I take students, and I volunteer to work with inmates—male and female. I have seen a female warden who in my estimation has a balance of power and concern or compassion in her management style, so I know it is possible to have administrators who understand coequal relationships and are sensitive to the needs of all concerned. Because of those needs, even though the structure is not the most modern, the environment is safer for all. And those who do come to work as coworkers come with a mentality of cooperation and harmony. Thus, instead of saying "No," I say when the structure is environmentally safe, the administration and coworkers value coequal relationships and not power over each other, take the job! But, they will be like hen's teeth—hard to find.

NO

Mary H. Clement

In 1972, the Equal Employment Opportunity Act made the coverage of Title VII of the Civil Rights Act of 1964 applicable to all agencies with fifteen or more employees. That act brought nearly all local, state, and federal-level agencies under its jurisdiction. Women were allowed entry into federal, state, and local agencies in all areas of criminal justice, including corrections. Thus, women have a constitutional right to be hired and work in male prisons, but should they? No.

Unlike their counterpart, female law officers, female correctional officers in male institutions have some unique challenges. When the President's Commission on Law Enforcement and Administration of Justice in 1967 challenged the traditional roles of women by stating that: "policewomen can be an invaluable asset to modern law enforcement and their present role should be broadened" (Washington, 1974, p. 58), the emphasis was on women in law enforcement, not in all-male prisons. I realize that the policy statement meant that a few police departments began the arduous task of full employment of females. For example, in 1972, twelve women were sworn in as Pennsylvania State Police, and two female agents graduated from the Federal Bureau of Investigation. Thus, before 1972, there were at least some female law officers on the local, state, and federal levels. However, it took the 1972 amendment before the first woman was hired in an all male prison.

Although there was the hope that the inclusion of women in the criminal justice system would help the system become more responsive to the needs of the public, the reality was that little research was done on corrections, a subculture of the criminal justice system, and the role women could or should play in that very repressive system. As usual, there were misconceptions as to how the criminal justice system works in general and the corrections component in particular. Now, knowing what I know, I suggest that women stay out for these critical reasons: (1) history and structure of correctional institutions, (2) lack of protection, and (3) the clientele.

History and Structure of Correctional Institutions

Besides the same kinds of resistance as female law officers, women in corrections were coming into a business of punishing men that was completely different from community involvement of the English policing system with its tithing system. Whereas police are to be more community orientated and view the alleged suspect as innocent until proven guilty, the correctional system cares little about the outside community. Even courts, until more recently, have taken a "hands-off policy" toward lawsuits initiated by inmates. Historically, prisoners in state and federal correctional institutions have been considered wards of the State. In 1871, the convict was labeled as a temporary slave of the state who had forfeited all state rights and "…subject to the regulations of the institution of which they are inmates" (*Ruffin* v. *Commonwealth*, 1871, p. 796). Legally, the convict was considered less than an alien.

Although the last decades in correctional law have expanded prisoners' rights, the statutes have been amended to incorporate complete control over an inmate as "public safety." Prisons that were originally created to exercise complete control over men are again in business under new rhetoric.

Prisons were built to deal primarily with men, with the cruelest methods to inflict pain as a way of changing behavior. The masters in historical penology, Barnes and Teeters (1959, p. 329), remind us that *penal* comes from the Latin root that means punishment, pain, and revenge. Ironically, the other branch of the root word means penitence and repentance. But, that model died out with the Quakers and the Eastern State Penitentiary, when the Auburn (New York) style that exploited the inmates' labor through prison labor took over. It was Elam Lynds, considered a strict disciplinarian and an early warden at Auburn and Sing Sing prisons, who believed that "reformation could not be effected until the spirit of the criminal was broken" (Barnes & Teeters, 1959, p. 341).

At the turn of this century, the arrest rate for women was one to fifty to sixty men. So, yes, a few women and children came into the justice system. But most were men. Prisons were created, in some cases actually built by the men, to house the men in some of the most inhuman conditions. It was only because of the cry from reformers of the sexual exploitation and unsanitary conditions of the female inmates that women were moved to their own correctional institutions (Clear & Cole, 1986, p. 473) instead of changing our concepts of punitive justice.

The geographic isolation of the prison and the administration policy work together with inadequate public transportation and the low finances of the visitors who might serve as watchdogs on the real system, to keep the public out of prisons. Without accountability, prisons are left to wardens (males) to run the institutions as they see fit.

In my experience, prisons are a place where adults are given the societal permission to abuse another human being in the name of correctional penology. Unless there is a very enlightened administrator, the prison is a very repressive management style such that even the correctional officers, both males and females, become their captives. The Stafford experiment in dividing the collage class into captors and captives that had to be discontinued because the students as role-playing the guards and the inmates were experiencing emotional trauma is relieved, today, by the real correctional officers (guards)—male and female. The occupational stress would then be even higher for women who had any training in human behavior or even any intuitive ideas that desired results in human behavior could be gained with some individuals in some different ways, instead of breaking the spirit of a person. Thus, an enlightened or educated female guard would be considered the "odd-man-out" or "bad apple" by the administration.

It is worthy to note that Purdy Institute in Washington State, developed by an educator, was one of the few correctional institutions based on human development stages, wherein inmates moved from maximum security to medium and then to minimum security based on merit. Yet, it is an all-female institution.

Generally speaking, a correctional officer is the front-line in the prison system, on whom the whole structure depends. Yet, that role is not clearly defined nor understood. Whenever there is that much ambiguity in a job, it permits the supervisor too much discretion in determining job effectiveness and evaluating job performance.

After 1972, there has been a push for women to work in male correctional institutions. Yet, full utilization of women in law enforcement, a counterpart to women in corrections, has not been actualized despite all the research studies that determine that women really could do the physical work required in law enforcement (Greenwald & Connolly, 1973; Milton, 1973; Sichel, Friedman, Quint, & Smith, 1978). Women may be law officers, but their numbers are few and their percentages only reach the middle twenties in such cities as Washington, DC. The end result is that female correctional officers are asked to do an almost unperformable task without proper training, for low pay, and at great risk.

Lack of Protection

Unlike the armed female law officer, the female correctional officer is more a captive than a captor. She is more isolated in that she is locked into an institution, with no weapon, where she lacks control and is outnumbered. In many institutions, officers do not even have access to radios to call for help if needed; they rely on whistles and their ability to scream for help. Conversely, female law officers can run; they are not locked into the patrol car with no weapon of their own.

In addition, inmates have been there longer than the officers. They outnumber the officers and in some cases control the institution or at least, are working with the administration in a cooperative endeavor to make profit for both the underground "black market" and the administration. Inmates know, for example, that if a warden is not working with them, they have a riot, and the state government views the warden as not being able to keep the inmates under control. Then, the undesirable warden is replaced and a new "fish" comes in, hopefully with a high learning curve so that business can continue as usual. So, in the end, it is the inmates who often try to protect their favorite officers, for many different reasons.

Male officers argue that female officers cannot handle the violence and confrontations with inmates. Yet, Zimmer (1986), in a study of female officers in two prisons for men, found that female officers had less trouble with the inmates than the male counterparts had, although there was harassment when they first appeared on the job.

Clientele

The clientele of a female correctional officer have a median age of thirty, minority, with 50 to 75 percent of all state prison inmates unable to read. The cycle of crime began at an early age, and many offenders passed repeatedly through the juvenile and adult criminal justice systems. "Eighty-one percent of all state prisoners have criminal histories that included previous incarceration or probation" (DiMascio, 1995, p. 13).

Clients in prison are not considered persons, hence, the word *inmates*. Sherman (1975), using participant observations, interviews with citizens, academy and department performance ratings, and interviews with command personnel, concluded that female law officers perform in a less aggressive fashion. "Sympathetic listening, compassionate understanding, and human responsiveness are the policing characteristics that the public really desires and, indeed, deserves" (p. 436). Yet, those qualities have not been valued by the administration in correctional officers.

Officers are expected to enforce all rules and policies in a manner that is punitive, regardless of circumstances. Many officers enjoy the power that this gives them over another human being. In many institutions, inmates are not given the status of being human. They are treated like predatory animals who deserve to be punished and humiliated whenever possible. Correctional officers who do not view them in that way are torn between their own sense of morality and the administration that demands that inmates be treated severely and punitively.

In addition, many of these offenders have been abused and neglected by the women in their lives (Widom, 1995). Thus, these offenders see the woman in the officer first, and that triggers a lot of anger, hostility, and desire to abuse her and her body. Inmates throw feces on officers, both male and female. But, for females, they get an added bonus—semen, thrown or placed in her hand through an unexpected handshake.

Inmates and correctional officers who have special difficulties accepting the feminine nature of themselves (feeling, intuition, seeing the whole of something, music) also project that warring within themselves onto the female officer. The murderers, the sex offenders, and the abusive husbands mentally undress her as a woman and fantasize having sex with her. For female officers, that becomes a tremendous burden in a working environment. It feels like rape, except one still has one's clothes on. Nonetheless, it is very stressful. Unlike the female law officer, wherein the citizen would view the officer as an officer first, the female correctional officer is viewed as a woman first, then as a correctional guard, if at all.

Sexual harassment comes from both the inmates and the other correctional officers. Some inmates think that female officers and staff enjoy watching them shower or dress. So they purposefully leave the curtain to the shower open so the officer can watch them masturbate in the shower. Inmates verbally harass them as well, accidentally bump into the female officers, or grab her in the crotch area. When female officers charge inmates with sexual harassment, the charges are dropped by the institution for various reasons. Male officers who do not feel comfortable having female officers harass them too. They are also slow to respond and make fun of an officer who is being harassed.

Because the history and administration of corrections is so punitive and the female correctional officers lack protection from both the other correctional officers and the clientele, I would conclude that she would be best to use her skills and talents in a more responsible, coequal environment. The macho image and the tests or challenges, "if-you-are-a-real-woman," are the kind that can break the spirit of the captor as well as of the captive.

REFERENCES

Barnes, H. E., & Teeters, N. K. (1959). *New horizons in criminology* (3rd ed.). Englewood Cliffs, NJ: Prentice-Hall.

Clear, T., & Cole, G. F. (1986). *American corrections.* Monterey, CA: Brooks/Cole.

DiMascio, W. M. (1995). *Seeking justice: Crime and punishment.* New York: Edna McConnell Clark Foundation.

Greenwald, J. E., & Connolly, H. A. (1973). *New York City police women evaluation.* Unpublished manuscript prepared for the Urban Institute for grant application to the Police Foundation.

Milton, C. (1973). *Policewomen on patrol.* Washington, DC: Police Foundation.

Sherman, L. J. (1975). An evaluation of policewomen on patrol in a suburban police department. *Journal of Police Science and Administration, 1,* 383–394.

Sichel, J. L., Friedman, L. N., Quint, J. C., & Smith, M. E. (1978). *Women on patrol: A pilot study on police performance in New York City.* Washington, DC: National Institute of Law Enforcement and Criminal Justice.

Washington, B. (1974). *Deployment of female police officers in the United States.* Gaithersburg, MD: International Association of Chiefs of Police.

Widom, C. S. (1995). Victims of childhood sexual abuse: Later criminal consequences. *Research in brief.* Washington, DC: National Institute of Justice.

Zimmer, L. E. (1986). *Women guarding men.* Chicago, IL: University of Chicago Press.

CASES

Ruffin v. *Commonwealth,* 21 Gratt 790 (1871).

Rejoinder to Dr. Clement
RICHARD TEWKSBURY

Professor Clement proposes that female correctional officers should not work in male correctional institutions because it has always been that way and change is not needed. Second, she suggests that women working in male correctional institutions are unable to protect themselves from the dangers of the violent and dangerous clientele. In short, it appears that, rather than a logical argument, Professor Clement offers an apology for women's inability to do the job. In suggesting that women are weak and incapable of doing the job, she suggests that both individual men and the correctional system as a whole would need to provide special care for female officers. If this were the case, yes, women's presence would certainly be problematic for corrections. However, there are several critical errors in her argument.

To begin with, suggesting that "prisons are a place where adults are given the societal permission to abuse another human being" is a wild exaggeration. Correctional officials are not granted "permission to abuse" anyone; perhaps this was the case until the early twentieth century, but not today. Certainly, prisons are often unsavory and less-than-desirable places to live and work. Professor Clement argues that "clients in prison are not considered persons, hence the term *inmates.*" Using this logic, could we not argue that to refer to a classroom full of budding scholars as "students" is to dehumanize them?

However, the problems in her argument are most clearly brought out when she exaggerates gender differences. She contends "an educated female guard would be considered the 'odd-man-out' or 'bad apple' by the administration" because she would most likely not agree with the "permission to abuse" inmates. First, why do we assume an educated woman is any different from an educated man? Second, any educated correctional officer (male or female) would be offended to be called a "guard." Third, if the concern is centered on not being 'odd-man-out,' perhaps corrections is not the best career choice. Furthermore, as the foundation of feminist thought, activism, and scholarship, women have always been the 'odd-man-out.' Why, then, should women be prohibited from correctional jobs?

It is also important to consider that simply because one is not Officer of the Year does not mean that she cannot, or should not, do the job. If things are to change, and if we believe corrections officers are given permission to abuse inmates, it would seem we would advocate for change; this needs to come from within. Changes in attitudes would seem best accomplished by women correctional officers demonstrating their abilities; if women never have the opportunity, it may well appear that they cannot do the job.

The apologetic nature of Professor Clement's argument does not stop here, however. Instead, she extends this position, suggesting that "occupational stress would then be even higher for women who had any training in human behavior." Again, are we to believe that only women are truly affected by education?

The argument that women have not yet achieved full utilization in law enforcement (which, interestingly, it appears that Professor Clement supports) is completely tangential and largely irrelevant. The one point where this discussion is relevant, however, is actually in support of why women should be correctional officers: "(D)espite all the research studies that determine that women really could do the physical work," they are not fully utilized in law enforcement. Yes, this is a problem, but is this not also contradictory to the argument she proposes that women cannot do the job of a correctional officer? If we rely on the fact that because women have yet to achieve full equality in law enforcement they should not be brought into corrections, perhaps we also need to advocate for the removal of African American, Native American, urban, and educated correctional officers. After all, none of these groups have achieved full equality yet either.

The argument that because women officers may experience sexual harassment they should not be in male correctional institutions is terribly uninformed. Based on this argument, it would seem only logical that we men "protect our women" by barring them from all types of "dangerous" employment opportunities. This would, of course, include university professorships; campuses are rife with sexual harassment, and while this clearly is a problem, her argument suggests that women should be barred here, as well as from many other occupations.

Professor Clement also adds the interesting twist of presenting women as victims of discrimination. She suggests that sympathetic listening, compassionate understanding, and human responsiveness are not valued by correctional administrators.

This suggests that women do have something to offer (despite their inherent physical, emotional, and psychological weaknesses), but these are traits "the system" does not want. This is incorrect; research has consistently shown that the use of force to compel inmate behavior is perhaps the worst approach, and traits such as sympathetic listening, compassionate understanding, and human responsiveness are much more effective. In fact, these are traits most modern (or, dare I say, progressive) correctional administrators want in correctional officers. Women are not victims here, except in Professor Clement's view.

In the end, to say that women should not be used as correctional officers in male institutions because the "end result is that female correctional officers are asked to do an almost unperformable task without proper training, for low pay, and at great risk" is a gross misrepresentation. To ask any correctional officer to work without proper training would be a major problem; this is not based on gender. To ask correctional officers to work for what they earn in most systems is insulting; this is not based on gender. And, to say that correctional work poses "great risk" is simply an exaggeration. Yes, correctional work can be dangerous, dirty, unappealing, and highly stressful. But none of these situations are gender specific, and to suggest that they are, or that women cannot effectively do the job, should also be insulting, to both women and men.

Coed Prison: Should We Try It (Again)?

John Ortiz Smykla argues YES. He is Professor and Director of Graduate Studies in Criminal Justice at the University of Alabama and received his Ph.D. from the School of Criminal Justice at Michigan State University in 1977. Dr. Smykla has been studying coed prisons for over twenty years and has authored and edited a number of books and articles on the subject. His current research focuses on the contributions of African Americans to nineteenth century Southern law enforcement and technology in criminal justice in the twenty-first century.

James Houston argues NO. He is Associate Professor of Criminal Justice at Appalachian State University. He has a Ph.D. in Urban Studies and Criminal Justice at Portland State University (1987). He is the author of *Correctional Management: Functions, Skills, and Systems*, 2nd ed., and is coauthor of *Criminal Justice and the Policy Process*. In addition, he has participated in a number of research projects on gangs and has twenty years of experience in adult and juvenile corrections and community services.

YES

JOHN ORTIZ SMYKLA

In 1833, Lieber (reprinted 1964) wrote that women in prison with men in the United States were "much and unfortunately neglected." By 1996, not much had changed. In a comprehensive review of the literature on the impact of coed prisons on women prisoners, I concluded that coed prison offers women prisoners few, if any, economic, educational, vocational, and social advantages (Smykla & Williams, 1996). I added that cocorrections benefits male prisoners and system maintenance. But, must coed prison disadvantage women prisoners and must one-sex prison with equally miserable records of correctional performance be the norm? I believe not. I argue here that coed prison holds a legitimate place in a comprehensive, rational system of sentencing and punishment. Until a prisoner demonstrates that he or she is incapable of living in a coed prison environment, coed prison should be the penal environment for most of our country's prison population. After all, the measure of punishment is not its objective appearance (that is, are women and men prisoners separated), but its subjective impact (Morris & Tonry, 1990). To believe otherwise is to accept the illusory ideal of single-sex incarceration at too high a price.

By coed prison I refer to the incarceration and interaction of female and male prisoners under a single institutional administration. The basic concept supporting coed prison is simple: the interaction of incarcerated men and women will have a positive effect on institutional functioning and the inmates' lives. Traditional single-sex incarceration exacerbates the sexual abnormality of offenders by fostering development of homosexual and often violent subcultures, ignores the fact that much criminal behavior stems, directly or indirectly, from the absence of healthy relationships with the opposite sex, or the inability to explore problems of sexual identification, impedes postrelease adjustment, engenders continued criminality, and caricaturizes traditional sex-role stereotypes. Coed prison aims to counteract these institutionalized deficiencies in punishment.

History of Coed Prison

When state institutions opened their doors to women prisoners in the early nineteenth century, women were incarcerated with men in institutions that were designed for men and held men in far greater numbers. In these facilities, women were mostly left entirely alone and kept in large rooms or individual cells, removed to separate quarters within or attached to the men's section (for example, an annex adjacent to the institution but outside its front wall, kitchen attic, or upper floor of an entrance building), or relocated to an isolated building on or near the main prison grounds (Rafter, 1990).

Not until the reformatory movement began in the last quarter of the nineteenth century was there a separation of female prisoners from male prisoners in which women would be moved to prisons of their own. Beginning with the Mount Pleasant Female Prison at Ossining, New York, in 1839 and the Indiana Reformatory Institution for Women and Girls in Indianapolis in 1873, prisons became involved in the politics of gender and in the discourse about the nature of criminal women (Rafter, 1990).

Today, after a century of sex segregation in prisons across the United States, incarcerating women and men together is reappearing. In 1971, the Federal Bureau of Prisons opened the first modern coed prison for young adults at the Robert F. Kennedy Youth Center in Morgantown, West Virginia. Today, there are fifty-two coed facilities operating in eighteen states, the District of Columbia, the Federal Bureau of Prisons, and the Departments of Army, Navy, and Air Force (Smykla & Williams, 1996). The number of women and men incarcerated in coed prisons across the United States is 29,794, of which 23 percent are women.

Why Go Coed?

There are a number of reasons to support coed prisons:

1. Coed prison can reduce the dehumanizing and destructive aspects of confinement by allowing continuity or resumption of heterosocial relationships.
2. Coed prison can reduce institutional control problems through the weakening of disruptive homosexual systems and predatory homosexual activity, lessening of assaultive behavior, and the diversion of inmate interests and activities.
3. Coed prison can create a more "normal," less institutionalized atmosphere.
4. Coed prison can expand the treatment potential for developing positive heterosocial relationships and coping skills.
5. Coed prison can cushion the shock of adjustment for release by reducing the number and intensity of adjustments to be made.
6. Coed prison can increase the diversification and flexibility of program offerings and equal program access for male and female prisoners.
7. Coed prison can expand career opportunities for women previously of ten "boxed into" the single state women's prison as correctional staff.

Rhetoric or Reality in Coed Prison?

The reasons listed above for supporting coed prison do not mean that they have been achieved or proved. The absence of that literature, though, is no reason to abandon the development of coed prison. The body of literature on single-sex prison demonstrates systemwide failure in prisoner rehabilitation and public safety, but we do not find correctional decision makers, legislatures, or the public calling for the abolition of single-sex prisons. Few doubted the wisdom and decency of moving women prisoners into all-female institutions in the nineteenth century, where they could be treated differently and housed in the promise of nurturant reformatories. But the promise of the benefits of single-sex incarceration has never appeared in anything like adequate numbers. The separating was achieved, the providing denied. It is the same with coed prison today: to become more than window dressing, the coed concept requires conceptual adequacy, detail to implementation factors, and an abandoning of any notion that they will be quick fixes to our nation's crime problem.

What, then, is the impact of coed prison? Evaluation research on coed prison stalled in the 1980s, even though "going coed" has continued. The body of ethnographic research suggests that coed prison is a more humane prison environment than single-sex incarceration. The recidivism research suggests high probabilities of success. At the same time, though, contradictions develop across coed facilities. These contradictions may be more a function of the state-of-the-art of evaluation research and politics than of the independent variable coed prison. For example, there is the problem of the constricted size of coed prison and external validity. The fifty-two coed prisons in existence today are spread across the entire United States. This geographical spread hinders access by researchers, makes it difficult to compare data from one coed prison with another, and limits the level of generalization from one coed prison to another.

Second, coed prison represents only one dimension of an institutional environment, and the degree to which coed factors can be isolated and evaluated apart from the total coed institutional setting can be problematic.

Third, within a relatively short time, there have been constant modifications within coed prisons of what may be designated critical variables: sex ratios, age distribution, program content and interaction levels, contact restrictions, use of transfer, and institutional security levels. Shifts in goal priorities and institutional operations impede both isolating the coed phenomenon for study and determining measures of success that are appropriate to the circumstances.

Fourth, to be sure, the existing body of knowledge on coed prison is informative and allows us to develop useful ideas on the effectiveness on the coed intervention. A pressing need exits to develop rigorous studies on the effectiveness of coed prison. Only then will we have a stronger reason to move beyond grasping for panaceas that ultimately prove disheartening failures. In the absence of such a body of knowledge, it will remain difficult to conclude with confidence that coed prison "works." When most of the current body of knowledge on coed prison is plagued by defects in design, any positive findings are open to only two interpretations: the program really works or the results are an artifact of biased methodology. In this situation, the positive findings are at best suggestive of what works and at worse could form the basis for an intervention that is ineffective or harmful. The challenge is to embrace a more informed approach that recognizes the limits of reform but also has a sounder, more scientific basis for understanding how the benefits of coed prison might be achieved.

A related problem is the absence of a research orientation and insufficient data collection capability stemming from the correctional bureaucracy's interest in giving coed prison a low profile or risk it being perceived as a "resort," "hotel," or "whorehouse." Single-sex incarceration and homosexual activity in prison is perceived as part of a prisoner's "unnatural lot," but coed prison and heterosexual contact is more offensive to society's values today than same-sex incarceration and predatory, homosexual activity. "Out of sight, out of mind" means correctional decision makers and politicians need not battle the politics of punishment or the safe illusion of single-sex incarceration. As a result, coed incarceration never receives state or federal research priority and is seldom discussed except in a few introductory textbooks on criminal justice and corrections. For example, in this researcher's experience, valid data on pregnancies in coed prison are difficult to obtain because such incidents are covered up. The orientation away from research exists toward both substantive matters and research in general.

Coed Prison Lessons from Denmark

Selke's (1993) fieldwork on the coed prison at Ringe, Denmark, offers two important lessons for further development of coed prison in the United States. First, in Denmark, coed prison is consciously and purposefully represented in the "open" prisons model of corrections. The open model emphasizes integration, privacy, activity, smallness, flexibility, casework, and healthful and safe prisons. Single-sex incarceration in the United States, however, is founded on the "control" model of incarceration, which emphasizes segregation, surveillance, idleness, largeness, rigidity, guards, and a belief that prison can control crime. Osmond and Siegler (1974) write that one of the worst features of the United States' prison system is the simultaneous presence of "open" and "control" correctional models in experimental correctional programs such as coed prison that are contradictory and wreak havoc with new programs, policies, and objectives. In the United States, we still find that coed prisons are beset with divergent policies, wide ranges in the level of policy implementation, inconsistent modes of action, and heated debates about the actual and ideal policies, programs, and objectives to be achieved. For example, the nature of the programmatic models of coed prison expresses the belief that there is value in the ability of the male–female relationship to normalize the prison environment, reduce postrelease adjustment problems, and contribute to a lowering of recidivism. However, the nonprogrammatic model of coed prison represents the belief that "going coed" need not alter standard prison operations or change our assumptions about punishments and is at odds with the programmatic model. The difference in these and other conceptual models must be articulated and checked for internal and external consistency. Anything less will thwart the effectiveness with which coed prison is implemented and its intended outcomes achieved.

In addition to the success of the "open" model of coed prison in Denmark, Selke (1993) also reports that the head of Ringe's coed prison attributes the role correctional staff play in translating coed theory into practice as the most important factor. At Ringe, correctional officers have a much broader and varied job scope than the typical United States' correctional officer. "The officers function as shop/vocational instructors, caseworkers, and security officers. Standard officers are assigned to one unit and work in that unit only.... They have responsibility for the training and supervision of inmates in workshops, for the planning of visits and furloughs...and for the care and management of the living unit. In addition, the officers of each unit together coordinate a flexible time system so that they have a fair degree of liberty in structuring their forty-hour work week" (p. 60).

Slowly, correctional decision makers in the United States are beginning to understand the important role correctional staff play in program success, as in Denmark's Ringe prison, by investing in the development of employees and the use of participatory management. In a study of five podular, direct-supervision jails that emphasize the characteristics of the "open" corrections model (integration, privacy, activity, smallness, flexibility, casework, and healthy and safe environments for staff and prisoners), Stohr, Lovrich, Menke, and Zupan (1994) found that investment in personnel results in greater job satisfaction, less workplace stress, greater organizational commitment, and less staff turnover. Employee investment through training in problem solving, interpersonal and communication skills, participatory management, ethics, and leadership prepared staff to be leaders and supervisors in their living units and develop more of a guidance role with prisoners. The podular, direct supervision concept that only a few years ago was thought of as too idealistic, liberal, and soft on criminals is now a permanent fixture on the United States' correctional landscape and advocated by the National Institute of Corrections. Application of employee investment to state prison systems for both coed and single-sex prisons is only a matter of time.

And Finally, Coed Prison in the Twenty-First Century

Coed prison has resurfaced in the United States, and it is here to stay. The question is, however, how many more prisons will go coed? As scholars, students, and practitioners think and act about the kinds of comprehensive and rational systems of punishment discussed by Morris and Tonry (1990), and as we look beyond our own borders for ways to control crime, more, not less, correctional options will become available in the twenty-first century, and the use of coed prison will expand.

References

Lieber, F. (1833, reprinted 1964). Translator's preface to Gustave de Beaumont and Alexis de Tocqueville. *On the penitentiary system in the United States and its application to France.* Carbondale, IL: Southern Illinois University Press.

Morris, N., & Tonry, M. (1990). *Between prison and probation.* New York: Oxford.

Osmond, H., & Siegler, M. (1974). *Models of madness, models of medicine.* New York: Macmillan.

Rafter, N. H. (1990). *Partial justice: Women, prison, and crime.* Belmont, CA: Brooks/Cole.

Selke, W. L. (1993). *Prisons in crisis.* Bloomington, IN: Indiana University Press.

Smykla, J. O., & Williams, J. J. (1996). Co-corrections in the United States of America, 1970–1990: Two decades of disadvantages for women prisoners. *Women & Criminal Justice, 8,* 61–76.

Stohr, M., Lovrich, B., Menke, B., & Zupan, L. (1994). Staff management in correctional institutions: Comparing DiIulio's "control model" and "employee investment model" outcomes in five jails. *Justice Quarterly, 11,* 471–497.

Rejoinder to Dr. Smykla

JAMES HOUSTON

Professor Smykla fails to provide an adequate argument for coed prisons. Decidedly absent from his argument is a discussion of the differences in the way men and women do time. Aggressiveness and exploitation characterize the way many men do time, and women mark time by less aggression, replication of the family structure, and cooperation. As a consequence, the effective women's institution provides more space and time for programs, space for spending time with children, and programs geared to the needs of today's woman as well as training for family-sustaining jobs. In addition, because of the socialization of most female offenders, programs should provide additional opportunities that foster independence and autonomy rather than forcing her into programs designed for men. This is the primary shortcoming of any argument for coed prisons; most institutional programs are designed for men, not women. Furthermore, although we can learn from other cultures and experiences, it is difficult to extrapolate lessons from a culture as homogenous as Denmark and apply those lessons to a culture as diverse as ours on a subject as important and sensitive as coed corrections. The "open" model noted by Smykla sounds suspiciously like many minimum-security institutions I am aware of that operate on the unit management model.

As Professor Smykla points out, the use of the "podular, direct supervision concept" is the answer to improving women's programs. This concept originated in the United States and has spread around the world and gained a life of its own. In the United States, unit management has been adopted by at least twenty-seven Departments of Correction. This is evidence enough that decision makers have begun to realize the importance of staff and their contribution to programs and institutional tranquillity, by the implementation of direct supervision jails and unit management. This approach to managing a jail or prison is recognized by corrections authorities as inherently offering a more humane environment and recognizing the individual and his or her needs. Contrary to Professor Smykla's argument, the possibilities exist not in coed prison, but in the implementation of unit management.

Any right-minded person is interested in decreasing the dehumanizing effects of prison, developing a more "normal" atmosphere, keeping inmates safe, and offering effective and useful programs to inmates while incarcerated. First, in a unitized institution, staff are on the unit approximately fourteen hours per day, taking a proactive stance to problems on the unit, and are available for normal social interaction. As a consequence, every inmate has the opportunity to see and talk to staff on an as-needed basis, and no inmate is lost in a shuffle of nameless faces. Second, disruptive, predatory inmates are more easily controlled, thereby making the environment more safe for those individuals apt to be preyed on. Third, the unit staff, which in this day is likely to be composed of both men and women, contributes to a more "normal" environment by their presence. The inmates have the opportunity to witness healthy, nonexploitive heterosexual social relationships between normally functioning people without hidden agendas. Finally, the unit team can assure that inmates will gain entrance into programs that will be most beneficial for them and develop and implement programs that "cushion the shock" of reintegration.

The answer to the question of how to address citizen calls for justice, and the female inmate is at present hiding in plain sight. Right under our noses is the opportunity to develop an approach to the effective delivery of services to women and the effective management of women's prisons: unit management. The unit management approach allows for a more intense interaction between staff and inmate, development of adequate programs designed with women's needs in mind, and the opportunity for staff to more adequately monitor and reward behavior that is autonomous and results oriented. What is missing in this scenario is the commitment necessary from elected officials and correctional administrators that will assure the availability of moneys to fund unit management and programs critical to allowing women to learn to become autonomous individuals capable of creating their own destiny.

NO

JAMES HOUSTON

As of the end of 1994, there were 957,318 inmates in our prisons serving sentences of one year or more; of that number, 60,069 were women (Maguire & Pastore, 1996). Between then and the time this book goes to press, the total number of inmates serving time in U.S. prisons will exceed 1.1 million. This is a sizable investment by any yardstick, and there is little reason to believe that the numbers will abate anytime soon. The result has been overcrowding and a paucity of programs for prison inmates. One solution for overcrowding and the related problems is coed prisons.

There are ninety-seven state institutions and sixteen Federal Bureau of Prisons (BOP) institutions that claim to be coed. In spite of the claims of proponents, how well they meet the needs of the inmates is open to question. It is my assertion that coed prisons do not work for the benefit of women inmates, that any advantages are directed to the male inmates, and that administrators use the concept to their own advantage as a shelter for the parsimonious use of funds. For the past fifteen years or so, elected officials have been trying to get as much mileage as possible out of crime and the fear of crime. For too long our senses have been assaulted by television images of youthful (usually black) men being led away in handcuffs and weekly calls for tougher sentences (read longer) for dangerous criminals. We have finally reached the point where some lawmakers are beginning to realize the terrible cost, both financial and social, that our continued "throw-away-the-key" policy is exacting.

Caught up in the drive to punish lawbreakers are increasingly larger numbers of women. What to do with them has been the subject of a great deal of discussion, and coed prisons are offered as a partial answer. Proponents claim that they are a reasonable alternative to an increasing female inmate population and decreasing resources. The advantages are believed to be a lower recidivism rate among inmates who are released, the ability to learn (or relearn) appropriate behaviors around members of the opposite sex, the development of healthy relationships, and an increase in self-esteem (Ruback, 1980). Heffernan and Kripple (1980) cite a decrease in homosexual relationships and an environment in which the inmates are more aware of their appearance.

From the earliest beginnings of our nation, the need for separate prisons for women has been made clear. In 1827, Congress authorized a new prison for the District of Columbia. Designed by Charles Bulfinch for 150 men in one wing and sixty-four women in the other wing, it was thought to be an answer to the problem of what to do with women prisoners. Beginning in the late 1800s, the women's prison reform movement experienced success by convincing a few state legislatures to allow separate prisons for women—Indiana, 1873; Massachusetts, 1877; New York, 1887 and 1893 (Heffernan,1994). From that time to the present, women have had separate institutions. However, they are often characterized by few programs, little attention by policy makers, and misguided assumptions about female criminality.

Conversley, prisons for women are often "softer" compared with men's prisons. For example, in my travels to various prisons and jails in many states, I have noted that prisons for men are characterized by rather spartan surroundings, whereas the women have small luxuries such as curtains at the windows, bedspreads, and other amenities that foster a more homelike environment. Conversely, many men's prisons are characterized by more programs that not only allow them to constructively fill their time, but may serve them well in the community. Not so for the women. Women's prisons usually have fewer programs and very few vocational programs that may help them secure meaningful employment on release.

Good Intentions or Just Cheap?

These shortcomings have caused many experts to call for the use of coed prisons to at least allow for greater program opportunities for women. Integrationists, that is, those who advocate the use of coed correctional facilities, argue that women have [greater] "access to programs, special projects, experts, and visitors commonly unavailable to them and that participation in programs with men offers women realistic training opportunities" (Schweber, 1984). Integrationists also call our attention to the fact that women have a calming effect on more violence-prone men; and that cocorrections is more like the real world to which the inmates return, thus facilitating their often difficult reentry.

Separatists, however, those who advocate separate institutions for men and women, concede the programmatic considerations but challenge the notion that integration gives women a greater share of programs and resources. They state that women's concerns are subordinated to those of men and that many women are in prison because of man-related difficulties.

Both have a point, but in my view the integrationists are dead wrong and ignore some important issues. Twenty years ago, I was the NARA Director (drug program) at the Federal Correctional Institution at Terminal Island, California. At the time of my arrival in 1973, FCI, Terminal Island was (and had been since 1955) both a men's institution and a women's institution. Both occupied the same site but were separated by prison industries and had separate staff. However, both shared medical facilities, the drug program resources, and other resources as called for. The system seemed to work, but in 1975, however, that began to change. The Central Office decided to turn FCI, Terminal Island into a coed prison.

At the direction of Warden Jack Wise, I served on the committee that converted a normally functioning institution into one that did not work well at all. In spite of our best efforts, careful planning, and good intentions based on the fact that we did believe that a coed institution would normalize the atmosphere and contribute to the ability of the inmates to make the adjustment to community life, we failed. Our failure was not attributable to faults in planning, implementation, or problems with staff, but to human nature and the pathologies of the inmates. True, the women did have access to the same programs as did the male inmates, but I am doubtful that those programs, save one in keypunch operation and the various educational programs, served them at all after release. There were other issues, mostly related to a "walk-partner," that I believe kept them from maximizing their program participation.

The issue of program availability and participation is of greatest interest to both integrationists and separatists. The foremost concern of proponents is that women have greater access to programs and that this access be "subject to the same controls and participate in the same programs;…a shared life which, to a degree varying between and within institutions might mirror the breadth of potential structured and spontaneous interactions that occur outside, in the 'free world'" (KOBA Associates, 1977). Indeed, they are not, nor were they ever, free; rather, in my experience, most women inmates were prisoners of their socialization and circumstances. Without adequate programming, such women will never be free. Adequate programming, should allow women inmates the opportunity to fully pursue whatever opportunities are available without being encumbered by a male inmate dictating what programs the woman should participate in. Anything less is simply cheap.

The Arguments for and against Coed Prisons

It may be useful to briefly review the arguments in favor of coed prisons. Historically women's prisons have not been known for an abundance of programs for women, but there have been isolated efforts to provide more than the weak imitations of programs available for men. However, Crawford (1980) makes an important point; the coed prison destroys any separate programming for the female offender and attempts to force the small number of incarcerated females into programs designed to meet the needs of the much larger number of male prisoners. This issue addresses another point discussed at greater length later. That is the observation that women who have been exploited by men for most of their lives continue to fall into that behavioral pattern, and only a few involve themselves in programs they believe important, not a program that maximized time with a walk partner.

Recidivism is another reason that integrationists use to justify coed prisons. It is difficult to assess the matter of recidivism in regard to inmates released from a coed prison. There are several confounding issues to consider, such as, did the inmate take advantage of coed opportunities or did he or she stay to themselves? Smykla (1979) cites studies of releasees from the Federal Correctional Institution at Fort Worth and the Massachusetts Correctional Institution at Framingham. Although some methodological problems were noted, neither study showed a significant difference between men and women released from either coed prison. Regardless, inmates properly classified for a minimum security institution may well have a lower recidivism rate than inmates released from a higher security institution simply because they are less criminal in their orientation than their brethren at a more secure institution.

The advantage of decreasing homosexual relationships in a coed prison is also a point whose benefits are subject to some skepticism. As anyone who has been around prisons is aware, consensual and forcible homosexual activity is a fact of life. But there is a difference between a minimum custody institution and a medium or maximum custody institution. Maximum custody prisons are characterized by inmates serving long (often very long) sentences and who are the most recalcitrant and psychologically damaged inmates in the system. These are prisons that must deal with inmates with all kinds of character disorders, gangs, and other inmates willing to rip off others who are not a member of their gang or set (see Irwin, 1980, for a more complete description of the contemporary prison).

Minimum custody prisons, however, are characterized by inmates serving shorter sentences, inmates whose crimes are nonviolent, and who are felt to be more amenable to the advantages of programs and counseling. These differences alone may account for less homosexual activity except between consenting adults. But there is more. A minimum custody institution is characterized by a more relaxed environment, including more female staff, more open visitation (it should be noted that anything more than handholding between visitor and inmate is still forbidden), and usually a more liberal furlough policy and procedures. Thus, it is my assertion that there is less homosexual activity, less probability of stronger, more pathological inmates exploiting weaker, more vulnerable inmates, and the self-concept of all inmates are not as apt to be as distorted and fractured as one finds in a medium or maximum security institution.

Finally, anyone who believes that male inmates in a coed institution learn or relearn more appropriate behaviors around members of the opposite sex is guilty of wishful thinking. Any one who has worked around this type of setting knows that most male inmates see women as someone to be exploited for one reason or another, usually for sex. Some inmates in coed institutions agree that the boy–girl types of behavior exhibited in prison are comical and that those who pursue members of the opposite sex are most often exhibiting pathological traits that most likely got them into trouble in the first place. For example, Mahan (1986) quotes an inmate who noted that most of the men who went to segregation went there because of a woman. Others complained that the sixth-grade mentality of walking around holding hands was ridiculous. Another inmate stated that he went for all the sex he could get.

This issue is the main point on which I base my objections to coed prisons. The "gentleman factor" has figured heavily in depressing the numbers of women being sent to prison. The field of criminal justice has been dominated by men who serve as police officers, judges, prosecutors, probation officers, prison workers, and parole officers. Many women have been able to exploit the system and the "the gentleman factor" to their advantage. This seems to be human nature, but in the past women were often able to receive break after break, until the judge finally had enough and sent the culprit off to prison. By then the woman was so damaged and so enmeshed in a lifestyle of exploitation, criminality, prostitution, drug abuse, and deviant behavior in general that any effort to rehabilitate her had become formidable.

From an early age, the average female inmate has been subjected to sexual and emotional abuse. Like her male counterpart, she has been raised in an environment in which women are subject to male domination and are exploited in a variety of ways. Conversely, from an early age, women learn to exploit their sexuality to their advantage and usually find a man to attach themselves to in a symbiotic relationship that is inherently unhealthy. Without effective intervention, they continue to exploit one another and live out a dysfunctional script, never to achieve a measurable degree of autonomy and self-actualization.

In the two years after conversion to a coed institution that I remained on staff at FCI, Terminal Island, I made a number of observations. First, most women did not participate in programs that were to their benefit, but rather they enrolled in programs that were dictated by their walk partner and that facilitated time together. Second, women who needed the most freedom to learn new patterns of behavior were most apt to team up with a walk partner, which further reinforced each other's pathology. Third, male inmates who had the strongest record of exploitation of women were always the ones with a walk partner who seemed willing to do anything for her walk partner. Fourth, in spite of our careful planning, there seemed to be far too many pregnancies, which were terminated by abortion on demand.

Separate and Equal

We cannot allow our desire to cut costs to increase the numbers of coed prisons. In my estimation, we have too many now. What we must do is provide funding for adequate programming for women inmates that meet their need for counseling, vocational training, and meaningful work while incarcerated. At the same time, we must begin to increase our use of alternative sanctions to bring down the numbers of inmates in prison. This initiative alone will take pressure off policymakers to develop coed prisons and allow women and men to be imprisoned in separate, but equal facilities.

REFERENCES

Crawford, J. K. (1980). Two losers don't make a winner: The case against the co-correctional institution. In J. Smykla (Ed.), *Coed prison.* New York: Human Sciences Press.

Heffernan, E. (1994). Banners, brothels, and a "ladies seminary": Women and federal corrections. In J. W. Roberts (Ed.), *Escaping prison myths: Selected topics in the history of federal corrections.* Washington, DC: The American University Press.

Heffernan, E., & Kripple, E. (1980). A coed prison. In J. Smykla (Ed.), *Coed prison.* New York: Human Sciences Press.

Irwin, J. (1980). *Prisons in turmoil.* Boston: Little, Brown and Company.

KOBA Associates, Inc. (1977). *Summary report: Phase I assessment of coeducational corrections.* Washington, DC: U.S. Department of Justice, Law Enforcement Assistance Administration (Contract # J-LEAA-009-77).

Maguire, K., & Pastore, A. L. (Eds.) (1996). *Sourcebook of criminal justice statistics, 1995.* Washington, DC: U.S. Department of Justice, Bureau of Justice Statistics.

Mahan, S. (1986, August). Co-corrections: Doing time together. *Corrections Today.* pp. 134–140; 164–165.

Ruback, B. (1980). The sexually integrated prison. In J. Smykla (Ed.), *Coed prison.* New York: Human Sciences Press.

Schweber, C. (1984). Beauty marks and blemishes: The coed prison as a microcosm of integrated society. *Prison Journal, 64* (1), 3–14.

Smykla, J. (1979). Does coed prison work? *Prison Journal, 59* (1), 61–72.

Rejoinder to Dr. Houston
JOHN ORTIZ SMYKLA

I thank my colleague, Professor James Houston, for responding. It is a privilege to discuss the concept with someone so well versed in both the theoretical and applied issues of co-corrections. However, I cannot agree with my colleague's conclusion that there is no room on the correctional landscape for coed prisons simply because co-corrections has not lived up to its promises. I too have been terribly disappointed with the outcomes of coed prisons, but I do not subscribe to the view that the outcomes cannot be improved so we should stop trying. Progress in social institutions has never followed that path, as every reader of this essay surely knows. Like Professor Houston, I saw the best efforts of institutional staff, careful planning, and good intentions at FCI Pleasanton (now FCI Dublin), California, which opened as a new federal coed prison in July 1974, get sidetracked by politics and politicians, public mood swings, and fiscal stinginess and become an all-women's prison. Yet has that not been the fate for almost all U.S. corrections, and have we not seen improvement? The first correctional institution for adult men at the Walnut Street Jail in Philadelphia in 1776 and the first reformatory for women and girls in Ossining, New York, in 1839 failed miserably shortly after they opened in spite of the work of international figures such as Elizabeth Fry, John Howard, Benjamin Rush, Eliza Farnham, and Georgiana Bruce. Were not probation and parole no sooner tried than sheriffs, prosecutors and judges called them failures?

Instead of coed prison, Professor Houston calls for an increase in our use of alternative sanctions to bring down the number of inmates in prison. With all due respect to my colleague, the alternative sanctions movement has not delivered on its promise to reduce prison crowding either, and the movement is stronger today than it was thirty years ago. Probation and parole today supervise almost four million adult men and women. The increase in 1996 was higher than the annual average increase since 1990, and *still* the number of adult men and women sent to prison climbed to an all-time high of almost 1.2 million. I agree that a rational sentencing system needs an expanded range of noninstitutional sentencing options that gives judges greater latitude to exercise discretion in selecting punishments that more closely fit the circumstances of the crime and the offender. Yet why should the level of proof for retaining coed prison be higher than the other sentences on the corrections landscape? I believe my colleague hit it on the head when he mentioned the "gentleman factor." The "gentleman factor" may include the chivalry component that Professor Houston claims, but it also says that "gentlemen and gentlewomen" do not commit crime and should not tolerate those that do. It is a kind way of covering up the deep negative and disgusting feelings we have for prisoners. Prisoners should be "punished" severely. No gymnasiums. No exercise equipment. No televisions or movies. Limited nutrition, visiting, and programming. And surely no contact with the "other" sex (albeit contact with the same sex is okay because that is the prisoner's natural lot for committing crime).

Coed prison by itself cannot control the crime problem; no sanction can. In 1975, when FCI Pleasanton was coed, I watched well-intentioned corrections professionals unknowingly duplicate sex role stereotypes in assigning inmates to prison jobs. Women inmates at FCI Pleasanton did not naturally go to prison jobs as clerks, typists and cooks for $10 to $15 per month while men inmates worked construction and mechanical repair for $30 per month. Staff brought with them definitions of appropriate sex role behavior and drew on those experiences in assigning women and men inmates to prison work and evaluating their expectations and performances. As a result, women inmates became disadvantaged in the way that Professor Houston complains. Similarly, single prisoners who did not find a "walk partner" were perceived as not taking advantage of the therapeutic value of the male–female relationship as defined by staff. Less concern was given to what happened in that relationship save the instances of assault and pregnancies.

With the adult prison incarceration rate in the United States today hovering at 420 per 100,000 adult population, the mad rush to add 1500 beds a week to keep up with the 6.6 percent annual average increase since 1990, a legislative attitude to use incarceration as a symbol of being tough on crime, and politicians now embracing alternative sanctions because they see small caseloads together with additional program restrictions, monitoring, and supervision as capable of providing as much incapacitation and deterrence as is possible under community release, it is no wonder we neither desire a conceptual change in our notions of "deserved" imprisonment nor provide it the resources it needs away from political and academic panhandling. There is nothing sacred about same-sex imprisonment. The American Quakers who created the concept learned quickly it would not work and today they are among its strongest opponents.

It is true that coed prison has not measured up to its promises, but the reason is not that the concept is a bad one (albeit the concept needs more open discussion without fear of being labeled "soft" on crime, and prisons, whether single-sex or coed, must stop promising that they can prevent offenders from committing crime when families, churches, schools, and communities have not been able to; for if the crime problem were easy to solve, it would have been solved a long time ago), but rather success lies in the details, implementation, research, and public education of coed prison being an appropriate correctional sanction in a continuum of sanctions.

Can (or Should) We Return to Corporal Punishment?

YES, argues Terry D. Edwards. He is Associate Professor in the Department of Justice Administration at the University of Louisville, where he teaches criminal law, criminal evidence, and constitutional law, as well as the legal aspects of police management in the Southern Police Institute. He has authored, or co-authored, articles and textbooks on environmental crime, legal ethics, HIV/AIDS in policing, state police training practices, and criminal law. He is past-president of the Southern Criminal Justice Association.

W. Richard Janikowski argues NO. He is Associate Professor of Criminology and Criminal Justice at The University of Memphis. His research interests are in the areas of jurisprudence, criminal law, constitutional law, and international human rights and genocide. He is the author of numerous articles on criminal procedure, is coeditor of *Legality and Illegality* (1994), and is currently completing two books, one on constitutional criminal procedure and the other on substantive criminal law.

YES

TERRY D. EDWARDS

Any academic discussion (the term I prefer over debate) involving the use of corporal punishment as a sentencing alternative in the United States would be remiss if it did not begin by revisiting the now infamous incident involving Mr. Michael Fay and his encounter with the criminal justice system of Singapore.

In March 1994, the criminal case of Mr. Fay, an 18-year-old citizen of the United States, drew the attention of the American public when, on his conviction for vandalism, part of the sentence imposed by the Singapore court included "caning." Although originally Mr. Fay was sentenced to receive six blows, his sentence was reduced to four blows by the President of Singapore after much media attention and a plea for leniency from many in this country, including President Clinton. On May 5, 1994, the four-blow caning portion of the sentence was administered to Mr. Fay, who satisfied the other portions of his sentence and eventually returned to the United States.

The sentencing and resulting punishment of Mr. Fay, although a rather routine and uneventful criminal case when judged by the criminal justice standards and practices in Singapore (as well as by the standards in many other countries), stirred the emotions of many Americans. The highly publicized caning of a United States citizen renewed the controversy surrounding the use of corporal punishment as a sentencing alternative in the United States.

Shortly after Mr. Fay's caning, numerous public opinion surveys were conducted, by the news media, producing mixed results. The general consensus regarding the mood of Americans toward corporal punishment, as reported by the surveys, was that most Americans surveyed approved of the government of Singapore imposing caning—a duly authorized and historically employed form of punishment under their system of criminal justice. Conversely, the surveys also revealed that Americans were about equally divided as to whether caning, as a sentencing alternative, would be acceptable in this country. One survey, conducted in April of 1994, reported that just under half of those surveyed (46 percent) supported caning of criminal defendants in the United States, with the respondents citing their "frustration over rising crime rates" in this country as the primary reason for their support of the practice (Bloom, 1995, p. 362).

In response to the incident involving Mr. Fay, and to appease what many politicians perceived was a "movement" favoring corporal punishment, state legislation was introduced in California and Louisiana to permit the "paddling" of juvenile offenders. At the local level, Cincinnati, Sacramento, and San Antonio also introduced such legislation (Bloom, 1995). Although none of the proposed legislation was ever enacted, the stage was set for continuing the debate over whether corporal punishment is an appropriate sentencing alternative in this country.

This chapter continues the discourse concerning the viability or effectiveness of corporal punishment as a sentencing alternative in the United States. First, I advocate the following: (1) corporal punishment as a sentencing alternative, if reinstated, would employ only those methods and practices that are consistent with the contemporary standards of decency of this society; (2) corporal punishment as a sentencing alternative, historically, played a legitimate and critical role as a "necessary evil" in the administration of justice in the United States, and the demise of the practice can be traced, not to judicial concerns about its legality, but rather to legislative repeal based on public opinion of the citizens; (3) despite the demise of corporal punishment as a sentencing alternative, the practice remains firmly entrenched in the fabric of American society today in both the family and public education setting, with the explicit "blessing" of legislatures and the courts; (4) there is no basis in law not for not adopting corporal punishment as a sentencing alternative; and (5) contrary to what the opponents of corporal punishment would have the American public believe, there is evidence supporting a conclusion that corporal punishment is at least as effective as other, more "acceptable" forms of punishment. I conclude that corporal punishment can, once again, assume its place in the American criminal justice system as an effective sentencing alternative—if imposed with the same judicious temperament and administered with the same safeguards as the death penalty, incarceration, and fines—to the current, and more "acceptable," forms of sentencing.

In short, corporal punishment as a sentencing alternative is quite clearly an idea whose time has come (again) in the United States.

What Is Corporal Punishment?

Opponents of corporal punishment often portray the practice in terms befitting a "Star Chamber" setting; floggings, gruesome whippings, razor-sharp cutting implements, branding, and disfigurements. No mental image would be complete without the thought of permanently scarred victims and pain inflicted to the point where the recipient is driven to unconsciousness: Roman galley ships, Nazi interrogations—anything to associate corporal punishment with the worst of humanity. Legitimate corporal punishment as a sentencing alternative has few, if any, of these trappings. For the purpose of this chapter, and because of the gruesome images that, unfortunately, have become associated with the extreme cases where the practice is abused, it is far more important for this chapter to focus on the end sought (pain) rather than to dwell on the means employed (most often paddling or electric shock) in the administration of corporal punishment as a sentencing alternative.

Corporal punishment, as modern criminologists use the term, encompasses nothing more than the intentional infliction of some degree of pain as part of a duly imposed sentence. Obviously, reasonable people will differ from the onset as to which crimes warrant corporal punishment as a sentence. Proponents of corporal punishment as a sentencing alternative quite clearly understand that, first and foremost, the practice must satisfy legitimate penological interests and be accepted by the public before it can be implemented. Furthermore, it is to be expected that there would be disagreement as to the method and means of administering corporal punishment. Certainly the degree to which the pain should be inflicted will be open to debate. Indeed, such disagreements and debates are not already uncommon when discussing the other, more "acceptable," forms of punishment such as incarceration and fines. To be certain, proponents of corporal punishment recognize that the practice, if it is to be legitimized and restored as a sentencing alternative in the United States, will be controversial. However, just because a sentencing alternative is controversial is no reason to unilaterally refuse to recognize the practice as being legitimate. If controversy were the determinative factor, few, if any, sentencing alternatives would ever be acceptable! Finally, proponents of corporal punishment as a sentencing alternative do not seek unrestricted, or unlimited, imposition of corporal punishment. As with any government-administered activity, the imposition of corporal punishment by the government must be safeguarded by legislative and judicial checks and balances to insure that abuses are eliminated, or at least minimized.

Universally accepted standards or parameters, agreeable across the political spectrum, will not be achieved easily. Liberals and conservatives cannot now agree as to what constitutes too much, too little, or the appropriate punishment for crime. However, that there will be disagreement regarding the imposition and application of corporal punishment is no reason to summarily dismiss a practice as without merit. Just as with incarceration, acceptable legislative parameters can be agreed on and enacted; and, just as with existing sentencing options, legislative action establishing the basic framework for the practice can be amended later, should public opinion change. Judicial review can accommodate for individual cases, "adjust" for errors, and provide the safeguard for abuses.

Finally, and most importantly, proponents of corporal punishment as a sentencing alternative also understand that the practice is subject to being abused— as are existing forms of sentencing. However, as with existing forms of sentencing, legislative and judicial safeguards will serve to prevent abuses, punish those who choose to abuse, and provide remedies for those abused.

What Is the History of Corporal Punishment in the United States?

Opponents of corporal punishment submit that the use of corporal punishment is somehow "foreign" to this country, a practice reserved for kings, dictators, potentates, and emperors. They argue that corporal punishment has no historical basis, or legitimate place, in the criminal justice structure of a democracy such as the United States. The opponents of corporal punishment insist that the "birth" of the United States as a democracy denoted the "death" of corporal punishment as a legitimate criminal justice practice in American society. Surely, they argue, the same individuals who so brilliantly orchestrated the creation of such a democracy and who were uniquely responsible for wresting the oppressed colonies from the tyrannical grip of the English monarchy would not tolerate such a barbaric practice as corporal punishment. Simply stated, nothing could be further from the truth.

In tracing the historical role of corporal punishment as a sentencing alternative for crimes in the United States, it is unnecessary, and quite beyond the scope of this chapter, to trace the roots of corporal punishment to antiquity. Suffice it to say that corporal punishment was alive and well and fully entrenched as an acceptable form of sentencing when the first settlements developed in what is now the United States. Europeans were quite comfortable with imposing mutilation, the ducking stool, and flogging as sentences for crimes during the seventeenth century, and even branding was authorized as a sentence for crimes in England until 1699. Ironically, tongue piercing, quite the rage among today's youth, was once the punishment inflicted for crimes such as blasphemy and perjury during this period (Hall, 1995).

During the late eighteenth century and early nineteenth century, various corporal punishment sentencing practices thrived in both Europe and the United States; it was reported that the British army alone inflicted over 17,000 lashes per month in India in 1812 (Bloom, 1995). Did the founders of the upstart democracy that came to be called the United States of America abandon all desire to employ corporal punishment as a sentencing alternative? Was not the American Revolution fought to insure that such heinous and oppressive action by the government would not exist? On the contrary, the same individuals who conceived of, and fought, the American Revolution, and who crafted the Declaration of Independence, the Constitution, and the Bill of Rights, were quite willing, after being elected to Congress, to continue the corporal punishment practices imposed by the very "oppressive" government they had violently overthrown. That the founders of this nation desired to retain corporal punishment as a sentencing alternative is evidenced by the fact that one of the first pieces of legislation to pass the newly formed Congress of the United States was to permit whipping as a court-martial sentence aboard U.S. Navy vessels, a federal sentencing practice that continued until 1839 (Hall, 1995).

To argue that the founders of this country sought to ban corporal punishment as a sentencing option in criminal cases through the adoption of the Eighth Amendment flies in the face of reasonable Constitutional interpretation, logic, and history. Although the late eighteenth and early nineteenth centuries saw the slow demise of corporal punishment as a sentencing option in both the United States and Europe, the last whipping imposed as a sentence in a criminal trial did not occur in the United States until 1952. Furthermore, it was not until 1972 that the last statutory authority for whipping at the state level (Delaware) was repealed (Hall, 1995).

It is central to the premise of this chapter to note that the relatively recent "final death" of corporal punishment as a sentencing alternative in the United States came during the "liberal" swing of the political pendulum. That "death" occurred, not by judicial edict based on constitutional infirmity, but rather by legislative declaration—through the repeal of the statutes authorizing the practice, in response to what was perceived as public opinion favoring such repeal. Historically, then, it is critical to understand that, in the United States, public opinion has played a vital role in determining whether corporal punishment is employed as a sentencing alternative.

What Is the Current Status of Corporal Punishment in the United States?

Those opposing corporal punishment as a sentencing alternative perpetuate still another myth: that in the United States today, corporal punishment, imposed rarely if at all, is used only by misguided "Neanderthals" who are not enlightened about modern disciplinary methods. The opponents zealously strive to paint corporal punishment in twentieth century America as an "oddity." Furthermore, they seek to stigmatize those individuals who choose to employ the practice. Again, nothing could be further from the truth.

First, with regard to the right of parents to employ corporal punishment in disciplining children, all fifty states permit corporal punishment, either explicitly in state statutes, or though court decisions (Edwards, 1996). Is this practice unlimited or unchecked? Are parents free to engage in corporal punishment at a whim? Is corporal punishment within the family setting administered with unbridled enthusiasm? Quite the contrary; the statutes and court decisions quite clearly recognize the potential for abuse and readily convict parents who cross the line from legitimate corporal punishment to abuse. The criminal justice system in this country has no problem convicting parents of assault, battery, or even murder when that line is crossed. To stigmatize parents who choose to employ a legitimate disciplinary tool because the practice is subject to abuse by some does a disservice to the millions of parents who successfully, and without abuse or excess, employ the practice.

Second, to what degree is government-sanctioned corporal punishment employed in the public school system? As of 1995, twenty-two states expressly permitted the practice, and for the 1987–88 school year, more than 900,000 students received some form of corporal punishment (Bloom, 1995). Does this, then, seem to be the rarely employed, isolated practice presented by the opponents of corporal punishment? When opponents of corporal punishment in public schools could not get public opinion swayed and have state legislatures repeal the authorizing legislation, the opponents quite naturally sought federal intervention challenging the constitutionality of the practice. Much to their disappointment, the U.S. Supreme Court, in *Ingraham* v. *Wright* 1977), expressly declared that corporal punishment, as a public school disciplinary measure, violates neither the Cruel and Unusual Clause of the Eighth Amendment nor the Due Process Clause of the Fourteenth Amendment. Constitutional reality is that even government-imposed corporal punishment is commonly practiced in American society today.

Corporal punishment, as a parental right, is not only tolerated in the United States, but explicitly sanctioned by the government in all states. Furthermore, even government-imposed (by public school teachers) corporal punishment is authorized in nearly half of the states. To claim that those who employ corporal punishment are "shamed" or are some sort of second-class citizens is a slap in the face to the millions of parents and teachers who routinely employ the practice, legally, and without excess or abuse. Corporal punishment quite clearly is a legitimate practice in the United States that, like many other disciplinary measures, must be monitored constantly and diligently for abuse—it is not, as its opponents insist, something civilized, or educated, people do not do.

Does Corporal Punishment Violate the U.S. Constitution?

The mightiest myth of all, the "half-truth" that is advanced by those who oppose corporal punishment as a sentencing alternative, is that the practice violates the Eighth Amendment's Cruel and Unusual Clause or the Fourteenth Amendment's Due Process Clause. Furthermore, opponents toss around cases that purportedly stand for the proposition that the courts agree with them on this point. It stretches the interpretation of both constitutional and case law to arrive at that conclusion.

Eighth Amendment

It is certainly well beyond the limited scope of this chapter to offer a detailed analysis of corporal punishment as a sentencing alternative and the Eighth Amendment (Bloom, 1995; Hall, 1995). Therefore, what follows is a "simplified" three-part analysis of corporal punishment under the Eighth Amendment, sufficiently detailed for the purposes of this discussion.

First, the starting point for evaluating a particular punishment against the Eighth Amendment's protections is to determine whether the punishment would have been considered cruel and unusual in 1791, at the time the amendment was adopted. If so, the practice would be, per se, unconstitutional. Quite clearly the previous discussion of the history of corporal punishment in the United States can leave no doubt that not only was corporal punishment acceptable in American society in 1791; the newly formed Congress readily passed legislation specifically authorizing its use.

The second prong of an Eighth Amendment analysis employs the "evolving standards of decency" test, developed by the Supreme Court in *Trop* v. *Dulles* 1958). In assessing the constitutionality of punishments in Eighth Amendment cases in modem settings, the analysis evaluates the punishment practice in light of contemporary public standards. Having earlier tied its interpretation of Eighth Amendment cases specifically to public opinion, in *Weems* v. *U.S.* 1910), the Court would later, in *Gregg* v. *Georgia* (1976), expressly note that the Eighth Amendment was "flexible and dynamic." The Court clearly recognized that any interpretation of the Eighth Amendment's protections required deference to certain "objective indicators" of public opinion, such as legislative action. Therefore, although no jurisdiction currently authorizes corporal punishment as a sentencing alternative, the Court's previous decisions certainly lead a reasonable person to conclude that carefully drafted legislation authorizing the practice would be given great deference by the federal courts.

Finally, the third constitutional hurdle under the Eighth Amendment is that a particular punishment must not be excessive. This requirement is satisfied when the punishment in question meets two tests: (1) it is neither unnecessary or a wanton infliction of pain and (2) it is proportional to the offense committed (Bloom, 1995). With regard to the first prong, corporal punishment, if it is to be authorized, must be imposed and administered under very specific legislative and judicial guidelines. Any enabling legislation must address which specific crimes are involved, how and when the punishment would be imposed, and details of the methods involved, and it must allow for supervision by medical personnel. Furthermore, judicial review must include provisions permitting both preimposition appeals and postimposition redress for abuse. With regard to the second prong of excessiveness, legislatures and courts must zealously guard to insure that all sentences imposing corporal punishment consider (1) the severity of the crime when measured against the harshness of the punishment, and (2) whether a sentence involving corporal punishment is comparable to the sentences imposed for the same crime within the jurisdiction, and in other jurisdictions.

The implementation and administration of corporal punishment as a sentencing alternative will, no doubt, require considerable legislative and judicial effort to clear constitutionality—but there is no constitutional, or legal, hurdle that cannot be overcome.

Case Law

No court has ever held that the imposition of corporal punishment as a sentencing alternative is a per se violation of the Eighth Amendment. That warrants repeating: No court has ever held that the imposition of corporal punishment as a sentencing alternative is a per se violation of the Eighth Amendment. Opponents of corporal punishment often cite the case of *Jackson* v. *Bishop* (1968) as standing for the proposition that corporal punishment as a sentencing alternative violates the Eighth Amendment. This argument, again, offers a "half-truth" regarding the issue of corporal punishment as a sentencing alternative.

In *Jackson,* the Court of Appeals for the Eighth Circuit did order prison officials to stop the practice of whipping prisoners, holding that the practice, as authorized and imposed, violated the Eighth Amendment. However, it is quite clear that in arriving at that conclusion the court was ruling that the practice of whipping prisoners, as applied in that particular setting, violated the Constitution. The court specifically, and explicitly, noted that the practice of whipping prisoners in that particular setting "...offends the contemporary concepts of decency..."

(p. 579). The court took great pains to assess the constitutionality of the practice, as measured by the rules and regulations that authorized and governed the whippings in question. With regard to the specific rules and regulations in question, the court noted:

1. They failed to expressly prohibit the abuse of corporal punishment.
2. Authorities took no action when they were violated.
3. They could be easily circumvented by those in authority.
4. They were, in fact, often abused.
5. They imposed no limits on those imposing corporal punishment.
6. They offered no clear guidelines as to how to impose corporal punishment; They served no legitimate penological interest.
8. They worked to pit correction officials against inmates.
9. Public opinion opposed corporal punishment.

Quite clearly, then, the justices in *Jackson* did not hold that the imposition of corporal punishment was a per se constitutional violation. To the contrary, in arriving at their conclusion that the whippings in question did, in fact, violate the Eighth Amendment, the justices followed both the spirit and letter of the law and weighed the rules, regulations, and practices against the contemporary community standards of decency. Who is to say that, today, in a different setting, one in which corporal punishment was authorized and implemented in accordance and compliance with these guidelines, that a court would find the practice constitutional, in that it did meet the contemporary standards of decency.

Will Corporal Punishment "Work" in the United States?

Here, again, opponents rush to decry the use of corporal punishment as a sentencing option by asserting that there is no empirical evidence to support a conclusion that the practice "works" in the United States. Without such hard evidence of success, opponents argue that corporal punishment fails to qualify as a legitimate sentencing alternative. This argument, too, is wrought with inconsistencies, fallacies, and false logic.

First, from a methodological perspective, it appears difficult, if not impossible, to produce research that would satisfy the opponents of corporal punishment as a sentencing alternative. Unlike the studies advanced in the debate over capital punishment, corporal punishment ended in the United States, for all intents and purposes, by the late 1800s, leaving advocates with little, or no, data on which to base a scientifically rigorous assessment of its effectiveness. There are simply insufficient current data relating to corporal punishment (as a sentencing alternative) in the United States to evaluate the success, or failure, of corporal punishment in terms of deterrence or recidivism.

When advocates of corporal punishment as a sentencing alternative do manage to produce a study indicating the practice has legitimate penological merit, opponents are quick to note that the methodology is faulty because (1) the study was conducted in another country, (2) the study related to parental discipline or school settings, not to criminal activity, or (3) there were insufficient or inaccurate data rendering the study invalid. As one scholar (Kahan, 1996) has noted, there *does* exist some evidence to support a conclusion that corporal punishment operates to discourage some forms of criminal activity. Furthermore, shifting the burden to the opponents of corporal punishment, Kahan goes on to state that there is no credible evidence that corporal punishment is any less effective than the sentencing options currently employed by the judicial system in the United States.

In other words, why should the advocates of corporal punishment as a sentencing alternative be required to produce methodologically rigorous studies that conclusively prove the practice works, to get legislative bodies to consider it as an option? Why should not legislative bodies consider corporal punishment as a viable sentencing alternative, in those jurisdictions where public opinion warrants such consideration, absent methodologically rigorous studies that conclusively prove that the practice does not work?

Given a chance, corporal punishment would prove to be a very effective sentencing alternative in the United States.

Should Corporal Punishment Be Permitted as a Sentencing Alternative in the United States?

Yes, under limited conditions. Hall (1995) outlined the parameters under which corporal punishment would be most effective and at the same time best survive judicial scrutiny. Those parameters are:

1. The public opinion supporting such punishment be expressed through legislative authority.
2. Corporal punishment be authorized, but not mandated, by such legislation.
3. Such legislation be "backed" by evidence that corporal punishment reduces recidivism, increased deterrence, or serves some other legitimate penological interest.
4. The legislation is limited to specific offenses, or classes of offenses.
5. The corporal punishment is imposed only as part of the sentence and only after all aggravating and mitigating factors have been considered by the sentencing body.
6. The defendant is accorded all traditional constitutional rights at trial.

7. The legislation restricts the degree of corporal punishment and prohibits any acts that would inflict permanent disabilities or scarring.
8. The legislation provides alternatives should the defendant be, or become, mentally or physically incapable of receiving the ordered punishment.
9. Correction officials administering corporal punishment are properly trained, and supervised, in the methods of imposing the punishment.
10. The corporal punishment is supervised by a medical person, qualified to render appropriate medical opinions and authorized to terminate the punishment for medical reasons. (pp. 459–460)

With these parameters in mind, corporal punishment certainly becomes at least as acceptable, or legitimate, as existing forms of punishment—and we would all agree that there is little or no debate regarding the current theories of punishment!

Conclusion

Corporal punishment was once an effective arrow in the quiver of American jurisprudence. For reasons having little or nothing to do with legitimate penological interests, American society made the decision to remove the arrow from the quiver, a decision made not by the courts as an outright ban of the practice based on constitutional or other legal concerns, but, rather by the citizens of this country, through the actions of their respective legislative bodies. The time has come to restore that arrow and use it—wisely, sparingly, and with all the safeguards afforded other severe sentencing options—but permit its use where appropriate.

Corporal punishment, properly imposed and administered, offends no provision of the United States Constitution. Furthermore, studies suggest that the practice is as effective, at least no more ineffective, as incarceration or fines with regard to reducing recidivism and providing deterrence. Furthermore, given that there is no legitimate penological or theoretical reason for prohibiting corporal punishment, why, then, not permit the citizens of this country, through their appropriate legislative bodies, to adopt such practice if that is what the prevailing majority in a jurisdiction demand?

After all, is not that how democracies and constitutional republics were designed to operate?

References

Bloom, S. (1995). Spare the rod, spoil the child? A legal framework for recent corporal punishment proposals. *Golden Gate University Law Review, 25,* 361.
Edwards, L. P. (1996). Corporal punishment and the legal system. *Santa Clara Law Review, 36,* 983.

Hall, D. E. (1995). When canning meets the eighth amendment: Whipping offenders in the United States. *Widener Journal of Public Law, 4,* 403.

Harvey, H. S. (1992). Of flogging and electric shock: A comparative tale of colonialism, commonwealths, and the cat-o'-nine tails. *University of Miami Inter-American Law Review, 24,* 87.

Kahan, D. M. (1996). What do alternative sanctions mean? *University of Chicago Law Review, 63,* 591.

Newman, G. E. (1983). *Just and painful: A case for the corporal punishment of criminals.* London: MacMillan.

CASES

Gregg v. *Georgia,* 428 U.S. 153 (1976).
Ingraham v. *Wright,* 430 U.S. 651 (1977).
Jackson v. *Bishop,* 404 F.2d 571 (8th Cir. 1968).
Trop v. *Dulles,* 356 U.S. 86 (1958).
Weems v. *U.S.,* 217 U.S. 349 (1910).

Rejoinder to Professor Edwards
W. RICHARD JANIKOWSKI

According to Professor Edwards, corporal punishment is "an idea whose time has come—again—in the United States." However, Professor Edwards fails to justify any need for disinterring the buried corpse of corporal punishment and breathing new life into it as a sentencing alternative in criminal cases.

Professor Edwards' own discussion of the history of corporal punishment provides the first justification for not reviving the practice. Although he implies that the extinction of corporal punishment was the result of some recent cataclysmic event (no doubt inspired by opponents of the practice), a careful review of the historical record shows a progressive trend in the United States and elsewhere increasingly condemning the practice and ultimately leading to its demise. As he himself observes. "the late eighteenth and early nineteenth century saw the slow demise of corporal punishment as a sentencing option;" although this slow demise only became final in 1972, its roots extend over two centuries of moral and ethical evolution. Lamenting this extinction of corporal punishment, Professor Edwards appears to argue that, because some contemporary popular support for corporal punishment led a few legislators to introduce bills reestablishing the practice (none of which passed), there is now a strong case for reintroducing corporal punishment.

However, nowhere does Professor Edwards provide a penological justification for reviving the practice. On the contrary, the evidence suggests that corporal punishment creates more penological problems than it can ever solve. As Justice (then Judge) Blackmun noted in his opinion in *Jackson* v. *Bishop* (1968), corporal punishment does not contribute to rehabilitation but instead frustrates the rehabilitative process while creating other correctional problems. Moreover, extensive research on the application of corporal punishment to children suggests the negative effects of the practice. Children subjected to corporal punishment are more likely to engage in criminal behavior in the future and experience a greater probability of engaging in violent and delinquent behavior. It does not require a great leap of the imagination to postulate that, as with children, the imposition of corporal punishment on adults will be counterproductive; instead of helping alleviate the crime problem in the United States, corporal punishment may well only serve to exacerbate it.

Instead, Professor Edwards accuses opponents of corporal punishment of purveying half-truths about the constitutional status of corporal punishment. Here two observations are worthy of note. First, he is correct in his assertion that no court has "held" that corporal punishment violates the Eight Amendment. However, it is then that he offers a "half-truth" regarding the decision of the Court of Appeals for the Eighth Circuit in *Jackson* v. *Bishop* (1968). He correctly states that the court's holding was limited to the issue of whipping prisoners as a prison disciplinary measure, but Professor Edwards fails to mention that the opinion went on to observe that no meaningful distinction could be drawn between this situation and "punishment by way of sentence statutorily prescribed" (p. 580.) Second, he attempts to buttress his argument for the constitutionality of corporal punishment by an oblique reference to the Supreme Court's decision in *Ingraham* v. *Wright* (1977). Eschewing the actual reasoning of the decision, Professor Edwards seems to suggest that because, to the dismay of many opponents, the Supreme Court upheld the use of corporal punishment in America's schools, there can be no doubt as to the constitutionality of its use in criminal sentencing. Unfortunately for Professor Edwards, even a cursory reading of the *Ingraham* Court's opinion shows the fallacy of this reasoning. In reaching its decision, the Court observed that, unlike the use of corporal punishment in criminal cases, the use of the paddle in American schools had never been completely discontinued, and no trend appeared to exist toward its elimination. Moreover, the Court carefully distinguished the use of corporal punishment in a school setting from its application in the criminal justice system: "The prisoner and the schoolchild stand in wholly different circumstances, separated by the harsh facts of criminal conviction and incarceration" (p. 669). The Court found that the openness of the public school and its supervision by the community provided schoolchildren with the necessary safeguards to protect them from the types of abuses from which the Eighth Amendment protects prisoners. *Ingraham* simply does not stand for the proposition that corporal punishment of prisoners is constitutional.

On the contrary, dicta from *Ingraham* may well point to the unconstitutionality of corporal punishment in the criminal context. As pointed out by the Court, one of the purposes of the Eighth Amendment is to limit the kind of punishments that can be imposed on individuals convicted of crimes. In reviewing punishments under the Cruel and Unusual Punishment clause of the Eighth Amendment, the Court has not been "fastened to the obsolete but may acquire meaning as public opinion becomes enlightened by a humane justice." (at p. 668, quoting *Gregg* v. *Georgia*, 1976). Clearly this does mean, as Professor Edwards would imply, simply looking at the public opinion polls at a given moment in time, but instead requires an analysis of the ethical and moral development of the nation over time. Here the verdict is clear; over the two hundred–year span of American history, corporal punishment of prisoners has progressively been rejected as a sentencing alternative. To reason otherwise would make all constitutional standards, even fundamental rights, subject to popular whim. Would he countenance the torture of suspects in criminal cases to illicit confessions because public opinion polls supported such measures and the law once winked at such practices? I think not. Although he may accuse opponents of corporal punishment of characterizing proponents as "misguided Neanderthals," we know better. Misguided proponents may well be, but they would not sacrifice our cherished constitutional rights on the altar of public opinion.

Corporal punishment was wrong when it was used; no amount of public support for its return can make it right. Let us leave it in the dustbin of history, where it belongs.

CASES

Gregg v. *Georgia,* 428 U.S. 153 (1976).
Ingraham v. *Wright,* 430 U.S. 651 (1977).
Jackson v. *Bishop,* 404 F.2d 571 (8th Cir. 1968).
Trop v. *Dulles,* 356 U.S. 86 (1958).
Weems v. *U.S.,* 217 U.S. 349 (1910).

NO

W. RICHARD JANIKOWSKI

Recent years have witnessed a rage to punish suffusing American society. Although nationwide empirical evidence shows a decline in crime, Americans, spurred on by media portrayals of violent crime, especially on the local news, have called for harsher penalties in the form of longer prison sentences, greater and speedier application of the death penalty, adult sentencing of juvenile offenders, and the bringing back of chain gangs. The caning of an American teenager in Singapore met with applause in some sectors of American society, with some state legislatures undertaking consideration of bills to subject convicted drug dealers to mutilation and flogging.

This proposed return to the brutality of the nineteenth century and prior ages, however, has not been isolated to politicians concerned with garnering votes or fearful citizens. In 1983, noted criminologist Graeme Newman argued for the employment of corporal punishment; "carefully selected" offenders, instead of being sentenced to probation or imprisonment, would have painful electric shocks applied to their bodies. Although not suggesting that imprisonment should be abolished for extremely violent or persisting offenders, he argued that the destructive effects of imprisonment on most offenders were unjust whereas probation fails to satisfy the needs of the conscience of the community.

"Cruel and Unusual" Punishment: Constitutional Dimensions of Corporal Punishment

This guarantee against the infliction of cruel and unusual punishment was made directly applicable to the states through the due process clause of the Fourteenth Amendment and reflects a judgment that some punishments are so barbaric and inhumane as to be prohibited in any civilized society. The United States Supreme Court in *Ingraham* v. *Wright* (1977) upheld the imposition of corporal punishment by school officials on students, but the infliction of corporal punishment in the criminal justice setting can readily be distinguished. In *Ingraham*, the Court noted that a:

> school child has little need for the protection of the [Eighth Amendment]. Though attendance may not always be voluntary, the public school remains an open institution. Except perhaps for the very young, the child is not physically restrained from leaving school during school hours; and at the end of the school day, the child is invariably free to return home. Even while at school, the child brings with him the support of family and friends and is rarely apart from teachers and other pupils who may witness and protest any instances of mistreatments (p. 670).

Surely no one can argue that Court's description of the setting in which corporal punishment might occur in a school can be equated to that of the criminal justice system. As the *Ingraham* Court recognized: "The prisoner and the schoolchild stand in wholly different circumstances, separated by the harsh facts of criminal conviction and incarceration" (p. 669). On the contrary, the court decisions regarding the cruel and unusual punishment clause in the criminal justice context are instructive.

As early as 1892, Justice Field, dissenting in *O'Neil* v. *Vermont* (1892), observed that the Eighth Amendment usually applied to punishments that inflicted torture and that were attended with acute pain and suffering. Acknowledging at the time that a state had the power to whip an offender for petty offenses, "repulsive as such mode of punishment is," he noted that combining a number of offenses to increase the punishment might be cruel and unusual. Subsequently, the Court in *State* v. *Resweber* (1947) noted the "traditional humanity of modern Anglo-American law" with its concern about "unnecessary pain" and the "wanton infliction of pain," with the dissent espousing a standard condemning conduct that "shocks the most fundamental instincts of civilized man." Thus, the Court in *Rochin* v. *California* (1952) held that the forcible pumping of a suspect's stomach to obtain evidence so "shocked the conscience" that it constituted a flagrant violation of the Fourteenth Amendment's due process clause, even though the evidence could not be otherwise obtained by police. Such concerns led the plurality in *Trop* v. *Dulles* (1958) to find that the Amendment constrained the state's power to punish by assuring that it be "exercised within the limits of civilized standards." Moreover, such limits were not static but instead had to be judged within the framework of "the evolving standards of decency that mark the progress of a maturing society." Accordingly, the plurality found that although a state might fine, imprison, and even execute an offender, "any technique outside the bounds of these traditional penalties is constitutionally suspect." Applying such reasoning, Justice Douglas, dissenting in *Dyke* v. *Taylor Implement Mfg. Co.* (1968), observed that although historically whipping had been applied for petty offenses, he was "loath to hold whippings…as 'petty.'"

In *Jackson* v. *Bishop* (1968), Judge (later Justice) Blackmun, writing for the court, found the use of the strap as a disciplinary measure in Arkansas penitentiaries to be cruel and unusual punishment. Moreover, the court refused to countenance any attempt to draw a distinction between such disciplinary measures and statutorily prescribed sentences authorizing such punishments. The *Bishop* decision represents the culmination of an evolving view of human decency and dignity; its concepts are the hallmark of a maturing society at the end of the twentieth century. A return to the use of corporal punishment would mean a rejection of these standards of good conscience, fundamental fairness, and civilized behavior.

The Effects of Corporal Punishment: Violence Begetting Violence

Judge Blackmun, in his opinion in *Bishop*, also noted the adverse effects stemming from the imposition of corporal punishment:

> Corporal punishment generates hate toward the keepers who punish and toward the system which permits it. It is degrading to the punisher and to the punished alike. It frustrates correctional and rehabilitative goals. This record cries out with testimony to this effect from expert penologists, from the inmates and their keepers…Whipping creates other penological problems and makes adjustment to society more difficult (p. 580).

Corporal punishment of children has been extensively studied by social scientists. Murray Straus (1979), reviewing the literature, found that some children subjected to corporal punishment suffer serious psychological problems, including depression and suicide. Straus's own research suggests that the experience often increases the likelihood that a child will engage in criminal behavior in the future. Other social scientists have discovered evidence that corporal punishment increases the probability of a child assaulting a sibling or spouse, committing street crime, and becoming involved in delinquent activities and school violence. A significant number of studies have also shown a connection between corporal punishment and child abuse.

Although little research has been performed considering the effects of corporal punishment on adults, it does not require a great leap in deductive thought to hypothesize the same type of relationship between corporal punishment and negative social outcomes with adults. Straus argues that one of the powerful factors causing child abuse in American families is the unintended but powerful training of Americans in the use of violence as a means of teaching and resolving conflicts. Thus, after an extensive review of the literature on domestic violence, Utech (1994) concluded that "[T]he learning and acceptance of violence as a means for resolving interpersonal and family problems, including the use of physical punishment on children, are antecedent conditions for the perpetuation of the intergenerational cycle of violence" (p. 83). As recognized by Judge Blackmun, corporal punishment does not represent a panacea for the crime problem plaguing contemporary life. Instead, corporal punishment represents the potential for creating an even more powerful antisocial reaction in offenders, and possibly society in general, which can become the basis for a recurring cycle of violence and crime.

The Legacy of Slavery: American Images of Back to the Future

Discussions of corporal punishment often appear to occur in a historical vacuum. Ignored are the legacies of racism and inequality endemic in American history. Newman in his work never addresses the American legacy of slavery or the connection between race and violence inherent in American history. Nowhere do proponents of corporal punishment appear willing to remember the use of the whipping post as a method of controlling runaway slaves or asserting white power in the South, the whipping and lynching of "uppity blacks" by members of the Ku Klux Klan. Given the overrepresentation of African Americans in the criminal justice system, can anyone ignore images of a future in which large numbers of poor, African American men are whipped or subjected to electric prods to satisfy the fears of a white middle class about crime? If the O. J. Simpson trial showed any truths about the American criminal justice system, it was the deep division along racial lines among Americans in their views of the system. A return to the use of corporal punishment can only exacerbate these divisions.

Conclusion

Corporal punishment raises grave constitutional issues implicating the Eighth Amendment's prohibition against cruel and unusual punishment. Its use would represent a retreat from the evolving standards of human decency and dignity, signifying a maturing society. Its use, even with attempted precautionary safeguards, raises questions of sadism, abuse, and excessive and disproportionate punishment. Research involving children suggests significant averse effects stemming from its use. Such research suggests that the use of corporal punishment, instead of controlling crime, may well be the harbinger of a cycle of future crime and violence. Moreover, the images created by its use, based on the legacy of slavery and racism that have characterized American history, may act as a catalyst for further dividing American society.

Corporal punishment was wrong when it was used. Bringing it back would be even worse.

REFERENCES

Newman, G. (1983). *Just and painful: A case for the corporal punishment of criminals.* London: MacMillan.

Straus, M. A. (1979). Family patterns and child abuse. *Child Abuse and Neglect, 3,* 213–225.

Utech, M. R. (1994). *Violence, abuse and neglect: The American home.* Dix Hills, NY: Nelson Hall, Inc.

CASES

Dyke v. *Taylor Implement Mfg. Co.,* 391 U.S. 216 (1968).
Ingraham v. *Wright,* 430 U.S. 651 (1977).
Jackson v. *Bishop,* 404 F.2d 571 (8th Cir. 1968).
State v. *Resweber,* 329 U.S. 459 (1947).
O'Neil v. *Vermont,* 144 U.S. 323 (1892) (Justice Field dissenting).
Rochin v. *California,* 342 U.S. 165 (1952).
Trop v. *Dulles,* 386 U.S. 86 (1958).

Rejoinder to Professor Janikowski TERRY D. EDWARDS

My friend and colleague, Professor Richard Janikowski, advances three arguments against the use of corporal punishment in the American criminal justice system—one legal, one emotional, and one ethical. Each is interesting; however, they are, individually and collectively, without sufficient merit or supporting evidence as to warrant a conclusion that corporal punishment serves no legitimate penological interest.

First, the legal argument—constitutionality. Professor Janikowski acknowledges, as did the U.S. Supreme Court in *Ingraham* v. *Wright* (1977), that the imposition of corporal punishment is not a per se violation of the U.S. Constitution. This is true, as in the *Ingraham* case, even where the practice involves juveniles who have not been convicted of any crime. Surely, if nonconvicted juveniles may be subject to corporal punishment without offending the Constitution, logic dictates that the imposition of corporal punishment for convicted offenders, under properly crafted guidelines and with regard for the health and welfare of the defendant, would not rise to a constitutional violation. Furthermore, reliance on *Jackson* v. *Bishop* (1968) to support the argument that the practice is unconstitutional is misplaced. The court in *Jackson* simply struck down the practice, as it was then imposed, holding that sufficient protections did not exist to justify its use. It is worth repeating—no court in this country has ever ruled that the imposition of corporal punishment, even in criminal justice settings, is a per se violation of the U.S. Constitution. Within an environment of legislative approval and judicial oversight, corporal punishment within the American criminal justice system quite clearly passes constitutional muster.

Next, the emotional argument—violence begets more violence: speculation and conjecture at best. In a brief three-paragraph "generalization" of the issue, Professor Janikowski offers but two studies in support of this argument, one relating to child abuse in the family setting and the other to domestic violence, and then suggests that it does not require a "great leap" to draw similar conclusions in the realm of corporal punishment in the American criminal justice system. Nonsense! Not a single study can be cited supporting the conclusion that the use of corporal punishment in the American criminal justice system will lead or has led to increased violence elsewhere in society. For the reasonable person, avoiding corporal punishment as a legitimate penological "tool" in the complete absence of evidence that it is harmful does seem, indeed, to require the "great leap" he mentions. Again, why should supporters have to empirically "prove" the practice works? Why should opponents not be required to empirically "prove" it does not work?

Finally, the ethical argument—corporal punishment is racist: an emotional argument at best. First, Professor Janikowski, in a brief one-paragraph summation, asserts, without citing historical basis or evidentiary support, that whipping is so inexorably intertwined with American slavery and the imposition of "white power" in the South that the imposition of corporal punishment on African-American inmates would somehow be so racially offensive as to preclude its use. Assuming such a statement to be true, then could corporal punishment be employed outside the South without becoming racially tainted? Could nonwhites employ the practice without being accused of being racist? If the form of corporal punishment did not involve whipping or electric cattle prods—would that suitably "de-race" the matter? It stretches the imagination, and offends the dignity of this discussion, to "play the race card" with regard to this issue.

In conclusion, the three arguments advanced by Professor Janikowski in opposition of corporal punishment, especially the argument relating to race, seem to rely more on emotion and sympathy rather than on logic or law. Such arguments certainly have a place, perhaps in editorials, but none of these arguments are supported empirically or legally. Corporal punishment in the American criminal justice system, legislatively adopted and administered with the protection of judicial review, although certainly controversial, is constitutional and certainly no more ineffective than existing penological practices.

CASES

Ingraham v. *Wright,* 430 U.S. 651 (1977).
Jackson v. *Bishop,* 404 F.2d 571 (8th Cir. 1968).

Are Inmate Lawsuits Out of Control?

Rick M. Steinmann argues YES. An Associate Professor of Criminal Justice at Lindenwood College, he has an M. A. in Criminal Justice from Youngstown State University and a J. D. from Hamline University School of Law. He has taught criminal justice courses for fifteen years, and current research interests include legal issues that impact on prisoners and juveniles.

Kathleen Simon argues NO. She is Assistant Professor in the Department of Political Science/Criminal Justice at Appalachian State University, where she teaches courses in criminal law, legal systems and research, and administrative law. Previous research has included analyses of the criminal procedure jurisprudence of Justice John Paul Stevens and of the Rehnquist Court, an examination of occupational crime in North Carolina, and a comparative survey of administrative procedure acts across the states.

YES

RICK M. STEINMANN

An inmate files a civil lawsuit that he received creamy peanut butter instead of crunchy. Another prisoner demands "soap on a rope." Yes, these are actual claims made by inmates who asserted a violation of their civil rights during confinement. The premise of this chapter is that a sizable amount of inmate suits filed in U.S. District Courts are "frivolous" and that a number of inmates are abusing the process. This chapter examines the nature and extent of inmate litigation along with recent Federal and State legislation to discourage abusive litigation. Additionally, alternatives to filing federal lawsuits, such as internal prison "grievance" systems, are both addressed and advanced as viable options to the filing of lawsuits.

Inmate Conditions of Confinement Lawsuits under *42 USCA §1983*

Inmates generally file lawsuits against a prison or jail through the federal courts, which are customarily viewed as being more hospitable to their complaints than state courts. This is accomplished by the filing of a *42 USCA, §1983* (1988) action, which provides that an action may be initiated against a person who has acted under color of state law (generally a state employee, such as a correctional officer) to deprive a person of rights secured by the U.S. Constitution or the laws of the United States. Civil rights suits filed by inmates generally involve conditions of confinement that revolve around such areas as the lack of medical care, assault by guards, religious deprivations, and unsatisfactory living conditions (Eisenberg, 1993; Maahs & Del Carmen, 1995). The focus of this chapter is on the latter category, unsatisfactory living conditions, because this is where many nonmeritorious claims are found.

A distinction should be made between *42 USCA, §1983* actions and federal *habeas corpus* actions (*28 USCA §2254,* 1988). Under *§1983,* monetary damages or injunctive relief are sought, whereas a habeas petitioner is asserting that he is being unlawfully detained and is seeking release from prison because of what he claims was an illegal conviction or sentence. *Habeas* petitions sometimes allege that the police, the prosecution, or the trial court violated their federal constitutional rights. Most frequently, prisoners federal file these petitions, arguing they are entitled to a new trial because of claims of "ineffective assistance of counsel" lodged against their trial attorney (Hanson & Daley, 1995). This chapter does not specifically address *habeas corpus* actions except to note that a 1996 federal statute entitled the *Anti Terrorism and Effective Death Penalty Act* (110 Stat. 1214, 1996) is an effort to discourage perceived abusive habeas litigation by placing tighter restrictions on its use, particularly as it applies to death row inmates.

Certainly, inmates have a constitutional right to bring meritorious claims concerning "conditions of confinement" to the attention of the federal district courts. However, so-called frivolous suits, the substance of this chapter, are another matter. What is the definition of a "frivolous" inmate lawsuit? Generally, a complaint is "frivolous…if the complaint lacks an arguable basis either in law or fact…dismissed for one or both of two broad reasons: the facts alleged are 'fanciful or delusional,' or the facts alleged do not amount to a legally cognizable claim" (Federal Judicial Center, 1996, p. 29).

The Nature and Extent of Inmate Lawsuits

In 1995, 40,569 civil rights (*42 USCA §1983*) actions were filed by State inmates in U.S. district courts (Maguire & Pastore, 1996). Compare this with 1966, when only 218 prisoner civil rights cases were filed (Eisenberg, 1993, p. 420). Ross

(1995) indicates that: "...In 1970, state prisoners filed 2,030 *§1983* lawsuits; by 1980 the total was 12,397, an increase of 500 percent in ten years. In 1985, over 18,000 of these suits were filed and by 1993, a total of 33,933 were filed by state prisoners, an increase of 89 percent" (p. 11).

Eisenberg (1993) reported that "In 25 years the number of prisoner civil rights actions filed in federal district court has increased 120 times, while the overall civil caseload in district court has tripled" (p. 466). Wilson (1994) describes how "in 1992, 22 percent of all federal civil suits were filed by inmates. Indeed, there were more civil suits filed by prisoners than criminal prosecutions brought by the federal government" (p. 150).

The central question is how many inmate *§1983* lawsuits are successful? Of 33,000 prisoner lawsuits filed in 1993, a staggering 97 percent of the suits were dismissed before trial (DeWolf, 1996). A 1991 study of *§1983* inmate actions brought in the U.S. district courts of eastern Missouri, southern Illinois, and eastern Arkansas determined that "...in not one case did the prisoner obtain any relief whatsoever by virtue of an order of the court. In a small number of situations the cases were settled, usually for nominal payment of damages or some alteration in the conditions of confinement or the promise of particular medical care" (Eisenberg, 1993, p. 458).

Some of the most outlandish suits that have been filed concern melted ice cream, bad haircuts, and a broken cookie. Others include an inmate seeking to obtain brand-name high-tops rather than inferior brand sneakers issued by the prison, a prisoner claiming that no prison salad bars and brunches were served on weekends and holidays, and a prisoner who killed five people suing after lightning knocked out the prison's TV satellite dish and he had to watch network programs, which he said contained violence, profanity, and other objectionable material (Bryant, 1995).

The question arises as to why inmates file frivolous lawsuits. One commentator (DeWolf, 1996) suggests that motivations include an attempt to show contempt and disrespect for the legal system, waging a personal vendetta, or simply a way to ease the boredom of prison life. He describes how one inmate filed more than 250 actions, another inmate in excess of 300 lawsuits, and yet a third inmate who filed more than 550 complaints.

What is the cost to the public when frivolous suits are filed? In 1992, Arizona needed fourteen full-time attorneys, four full-time corrections staff, and a fluctuating number of full-time support staff to address 1200 inmate lawsuits (Wilson, 1994). The Missouri Attorney General claims his office spends $2 million a year to defend prison officials sued by inmates (Bryant, 1995), and the Ohio attorney general's office spent more than $1.35 million to defend against more than 600 inmate civil lawsuits in 1993 (DeWolf, 1996). In Texas, the ten most prolific inmate litigants cost the Texas attorney generals' office more than $300,000 (Maahs & Del Carmen, 1995) Additionally, costs to the public include the time of the U.S. district court staff attorney (or *pro se* law clerk) who must screen the cases, and ultimately the time of the U.S. district court judge. Add to this the cost of gathering documents and transporting inmates for court appearances (DeWolf, 1996).

Federal Laws to Discourage Meritless Inmate Lawsuits: 1996 Prison Litigation Reform Act

The Prison Litigation Reform Act (18 USCA §3636) became effective on President Clinton's signature in April of 1996. The statute sets out criteria for the granting of relief in prisoner litigation (the *Act* also applies to jails). The 1996 U.S. Court of appeals case of *Madden* v. *Myers* (1996) concluded that the clear import of the *PLRA* is to curtail frivolous prison litigation, namely, that brought under *42 USCA §1983 (Habeas & Prison Litigation, 1997)*. The *PLRA* does not apply to *habeas corpus* petitions.

The *PLRA* has had an extraordinary impact on inmate litigation. It substantially amends the language found in the old 1980 *Civil Rights for Institutionalized Persons Act (42 USCA §1997)*, CRIPA, and also materially changes the process concerning inmates who seek to avoid the payment of filing fees when filing suit, a procedure referred to as an *in forma pauperis* petition (*28 USCA §1915,* 1996).

The *PLRA* now mandates early dismissal of frivolous suits by the judiciary. Pre-*PLRA* law authorized, but did not mandate, dismissal of suits. Provisions also allow for earlier, more thorough screening, and dismissal of cases based on such grounds such as the action or complaint is frivolous or malicious (See *42 USCA §1997e,* as amended in 1996; now retitled: *Suits by Prisoners*). Also, and perhaps most important, the *PLRA* now mandates "exhaustion" of administrative remedies before to filing a *§1983* action in federal court. In other words, an inmate has to first avail himself of whatever prison internal grievance process is in place at his correctional institution before filing suit in federal court.

Under *CRIPA,* inmates could forego submitting their claim for relief through the prison "internal grievance process" if the grievance program had not been certified as providing minimum acceptable standards by the U.S. attorney general or a U.S. district court. *PLRA* has eliminated this requirement (Federal Judicial Center, 1996).

As to *in forma pauperis* petitions, new *28 USCA §1915(g)* "precludes a prisoner from proceeding *in forma pauperis,* regardless of ability to pay, if the prisoner has, on '3' or more previous occasions…brought an action…that was dismissed on the grounds it was frivolous…" (Federal Judicial Center, 1996, p. 16). The *PLRA* also "authorizes the court to revoke the earned good-time credit under *18 USCA §3624(b)* of a prisoner who brings a civil action if the court finds that (1) the claim was filed for a malicious purpose or (2) the claim was filed solely to harass the party against which it was filed…" (Federal Judicial Center, 1996, pp. 53–54).

Other provisions of the *PLRA* prohibit any prisoner from bringing an action for mental or emotional injury suffered while in custody without a prior showing of physical injury (*42 USCA §1997[e]*) and requiring a filing fee and payment of court costs if judgment is entered against the prisoner (*42 USCA §1915[b]* & *[f]*). Lastly, in the event an inmate prevails in his lawsuit, any compensatory damages are to be applied directly to the payment of any outstanding restitution orders against the prisoner. Likewise, up to 25 percent of any monetary judgment awarded to a prisoner must be applied toward his attorney's fee award (Federal Judicial Center, 1996).

Federal appellate courts have overwhelmingly upheld the constitutionality of the provisions found in the *PRLA*. For examples, see *Plyler* v. *Moore* (1996) and *Adepegba* v. *Hammons* (1996).

State Laws to Discourage Meritless Inmate Lawsuits

Wharton (1996) reports that about twenty-one states have passed or are considering passing legislation similar to the *PLRA*. He indicates that "most statutes require inmates to file partial filing fees and revoke good conduct credit or other privileges if inmates persist in filing lawsuits found to be frivolous" (p. 41).

Missouri is an example of a state that has aggressively sought to discourage meritless inmate lawsuits. In 1995, Missouri passed legislation that specifies that on a court's finding of a frivolous claim, an additional sixty days shall be added to the time that an offender is first eligible for parole consideration. An additional provision provides that a deduction from the inmates institutional account shall be made for each instance that a frivolous suit has been filed. Soon after the law took effect, the Missouri attorney general mailed letters to inmates who had filed sixteen claims that he believed were particularly implausible. The letters warned that pursuing the suits could lead to sanctions under the new law. Missouri inmates subsequently brought suit, claiming that legitimate suits over prison conditions will not be filed for fear of such sanctions. In May 1997, the U.S district court for eastern Missouri in *Johnson* v. *Missouri* (1997) rejected the prisoners' claim that legitimate suits over prison conditions will not be filed for fear of such sanctions. The same year, the Missouri legislature passed additional legislation (*Senate Bill 56*) that provides that prisoners who file frivolous lawsuits can be forced to pay the defendant's court costs and attorney fees. The bill awaits the Governor's signing.

Maahs and Del Carmen (1995) examined several different states in assessing the various sanctions that are imposed to deter frivolous suits and found that the laws in most states focus mostly on the imposition of filing fees. This legislative approach has already had a significant impact on prisoner litigation. Statistics from the state of New York show a dramatic decrease in lawsuits by inmates since the imposition of a filing fee requirement in 1985. Even more striking are statistics from Arizona, which experienced a 35 percent drop in filings during the first year in which its filing fee legislation was enacted (DeWolf, 1996).

A question that has arisen is whether imposing filing fees on inmates violates their First Amendment guarantee of the right to petition the government for redress of grievances. The U.S. Supreme Court case of *Bill Johnson's Restaurant* v. *National Labor Relations Board* (1983) may be instructive on this point. The Court in that case stated that

> The first amendment interests in private litigation...are not advanced when the litigation is based on intentional falsehoods or on knowingly frivolous claims. Furthermore, since sham litigation by definition does not involve a bona fide grievance, it does not come within the First Amendment right to petition (p. 743).

Alternative Procedures to Avoid Inmate Litigation

As mentioned earlier in this chapter, an inmate must now "exhaust" any administrative remedy before filing a *§1983* action in federal court. This requirement mandates that an inmate first participate in any internal grievance process that is available within his prison.

The prison grievance process serves several purposes. First, it deters prisoners from becoming abusive litigants by filtering out those lawsuits that are frivolous and malicious, before they burden court dockets (DeWolf, 1996). The thinking is that inmates may recognize during the internal prison grievance process that their claim lacks merit and voluntarily choose to terminate the matter at this stage. Likewise, the thinking is that a valid claim can be resolved in favor of the inmate, and hence the costs of litigation in federal court are averted. Certainly, there is also more room for a compromise-type determination through the grievance process, as compared with the more formal litigation process, where only one party prevails. In other words, a resolution that is generally satisfactory to both sides is more likely to occur during the prison internal grievance process than during litigation. The inmate, of course, always retains the right to file a *§1983* action in federal court after first participating in the prison grievance process.

Mandatory participation in internal grievance programs should decrease the number of 1983 suits that are initiated and therefore reduce federal court oversight of prisons and jails. The thinking of many correctional administrators is that federal courts are not equipped to properly engage in microscopic oversight or management of prisons or jails. That is, the federal courts ought to more frequently recognize that correctional administration is a complex matter best left to the discretion of correctional experts rather than the courts and hence be more conducive to deferring to the expertise of prison administrators. In fact, since the early 1980s, U.S. Supreme Court decisions pertaining to inmates have actually shown a greater willingness to permit correctional administrators to operate institutions as they see appropriate relative to conditions of confinement.

It is also constructive to recognize that the prison internal grievance process is useful as a management tool. Clear and Cole (1997) advance the proposition that: "By attentive monitoring of the complaint process, a warden or commissioner is able to discern patterns of inmate discontent that may warrant actions to prevent the development of more serious problems" (p. 408).

Of course, any prison internal grievance process must be designed so that safeguards are in place to prevent inmate concerns that reprisals will be taken against them for bringing allegations of civil rights violations before the internal prison grievance board.

Aside from the prison inmate grievance process, other alternative procedures to avoid inmate litigation have been promoted and deserve consideration. These include the use of an ombudsman, the use of mediation, and implementing prison legal assistance programs (Clear & Cole, 1997). Each of these approaches may be helpful, in their own way, in deterring frivolous lawsuits while at the same time framing issues in a comprehensible manner for those inmates who indeed have legitimate constitutional claims concerning conditions of confinement.

Increased use of alternatives to litigation should result in a decreased filing of *§1983* actions. The beneficiary of reduced filing of *§1983* actions will be, in part, the U.S. district court staff attorney (or pro se law clerk) who initially screens inmate lawsuits to determine whether they appear, on their face, to be meritorious in nature. Reduced filing of suits under *§1983* should enable the U.S. district court staff attorney (or pro se law clerk) to have the luxury of expending additional time in carefully examining the lawsuits that have been filed, to assess whether any meritorious issues concerning conditions of confinement are present.

Conclusion

The premise of this argument has been that a sizable number of inmate lawsuits brought under *42 USCA §1983* concerning conditions of confinement are frivolous in nature. Additionally, the sheer number of such lawsuits imposes a substantial financial expenditure to the states that must defend such claims and also to the federal district courts, which must oversee and manage the processing of such actions. This chapter, moreover, has suggested that alternative approaches to inmate litigation, such as prison internal grievance procedures that are now mandated by law, may be more suited to resolve legitimate inmate concerns while at the same time filtering out frivolous claims.

The Court in *Wilson* v. *Seiter* (1990), in quoting the language of a 1981 U.S. Supreme Court opinion that addressed conditions of confinement, reiterated that "…to the extent that such conditions are restrictive and even harsh, they are part of the penalty that criminal offenders pay for their offenses against society" (p. 861). Another Court opinion, *Johnson* v. *Ozim* (1991), pronounced that "it is our very strong feeling that comfort and convenience are not elements that should be supplied by society to prison inmates" (p. 181).

In 1994, Kathleen McDonald O'Malley, first assistant attorney general in Ohio, gave testimony before an Ohio senate judiciary committee, which was considering and subsequently passed legislation that addressed frivolous inmate litigation. She testified that "…The time and expense of litigating frivolous lawsuits have diverted valuable and limited public resources from being focused on meritorious claims and on providing better facilities and rehabilitative opportunities throughout our prison system" (DeWolf, 1996, p. 271).

At least fourteen states and the federal government have enacted so-called "three strikes and your out" sentencing laws. As more states contemplate doing likewise, it is clear that enormous numbers of inmates will be spending a considerable amount of time incarcerated. In June of 1995, 1,104,074 individuals were incarcerated in U.S. state and federal prisons, whereas 490,442 individuals were housed in local jails in December of 1994 (Maguire & Pastore, 1996). Obviously, inmates encountering longer periods of incarceration may have more incentive to file actions challenging the conditions of their confinement. Hence, legislation such as the *PRLA* may be even more meaningful in discouraging frivolous litigation.

The beginning of this chapter described an inmate who filed a lawsuit because he received creamy peanut butter instead of crunchy. Perhaps former U.S. Supreme Court Chief Justice Warren Burger said it best when he stated:

> Federal judges should not be dealing with prisoner complaints which, although important to a prisoner, are so minor that any well-run institution should be able to resolve them fairly without resort to federal judges (Clear & Cole, 1997, p. 405).

References

Bryant, T. (1995, October 22). Nixon smells a rat when it comes to some jail lawsuits. *St. Louis Post Dispatch,* pp. 1d, 8d.

Clear, T. R., & Cole, G. F. (1997). *American corrections* (4th ed.). Belmont, CA: Wadsworth.

DeWolf, G. L. (1996). Protecting the courts from the barrage of frivolous prisoner litigation: A look at judicial remedies and Ohio's proposed legislative remedy. *Ohio State Law Journal, 57,* 257–289.

Eisenberg, H. B. (1993). Rethinking prisoner civil rights cases and the provision of counsel. *Southern Illinois University Law Journal, 17,* 417–490.

Federal Judicial Center. (1996). *Resource guide for managing prisoner civil rights litigation, with special emphasis on the Prison Litigation Reform Act.* Washington, DC: Author.

Hanson, R. A., & Daley, H. W. (1995). *Federal habeas corpus review: Challenging state court convictions.* Washington, DC: U.S. Department of Justice.

Maahs, J. R., & Del Carmen, R. V. (1995). Curtailing frivolous *§1983* inmate litigation: Laws, practices, and proposals. *Federal Probation, 59,* 53–61.

Maguire, K., & Pastore, A. L. (1996). *Sourcebook of criminal justice statistics, 1995.* Washington, DC: U.S. Department of Justice.

Ross, R. L. (1995, May/June). A twenty-year analysis of *Section 1983* litigation in corrections. *American Jails, 9,* 10–16.

Wharton, J. (1996, August). Courts now out of job as jailers: New law to end prison oversight applauded by attorneys general. *American Bar Association Journal, 82,* 40–41.

Wilson, J. C. (1994, July). Inmates license to sue. *Corrections Today,* 150–153.

CASES

Adepegada v. *Hammons,* 103 F.3d 383 (5th Cir. 1996).

Bill Johnson's Restaurant v. *National Labor Relations Board,* 461 U.S. 731 (1983).

Johnson v. *Missouri,* __ F. Supp. __ (E.D. MO. 1997) (Ct.# 4:96CV-589-CDP).

Johnson v. *Ozim,* 804 S. W.2d 179 (1991).

Madden v. *Meyers,* 102 F.3d 74 (3rd Cir. 1996).

Plyer v. *Moore,* 100 F.3d 365 (4th Cir. 1996).

Wilson v. *Seiter,* 893 F.2d 861 (6th Cir. 1990).

Rejoinder to Professor Steinmann   KATHLEEN SIMON

The topic to be addressed is whether inmate lawsuits are out of control. Rather than establish the premise that in fact such lawsuits *are* out of control, my opponent's overall presentation appears to defend the proposition that prisoner abuse of prison litigation processes can be controlled by tightening those processes through state and federal legislation—which he describes at great length. He takes hold of the debate by changing the premise to be debated. He does this by narrowing the categories of inmate lawsuits to "frivolous" lawsuits filed under *§1983*, and narrowing that category even further to include only claims under "unsatisfactory living conditions." Like the politicians who supported the reform legislation detailed in this article, Professor Steinmann draws generalizations from particular facts.

Unlike your author, I refused to recite descriptions of the more outlandish prisoner claims or to note the hundreds of cases filed by a handful of "creative" inmates as typical of all inmate lawsuits dismissed. The National Association of Attorneys General (NAAG) used this examples strategy in issuing their "unmeritorious claims" hit lists, and it is nothing more than demagoguery. Yet, by introducing the outlandish for effect, Professor Steinmann sets the stage for building his case. After these examples and after giving the statutory definition of "frivolous," by implication the author would have us conclude that all of the unsuccessful *§1983* lawsuits (e.g., 97 percent dismissed in 1993) were indeed frivolous. On the contrary, Hanson/Daley's work, among the most in-depth of the very few empirical studies available that actually examined the files of federal district court cases, shows us that fewer than 15 percent of the cases filed fit the legal definition of "frivolous." Most cases dismissed were on procedural grounds; that is to say, the inmate could have a justifiable grievance against the prison but not under the criteria stipulated by *§1983*. In the absence of grievance procedures within the state correctional apparatus, an inmate may be hard pressed for forms of redress. In addition, I caution readers when evaluating public funds spent to defend against inmate lawsuits. Again, the author implies that the identified states spent their monies to defend against frivolous lawsuits, whereas a fairer conclusion is that (except for Texas) the funds were applied to total inmate lawsuits. It would be more helpful to compare attorneys general staffing and expenditures across the states per inmate case in the years 1966, 1970, 1985, 1993, and 1995. This would complement the years my adversary uses to illustrate benchmarks in case volume increases. A clearer picture may appear, showing whether the staffs are overworked or merely not sufficient enough in numbers to handle a caseload that had increased, predictably, in proportion to the numbers of prisoners incarcerated. Also, calling to mind both Hanson/Daley as well as Flango's research, one must reiterate that it is generally the *complexity* of cases rather than volume that dictates the costs of litigation. Thus, actual staff time and efforts spent on individual cases vary considerably and should be taken into account in evaluating staff productivity as well.

The repeated charge that a sizable number of inmate lawsuits brought under *§1983* are frivolous without articulating the meaning of "sizable" is similar to the position that the number of lawsuits is "out of control." It begs the question, "How many is too many?" Or, for that matter, "What is a 'sizable' amount?" The *Random House Dictionary* defines *sizable* as "fairly large." Without actually pinpointing how many dismissed cases are actually frivolous, one is hard pressed to conclude whether in fact there is a large amount of frivolous prisoner cases that need to be controlled. Along the same lines, the secondary sources quoted to identify the "nature and extent of inmate lawsuits" first identify numbers of civil rights cases filed over twenty-five years, but switch to civil suits in the next paragraph. Indeed, 22 percent of all federal civil suits filed in 1992 *were* brought by inmates, but only 13.3 percent were civil rights cases. Also, statistics from the Administrative Office of the Courts show that 67,635 criminal cases and 230,509 civil actions were commenced in federal district courts in 1992. Of the total civil actions, 48,423 were from prisoner petitions (12,806 *habeas corpus,* 30,556 civil rights, 1,078 mandamus, and 3,983 motions to vacate sentence). From these numbers it is difficult to understand how "there were more civil suits filed by prisoners than criminal prosecutions brought by the federal government." Even if the exact numbers were incorrect, it would surprise few that federal criminal prosecutions are low, because most criminal law is enforced at the state level.

Given that the remaining presentation by my opponent consists of a description of current legislative initiatives taken by state and federal officials to provide alternative grievance resolution or designed to discourage and sanction prisoners from approaching the federal courts, my rejoinder must end. I concluded that the campaign by these officials to make inmate lawsuits (from both civil rights and *habeas corpus* petitions) a political issue by distorting the significance of actual case statistics resulted in both the *Prisoner Litigation Reform Act* and the *Antiterrorism and Effective Death Penalty Act.* There is no doubt that both designs will stem the tide of prisoner litigation. In fact, early statistics from the Administrative Office of the Courts for FY1996–97 already reflect a downturn in filings of civil rights cases; however, those cases had already begun a decline in FY1995–96 even without litigation reform. Thus, my opponent can claim support for the proposition that inmate litigation can be controlled, but falls short of defending the position that inmate lawsuits are in fact out of control.

NO

KATHLEEN SIMON

In March of 1994, the National Association of Attorneys General (NAAG) took a stand calling for major changes in postconviction criminal procedures to stem the tide of so-called frivolous inmate lawsuits inundating both state and federal courts. Concurrent with this effort was a major (and now often-quoted) *New York Times* article by Ashley Dunn (1994) highlighting issues from a few of the more outrageous prisoner claims and illustrating how steadily increasing caseloads taxed state defense resources. Further emphasis was placed on the issue of inmate litigation later that year when Republicans running for Congress included prison litigation reform under the anticrime tenet of their Contract with America campaign strategy. Targeting frivolous suits complemented earlier, yet unsuccessful, NAAG as well as Reagan and Bush administrations' initiatives to lobby for changes in federal *habeas corpus* procedures, thereby curtailing multiple capital and noncapital inmate appeals by both state and federal prisoners. In ensuing years, fervent rhetoric by state and federal executives, legislators, and judges kept the issue alive and in the national dialogue (Maahs & del Carmen, 1995), culminating in significant legislation.

Despite the many death penalty convictions upheld and *habeas corpus* claims denied by the federal courts and the concerted effort by the U.S. Supreme Court to limit the use of the writ of *habeas corpus* throughout the 1980s and early 1990s (Mays & Winfree, 1997), the few death penalty cases overturned or prisoner rights recognized by Court decisions received disproportionate attention by both the media and particular politicians (Hanson & Daley, 1995a). In retrospect, one may question whether such concerns identified a legitimate problem, and whether inmate litigation is a persistent problem today.

The Evolution of Prisoner Litigation

Historically, the bulk of litigation filed by prison inmates has been under the federal *habeas corpus* statute (*28 USCA §2254*) as well as state *habeas corpus* laws. A prisoner may petition for the writ to challenge the legality of his or her conviction as a means to gain release from unlawful custody. However, a prisoner must have exhausted state remedies through direct appeal in the state court system, and review of the same *habeas corpus* issues, before petitioning a federal district court. Beginning in the 1960s, a second source for prisoner suits manifested itself (Mays & Olszta, 1989). More and more prisoners began to challenge the conditions of their confinement using the *Civil Rights Act of 1871 (42 USCA §1983)*, under which one may argue that a person, acting under color of state law, violated a protected constitutional right. Whereas the former suit may lead to release of the inmate, the latter suit seeks changes in the prison environment and possible damages for injuries incurred within the correctional institution. And, unlike *habeas corpus* procedure, a prisoner did not have to exhaust state remedies (other than federally certified prison grievance procedures) before filing a civil rights suit. The consequences of each type of suit differ in reach as well. If a court grants a writ, one prisoner is released, but if a court grants *§1983* relief, a whole state prison system could be under federal court control indefinitely until the remedies are in place.

By the same token, issues affecting federalism are manifest in both procedures. States must use extensive resources in defending against the suits, even if many are dismissed. Federal judges are seen to be second-guessing extensive state court processes and the decisions of competent persons when state prisoners, especially those on death row, are released, and federal judges are resented for making demands on state corrections budgets and personnel in areas traditionally the responsibility of the states. Thus, one cannot deny that concerns related to state–federal relations have been at the crux of the inmate litigation complaints.

The Extent of Prison Litigation

There is no one source that maintains a record of prisoner litigation from the fifty state court systems; however, the annual report of the Administrative Office of U.S. Courts includes the numbers of *habeas corpus* and civil rights cases filed by state and federal prisoners in the federal courts. Flango (1994; 1996) and Hanson & Daley (1995a; 1995b) provide the most current published empirical research analyzing these prisoner litigation statistics, and some of their findings indicate that prisoner filings may not be as out of control as the critics contend. Flango's (1994) work acknowledges that the rise in state prisoner *habeas* petitions began in 1963 after a series of U.S. Supreme Court cases that broadened the authority of federal district courts to review the cases. Looking at filings over a twenty-five-year period, he concluded that, though the volume had quadrupled to 10,323 in

1991, the rate of filings per prisoner had declined from a high of 5.1 percent in 1970 to 1.3 percent in 1991. In addition, he noted that *habeas* cases represented only 4.7 percent of the civil cases filed in federal courts in 1990 and 1992, and that more than half of the petitions filed were from only nine states.

Flango (1996) also found that, though earlier studies had shown that 40 percent of death penalty cases from state petitioners had been overturned by federal courts, more recent statistics show, for example, that of the ninety-four petitions filed in federal courts by death row inmates in 1992, only seven (or 7.4 percent) of the forty-six cases that actually reached judgment favored the inmate, and of the 10,968 total petitions filed, only 241 (2.6 percent) of the 4620 cases decided on the merits were decided for the petitioner. In answer to the concerns that processing of *habeas* cases, especially death penalty cases, absorb an inordinate amount of court time, Hanson and Daley (1995b) found that case complexity (number of issues, whether the petition is decided on the merits, the appointment of counsel, and the holding of an evidentiary hearing) far outweigh the influence of case characteristics, the most serious offense at conviction, whether the sentence was death, life in prison, or a term of years, or whether the trial court proceedings was a jury trial or a guilty plea. They determined that what appeared to be driving the numbers of petitions filed was petitions from individuals under life sentences, not from those under a death sentence, as supposed by conventional wisdom.

Directing their attention to *§1983* civil rights suits, Hanson and Daley (1995a) noted the increase in prisoner rights cases over a twenty-five-year period from a low of 218 cases in 1966 to 26,824 in 1992, with such cases constituting more than 10 percent of all civil case filings in the U.S. District Courts. This increase corresponds not only to the recognition of prisoner rights in a series of U.S. Supreme Court cases in the 1960s, but also to the tremendous growth in prison populations, especially in the 1980s. In analyzing outcomes of over 50 percent of the cases filed in the federal courts in 1992, they found that 94 percent of the issues were dismissed (74 percent by the court and 20 percent on motion by the defendant), 4 percent of the cases resulted in a stipulated dismissal or settlement, and less than one-half of 1 percent favored the claims of the inmates for the 2 percent of cases that went to trial. Of the 74 percent of cases dismissed by the court, 19 percent (or 13 percent of the total cases filed) were determined to be "frivolous" (i.e., no arguable basis in law or fact). The most frequently raised issues were inadequate medical treatment, a lack of physical security, and transfer to administrative segregation without due process. The average case processing time was 181 days, and half of the total cases took less than six months to resolve. Like the *habeas corpus* cases discussed, the researchers discovered that the complexity of a case, rather than the volume of cases, determined the extent of court personnel time devoted to *§1983* cases. In finding that the overwhelming number of court dismissals were based on procedural grounds, the researchers suggested that use of *habeas corpus* or alternative prisoner grievances processes were better suited to provide relief for those prisoners whose complaints were not frivolous, yet failed to meet the strictness of §*1983* criteria (i.e., failure to sue an individual acting under state law, failure to raise an issue cognizable under §*1983,* failure to sue an individual without immunity, and failure to raise an issue that rises to the level of constitutional violation).

Federal and State Legislative Response

In the aftermath of the 1994 elections and the April 1995 bombing of the Oklahoma City federal building, the curtailment of inmate litigation was the target of two major pieces of federal legislation and a number of state statutes. In 1995, various state attorneys general kept up the heat on both federal and state legislators by giving speeches and press conferences noting the high number of lawsuits filed by inmates, the states' costs to defend against them, and the advantages of adopting NAAG's model legislation. Among the groups countering these efforts was the *National Prison Project* of the American Civil Liberties Union, long an advocate of prison reform and prisoner rights, which attempted to educate the public on the practical consequences of curtailing prisoners' access to the courts.

In Congress, House Republicans were successful in passing prison litigation reform as part of their 1995 anticrime bill; however, it was not until April 1996 that *The Prison Litigation Reform Act* was finally signed into law and tagged onto a budget reconciliation bill for the Departments of Commerce, Justice, and State. In addition to limiting the authority of the federal district courts to issue consent decrees and allowing immediate state challenges to existing consent decrees, the law set up a number of procedures to screen out cases even before docketing, to require filing fees, to sanction prisoners with loss of good time credits for filing malicious or harassing suits, and to prohibit or limit attorneys' fees. Also in April, after more than a year of negotiating, Congress passed the *Antiterrorism and Effective Death Penalty Act of 1996.* Under the law, state prisoners must file a petition within one year after their final state appeal and within six months of appeal for death penalty cases and are limited to the number of writs they may file; in addition, federal judges must defer to state judge rulings unless the latter are viewed as unreasonable (Idelson, 1996).

State legislatures had also been active in efforts to curb frivolous law suits (*CJ Letter,* 1997). Between 1994 and 1997, at least ten states had passed laws requiring prison inmates to pay filing fees (Alaska, Mississippi), or pay court costs (California, South Carolina), or both (Arizona, Delaware, Florida, Iowa, Kentucky, Minnesota), and at least four states now require inmates to pay fees or court costs if a suit filed is determined to be frivolous (Mississippi, New Jersey, Tennessee, Texas). In at least thirteen states, inmates can lose good time credits (Arizona, California, Delaware, Florida, Illinois, Iowa, New Jersey, Nevada, South Carolina, Tennessee, Texas), or are subject to other sanctions (Colorado,

Oklahoma, South Carolina) for filing frivolous and malicious suits. A few other states recently placed various limits on filing periods (Florida, Tennessee, Utah) or extent of liability of the correctional institutions (Florida, Mississippi).

Prisoner Litigation Statistics Update

Both Flango's (1994/96) and Hanson/Daley's (1995) research began with the observation that the steady increase in numbers of prison litigation cases between 1961 and 1992 corresponded to the rise in prison populations across the states. However, the proportion of *habeas* petitions filed to the number of state prisoners has steadily declined from a high of 5 percent in 1970 to a low of 1.37 percent in 1991, whereas statistics showed there was approximately one *§1983* lawsuit for every thirty state prisoners. One may inquire as to whether these trends continue. A cursory analysis of litigation and population statistics indicates that they do.

If one were to pick up where Hanson and Daley and Flango left off and examine the 1992–1996 statistics, it would be noted that as state prison populations continued to rise, so did the volume of lawsuits. This follows the same pattern as in previous years. In 1992, the overall prison population was 882,500 (802,421 state prisoners) who filed 12,806 *habeas corpus* petitions (9,480 from state prisoners) and 30,556 civil rights petitions (22,972 from state inmates). In 1996, the overall prison population was 1,182,169 (1,076,625) who filed 16,429 *habeas corpus* petitions (14,726 from state prisoners) and 41,215 civil rights petitions (39,996 from state inmates). However, when filings are seen as a percentage of state prison population, the *habeas corpus* cases show less than a 0.1 percent fluctuation from the 1.37 percent of cases filed per prisoner in 1991. (Note: The numbers of *habeas* filings per state prisoner between 1992 and 1996 were 1.41, 1.32, 1.24, 1.33, and 1.39, respectively.) Similarly, an examination of the *§1983* cases show a 0.2 percent fluctuation over five years since 1991. (Note: The numbers of *§1983* filings per state prisoner between 1992 and 1996 were 3.70, 3.75, 4.00, 4.00, and 3.71, respectively).

Viewed over a ten-year period, it is evident that the percentage of state *habeas corpus* cases generally showed a slight decline until 1996. It has been explained that the rise in state and federal *habeas corpus* cases from 14,975 in 1995 to 16,429 in 1996 reflected efforts by prisoners to beat filing deadline imposed by the *Antiterrorism Act* (Report of the Director, 1997). The high watermark of state *§1983* cases filed during this decade appears to be 1987, when the percentage of cases to prison population was 4.28 percent. However, the overall average has been 3.81 percent since 1987, and 3.83 since 1992. When federal and state cases are viewed together, only a minimum of fluctuation can be noted between 1992 and 1996: the average for *habeas corpus* cases to prison population was 1.36 percent (reflecting 1.45, 1.35, 1.27, 1.33, 1.39, respectively), and the average for civil rights cases was 3.57 percent (reflecting 3.46, 3.50, 3.70, 3.70, 3.49, respectively).

Summary

Ultimately, then, the question of whether inmate law suits are out of control is a relative one. How many lawsuits are too many? The same state and federal officials who added more crimes (especially drug associated crimes) to the criminal codes, waged anticrime campaigns, and successfully supported and passed more death penalty and presumptive sentencing legislation, are the very ones who demagogued the lawsuit issue when the prisons became overcrowded. It should have come as no surprise that as the numbers of inmates rose, inmate litigation would increase, thereby necessitating more public funding for the appellate and civil litigation divisions, as well as for alternative methods to remedy prisoner grievances. By taking aim at frivolous lawsuits (about 13 percent of prisoner cases filed) and multiple petitions for *habeas corpus* (where filings have consistently gone down through the years, and death penalty cases are at a minimum), legislators were able to initiate procedural reforms and threats of sanction that will inevitably reduce the number of prisoner suits. They were able to do this while not acknowledging that the proportion of lawsuits to prison population had stayed relatively the same within the past several years. Relieving overburdened public employees and saving taxpayer money are welcome political goals behind such legitimate policy changes, but exaggerating the "problem" to achieve the goals may be somewhat less than altruistic.

References

Administrative Office of the United States Courts. (1997). *Judicial business of the United States Courts.* 1996 Report of the Director. Washington, DC: Author.

Antiterrorism and Effective Death Penalty Act. (1996). Pub. L. No. 104-132, 110 Stat. 1217.

CJ Letter (1997, February). *Crackdown seen on frivolous inmate lawsuits.* National Conference of State Legislatures, online subscription newsletter, NCSLnet: Author

Dunn, A. (1994, March 21). Flood of prisoner rights suits brings effort to limit filings. *The New York Times,* A1, B4.

Flango, V. E. (1994). Habeas corpus *in state and federal courts.* Williamsburg, VA: National Center for State Courts.

Flango, V. E. (1996, Winter). *Habeas corpus* petitions in death penalty litigation. *The Judges' Journal,* 8–14; 43.

Hanson, R. A., & Daley, H. W. K. (1995a). *Challenging the conditions of prisons and jails: A report on 1983 litigation.* Washington, DC: U.S. Department of Justice.

Hanson, R. A., & Daley, H. W. K. (1995b, Fall). How federal courts handle *habeas corpus* petitions. *The Judges' Journal,* 4–11; 40–41.

Idelson, H. (1996, April 20). Terrorism bill is headed to president's desk. *Congressional Quarterly Weekly Report, 54,* 1044–1046.

Maahs, J. R., and del Carmen, R. V. (1995). Curtailing frivolous *section 1983* inmate litigation: Laws, Practices, and Proposals, *Federal Probation, 4,* 53–61.

Mays, G. L., & Winfree, L. T., Jr. (1997). *Contemporary corrections.* Belmont, CA: Wadsworth/West Pub. Co.

Mays, G. L., & Olszta, M. (1989). Prison litigation: From the 1960s to the 1990s. *Criminal Justice Policy Review, 3,* 279–98.

The Prison Litigation Reform Act (1996). Pub. L. No. 104-134, 110 Stat. 1321.

Rejoinder to Dr. Simon

Rick M. Steinmann

Dr. Simon, in the introductory part of her chapter, implicitly, if not explicitly, questions the motivation of politicians and the media relative to their concern over the issue of frivolous inmate litigation. It appears that her position is that politicians, in particular, are simply attempting to curry favor with the public by attacking inmate litigation. I would suggest, instead, that it is the responsibility of elected officials to monitor the cost to the public of defending frivolous lawsuits. After all, the state of Missouri was spending approximately two million dollars a year in 1995 to defend against such suits.

In the introductory part of her chapter, Dr. Simon also asks whether inmate litigation is indeed a persistent problem today. I submit that it is indeed a problem from both a sheer numbers perspective as well as from the standpoint of the outlandish types of lawsuits that are filed. Granted, the total number of *§1983* civil rights inmate lawsuits decreased slightly between 1995 and 1996. Nonetheless, statistics still indicate that the total number is close to 40,000 per year.

Of equal, if not greater concern, is the bizarre nature of some inmate lawsuits. The tenor of Dr. Simon's chapter appears to downplay the rather unusual types of inmate lawsuits that are sometimes filed and instead looks at the issue as a mere mathematical equation as to whether the number of lawsuits per inmate is simply rising or declining. I contend that the specific type of inmate "condition of confinement" lawsuit filed is of particular interest to the general public, policymakers, and elected officials. This may consequently have immense influence over how these parties view inmates and the correctional system in general. For example, a Pennsylvania inmate claimed that his religion forbade him from eating anything cooked with onion or garlic, and another inmate filed suit over a misconduct violation he was given for masturbating in front of an officer, claiming that his religion justified such behavior. A significant number of frivolous lawsuits have been filed by inmates to justify inappropriate behavior under the guise of religious practice. Fortunately, the U.S. Supreme Court's 1997 nullification of the

1993 *Religious Freedom Restoration Act* should discourage such lawsuits in the future.

I would suggest that the statistics presented in the section of Dr. Simon's chapter dealing with the extent of prison litigation, in effect, advances my view that inmate lawsuits are out of control. Furthermore, I question the degree of significance that can be placed on Dr. Simon's strong reliance on a research study that concluded that the complexity of a case, rather than the volume of cases, determined the extent of "court personnel time" devoted to *§1983* cases. My uneasiness with the above study derives from the fact that, in addition to court personnel time, one must also truly appreciate the huge amount of legal resources (and other collateral correctional institutional costs) expended to defend against inmate lawsuits. For instance, in 1992, Arizona needed the services of fourteen full-time attorneys and a number of support staff to cope with inmate litigation.

In Dr. Simon's section on the federal and state legislative response to inmate litigation, she mentions the National Prison Project of the American Civil Liberties Union as being a group attempting to educate the public on the practical consequences of curtailing prisoners access to the courts. Certainly, the courts should not be precluded from addressing meritorious inmate lawsuits. However, given the fact that most inmate lawsuits are dismissed by the courts, I would suggest that a more prudent mechanism to resolve inmate "conditions of confinement" issues could be addressed by taking the following three-step approach:

1. First, state prison systems should consider instituting what Missouri has called a *Constituent Services Program.* This program was started in 1994 and is being heralded in various criminal justice publications as a new effective way of resolving inmate "conditions of confinement" issues. In brief, the program mediates inmate disputes in an informal proactive problem-solving manner. Since the inception of the program, Missouri's pending inmate lawsuits have been reduced by sixty-nine percent. The program is unique in that it handles a variety of inquiries and concerns from a very diverse community that includes not only inmates, but also local, state, and federal government offices; legislators; families and friends of inmates; and staff and inmate advocacy agencies.

2. If a "Constituent Services" or similarly designated agency is unable to suitably resolve the dispute, the next step would be to participate in the now legally mandatory *Prison Internal Grievance Process.* This grievance process is legislatively dictated by the *1996 Prison Litigation Reform Act* (which amended the *1980 Civil Rights for Institutionalized Persons Act*). The *PLRA* requires the above process before an inmate instituting a *§1983* condition of confinement lawsuit.

3. Lastly, a *§1983* action can be instituted in Federal Court by an inmate who is not satisfied with the resolution of the problem through the *Prison Internal Grievance Procedures.*

I propose the above approach as a logical way of controlling the number of frivolous inmate lawsuits. As it now stands, it is difficult to persuade the general public and elected officials to support innovative prison correctional efforts that aim to rehabilitate incarcerated prisoners, when at the same time the public and politicians read about an inmate suing the state over receiving creamy peanut butter instead of crunchy.

The Punishment of Youthful Murderers: Should They Be Executed?

Michael Donahue argues YES. He is Associate Professor and Chair of the Department of Government at Armstrong Atlantic State University and holds a Ph.D. in social science from Michigan State University, an M.C.J. from the University of South Carolina, and a B.A. in philosophy from the University of North Carolina. He is a former police officer and trainer and serves as a consultant to local governments on police recruitment, selection, promotion, program evaluation, and human resource allocation.

Margaret Vandiver argues NO. She is Assistant Professor in the Department of Criminology and Criminal Justice at the University of Memphis and holds M.A. and Ph.D. degrees in Criminology from Florida State University. Dr. Vandiver has worked extensively with attorneys defending capital cases and has written about racial discrimination in the use of the death penalty, and about the effect of executions on the families of defendants and victims. Her main research interest is state violence is its various forms, including the death penalty, genocide, and human rights violations.

YES

MICHAEL DONAHUE

This question, it seems to me, is not over whether juvenile offenders who commit murder should be severely punished but rather addresses the propriety of executing juveniles who commit these heinous crimes. Does justice dictate the execution of juvenile murderers? I believe it does.

To echo John Stuart Mill's sentiments in his well-known 1868 speech to Parliament against the proposed ban on capital punishment, I too would have great satisfaction were I able to endorse a comparable ban on the execution of juvenile offenders. Like Mill, whose opposition placed him at odds with well-meaning philanthropists whom he respected, my views on the subject place me squarely against the vast majority of social scientists whose work I otherwise admire. A review of the legal, political, criminological, and sociological literature leaves no doubt about the dominance of the abolitionist views among my cohorts.

Assuming that most teenagers above the age of fifteen have attained moral maturity—the Supreme Court no longer permits the execution of younger murderers as per *Thompson* v. *Oklahoma* (1988)—the debate regarding the death penalty for juveniles convicted of murder essentially mirrors the debate pertaining to adult murderers. I believe the controversy over capital punishment for either adult or juvenile murderers is intractable, and I see no way of resolving it. Moreover, I am certain that I will not persuade those who oppose executing adults of the necessity of executing juvenile murderers. Nonetheless, I shall try by attempting to show that many of the arguments against the death penalty draw us away from the central issue of justice, in this case, the propriety of executing juvenile murderers. In essence, they are what philosophers call red herrings. By so doing, I hope to have demonstrated that only executions of these offenders, not long-term imprisonment, can satisfy the demands of justice.

Juvenile Murderers Generally Lack the Moral Maturity to Understand the Consequences of Their Actions; Therefore, Capital Punishment for Them Is Wrong

The classical retributivist view holds that just deserts require the murderer, by way of punishment, to "pay back" the state and thus the victim for his abhorrent act. In this way the law is vindicated and the worth of the innocent victim acknowledged. Certainly it is the intent of the criminal law to value more highly the lives of innocent victims than the lives of convicted murderers. In capital murder cases, the offender must pay for his transgression with his life.

Retribution assumes choice. Choice is predicated on the existence of the freedom—limited though it may be by the circumstances particular to each case—to choose (or not to choose) to act. Only in this way does it make sense to punish egregious conduct, or for that matter, to reward human achievement. Without free will, reward and punishment are meaningless gestures.

Assuming there is free will, and assuming that actions have consequences, the fundamental question inherent in this debate is whether sixteen- and seventeen-year-old juveniles possess the maturity to make choices of significant moral and material dimensions. What troubles me is the inclination of at least some my colleagues who oppose the execution of juvenile murderers to simply assert that these predators possess no such maturity. For instance, Streib (1990) declares that "it generally seems accepted that adolescents typically do not have the adult level of maturity and sophistication in their thought processes" and, although adolescents can "intend behavior," he says, it is not likely "that they have thought about it deeply with insight and understanding" (p. 156).

First, Streib stumbles over a fundamental epistemological point. It is not clear what authorities accept these claims as generally true or on what basis they do. In other words, how does he know that juveniles do not typically possess the requisite maturity to understand or to make choices? Second, murder does not require anything beyond premeditation and malice. The law and the courts do not expect convicted murderers to be philosophers in applied ethics or even to ponder the moral significance of their acts. It is doubtful that any murderer does. It seems far-fetched, then, to think that sixteen-year-old murderers do not have an acute and immediate sense of the causal connection between their acts (e.g., shooting a gun at an innocent victim) and their immediate consequences (e.g., the rather sudden demise of that victim). One need not be a criminologist to know that these violent adolescents commonly have a working familiarity with guns, and most assuredly are acquainted with the discourse of street violence. Third, notwithstanding the dynamic nature of the field of developmental psychology, there is extensive, indeed, impressive empirical evidence that moral development generally reaches its plateau around the age of sixteen. Moreover, these findings have been demonstrated by cross-sectional, longitudinal, and cross-cultural investigations (Gardner, 1978, p. 488).

The Capricious Imposition of Capital Punishment Necessitates Its Abolition

A familiar argument against execution is that its capricious, arbitrary, and freakish imposition is enough to warrant its abolition. This claim, as van den Haag (1993) observes, confuses two ideals, justice and equality. Justice is defined here as giving someone that which is due him; that is, his "just deserts." Rendering just deserts is based on that person's actions alone. Equality, however, means treating persons under the same conditions the same way. Justice can be either pleasant (as in reward) or unpleasant (as in punishment). The same is true of equality. For example, entire classes of people can be treated equally well (e.g., all Americans have a right against self-incrimination and unreasonable searches) or equally badly (e.g., America's enslavement of Africans; the Nazi's persecution of Jews).

In van den Haag's distinction between the two, he notes that equality in the imposition of capital punishment is not attainable. We cannot apprehend, try, convict, and sentence all murderers "by the same court at the same time." In short, he says, "unequal justice is the best we can do; it is still better than injustice, equal or unequal, which occurs if, for the sake of equality, we deliberately allow some who could be punished to escape" (p. 259).

"The relevant question is: does the person to be executed deserve punishment? Whether others equally deserving of the death penalty escape it does not make those who are executed less deserving of it" (p. 256). Van den Haag emphasizes that:

> Justice is independent of distributional inequality. The ideal of equal justice demands that justice be equally distributed, not that it be replaced by equality. Justice requires that as many of the guilty as possible be punished, regardless of whether others have avoided punishment. To let these others escape the deserved punishment does not do justice to them or to society. But it is not unjust to those who could not escape (p. 256).

Furthermore, "if capital punishment is immoral per se, no distribution among the guilty would make it moral. If capital punishment is moral, no distribution would make it immoral. Improper distribution cannot affect the quality of what is distributed, be it punishment or rewards." His conclusion is clear: "Discriminatory or capricious distribution thus can not justify abolition of the death penalty" (p. 255).

Because Executions Do Not Deter Prospective Murderers, They Do Not Protect Society and Should Be Abolished

There are reasons why the question of general deterrence cannot be decisive to the ongoing debate, the least of which is conflicting empirical findings. Chief among them is the infrequent and irregular administration of it. One would be pressed to cite a period in American history since the days of western frontier when our society consistently or frequently hanged or shot the most notorious of its ne'er-do-wells, miscreants, or reprobates. Thus, it could be argued that the capricious application of capital punishment inhibits its deterrent effect. It is not the punishment per se that diminishes deterrence, proponents might claim, but rather the irregular imposition of it. There is, of course, no way to refute or to corroborate this argument.

Deterrence theorists hold that punishment, to have the desired effect of discouraging criminality in the general population, must be proximate to the time of the crime (celerity), very likely to be administered (certainty), and sufficiently severe (proportionality). These conditions are rarely obtained in most criminal cases and never in capital cases for either adults or juveniles. For example, the average time on death row for those few murderers actually executed is almost a decade. Furthermore, in 1994, of the 2,890 adults under the sentence of death in the

United States, only thirty-one, or 1 percent, were executed. From 1977 (when the Supreme Court lifted the ban on executions) through 1994, state courts handed down 4549 death sentences, yet only 257 (5.7 percent) were executed. During the ten years from 1985 through 1994, well over a third (37.8 percent) of all death sentences were dismissed, reversed, resentenced, or retried (Maguire & Pastore, 1996; Table 6.80).

Since 1977, only nine juvenile murderers have been executed; at present only thirty-seven to forty-six sit on death row. Regardless of the reasons why deterrent conditions are not obtained—concern for due process and inadequate criminal justice resources to incapacitate violent criminals are two—is it any wonder that the deterrent effect of execution is rarely detected in the several studies done on it? Is there any reason for anyone to think, including prospective juvenile murderers, that execution is likely, much less immediate?

Because Capital Punishment Is More Expensive, It Should Be Replaced by Long-Term Imprisonment

Opponents of capital punishment argue that it is less expensive to maintain convicted murderers in prison for life than to pay the costs of inmate maintenance and appeals for death row inmates—approximately $3.2 million or six times the cost of life imprisonment, according to Bedau (1989). It is not likely to be less for juvenile murderers, though I know of no study on the matter. Proponents, however, contend that the burdensome cost of maintaining murderers in prison for life is unfair to taxpayers. They note, moreover, that there is no reason to expect murderers sentenced to life to terminate their appeal efforts and the associated costs. Indeed, under life imprisonment, they have the rest of their lives to file what will be, for the most part, frivolous *habeas corpus* petitions. Finally, supporters of the death penalty rightly complain of the exorbitant costs taxpayers pay to legal associations, some that are little more than special interest groups, to spare those guilty beyond a reasonable doubt of the most reprehensible crime in a state's criminal code. Expeditious imposition of the death sentence would attenuate these costs.

All the same, the costs connected with capital punishment are not a decisive factor for me. As with deterrence, cost reductions are only a side benefit to expediting the sentence, which at least theoretically, would enhance the penalty's celerity. Most would agree, I think, that economic considerations are secondary to doing justice for the murderer and for the victim. Again, I know of no opponent who would change his or her mind were it shown that capital executions were less expensive than life in prison. A concern for justice trumps the economic advantages of either life imprisonment or execution.

Although Public Opinion Appears to Support the Death Penalty for Juvenile Murderers, It Is an Ephemeral Measure and Should Be Disregarded

Adler, Mueller, and Laufer (1994) assert that, "two decades ago public opinion was not in favor of the death penalty" (p. 368). That claim, however, does not square with reality. Since 1953, in only one year (1966) has there been greater opposition than support—42 percent to 47 percent (Maguire & Pastore, 1996, Table 2.70). In fact, from 1976 to 1994, public support for the death penalty in the U.S. bumped steadily upward from 66 percent to 74 percent (Maguire & Pastore, 1996, Table 2.72). A *Gallup Poll Monthly* showed even stronger support during the same period—up to 80 percent in 1994 (Maguire & Pastore, 1996, Table 2.70). In addition, a 1994 *Los Angeles Times* public opinion poll reported that fully two-thirds of Americans (68 percent) believe the courts should treat juveniles who commit violent crimes the same as adult violent criminals. Moreover, a 1994 Gallup Poll shows that three in five Americans favor executing juveniles convicted of murder (Maguire & Pastore, 1996, Table 2.73). Significantly, this finding varied little by race, sex, region of the country, political party, education, age, or income.

This unabated support for adult executions is well known. Yet abolitionists (e.g., Adler et al.) overlook it, or worse, attribute it to what they erroneously believe is the public's woeful ignorance of the death penalty's alleged failure to deter murder (see, for example, Cox & Wade, 1998, p. 229). We simply do not know whether it does. Furthermore, I know of no study that shows public support would deteriorate if Americans were convinced of evidence showing that it fails as a deterrent. Indeed, as Table 2.74 in the *Sourcebook of Criminal Justice Statistics* demonstrates, support for the death penalty remains high even when respondents are told of the possibility that innocent persons may be executed (Maguire & Pastore, 1996).

This public endorsement of execution for teenage murderers may well arise from soaring juvenile arrest rates for murder and the impression that the criminal justice system has failed to do anything about it. These beliefs may not be groundless. For example, from 1985 through 1994, there was a 207 percent increase for fifteen-year-olds; 197 percent for sixteen-year-olds; and 146 percent for seventeen-year-olds, yet juveniles constitute less than two hundredths of a percent (0.02 percent) of those on death row, and relatively few are ever executed (Maguire & Pastore, 1996, Table 6.75). In sum, the strength and durability of the public's support for the death penalty is undeniable. However, although it may be as unpersuasive to my social science colleagues as it is persuasive to politicians, it cannot decide the propriety of the penalty. It is always possible for the majority—of social scientists as well as citizens—to be wrong.

Capital Punishment Is Irreversible, and Insofar as the Innocent Risk the Possibility of Execution, It Must Be Abolished

Over the long term, mistakes will be made in the administration of capital punishment. Estimates vary, but it is generally accepted, even by abolitionists, that only about twenty-five of the more than seven thousand adults executed in this country since 1900 were innocent; a wrongful execution probability of thirty-six hundredths of a percent (0.35 percent). There are no such data of which I am aware regarding juvenile murderers, perhaps because so few have been executed in modern times. It can be inferred from the above poll (Maguire & Pastore, 1996, Table 2.74) that "irreversibility" does not inhibit public support for the death penalty. This should not surprise us. As van den Haag notes, "nearly all human activities...cost the lives of some innocent bystanders. We do not give up these activities because the advantages, moral or material, outweigh the unintended losses" (1993, 257).

In addition, he believes that, "for those who think the death penalty just, miscarriages of justice are offset by the moral benefits and the usefulness of doing justice. For those who think the death penalty unjust, even when it does not miscarry, miscarriages can hardly be decisive" (p. 257).

Because the Imposition of Capital Punishment Is Racist, It Should Be Abolished

Almost two-thirds (65 percent) of juvenile murderers on death row are black or Hispanic. Of the 2890 adult murderers under sentence of death, 43 percent are minority (Maguire & Pastore, 1996, Table 6.75). Regarding adult executions, the chief complaint seems to be that murderers of whites are more likely to be executed than murderers of blacks. Death penalty opponents complain, therefore, that "black victims...are less fully vindicated than white ones" (van den Haag, 1993, p. 256). Moreover, abolitionists protest that black murderers of whites are more likely to be executed than whites who kill either whites or blacks. Some (e.g., Walker, Spohn, & DeLone, 1996), cite data from the Baldus, Woodworth, and Pulaski study (1990) in support of this claim. These data, taken from Walker et al. (1996) and shown below in plain type, would appear to confirm the race discrimination thesis, for they show that blacks killing whites are almost *five times* more likely than blacks killing blacks to be sentenced to death (35 percent/ 7 percent).

Additional analyses (shown in bold in Table 16.1) of their data, however, cast doubt on this thesis. On a related point, three of five cases (59 percent) have white victims (130 + 230/606). Interestingly, blacks and whites are equally likely

TABLE 16.1 Offender/Victim Race and Death Penalty Imposition

Offender/Victim Race	Overall Death Sentencing Rate		Proportion of All Cases	
	Cases	%	Cases	%
Black/white	45 of 130	35	**130 of 606**	**21**
White/white	51 of 230	22	**230 of 606**	**38**
Black/black	17 of 232	7	**232 of 606**	**38**
White/black	2 of 14	14	**14 of 606**	**2**
Total	116 of 606	19		

to commit intraracial murder (38 percent each), yet blacks are *10.5 more times* likely to kill whites than whites are to kill blacks (21 percent/2 percent).

Further analysis shows that white murderers are more likely to receive the death sentence than black murderers, *even when death sentences of black perpetrators with white victims are excluded.* Consider that cases with black murderers (362) outnumber white murderers (244). Yet the number of blacks receiving the death sentence is only marginally larger (62 to 53). The ratio of black murderers receiving the death sentence to all black murderers is 1 to 5.9 (62 to 362). The comparative ratio for whites is 1 to 4.6 (53 to 244); therefore, white murderers are more likely to receive the death penalty than their black counterparts. Furthermore, the ratio of black murderers receiving the death sentence to all black murderers *minus* black murderers receiving the death sentence for murdering whites is 1 to 5.1 (62: 317). Thus, even when so-called racist cases are excluded, black murderers still remain somewhat less likely to receive the sentence of death than their white murderers.

In short, what little racial discrimination exists in the imposition of the death penalty seems to disadvantage white murderers. As van den Haag (1993) observes, "because most black murderers kill blacks, black murderers are spared the death penalty more often than are white murderers. They fare better than most white murderers. The motivation behind unequal justice may have been to discriminate against blacks, but the result has favored them" (p. 256). Empirical findings thus show that the distribution of the death sentence by race as a reason to abolish capital punishment is irrelevant.

Beyond all of this, guilt is personal. It applies to the concrete, individual actions of the murderer, not to classes or groups of people to which the murderer happens to belong. In the case of murder, guilt and punishment can be neither ascribed nor borne collectively.

Capital Punishment Precludes the Opportunity for the Rehabilitation of Juvenile Murderers

Rehabilitation of either juvenile or adult murderers is, at best, uncertain. The treatment model of corrections has failed to deliver on its promises across a range of criminal behaviors, a finding well documented! One should not be surprised to find, for example, that two-thirds of all death row inmates have prior felony convictions. In 1992, more than two of every five convicted murderers returned to prison (Maguire & Pastore, 1996, Table 6.66), and, at the time of their offense, one in five were on parole, one in ten on probation, one in fifteen had other charges pending, and one in a hundred, a prison escapee (Table 6.75). Contrary to Streib's assertion of the "universally accepted truisms" that the behavior of juvenile murderers becomes "more acceptable to society" as they become older, it is not at all clear that the incorrigibility of juvenile murderers is any more tractable than that of adults or that they get any better, with or without therapy. Nor is it clear why he or other opponents of capital punishment think long-term imprisonment will make them model citizens or that any rehabilitation programs can overcome the moral depravity that is the root of such heinous acts.

Finally, whether rehabilitation really works or is even cost-effective is beside the point. Rehabilitation is not a right. The state does, however, have a right to self-protection, a right afforded by the specific deterrent value of execution. Capital punishment guarantees the permanent incapacitation of youthful criminals who, for example, sodomize, torture, and then murder. Endorsers of long-term imprisonment, so-called life imprisonment without parole, and rehabilitation programs properly do not make this promise; it cannot be kept.

Because Capital Punishment Is Excessive, Cruel, and Unusual, It Must Be Abolished

The U.S. Supreme Court has ruled that executions using torture or causing lingering death are unconstitutional (*In re Kemmler,* 1890). As readers know, most of the Court had never held the punishment itself as unconstitutional, only its administration or its methods. In *Thompson* v. *Oklahoma* (1988), however, the majority opinion for the first time banned executions of juveniles under the age of sixteen because it believed such violated the Fourteenth and Eighth Amendments to the Constitution.

Is the execution of juveniles murderers, sixteen years of age and older, excessive, cruel, or unusual punishment? Does retribution require death instead of, for example, long-term or life imprisonment? Van den Haag (1993) argues that "retribution is an independent moral justification." A murderer, in committing the crime, freely assumes "the risk of receiving legal punishment that he could have avoided by not committing the crime. The punishment he suffers is the punishment he voluntarily risked suffering and, therefore, it is no more unjust to him than any other event for which one knowingly volunteers to assume risk. Thus the death penalty cannot be unjust to the guilty criminal" (p. 258).

Bedau (1986, p. 285), although a strident opponent of capital punishment, admits that murderers must be punished. He agrees with the retributivists that punishment serves the principles of *fairness* (both the law-abiding and the innocent victim require it), *deprivation* (society must cause the offender hardship and suffering for such a grievous offense), *denunciation* (society must mete out a severe penalty to express its abhorrence of the act), and *proportionality* (the severity of the punishment must be proportionate to the gravity of the offense).

Disagreement arises over the principle of proportionality. Bedau maintains that long-term imprisonment satisfies all four principles. In other words, he does not view any murder as sufficient to compel the death sentence for the perpetrator. Like most social scientists, he views the death penalty as *always* excessive because all human beings have a right to life.

I disagree. I think that the death of the murderer is the only penalty that meets the necessary and sufficient conditions of proportionality. It is, therefore, the only penalty that is sufficiently just. With long-term imprisonment, the murderer has a realistic hope of liberty—a hope his victim can no longer know. He possesses privileges, no doubt circumscribed, that attach only to the living—study, work, and leisure. His victim does not. And even though the murderer's family no doubt suffers, they live in the knowledge that he is alive, fed and cared for, that they can see him, that they can be with him, and that eventually he is very likely to return to them, alive. The victim's family will always be without the warmth and presence of their innocent loved one. For them, there is no hope and no proper payment for their loss.

Opponents of the death penalty object that true proportionality would require retributivists to endorse, for example, torture and execution for murderers who tortured their victims. Retributivists, to remain consistent, it is said, must replicate by punishment the kind and degree of suffering the murderer imposed on his victim. By such logic then, the state would rape its rapists, and routinely assault those guilty of aggravated assault. Indeed, a serial killer would be executed as many times as there were victims! The state does not sanction any of this, of course, because retribution requires no such response. It is the punishment per se, not its infliction, method of imposition, or the number of times it is imposed that must be proportionate. And in this, the death penalty provides exact sufficiency. In this way the perpetrator pays back for the harm he has done in precisely equal measure—with his life.

A corollary to this argument is that capital punishment is so dehumanizing that when the state kills a murderer, it somehow legitimizes murder. But although punishment is meant to be unpleasant, few misconstrue that as legitimizing "the unlawful imposition of identical unpleasantness" (van den Haag, 1993, p. 258). Imprisonment is not thought, for example, to legitimize kidnapping; neither are fines thought to legitimize robbery or larceny.

Opponents of capital punishment claim that all persons, including murderers, have an inviolable right to life. Were this right inviolable, it follows that taking life in self-defense, in defense of others, in combat, or in the apprehension of a felon that poses an imminent danger is impermissible. It would mean that war criminals guilty of heinous crimes against humanity could not be executed for those crimes. Likewise, it would proscribe the execution of the likes of mass murderer Timothy McVeigh, cannibal Jeffery Dahmer, serial killers Aileen Wournos and Wayne Gacy, and child-killer Richard Allen Davis. A nation's routine failure to execute those clearly guilty of murder signifies, in my view, a devolution, not an evolution, of standards of decency. It represents a less, not more, civilized society. This is because such a society fails to vindicate its law and demeans the worth of the innocent victim. It signifies that we value the life of the criminal predator more than the life of his innocent prey.

To assert, as Bedau does, that capital punishment is always excessive, "one must believe that no crime, no matter how heinous, could possibly justify capital punishment. Such a belief can be neither proved nor contradicted; it is simply an article of faith" (van den Haag, 1993, p. 258). To declare an inviolable right to life is, quoting Jeremy Bentham, "nonsense upon stilts" (p. 259).

REFERENCES

Adler, F., Mueller, G. O. W., & Laufer, W. S. (1994). *Criminal justice.* New York: McGraw-Hill, Inc.

Bedau, H. A. (1986). Justice and the death penalty. In M. E. Katsh (Ed.). *Taking sides: Clashing views on controversial legal issues (2nd ed.)*, Guilford, CT: Dushkin Publishing Group, Inc.

Baldus, D. C., Woodworth G. G., & Pulaski, C. A., Jr. (1990). *Equal justice and the death penalty.* Boston, MA: Northeastern University Press.

Cox, S. M., & Wade, J. E. (1998). *The criminal justice network: An introduction.* Boston, MA: WCB/McGraw-Hill.

Gardner, H. (1978). *Developmental psychology: An introduction.* Boston, MA: Little, Brown & Co., Inc.

Maguire, K., & Pastore, A. L. (Eds.) (1996). *Sourcebook of criminal justice statistics, 1995.* Washington, DC: Bureau of Justice Statistics, U.S. Department of Justice.

Streib, V. L. (1990). Imposing the death penalty on children. In R. A. Weisheit and R. G. Culbertson (Eds.), *Juvenile delinquency: A justice perspective* (2nd ed.), Prospect Heights, IL: Waveland Press.

van den Haag, E. (1993). The ultimate punishment: A defense. In M. E. Katsh (Ed.), *Taking sides: Clashing views on controversial legal issues* (5th ed.), Guilford, CT: Dushkin Publishing Group, Inc.

Walker, S., Spohn, C., & DeLone, M. (1996). *The color of justice: Race, ethnicity, and crime in America.* Belmont, CA: Wadsworth Publishing Co.

CASES

In re Kemmler, 136 U.S. 436 (1890).
Thompson v. *Oklahoma,* 48 U.S. 815 (1988).

Rejoinder to Dr. Donahue

MARGARET VANDIVER

Much of Dr. Donahue's essay defends the death penalty in general, rather than focusing on the specific question of whether juveniles should be executed. I will not attempt in this limited space to respond to his general arguments,[1] because these have been thoroughly discussed in the massive and ever-growing literature that documents the failures of our current system of capital punishment. In this rejoinder, I will focus only on Dr. Donahue's arguments that pertain to the execution of juveniles.

In support of his conclusion that sixteen- and seventeen-year-olds convicted of homicide should be executed, Dr. Donahue states that "moral development generally reaches its plateau around the age of sixteen." The degree to which adolescents are capable of higher-order moral reasoning in their answers to hypothetical questions, however, does not answer the question of whether adolescents are as responsible for their behavior as are adults. There is a large gap between how people respond to paper and pencil questions and how they respond in real situations, where experience and maturity are most likely to make a difference. The relevant question is whether juveniles have the maturity, judgment, decision-making skills, and experience necessary to translate abstract concepts into action (or, often even more importantly, into refraining from action).

Adolescents must cope with their own developmental changes, while at the same time learning to function in different and broader social contexts than those of childhood. And these challenges must be met in an increasingly complex, difficult, and dangerous environment. While most adolescents cope successfully, it must be remembered that those minors who wind up on death row are not average adolescents. Nearly without exception, they have suffered serious trauma and deprivation, in many cases so severe as to have resulted in neurological, cognitive, and emotional impairment. They are less prepared than other adolescents for the challenges of adult responsibilities, and they are more likely to be trying to function in disruptive, unstable, and dangerous environments. Because of their youth, their crimes were committed either while they were still coping directly with the problems of their family of origin or soon after they left home. In either case, there was insufficient time for them to have recovered from their childhood experiences or to have learned the skills, judgment, and restraint so necessary for successful adjustment.

But for the sake of argument, assume that juveniles are fully responsible for their choices and actions. If this is the case, how can our numerous laws distinguishing them from adults possibly be justified? Advocates of the death penalty for minors take the strange position of supporting the government's use of lethal violence against a few juveniles, while the same government will not allow any juveniles to vote or to buy a beer or to drop a quarter into a slot machine or to serve on a jury. One of the grimmest absurdities of our current death sentencing system is the irony of minors waiting on death row to be killed by the same authorities who are not legally able to sell them cigarettes from the prison canteen. If advocates of juvenile executions really believe that juveniles are fully responsible for their actions, they should support the abolition of all laws distinguishing minors from adults. And if they do not support the equal treatment by law of juveniles and adults in all situations, the burden is on them to explain the contradiction in their position.

Dr. Donahue states that "murder does not require anything beyond premeditation and malice." But we are not debating whether juveniles should be convicted of murder; we are debating whether they should be sentenced to death. And the death sentence, under all currently operating statutes, is supposed to be reserved for the very worst of murders committed by the most culpable of offenders. This point is particularly important when considering the morality of the execution of minors, because so many adults who are more experienced, sophisticated, and culpable are spared the death sentence. Despite Dr. Donahue's assertion that failure to impose the death penalty fairly across cases does not make it unfair in any particular case in which he believes it is deserved, it is difficult to understand how a penalty that is unjustly applied can be defended on the basis that it is a just penalty.

In conclusion, I urge readers to ponder again the personal histories of the juveniles executed and condemned under our current death penalty statutes. It is comforting to blame the dreadful actions of these juveniles on their "moral depravity," as Dr. Donahue does, thus allowing ourselves to blame the individual actor and to look no further for causes. This reasoning, however, is circular; it is not explanatory and it does not advance our understanding. (How do we know they are morally depraved? Because of what they did. And why did they do it? Because they are morally depraved.) We must ask questions that can lead to real explanations. For a start, we should ask why it is that "moral depravity" correlates so highly with histories of brutal childhood victimization, family and institutional neglect, neurological damage, race, poor representation by defense counsel, and low family income. The answers we find might encourage us to turn our efforts toward protecting children (and thus their potential future victims) from violence, rather than waiting until the victims are dead, and then responding with our own violence.

NOTES

1. I must briefly comment on Dr. Donahue's analysis of data from the Baldus study. Although he acknowledges that "the chief complaint seems to be that

murderers of whites are more likely to be executed than murderers of blacks," he then computes ratios based on the *defendants'* race. These figures indicate that white murderers in this data set were slightly more likely than African American murderers to be sentenced to death, a finding that is entirely consistent with a claim of racial disparities by victim, because most homicides are intraracial. Had Donahue computed ratios based on the *victims'* race, he would have found the following disparity: The ratio of murderers of black victims receiving the death sentence to all murderers of black victims is 1:12.9 (19 of 246). The ratio of murderers of white victims receiving the death sentence to all murderers of white victims is 1:3.75 (96 of 360). Clearly, those people convicted of killing white victims were several times more likely to receive death than those convicted of killing African American victims.

NO

MARGARET VANDIVER

Executions of persons who were younger than eighteen at the time of their crimes have always been rare in the United States. Only 353 of 19,121 documented American executions, or about 1.8 percent of the total, have been carried out against juveniles (Espy, 1997). Victor Streib (1987), the preeminent authority on executions of juveniles in the United States, analyzed 281 juvenile executions.[1] Twelve of the 281 children were executed for crimes committed when they were under the age of fourteen. The youngest were two boys executed for crimes committed at age ten, one in Louisiana in 1855, and another by federal authorities in Arkansas in 1885. Nine (3 percent) of the juveniles executed were girls; 185 (69 percent) were black. Murder was the most frequent crime for which juvenile death sentences was imposed, accounting for 80 percent of the total. Fifteen percent of the juvenile death sentences were imposed for rape. Every juvenile executed for rape was black, and in all but one case, the victim was white. All juvenile executions for rape occurred in the South (pp. 57–61).

Between May 1964 and September 1985, no one was executed in the United States for a crime committed as a minor. Under current death penalty statutes, nine people have been executed for crimes committed before they were eighteen. All were male, and all were seventeen at the time of their crimes. Five were white, three black, and one Latino. Five of these executions occurred in Texas, and one each in South Carolina, Louisiana, Missouri, and Georgia.

As of June 1997, there were fifty-eight people on death row for crimes committed when they were sixteen or seventeen. All of them were male, twenty-six (45 percent) were African American, thirteen (22 percent) were Latino, and nineteen (33 percent) were white. Only 22 percent of their victims were younger than eighteen, and 64 percent of their victims were white. Fourteen states and the federal government restrict the death penalty to those eighteen and older at the time of the crime. Another four states specify age seventeen as the statutory minimum. The minimum age in the other states with the death penalty is sixteen, either by statute or by court rulings (Streib, 1997).

American and International Law

The constitutionality of juvenile executions was considered by the U.S. Supreme Court in the 1980s. In *Thompson* v. *Oklahoma* (1988), four justices held that the execution of a defendant who was fifteen at the time of his crime would violate the Eighth Amendment's prohibition of cruel and unusual punishment. Justice O'Connor concurred, but on narrower legal grounds, holding that a state that did not specify a minimum age in its statute could not execute a fifteen-year-old. A year after *Thompson,* the Court ruled five to four in *Stanford* v. *Kentucky* (1989) that the Eighth Amendment is not violated by the execution of persons who were sixteen or seventeen at the time of their crimes. The practical effect of these rulings has been to establish sixteen as the minimum age at which a person can face the death sentence.

The United States is the only developed country in the world that executes juveniles. This policy puts us in the company of countries known for their lack of respect for human rights. Between 1980 and 1995, the United States joined the following countries in executing minors: Bangladesh, Barbados, Iran, Iraq, Nigeria, Pakistan, Saudi Arabia, and Yemen (Human Rights Watch, 1995, pp. 2–3). Since 1990, the United States has executed more juvenile offenders than any other country for which information was available.

The United States contravenes international law and practice on the issue of juvenile executions.[2] "The execution of juvenile offenders is one of the few areas where United States domestic law clearly conflicts with binding international norms" (Spillane, 1991, p. 130, note omitted). The United States signed the Fourth Geneva Convention, which bans executions for crimes committed under age eighteen during wartime, and the *American Convention on Human Rights* and the *International Covenant on Civil and Political Rights,* both of which ban all executions of persons under eighteen when the crime was committed. The U.S. ratified the *I.C.C.P.R.* in 1992, with the following reservation: "The United States reserves the right, subject to its Constitutional constraints, to impose capital punishment on any person (other than a pregnant woman) duly convicted under existing or future laws permitting the imposition of capital punishment, including such punishment for crimes committed by persons below eighteen years of age" (quoted in Human Rights Watch, 1995, p. 8). The United States is the only country to have made such a reservation, and at least ten countries have declared their opposition to the reservation.

In addition to these treaty obligations, the United States is bound by customary international law, which prohibits the execution of minors. The Inter-American Commission on Human Rights has held that the execution of juveniles by the United States is a violation of *jus cogens,* "a norm of international law from which no derogation is permitted" (Fox, 1988, p. 601). The position of the United States on this issue contradicts and undercuts our attempts to take the lead in supporting human rights worldwide. We leave ourselves open to well-founded accusations of hypocrisy when we continue to violate this fundamental principle of international law.

Adolescent Development

There is insufficient space in this chapter even to outline adequately the massive evidence that adolescents differ significantly from adults in their psychology, reasoning abilities, decision making, and responsibility for their actions. Suffice it to say that science, law, and common experience are in agreement that adolescents are different from adults and deserve special considerations and protections. "Adolescence is well recognized to be a time of physiological and psychological change and stress. Normal adolescents are distinguished from adults by their intensity of feeling, immature judgment, and impulsiveness" (Lewis et al., 1988, p. 588). We acknowledge these differences in many aspects of the law, including restricting voting rights and jury service to those eighteen and older, enforcing restrictions on tobacco and alcohol sales to minors, and treating minors accused of crime differently from adults.

A number of organizations that work on behalf of children and adolescents have taken a stand against subjecting minors to the death penalty. Among the organizations that urged the Supreme Court to declare a minimum age of eighteen for the death penalty were the Child Welfare League of America, the American Society for Adolescent Psychiatry, Defense for Children International—USA, National Parents and Teachers Association, Children's Defense Fund, National Black Child Development Institute, National Youth Advocate Program, and the American Youth Work Center.

Justification for the Death Penalty

The death penalty has been justified by the Supreme Court on the two principal grounds of retribution and deterrence. Decades of increasingly sophisticated research on deterrence have failed to demonstrate that the death penalty deters more than a long term of imprisonment. But leaving aside the question of adult deterrence, it strains credulity to argue that adolescents would alter their behavior based on the chance that they might face execution. As Justice Stevens wrote for the

Court in *Thompson* v. *Oklahoma,* "The likelihood that the teenage offender has made the kind of cost–benefit analysis that attaches any weight to the possibility of execution is so remote as to be virtually nonexistent" (p. 837). And even if an adolescent did make such a calculation, it is likely that the prospect of death would have very little deterrent effect; teenagers do not fully comprehend their own mortality and frequently engage in extremely risky behavior (Papalia & Olds, 1989, p. 597).

Nor is retribution a justification for imposing capital punishment on juveniles. As noted by Justice Stevens:

> …less culpability should attach to a crime committed by a juvenile than to a comparable crime committed by an adult. The basis for this conclusion is too obvious to require extended explanation. Inexperience, less education, and less intelligence make the teenager less able to evaluate the consequences of his or her conduct while at the same time he or she is much more apt to be motivated by mere emotion or peer pressure than is an adult. The reasons why juveniles are not trusted with the privileges and responsibilities of an adult also explain why their irresponsible conduct is not as morally reprehensible as that of an adult" (*Thompson* v. *Oklahoma,* at 835, notes omitted).

Only a very small fraction of homicides result in death sentences. Supposedly, those cases resulting in the death sentence are the worst cases in two ways: the crimes are the most horrible, and the offenders are the most culpable. Although juvenile offenders may indeed commit extraordinarily cruel murders, they are unlikely ever to be the worst and most culpable of offenders. To condemn them to death is to declare them utterly lost and irredeemable before their personalities have even fully matured.

Theory and Reality

Supporters of juvenile executions sometimes argue that our current laws provide safeguards ensuring that only those juveniles most deserving of the severest punishment will be selected to die. In theory, this is a reasonable argument, but it ignores everything we know about how the death penalty operates in practice. There are two main ways in which the reality of the death penalty for juveniles contradicts supporters' theoretical arguments: (1) the juveniles who are sentenced to death are not the worst offenders, but in many ways are the most vulnerable and damaged offenders, and (2) their age, which is supposed to operate as a mitigating factor, may actually work to their disadvantage when juries deliberate on sentencing.

The personal histories of the juveniles who have been executed under our current laws reveal severely emotionally damaged and mentally impaired youths whose life experiences have been brutal in the extreme. Consider these descriptions of three juveniles executed in the 1980s: "Terry Roach was a mental retardate with a mental age of twelve who was probably insane at the time of his execution; Charles Rumbaugh was a manic depressive with a history of self-mutilation; and Dalton Prejean had an IQ of seventy-one, suffered from organic brain damage and had been diagnosed as schizophrenic" (Spillane, 1991, p. 128, footnotes omitted). Can anyone seriously argue that these three young men were more deserving of death than all the thousands of adult murderers sentenced to serve prison terms?

The most sophisticated study of the background and mental condition of condemned juveniles was done under the lead authorship of Dorothy Lewis (1988). Lewis and her coauthors examined fourteen of the then thirty-seven juveniles on death row in the United States. The number and severity of impairments found by the researchers were astonishing: "juveniles condemned to death in the United States are multiply handicapped. They tend to have suffered serious CNS [central nervous system] injuries, to have suffered since early childhood from a multiplicity of psychotic symptoms, and to have been physically and sexually abused" (p. 587). Eight of the fourteen juvenile subjects "had injuries [to the central nervous system] that were severe enough to result in hospitalization, and/or indentation of the cranium." Nine of the fourteen showed serious neurological abnormalities. Seven of the fourteen "were psychotic at the time of their evaluations or had been so diagnosed in earlier childhood.... An additional four subjects had histories consistent with diagnoses of severe mood disorders.... The three remaining subjects experienced periodic paranoid ideation" (p. 585).

The family histories of the condemned juveniles revealed that "twelve of the subjects had been brutally, physically abused and five had been sodomized by older male relatives.... Alcoholism, drug abuse, psychiatric treatment, and psychiatric hospitalization were prevalent in the histories of the parents" (pp. 596–597). All but one of the subjects had experienced either physical or sexual abuse. One subject was "hit in the head with hammer by stepfather; sodomized by stepfather and grandfather throughout childhood"; there was violence between his parents and his mother was psychiatrically hospitalized. Another juvenile had been "beaten and stomped by older brother; whipped by mother; kicked in head by relative; sodomized by older cousin in early childhood; sexual assault attempted by male relative"; there was "extreme violence with weapons by several family members" in his home. Another was "punched and hit in head with board by father," breaking his teeth; there was "violence between parents; mother had multiple hospitalizations and seizures." Yet another had been seated on a hot burner by his stepfather, "sodomized by stepfather and his friends; [there was] possible sexual abuse by mother and brother." It is a strange sort of justice that allows children to be so horribly victimized when they are entirely defenseless, and then kills them when, predictably enough, they become violent themselves. Such a response is not retribution; it is only more violence.

Many states specifically list youthful age as a mitigating circumstance in their death penalty statutes, and under current death penalty law, youth can be considered as mitigation in all states. Proponents of the executions of juveniles often note this and other mitigating circumstances as safeguards, which they should be.[3] Sentencing decisions, however, often are not made in the way the legislators and courts assume. Youth can actually weigh against a defendant in the jury's calculations.

Conclusion

The execution of juvenile offenders does not serve any legitimate purpose and contradicts all we know about adolescent development. The process of selecting juveniles for death is flawed and often results in the condemnation of those who are themselves the severely damaged survivors of violent crimes. We bring international shame on the United States by strangling, gassing, electrocuting, shooting, and poisoning juveniles. Executing minors cannot be justified as a deterrent or as retributive punishment. The time, effort, and resources we currently devote to trying to execute juveniles could be much better directed to efforts to prevent violence committed against and by young people. There are steps we can take to protect children from violence, and to provide them with positive social and educational environments. These efforts are far more likely to protect potential victims than is capital punishment. Three and a half centuries of executing juveniles is more than enough. It is past time to bring this sad and shameful history to a close.

NOTES

1. Victor Streib studied 281 confirmed cases of juvenile executions occurring between 1642 and 1986. He relied on Watt Espy's ongoing research into American executions for his data. Since Streib's analysis, six more American juveniles have been executed, and Espy has confirmed another sixty-six historical cases.

2. "International agreements and standards on the death penalty unequivocally prohibit the use of death sentences for offenders who were under eighteen years of age at the time of the offense for which they were convicted. Several international and regional human rights instruments contain clear dictates against the use of the death penalty for juvenile offenders, including: the International Covenant on Civil and Political Rights (ICCPR), the American Convention on Human Rights (ACHR), the U.N. Convention on the rights of the Child (CRC),

and the U.N. Standard Minimum Rules for the Administration of Juvenile Justice of 1986.... In addition, the U.N. Economic and Social council adopted a series of safeguards in 1984...ruling out the death penalty for those under eighteen years of age at the time of the offense. In 1989, the U.N. Subcommission on Prevention of Discrimination and Protection of Minorities adopted Resolution 1989/3 which urged countries still applying the death penalty to juveniles to take legislative and administrative steps to end this practice" (Human Rights Watch, 1995, p. 4).

3. One reason why mitigating factors often do not have the weight they should is the appallingly poor legal representation received by many capital defendants. This issue is beyond the scope of this chapter, but interested readers are referred to Bright, 1994. Lewis et al. (1988) discuss why juveniles are particularly inept at assisting their counsel in developing mitigation.

REFERENCES

Espy, W. (1997). *List of confirmations, state by state, of legal executions as of January 15, 1997.* Available from Capital Punishment Research Project, P. O. Drawer 277, Headland, AL.

Fox, D. T. (1988). Inter-American Commission on Human Rights finds United States in violation. *The American Journal of International Law, 82,* 601–603.

Human Rights Watch Children's Rights Project (1995, March). United States: A world leader in executing juveniles. Available from Human Rights Watch, 485 Fifth Avenue, New York, NY 10017.

Lewis, D. O., Pincus, J. H., Bard, B., Richardson, E., Prichep, L., Feldman, M., & Yeager, C. (1988). Neuropsychiatric, psychoeducational, and family characteristics of 14 juveniles condemned to death in the United States. *American Journal of Psychiatry, 145,* 584–589.

Pupalia, D. E., & Olds, S. W. (1989). *Human Development* (4th ed.). New York: McGraw Hill Book Co.

Spillane, M. J. (1991). The execution of juvenile offenders: Constitutional and international law objections. *University of Missouri–Kansas City Law Review, 60,* 113–137.

Streib, Victor (1997). *Current death row inmates under juvenile death sentences.* Posted on Death Penalty Information Center Website. Available at http://essential.org/dpic/juvchar.html.

Streib, V. L. (1987). *Death penalty for juveniles.* Bloomington: Indiana University Press.

CASES

Stanford v. *Kentucky,* 492 U.S. 361 (1989).

Thompson v. *Oklahoma,* 487 U.S. 815 (1988).

Rejoinder to Dr. Vandiver

MICHAEL DONAHUE

Although I enjoyed Dr. Vandiver's essay, I believe her argument is fundamentally flawed in at least three places. First, and least important, she asserts that the United States "contravenes" (that is, violates or infringes on) "international law and practice on the issue of juvenile executions" and that we are "open to well-founded accusations of hypocrisy when we continue to violate [this] fundamental principle of international law." Well…no. Within the very paragraphs in which these assertions are made, she, herself, carefully notes the United States ratified the *I.C.C.P.R.* with the clearly stated reservation that its Constitution cannot be restrained from permitting the execution of juveniles. The U.S. position, far from being hypocritical or even mendacious, is not only unequivocal, but, in my view, quite principled. Of course, the intended supposition is that the United States ought to join the rest of the "civilized world" in matters of law and morality. I can imagine little else more repugnant than such specious compulsions. There is already enough mischief and chaos in the civilized world with which this nation is associated. Moreover, and as I argued earlier, there is nothing intrinsically superior about a majority's view on any matter of grave ethical or moral substance. Were that the case, I would, for my part, find the American public's clearly demonstrated and persistent support for capital punishment for both adults and juveniles more compelling than any proclamation from the United Nations, the American Bar Association, or any of the assorted "human rights" organizations listed in my colleague's essay. Morality is not decided by the force of the majority but by reasoned discourse, and the edicts of national and transnational organizations are inconsequential to the matter.

My colleague also contends that there is insufficient space in this chapter to marshal the evidence demonstrating the differences between adolescents and adults in terms of psychology, reasoning ability, decision making, and responsibility for actions. Whether this claim is true for much of human behavior is not corroborated; it is simply an assertion. We do know, however, that the best evidence available regarding moral maturity (the criterion on which it seems to make sense to judge the culpability of murderers) shows that it stabilizes around the age of sixteen years. It is in this vein that Dr. Vandiver rightly notes that our law properly distinguishes between adults and juveniles in terms of rights and obligations. They may not, for example, vote, smoke, or drink. In extending the logic, Dr. Vandiver may insist (she did not) that differential treatment entails differential justice, and thus differential punishment. Without the rights of adults, she would say juveniles cannot be punished as adults. Conversely, if the state can "strangle, gas, electrocute, shoot, or poison" (her words) youthful murderers, then it seems unfair that they are not extended adult privileges (e.g., smoking, drinking, voting, and by logical extension, gambling, carrying firearms, and having consensual sex). That juvenile murderers probably do all this and more conveniently escapes the circumspection and judgment of most social scientists. Indeed, the specific purpose of differential treatment (that is, the denial of these privileges to adolescents) is to protect the same and to discourage wanton conduct. But it does not compel the conclusion that the absence of these mostly trivial privileges mitigates the responsibility, culpability, and punishment for juveniles who engage in the vicious act of murder. The relationship, simply put, is spurious.

Most serious, I believe, is Dr. Vandiver's conflation of two distinctively different claims: the argument(s) against the execution of juveniles with the argument(s) against the execution of the mentally defective. For her, they appear to be virtually identical. In general, she maintains that all juvenile murderers are classical victims in the sense that they suffered some category of earlier physical abuse leading to psychological trauma. Indeed, sprinkled generously throughout her characterizations of juvenile killers are descriptions of psychological diagnoses, many with doubtful clinical validity, e.g., unknown "neurological abnormalities," vague "psychotic symptoms," "severe mood disorders," and periods of "paranoid ideation" such as they are. Of course, the insinuation is that the "symptoms" caused these teenagers to murder. But what would explain the many thousands of juveniles with these same symptoms who neither murder nor commit other crimes of violence? Is it only the most seriously traumatized who commit these acts of savagery? Perhaps, but it is hard to know, for there is no empirical evidence of which I am aware to support such calibrations. Nothing, in my view, more clearly epitomizes the bias of most social scientists than the assumption that children are instinctively congenial. Better then to seek the *locus classicus* of the cause for juvenile murder among the usual suspects: Social arrangements and structures for which we as a community owe a correction—or, failing that, in organic or psychological mechanisms, the autonomous nature of which diminishes or altogether erases the criminal's responsibility. For the typical social scientist, all behavior is in some sense caused; therefore, causation attenuates, often to the vanishing point, responsibility. In sum, I fear my colleague favors punishment for juvenile murderers (but certainly not capital punishment), and only if it is stripped of its retributive elements and marketed as community therapy. Paraphrasing the columnist George Will, such "punishment" fails to civilize the wholesome (yes, wholesome) desire for vengeance against the vicious.

Allyn & Bacon Order Form

The Controversial Issues in Criminal Justice Series
Steven A. Egger, Series Editor

Complete your set of books in the Controversial Issues in Criminal Justice Series with these additional titles—only $24.00 each!

Available Now!

Controversial Issues in Corrections
by Charles B. Fields
Order No. 0-205-27491-9

Controversial Issues in Criminology
by John R. Fuller and Eric W. Hickey
Order No. 0-205-27210-X

Controversial Issues in Policing
by James D. Sewell
Order No. 0-205-27209-6

Available Fall 1999*

Controversial Issues in Criminal Justice
by Frank Horvath
Order No. 0-205-29214-3

Controversial Issues in Gender
by Donna Hale
Order No. 0-205-29215-1

*Prices and Titles are subject to change

To Place an Order:

MAIL:
Allyn & Bacon Publishers
111 10th Street
Des Moines, IA 50309

CALL:
Toll-Free: 1-800-278-3525
Fax: 1-515-284-2607
WEBSITE: www.abacon.com

Name: _____

Address:_____

City: _____ State: _____ Zip Code: _____

Phone: _____ E-Mail:_____

Charge my: _____Amex _____Visa _____Mastercard _____Discover

Card # _____ Exp. Date _____

Enclosed find my: _____Check _____Money Order

*Shipping and handling charges will be added unless order is prepaid by check or money order.